MW01717344

Instructor's Manual

to accompany

ARCHITECTURAL DRAWING AND LIGHT CONSTRUCTION

Fifth Edition

Edward J. Muller
James G. Fausett
Philip A. Grau III

Prentice Hall
Upper Saddle River, New Jersey   Columbus, Ohio

Simon & Schuster/A Viacom Company
Upper Saddle River, New Jersey 07458

Printed in the United States of America

10 9 8 7 6 5 4 3 2 1

ISBN: 0-13-597949-8

This edition of the Instructor's Manual has been reorganized to reflect the changes made in the new, fifth edition of *Architectural Drawing and Light Construction*. There is new material that I hope will be helpful to both instructors and students. For example, I have added a description of how we use this textbook in our 2-year Associate Degree program. Also included is an outline of our course syllabi for the first two semesters showing how our lab lectures and assignments correlate with the textbook chapters. And, there is also a table showing a comparison of chapters from the fourth edition and current fifth edition of the textbook, which I hope will make the transition to the new edition less problematic. At the end of the material in Chapters 3, 6, 9, 14, and 18 of this manual I have included supplement items you may find useful as either handouts for students or as masters for overhead transparencies.

Philip A. Grau III

Milwaukee Area Technical College
Technical Division

ARCHITECTURAL TECHNOLOGY PROGRAM

The following outlines are condensed versions of the syllabi we use in first year (two semesters) of our two year Associate Degree program. We use the **Architectural Drawing and Light Construction** textbook as our major exercise text for the first year of our program and as the major reference source for the second year.

The focus of the first half of the first semester is on basic drafting. About one-third to one-half of the students entering our program have had no prior instruction in drafting of any sort. We have found it important to initially develop a good foundation in drafting, lettering, using drawing scales, and freehand drawing.

The second half of the first semester is used to familiarize the students with the basic language of architectural and construction drawings including terms, symbols, and drawing types such as plans, elevations, sections and details.

During this first semester we are also introducing the students to the AutoCAD drafting program as an architectural drafting tool. Most of this semester is spent reviewing how AutoCAD works, what the commands are, how to perform simple drafting exercises, and how to produce acceptable "output".

In the second semester of our program we begin with a review of basic architectural drafting and detailing and drawing. At this point we introduce in more depth one-point perspective drawing, shade and shadow construction, and presentation drawing concepts. The second third of this semester is used to introduce the principles of residential design. A project is assigned that incorporates a design response to a program statement that is then presented with plans, sections, elevations, details, and perspective renderings. The final third of the semester is spent developing construction drawings for a medium sized building.

The computer related instruction in this semester includes more work with AutoCAD as an architectural drafting and detailing tool. Three dimensional drawing is also introduced. The medium sized project described above and assigned for the final third of the semester is usually developed on the computer rather than drawn manually.

Philip A. Grau III
NCARB, AIA, CSI

ArchT 101 - Architecture: Theory and Drawing 1

COURSE OUTLINE

WEEK #1: **Introduction to Architectural Technology**

Lecture:

Review what architecture is and what architectural technicians are.

Assignments:

Read textbook Chapters 1 & 2.

This is typically a very short week, 2-3 days, and is primarily used to orient the students to the school and the program.

WEEK #2: **Architectural scales ,lettering ,terms, and symbols**

Lecture:

Identify common architectural terms and symbols.
Explain the use of both architectural and engineering scales.
Review architectural lettering.

Assignments:

Read textbook Chapter 1.
Read textbook Chapter 2.
Read textbook Chapter 3.
Review textbook Chapter 12, Section 12.1.

This week is usually an intense introduction to the theory of drawing scale, the language of architecture and construction, and to lettering. Various assignments are handed out during the week addressing these topics.

Exercises in the use of scales require the students to correctly measure items such as lines, sides of objects, etc. at various scales.

Lettering exercises at this stage consist of using the templates provided in the Instructor's Manual and practicing basic lettering of the alphabet and numerals at the four sizes. Students are expected to complete one sheet at each scale each day. The exercises at the end of Chapter 3 are also used and provide a good transition from lettering individual items to combining the letters and numbers into words and sentences.

The terms used in architecture and construction are introduced by assigning a number of terms from the text glossary to each student each day and reviewing those terms in class the following day.

WEEK #3 &
WEEK #4: **Using drafting equipment**

Lecture:

Develop skill in the basic use of drafting equipment.
Line weights and types.

Assignments:

Review textbook Chapters 1 & 2.
Read textbook Chapter 4.
Read textbook Chapter 5.

The exercises from the end of Chapter 1 provide a good start at using the basic drafting equipment to draw fairly simple shapes with minimum concern for line expression. The exercises at the end of Chapter 4 are more architecturally oriented and require some basic familiarity with the concept of line weights.

Lettering exercises are continued each week until mid semester. The focus is on correct spacing for words and phrases that students will encounter in the types of notes one typically finds on construction documents.

The reading in Chapter 5 is used to introduce the student to the modular and metric concepts of drafting. Generally, exercises in this area are concerned with becoming familiar with the basic metric measuring system and the concept of a 'module' in construction.

WEEK #5 &
WEEK #6: **Architectural projection drawings**

Lecture:

Orthographic drawings
Axonometric/Isometric drawings

Assignments:

Read textbook Chapter 6.
Read textbook Chapter 7.

The exercises in these two weeks are split between standard three-view orthographic projection work and isometric construction drawings. The Instructor's Manual contains, at the end of Chapter 6, an example of using solutions from an orthographic projection exercise to carry the student into the discipline of axonometric construction. These exercises are first assigned as three-view problems and then assigned as axonometric problems.

WEEK #7: **Freehand sketching**

Lecture:

Develop basic skill in freehand sketching

Assignments:

Read textbook Chapter 8.

We have found that the exercises at the end of this chapter offer a good range of styles from simple line sketching to more complicated architectural and 'three-dimensional' sketching problems.

WEEK #8 &
WEEK #9: **Perspective drawings**

Lecture:

Two-point perspectives.

Assignments:

Read textbook Chapter 9.

The exercises assigned for this chapter are more dependent on individual ability than in any other chapter. Some students need to repeat multiple simple exercises before the process becomes clear while other students can progress to rather complex constructions much quicker. We generally assign a simple exercise to all students initially and then determine subsequent exercises on an individual basis.

WEEK #10 -
WEEK 17: **Working Drawing Set**

The final segment of this first semester is spent introducing students to the production of the basic documents used in the construction of a small residence. The eight plus weeks are split into segments during which the students are required to draw various types of residential construction documents. We normally try to cover floor plans, exterior elevations, interior elevations, building sections, and wall sections. Students are required to submit a print of each drawing at the end of each time period. The instructors then review and 'mark-up' each submittal before returning them to the students.

The first week of this segment is reserved for student reading and review of the assigned readings in class. Students are told to review Chapter 4 - Drafting Expression. They are also assigned Chapter 12 - Light Construction Principles, Chapter 18 - Working Drawings of Small Homes, and Chapter 19 - Residential Mechanical and Electrical Systems. Chapters 4 and 12 are reviewed in class before any drawing assignments are made. Sections from Chapter 18 and 19 are reviewed during lectures as the drawing assignments related to those specific sections are made. The final week of the semester is reserved for the students to make the indicated corrections prior to final submittals . Final submittals include both the instructor noted initial print and the final, corrected print

ArchT 102 - Architecture: Theory and CADD 2

COURSE OUTLINE

WEEK #1:
WEEK #2:
WEEK #3: **Stair Details**

Lecture:
- Review basic wood stair construction.
- Review the details commonly required for stair construction.

Assignment:
- Review textbook Ch. 14, Section 14.7.

We usually begin the second semester with a drafting exercise that relates to the project completed at the end of the first semester. The students are required to redraw the stairs from the earlier floor plan at a larger scale, usually 1/2" = 1'-0", along with a full section through the stair from the basement to the top floor. In addition they are required to draw a number of details at 1 1/2" = 1'-0" such as tread/riser, baluster, railing, and carriage/wall connections.

WEEK #4:
WEEK #5:
WEEK #6: **Shades/Shadows.**
Perspectives: One-point.

Lecture:
- How to construct shades and shadows on drawings.
- How to construct one-point perspectives.

Assignment:
- Review textbook Chapter 9.
- Read textbook Chapter 10.

The exercises assigned for this period are split into two segments. The first two weeks are spent working with constructing shades and shadows. The first week assignments consist of simple geometric shapes. The second week assignments are more complex and architectural. During the third week we assign two one-point perspective exercises. The first is very simple, with no interior furnishings. The second is more complicated and includes doors, windows, and furnishings. Often we use one of our labs with all the chairs, desks, computers, bookcases, and drawing files.

WEEK #7 -
WEEK #13: **Design Sketch Problem**

Lecture:

What are basic design principles and how do you accommodate them in a study sketch.

Assignment:

Review textbook Chapter 12.
Read textbook Chapter 13.
Read textbook Chapter 14.
Read textbook Chapter 15.

This segment focuses on two skill areas: basic residential design and construction planning principles and presentation drawings. Students are given a program for a simple house on a specific site. The program leaves the choice of building materials and construction systems to the student but strong emphasis is placed in the program on energy efficient design and resource use. Students are required to develop a site analysis, spatial relationship diagrams, a floor plan, elevation, building section and wall section along with a two-point exterior perspective and a one-point interior perspective. All drawings are done in a presentation style as opposed to a construction document style.

WEEK #14 -
WEEK #18: **Working Drawing Set**

The final segment of this second semester is spent intoducing students to the production of the basic documents used in the construction of a medium-sized, non-residential building.

The five weeks are split into segments during which the students are required to draw some of the types of construction documents developed for a commercial building including floor plans, exterior elevations, interior elevations, building sections, and wall sections. As in the first semester students are required to submit a print of each drawing at the end of each time period for instructor review and 'mark-up'. A major difference from the first semester is that these drawings are developed on the computer using AutoCad and plotted to an assigned scale.

Students are assigned Chapter 13 - Structural Selection, Chapter 19 - Writing Specifications, and Chapter 20 - Drawing a Small Commercial Building. These chapters are then reviewed in class the first two days of the project assignment before any drawing assignments are made. Students are also reminded to review Chapters 12 and 14.

ARCHITECTURAL DRAWING AND LIGHT CONSTRUCTION

Chapter Comparison

	Fifth Edition - 1998	Fourth Edition - 1993
1.	Drafting Equipment and its Uses	1.
2.	Computer-Aided Drafting and Design	18.
3.	Lettering	2.
4.	Drafting Expression	9.
5.	Modular and Metric Drafting	9.
6.	Basic Technical Drawing	3.
7.	Axonometric and Oblique Pictorial Drawing	4.
8.	Freehand Sketching	5.
9.	Perspective Drawings	13.
10.	Shades and Shadows	13.
11.	Presentation Drawings and Rendering	14.
12.	Light Construction Principles	7.
13.	Structural Member Selection	8.
14.	Typical Architectural Details	10.
15.	Basic Residential Planning	6.
16.	Building Models	16.
17.	Writing Specifications	17.
18.	Working Drawings of Small Homes	11.
19.	Residential Mechanical and Electrical Systems	12.
20.	Drawing a Small Commercial Building	15.

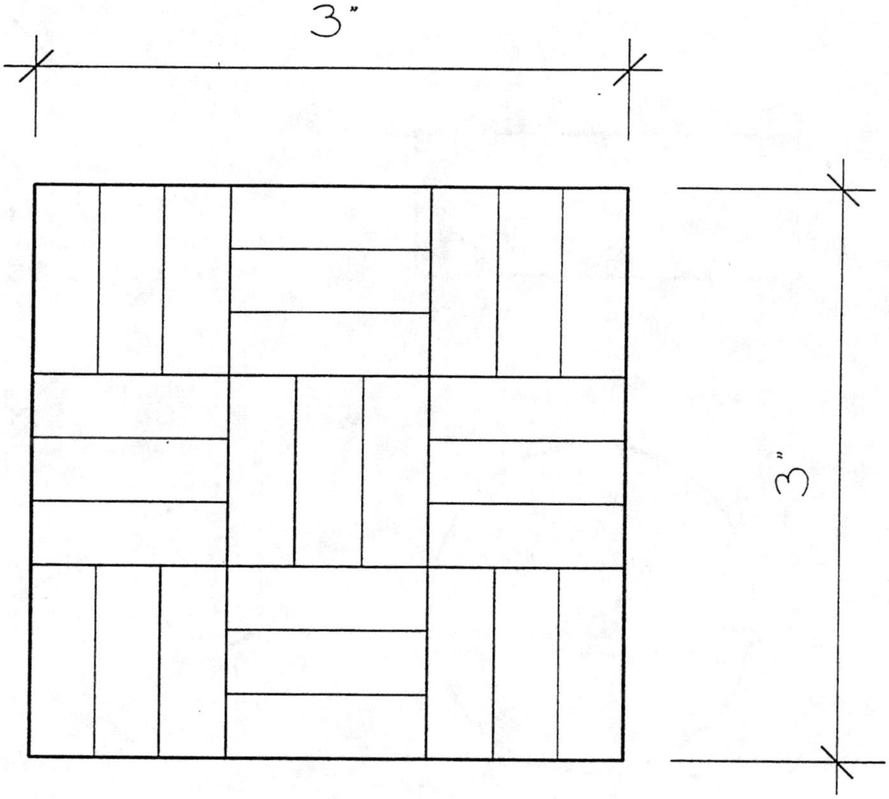

CHAPTER 1, EXERCISE 1, FIG. 1-40

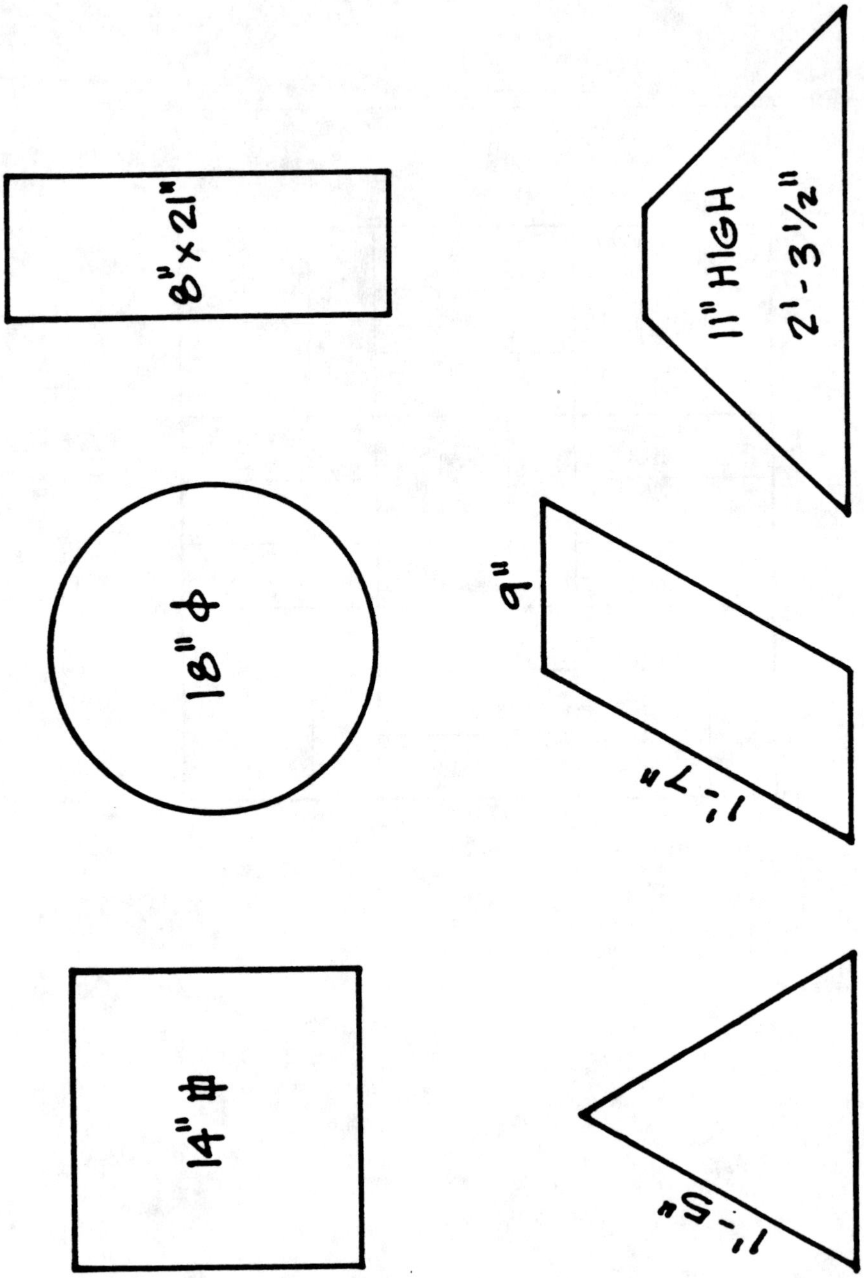

CHAPTER 1, EXERCISE 2, FIG. 1-41

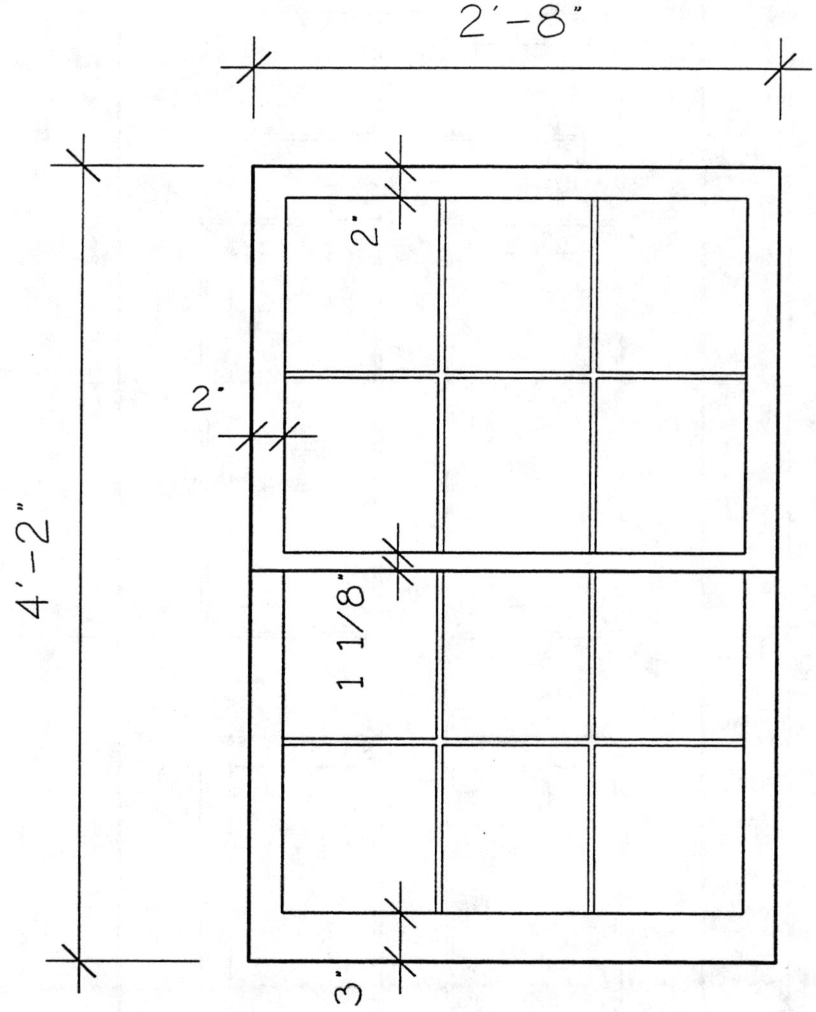

CHAPTER 1, EXERCISE 3, FIG. 1-42

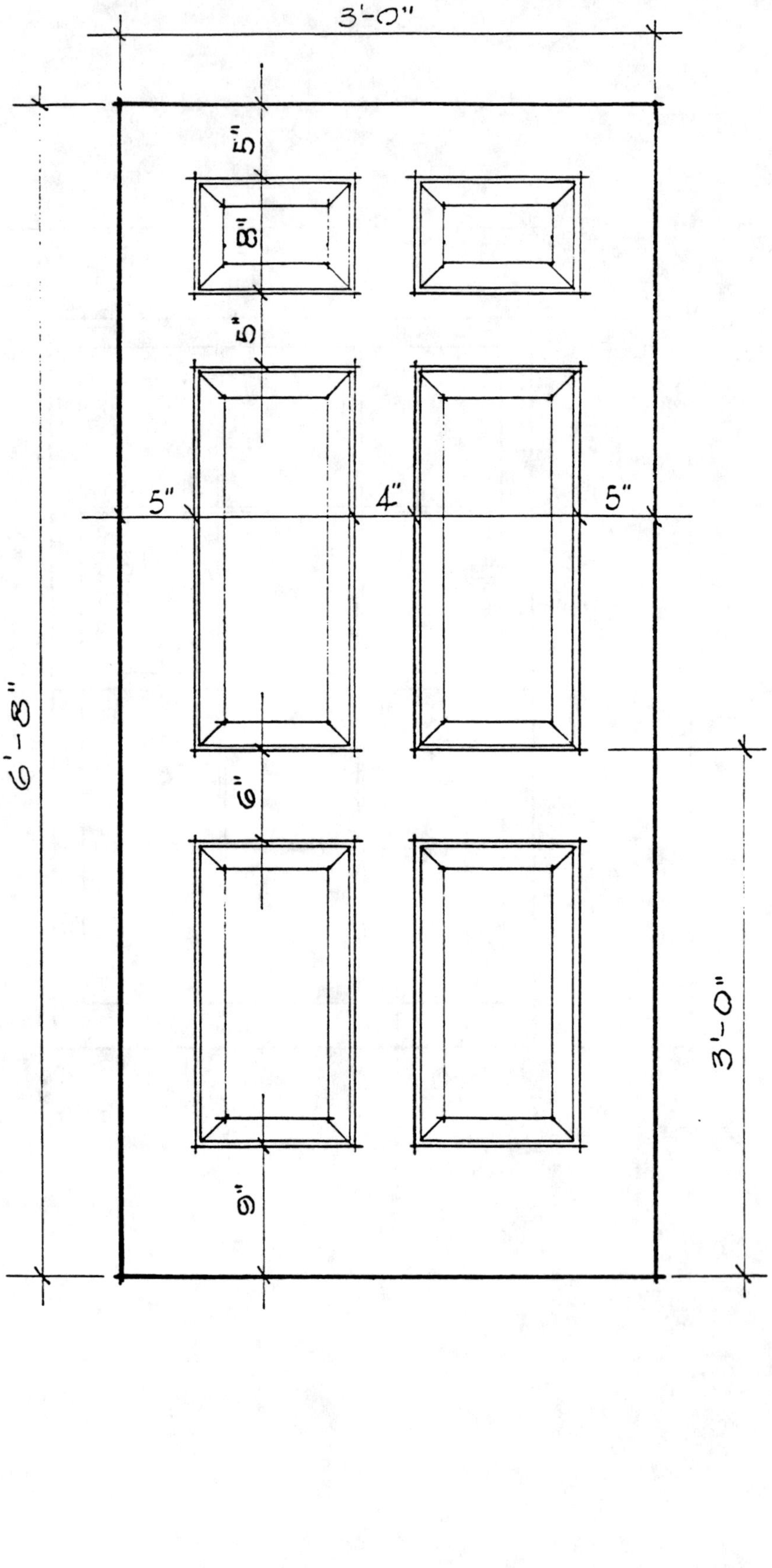

CHAPTER 1, EXERCISE 4, FIG. 1-43

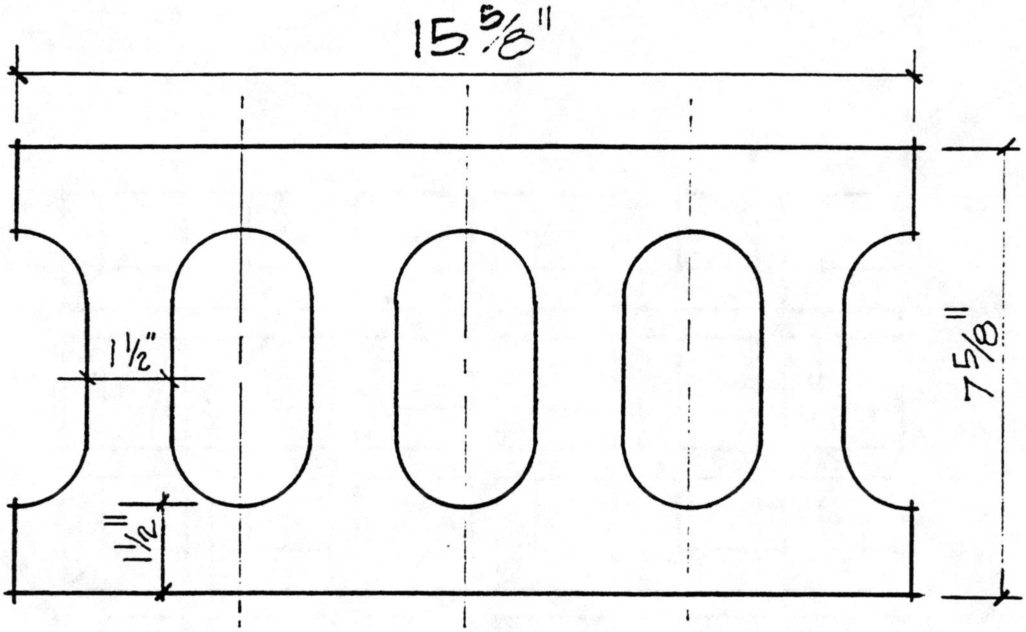

CHAPTER 1, EXERCISE 5, FIG. 1-44

CHAPTER 1, EXERCISE 6, FIG. 1-45

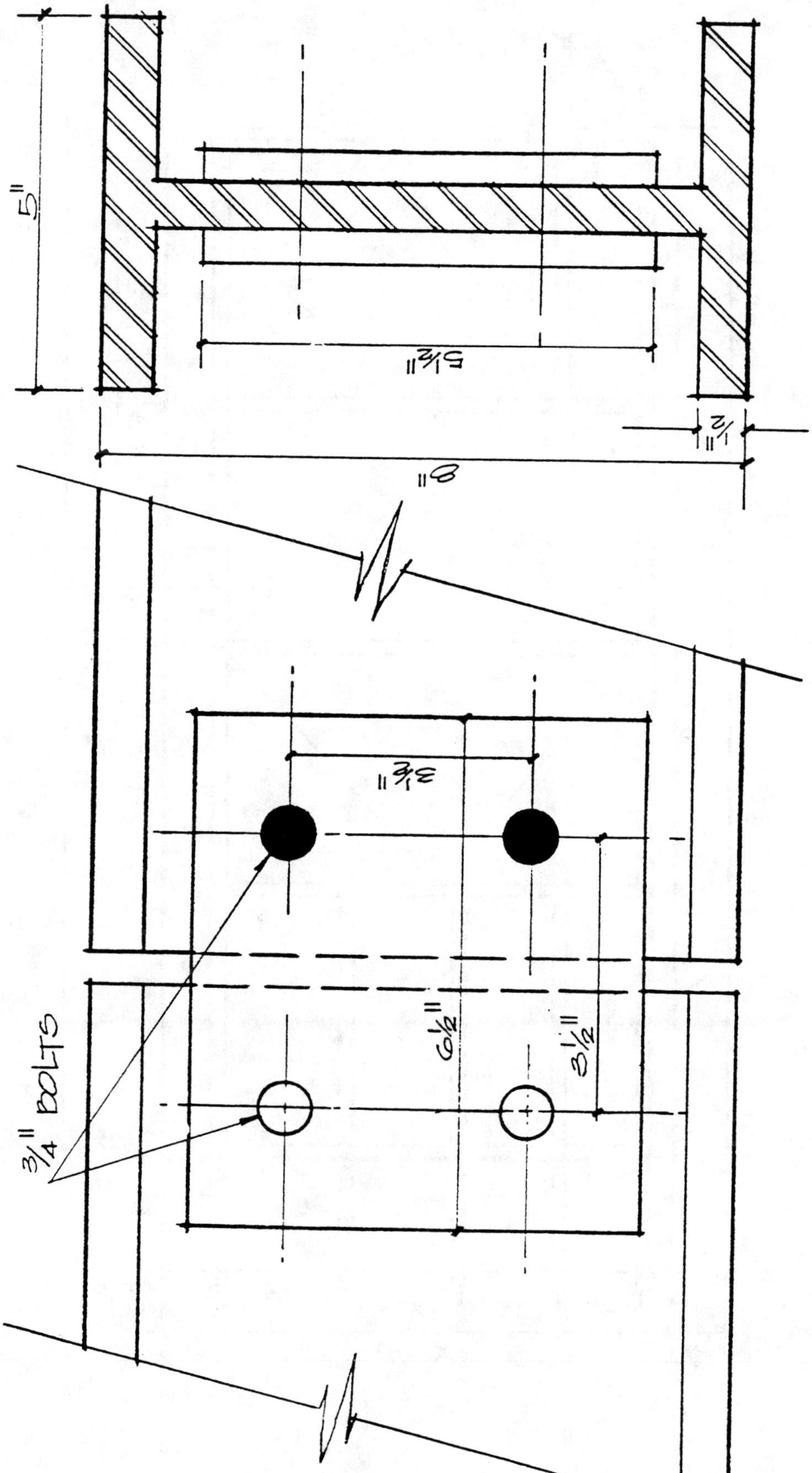

CHAPTER 1, EXERCISE 7, FIG. 1-46

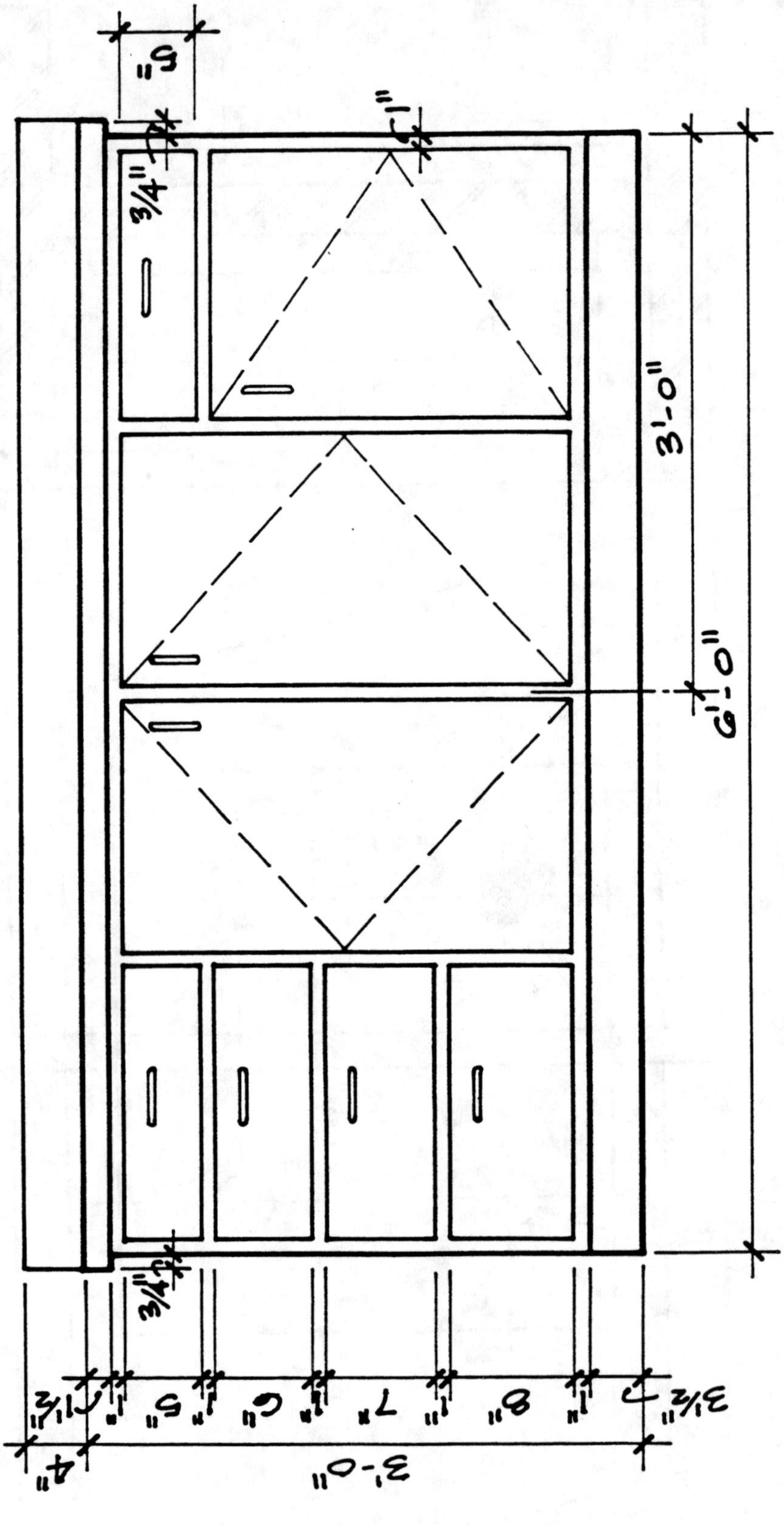

CHAPTER 1, EXERCISE 8, FIG. 1-47

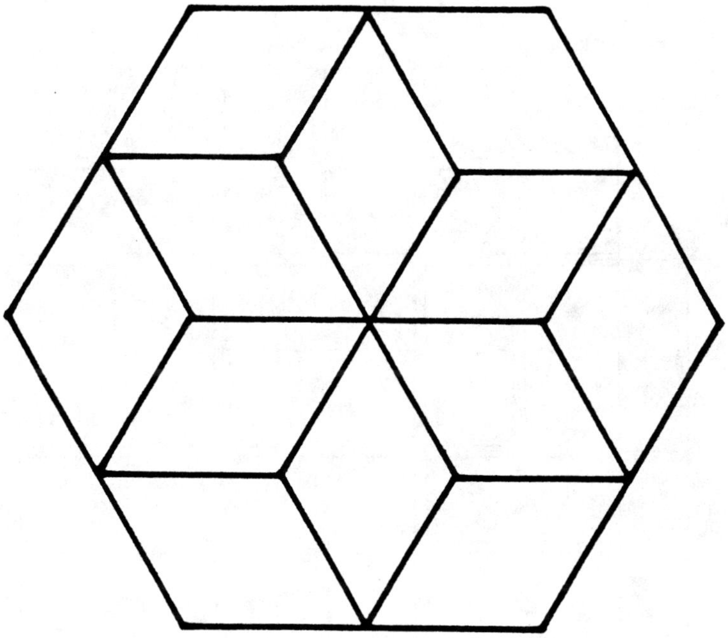

CHAPTER 1, EXERCISE 9, FIG. 1-48

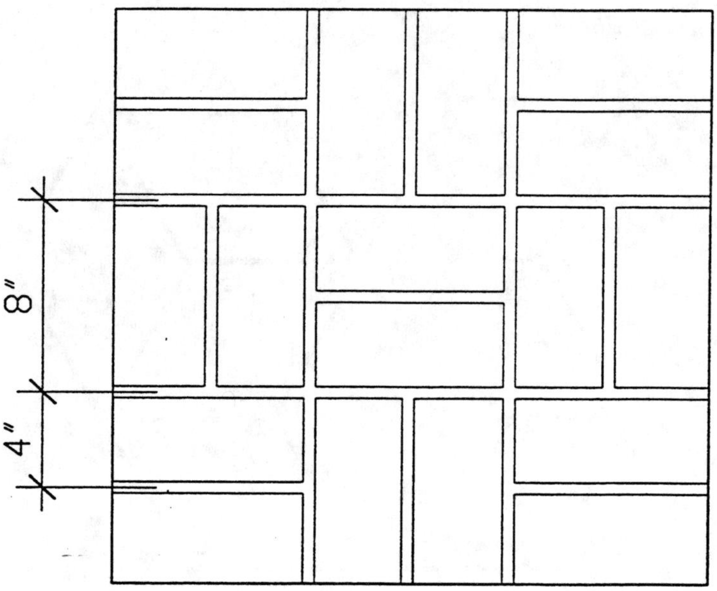

CHAPTER 1, EXERCISE 10, FIG. 1-49

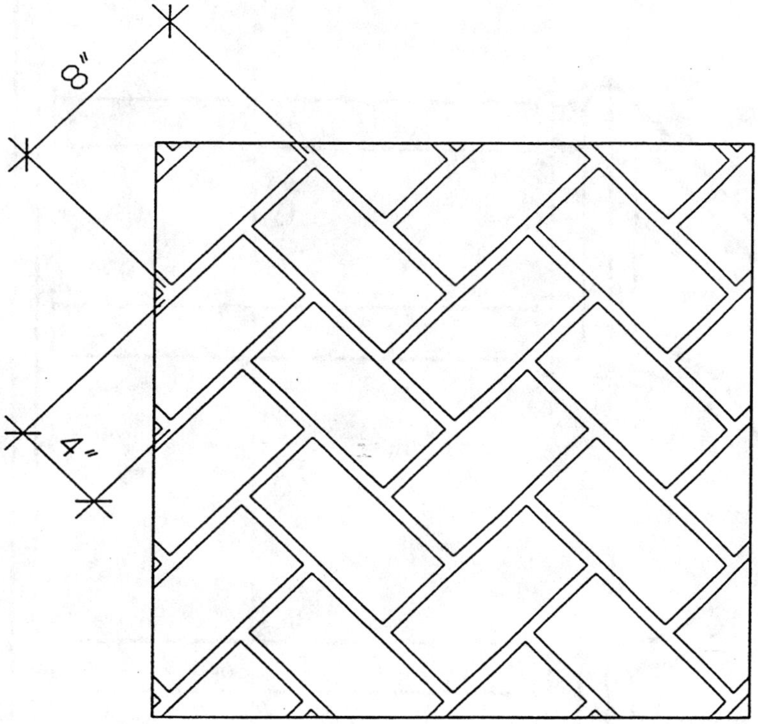

CHAPTER 1, EXERCISE 11, FIG. 1-50

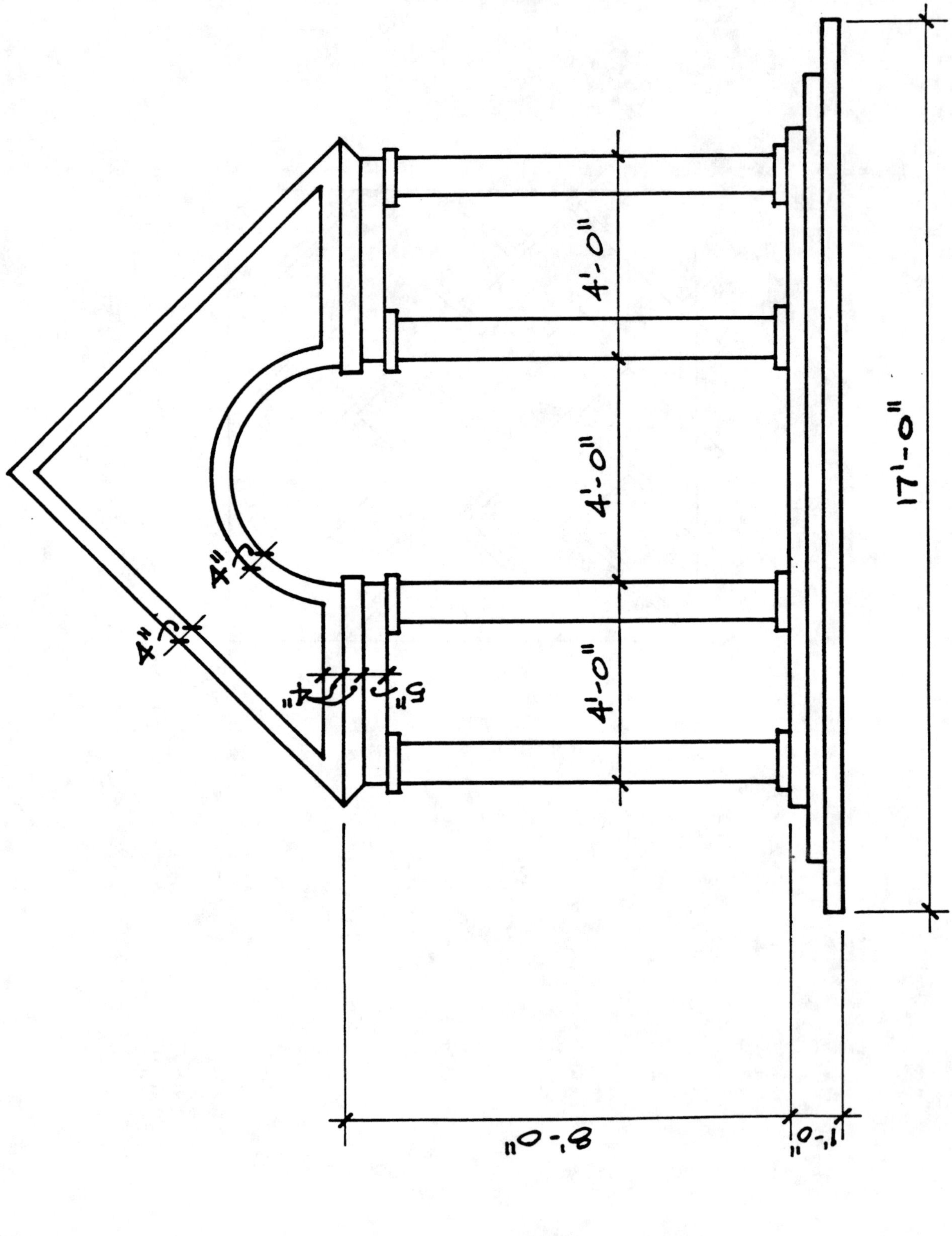

CHAPTER 1, EXERCISE 12, FIG. 1-51

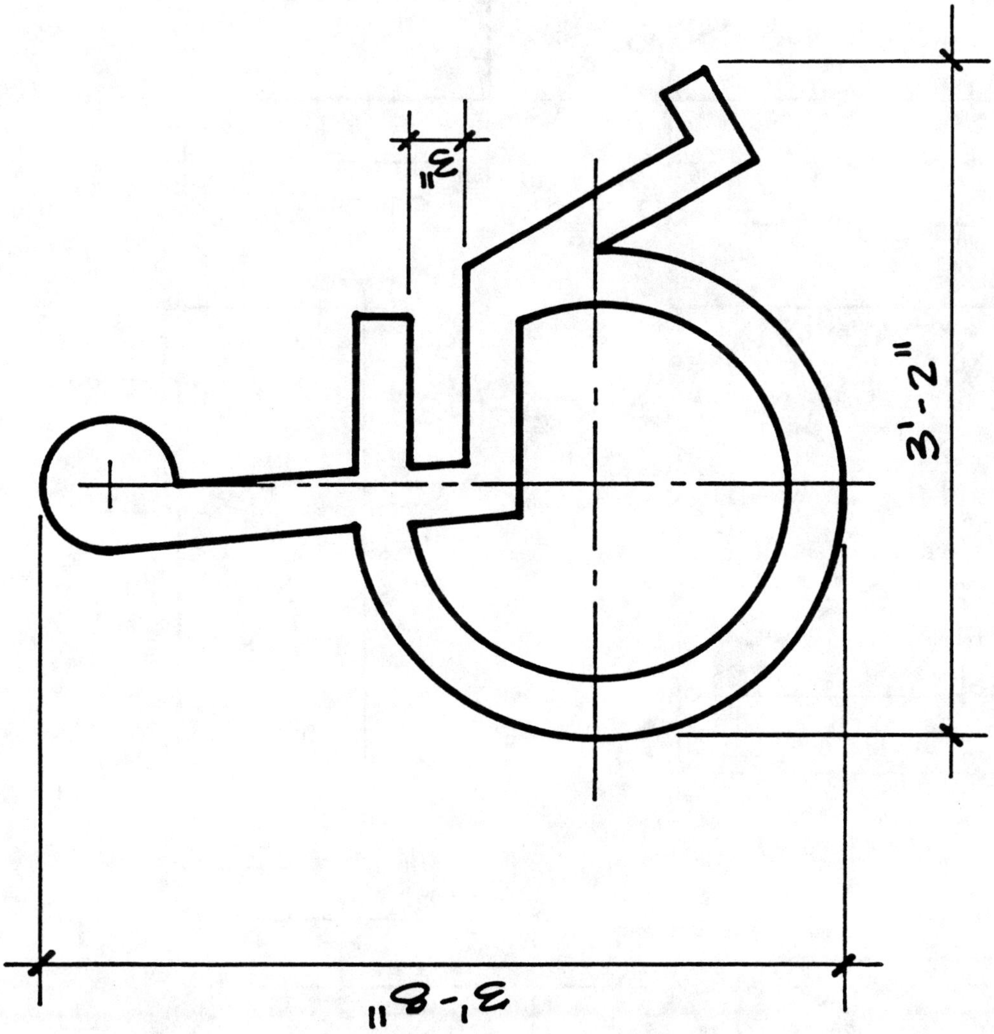

CHAPTER 1, EXERCISE 13, FIG. 1-52

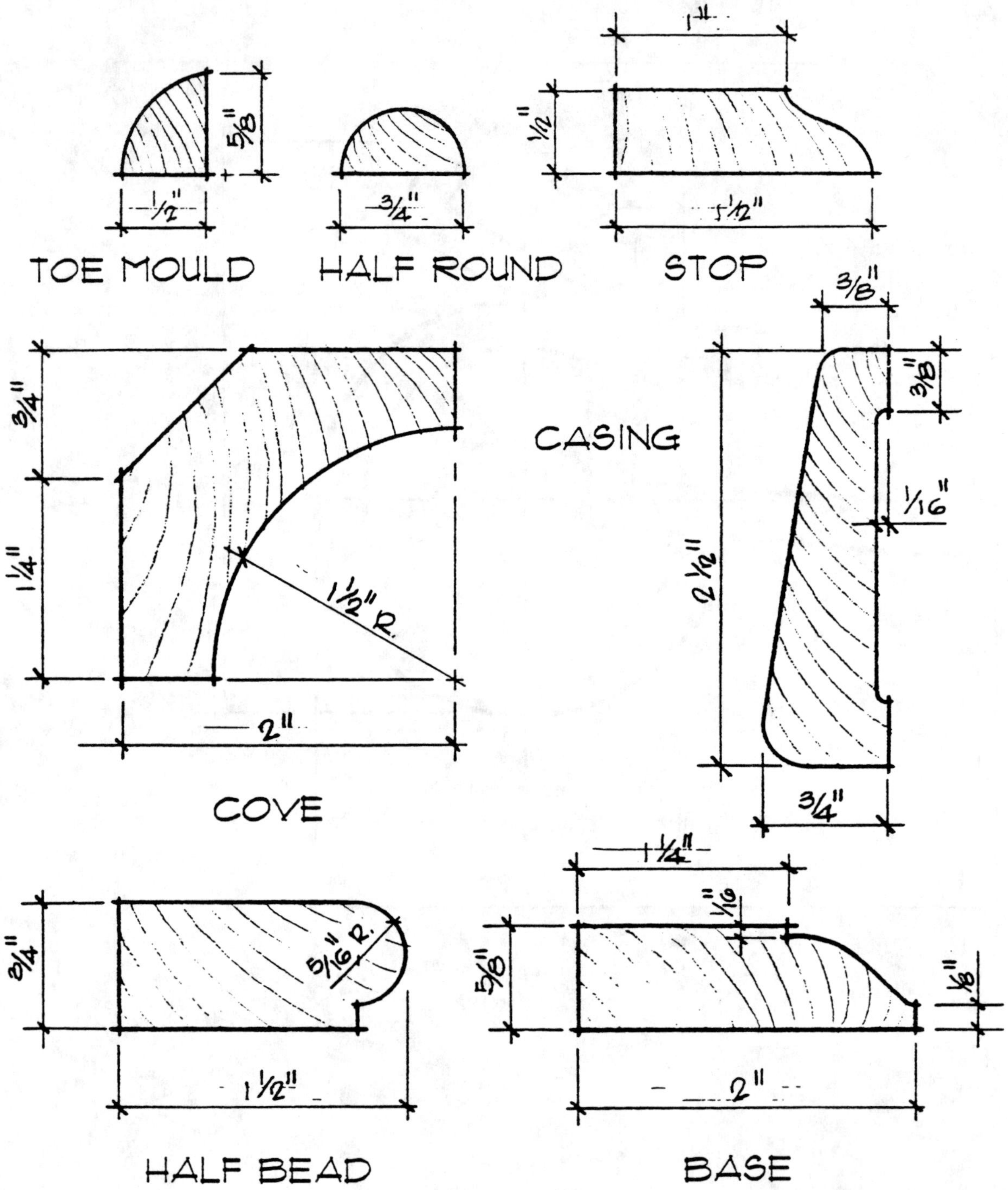

CHAPTER 1, EXERCISE 14, FIG. 1-53

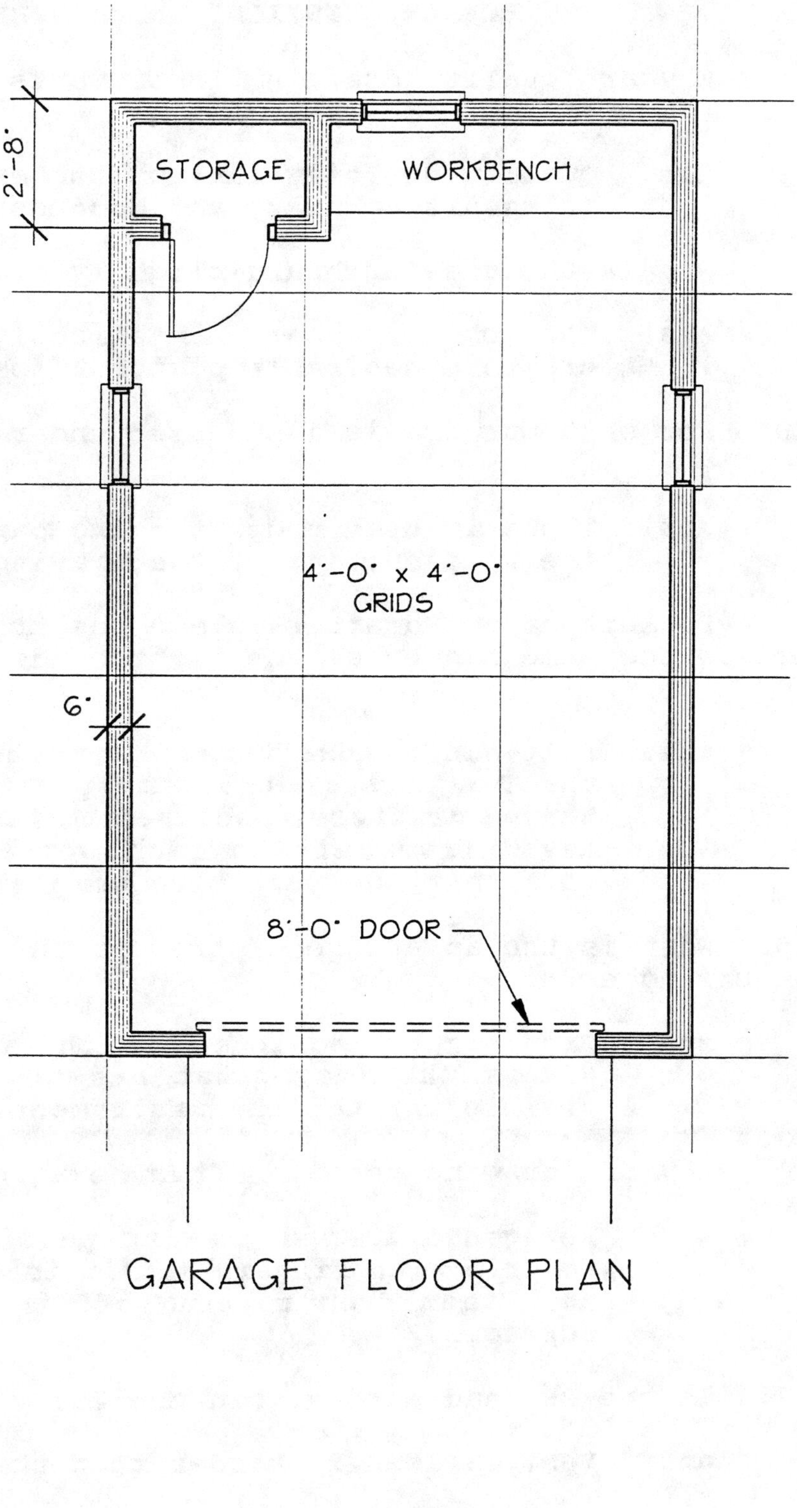

GARAGE FLOOR PLAN

CHAPTER 1, EXERCISE 15, FIG. 1-54

CHAPTER 1
REVIEW QUESTIONS AND ANSWERS

1. Why are quality drafting instruments important for good work?

ans. Quality drafting instruments are important to assure accuracy and good design.

2. Why is the drawing board slightly inclined?

ans. The drawing board is slightly inclined to create a desirable position for the drafter.

3. For what purpose is a pad used under tracing paper?

ans. A pad is used under tracing paper to protect the wood surface of the drawing board.

4. Do left-handed drafters place the triangles on the T square in the same manner as the right-handed drafter? If so, why?

ans. Left-handed drafters place the triangle on the T square in the same position as right-handed drafters, because the triangle must be moved from left to right to avoid smudging work that has just been completed.

5. What is the advantage of transparent equipment such as triangles?

ans. Transparent equipment such as a triangle allows the image that has been drawn to be visible through the instrument.

6. Why are drawing pencils often hexagonal in shape?

ans. Hexagonal shaped drawing pencils are easier to grip with fingers and it is also easier to keep them from rolling off inclined drawing surfaces.

7. Is the 2H lead harder than the 2B?

ans. Yes, 2H lead is harder than the 2B lead.

8. For what purpose is the pencil turned between the fingers when drawing a line?

ans. Turning the pencil between the fingers when drawing a line keeps the point sharp and prevents the point from wearing down on one side.

9. Why is the adjustable triangle time saving?

ans. The adjustable triangle is time saving by allowing the drafter to select various angles.

10. What is the difference between the architect's scale and the civil engineer's scale?

ans. The architect's scale is divided into 1/16" inch increments while the engineer's scale is in 1/10" inch increments.

11. List the necessary qualities of suitable tracing paper.

ans. Desirable tracing paper should be transparent, durable, erase well, and suitable for reproduction.

12. What are the most ideal lighting conditions for drafting?

ans. Ideal lighting conditions for drafting are natural north light or soft light of the proper intensity from the upper left for right-handed drafters and vice versa for left-handed drafters. Direct sunlight should never fall on the drafting board; it is too intense.

13. What is a parallel bar and why is it preferred over a T square?

ans. The parallel bar is a drawing tool similar to a T square generally constructed of hard plastic and mounted to the drawing board. It is more convenient and accurate than the T square.

14. What is the most suitable type of lead for drafting on films?

ans. Plastic lead is the most suitable type of lead for drafting on films.

15. What are templates and where are they used?

ans. Templates are thin plastic sheets cut with various scaled openings of architectural symbols. They are used on architectural drawings to represent circles, squares, rectangles, furniture, plumbing fixtures, and so on.

16. How are drafting papers or films attached to the drawing surface?

ans. Drafting paper or films are attached by drafting tape or dots which leave no marks or residue on the drawings.

17. What is an irregular curve and why is it used?

ans. An irregular curve is one that has a number of small curvatures as well as a few long, slightly curved edges. It is used to draw irregular curved shapes.

18. What is the difference between the arm drafting machine and the track drafting machine?

ans. The arm drafting machine has a pair of pinned arms and elbow. The track drafting machine has a fixed horizontal track at the top edge of the drawing board and a movable vertical track attaced to the horizontal track. Arm drafting type machines are more popular with engineers and track drafting machines with architects.

19. Draw a line 3" long and measure the line with the scale 3/4" = 1′-0". What is the length of the line?

ans. A 3" line drawn to the 3/4" scale is 4′-0" long.

20. Draw a line 4 1/2" long and measure the line with the scale 1/4" = 1′-0". What is the length of the line?

ans. A 4 1/2" line drawn to 1/4" scale is 18′-0" long.

CHAPTER 2
REVIEW QUESTIONS AND ANSWERS

1. Why doesn't learning to draw with a computer eliminate the need to learn to draw by hand?

ans. Freehand and technical sketches are still required to communicate basic ideas, quickly.

2. What is meant by the term "model" in computer aided design?

ans. A full scaled representation of an object which can be changed and improved during the creation is termed a model.

3. In what ways can computer aided design aid creativity?

ans. Creativity can be aided by the rapid trial of ideas using CAD.

4. Which two major technological developments with computer hardware have fueled the rapid rise in popularity of micro computers?

ans. Increased speed of microprocessors and reduction in cost of memory has fueled the rapid rise in micro computer popularity.

5. What is the proper name for the main circuit board, which contains the microprocessor, numeric coprocessor, and expansion slots?

ans. It is known as the <u>system</u> board.

6. How many pages of text can be stored on a typical CD-ROM disk?

ans. 225,000 pages of text can be stored on a typical CD-ROM disk.

7. Why is it important that CAD users develop good typing skills?

ans. CAD users must develop good typing skills to be able to enter text and commands from the keyboard.

8. Discuss the advantages and disadvantages of pen and electrostatic plotters.

ans. Pen plotters are accurate; however, they require frequent maintenance. Electrostatic plotters are reliable and can be used to plot shaded areas.

9. Name a device (other than a FAX) used to transmit files electronically over telephone lines.

ans. The modem is used to transmit files electronically over telephone lines.

10. What are the major purposes of an operating system?

ans. The main purpose of an operating system is for file management (housekeeping), organization of memory, and coordination of hardware components.

11. Using AutoCAD conventions, give an example of each of the following:

a. linear displacement by absolute coordinates

from point: x,y
to point: x,y

b. linear displacement by relative coordinates

from point: @x,y
to point : x,y

c. angular displacement by polar coordinates

from point: x,y
to point: x < angle

12. What are four different techniques to issue commands using AutoCAD?

ans. AutoCAD commands are issued using a keyboard, table menu, screen menu, and pull-down menu.

13. In a typical CAD drawing session, which type of commands are used most frequently, draw or edit?

ans. The edit command is the most frequent command used in CAD drawing sessions.

14. Why does a square one inch long on each side require the same amount of computer memory as a square one

mile long on each side?

ans. Each square is stored in the computer as four points.

15. What is the name of a compact groups of entities in AutoCAD?

ans. <u>Polyline</u> is the term for entities in AutoCAD.

16. Polyline can greatly increase the <u>speed</u> of CAD work; however, it can hinder <u>detailed work</u>. Why?

ans. Polylines are compact groups of entities that require less memory and processing time. Unless broken down, they can hinder detailed work because the individual entities comprising the polyline cannot be changed.

17. What are the advantages of combining drawings?

ans. By combining drawings, parts of drawings can be re-used in other drawings.

18. Explain how symbol libraries are created in CAD.

ans. Symbol libraries are created in CAD.

19. Explain the difference between graphic images stored in vector format and raster format.

ans. Graphic images are stored by their exact geometric description in a vector format and by a series of dots in raster format.

20. When objects are drawn at full scale in CAD how are these scaled drawings generally produced?

ans. The drawings are scaled as they are plotted.

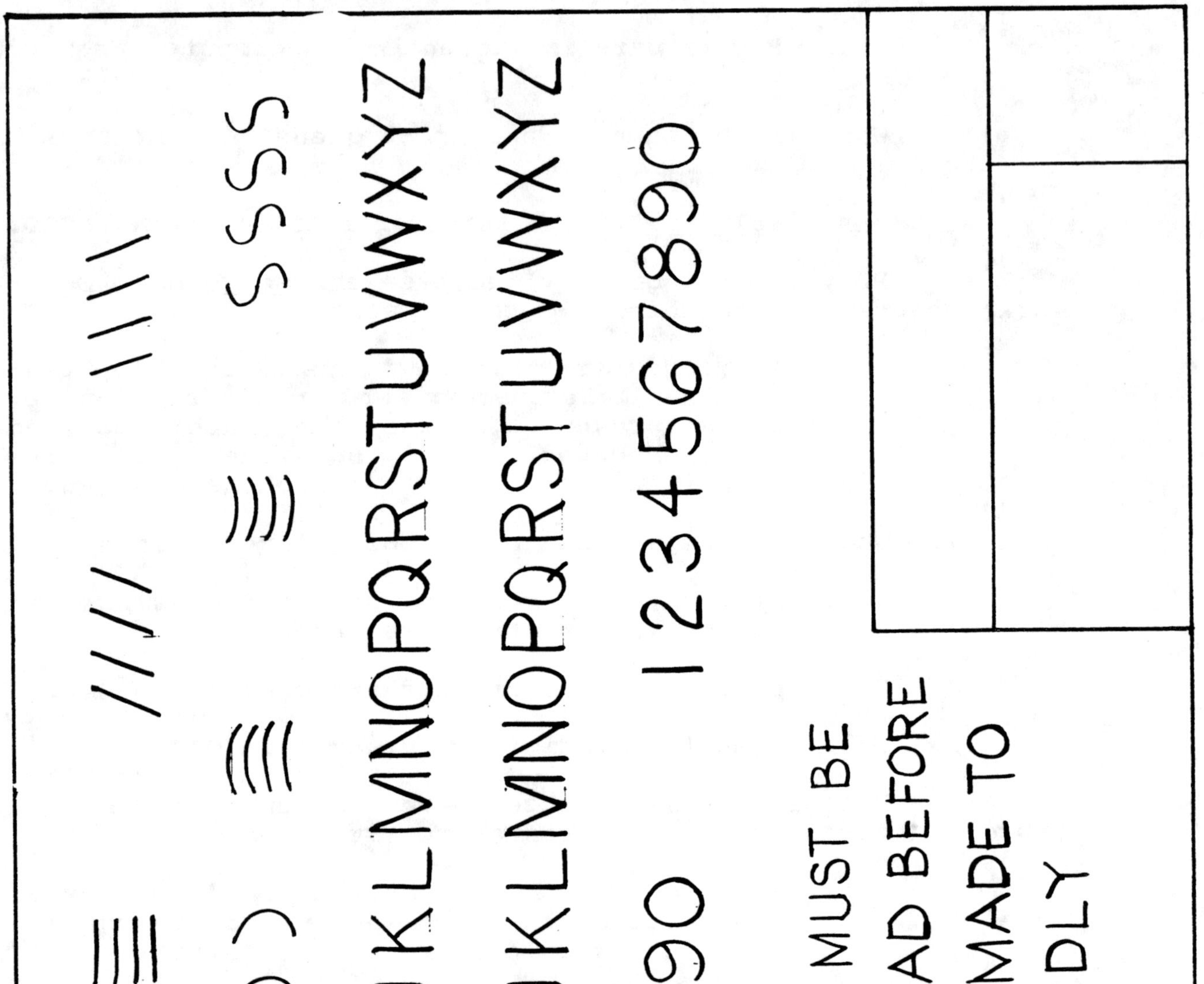

CHAPTER 3, EXERCISE 1

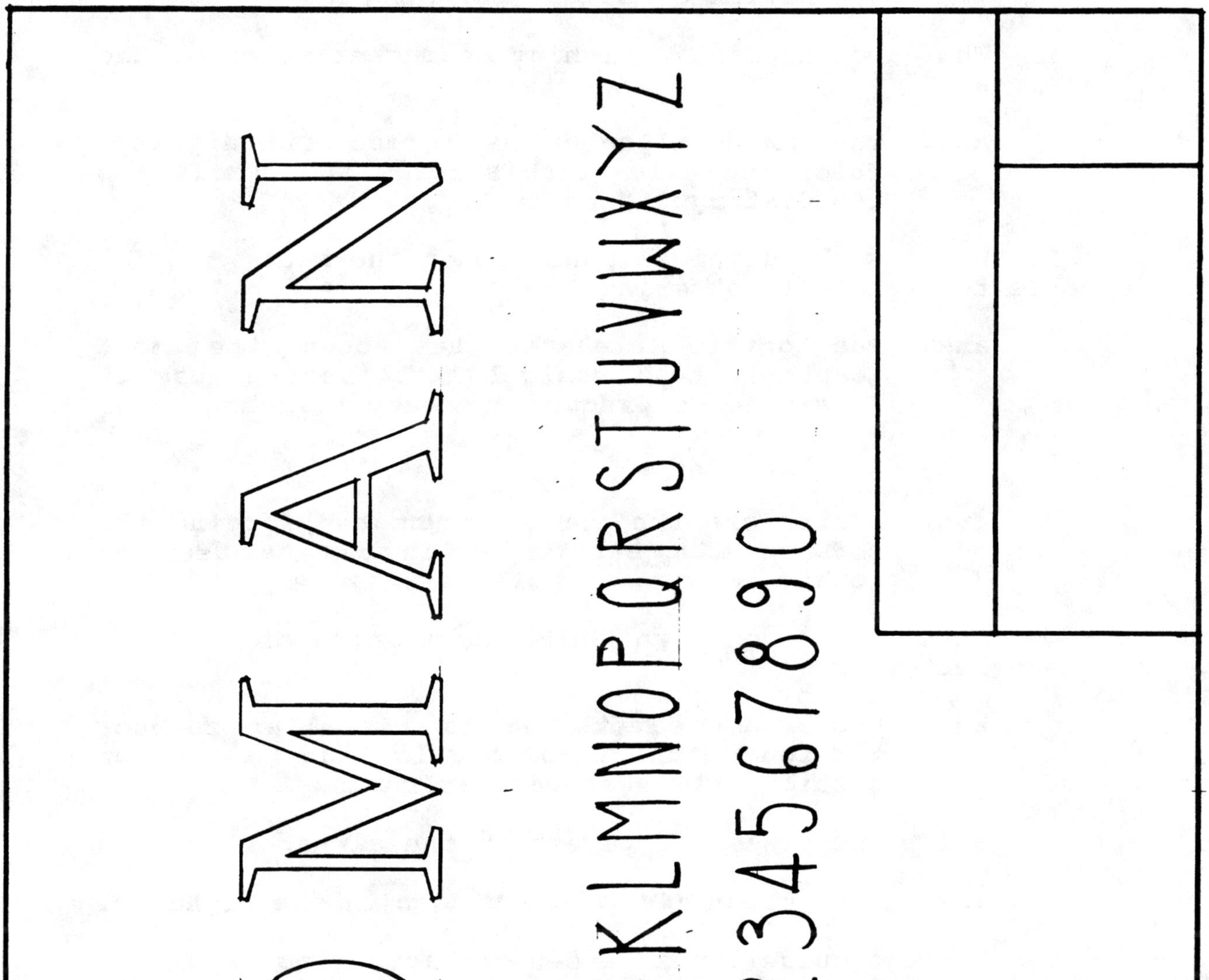

CHAPTER 3, EXERCISE 4, FIGS. 3-26 and 3-22

CHAPTER 3
REVIEW QUESTIONS AND ANSWERS

1. What are the distinguishing characteristics of the roman alphabet?

ans. The roman alphabet has grace and dignity. Thick and thin-width strokes and serifs are its distinguishing features.

2. Why has the gothic alphabet been the most adaptable to technical lettering?

ans. The gothic alphabet has been the most adaptable to technical lettering because it is simple to execute and easy to read.

3. What are serifs?

ans. Serifs are the spurs or "boots" forming the ends of the strokes which can be used on gothic letters as well as roman.

4. Describe in your own words the meaning of lowercase lettering.

ans. "Lowercase" lettering is a smaller rounder version of the strokes which can be used on gothic letters as well as roman.

5. Which letter is the widest in the alphabet?

ans. The letter "W" is the widest in the alphabet.

6. Why are guide lines needed for lettering on working drawings?

ans. It is nearly impossible to maintain straight lettering without guidelines. Use them like the experts do.

7. What is meant by a boldface alphabet?

ans. The boldface alphabet has heavier and thicker letters. It is formed with a thick point instrument.

8. List several methods of giving titles emphasis.

ans. Emphasis is given to titles by the use of

extended lettering, thicker strokes, and/or underlining.

9. What is meant by architectural style in lettering?

ans. **Architectural style is each drafter's individualized lettering style which he or she reproduces with speed and consistency and is generally a variation of several styles.**

10. Where is the title block usually placed on a working drawing?

ans. **The title block is usually placed in the lower right corner of the sheet.**

11. Which of the five styles of architectural lettering illustrated in this chapter would be most appropriate for notes on an architectural working drawing?

ans. **The triangle style lettering would be most appropriate for notes on working drawings.**

12. What are lettering devices?

ans. **Lettering devices are lettering sets which are for making uniform technical letters in ink or pencil.**

13. What are transfer letters and where are they used?

ans. **Transfer letters are pressure sensitive alphabets which are usually used for titles.**

14. Why are letters not spaced equally apart in each word?

ans. **Because each letter has a different profile and width; therefore, spacing of characters within a word cannot be equal.**

15. When would it be appropriate to use the bold freehand letters that are executed with broad-and fine-tip felt pens?

ans. **Bold freehand letters are usually used on preliminary sketches.**

16. How much space should be allowed between each word when lettering?

ans. A good rule of thumb would be to make the space between words twice the area between letters within the word.

17. Architects generally use vertical stroke letters. What type of strokes are generally used by engineers?

ans. Engineers commonly use inclined stroke letters.

18. What height letters would be appropriate for the title NORTH ELEVATION on architectural working drawings: 1/16", 1/4", 3/4", or 1" high?

ans. 1/4" height letters would be appropriate for the title NORTH ELEVATION on an architectural working drawing.

19. When would it be appropriate to use an extended lettering style?

ans. Extended lettering style would be appropriate for titles on long drawings.

20. What is the best method for developing perfection in lettering?

ans. There is no substitute for diligent practice in developing perfection in lettering.

The following pages contain templates that can be used for additional lettering exercises.

The templates are for 1/8", 3/16",1/4", and 3/8" high lettering. The appropriate template should be copied for the students. A sheet of vellum or trace should be placed over the template. The student then letters the alphabet and numerals placing one item in each 'box'. These templates were originally developed for use with the "BASIC" style lettering as shown on the accompanying page. Other lettering styles can also be used. The "BASIC" style letters can be made using a triangle to draw the verticals, freehand, or both.

Also included is a handout sheet which notes suggested guidelines for lettering sizing and spacing when used for notes on construction drawings.

"BASIC"

ABCDEFGHIJKLMNOPQRSTU

VWXYZ 1234567890 ¢ 1/2 3/4

1/8" HIGH LETTERING

NAME:________________________

NAME:________________________

3/16" HIGH LETTERING

1/4" HIGH LETTERING

NAME:________________________

3/8" HIGH LETTERING

NAME: ______________________

FOR MAIN TITLES
USE 1/4" HIGH
LETTERING AND
1/8" SPACING

1/4"
1/8"
1/4"

FOR SUB-TITLES
USE 3/16" HIGH
LETTERING AND 3/32"
SPACING

3/16"
3/32"
3/16"

FOR MOST NOTES AND OTHER
TEXT USE 1/8" HIGH LETTERING
AND 1/16" SPACING, ESPECIALLY FOR
DOCUMENT REDUCTIONS

1/8"
1/16"
1/8"

IN SOME INSTANCES THE USE OF 3/32"
HIGH LETTERING FOR NOTES IS ACCEPTABLE
IN THIS CASE THE SPACING SHOULD BE
EITHER 3/32" OR 3/64"

3/32"
3/64"
3/32"

LETTERING SIZES AND SPACING

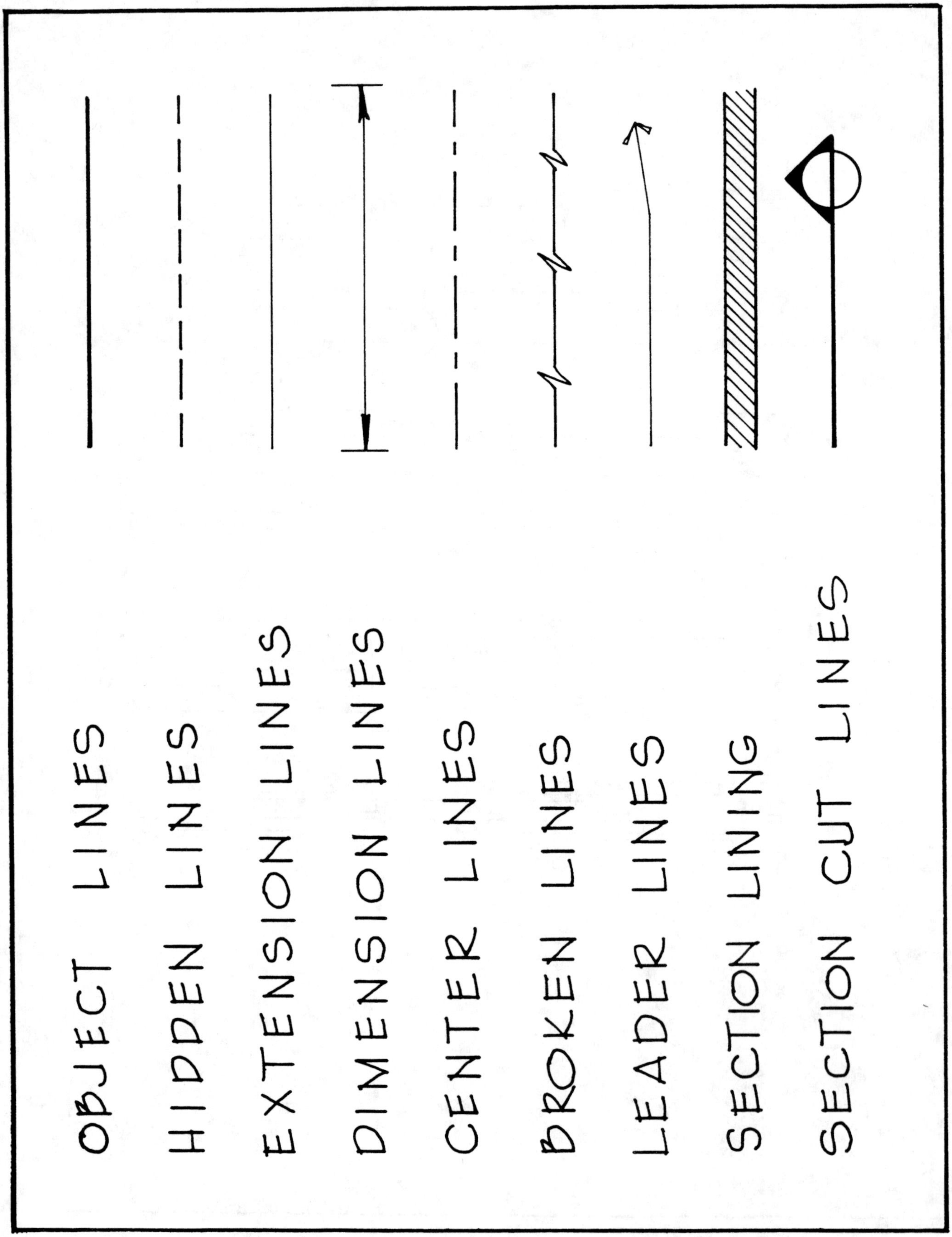

CHAPTER 4, EXERCISE 1

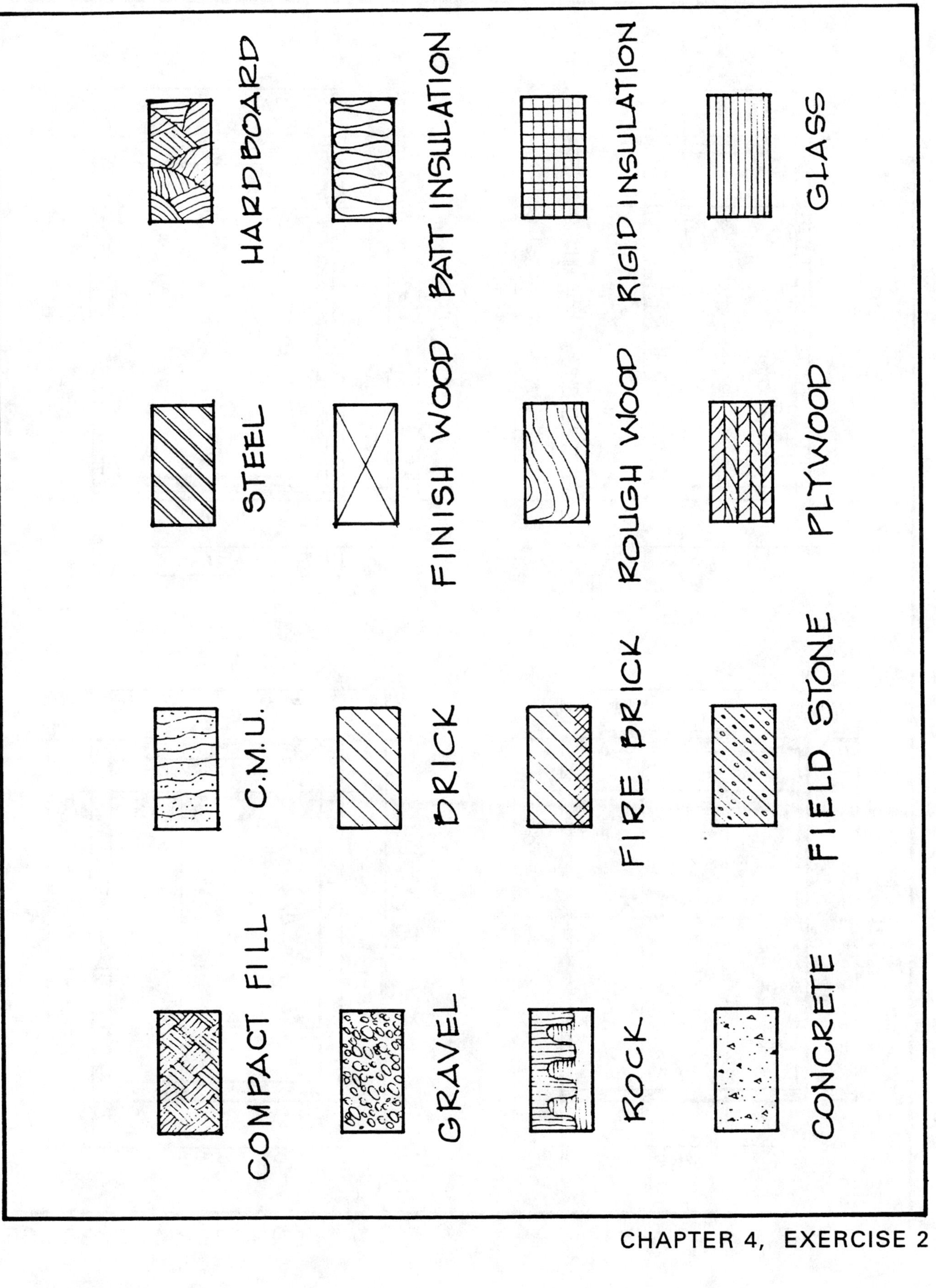

CHAPTER 4, EXERCISE 2

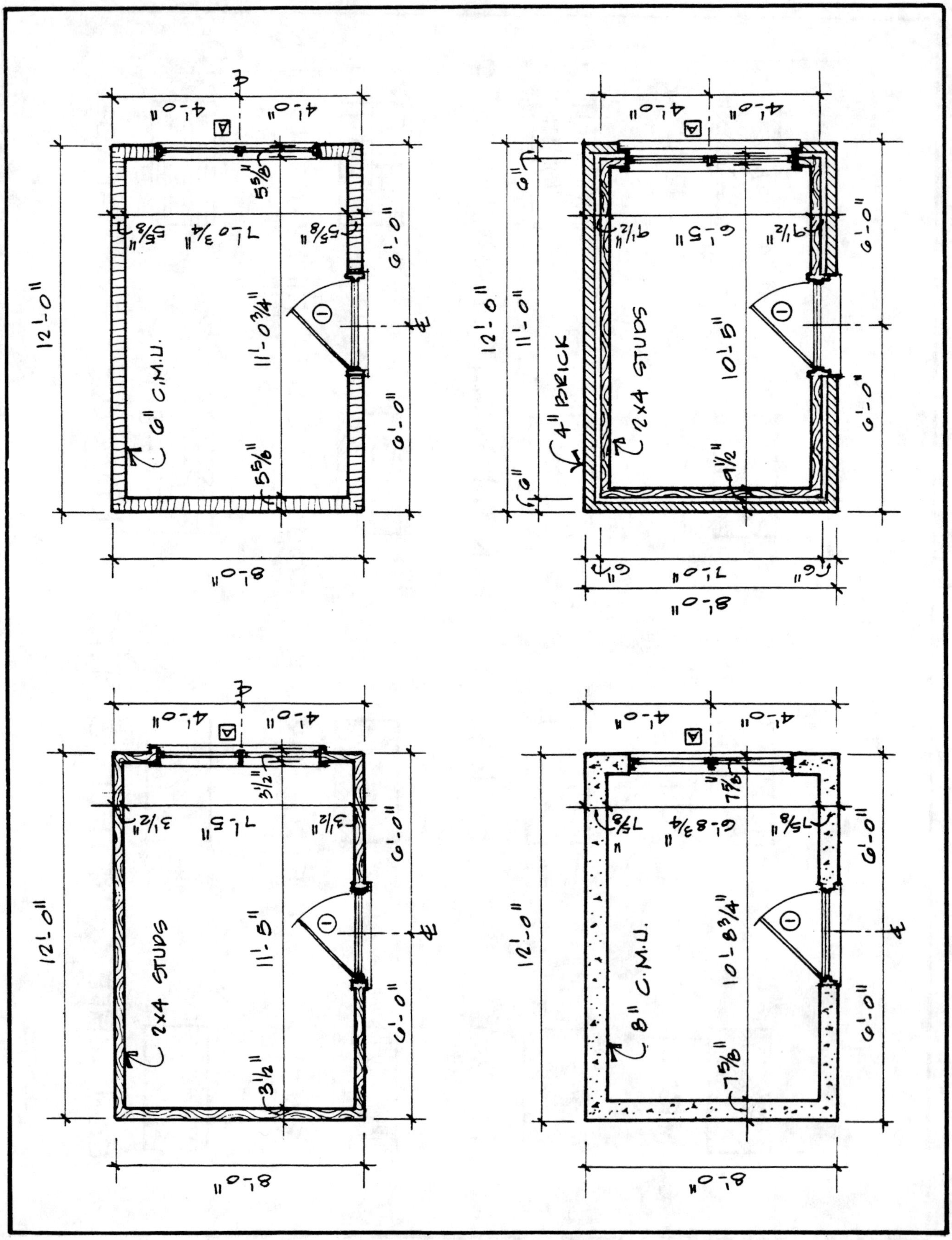

CHAPTER 4, EXERCISE 3

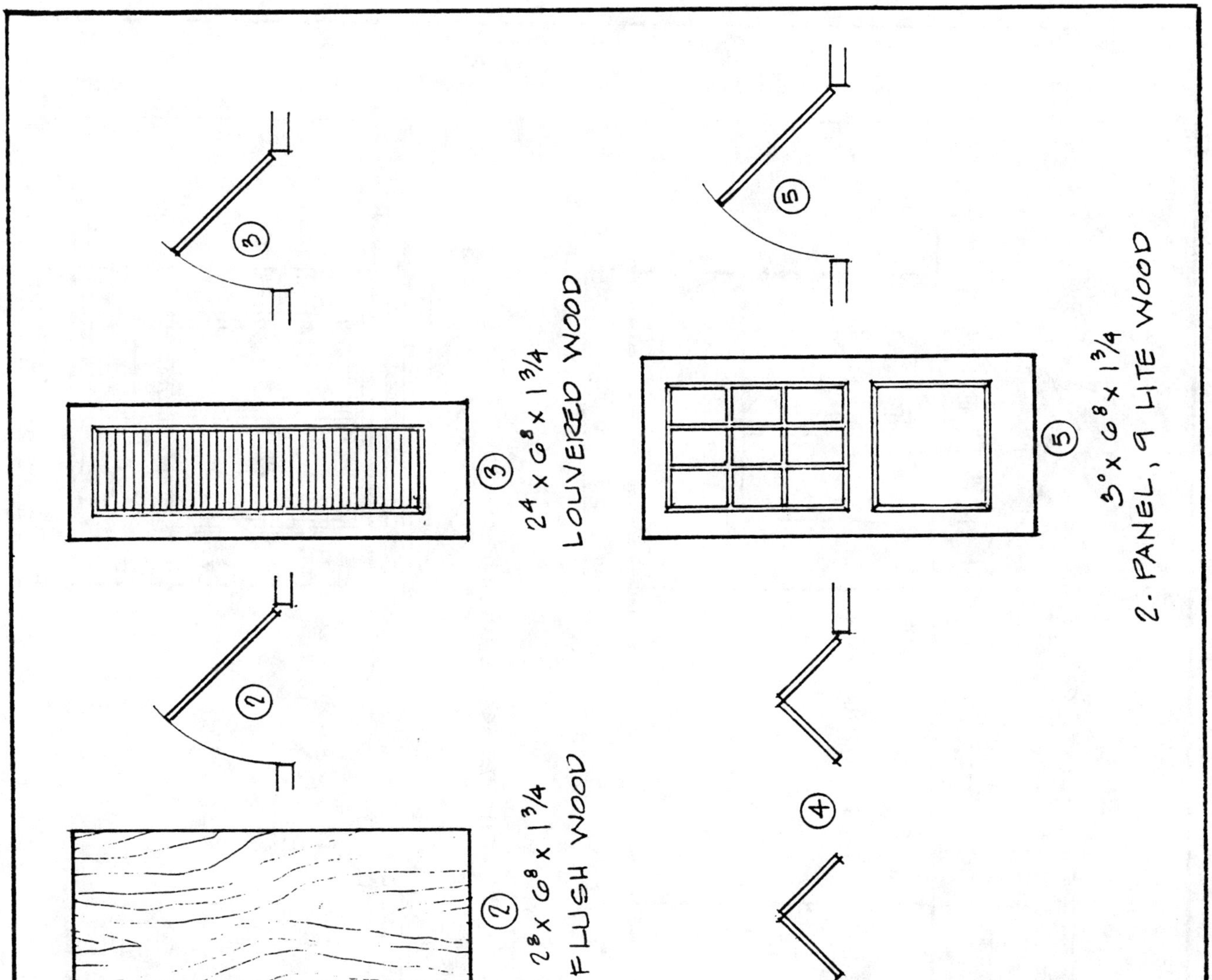

CHAPTER 4, EXERCISE 4

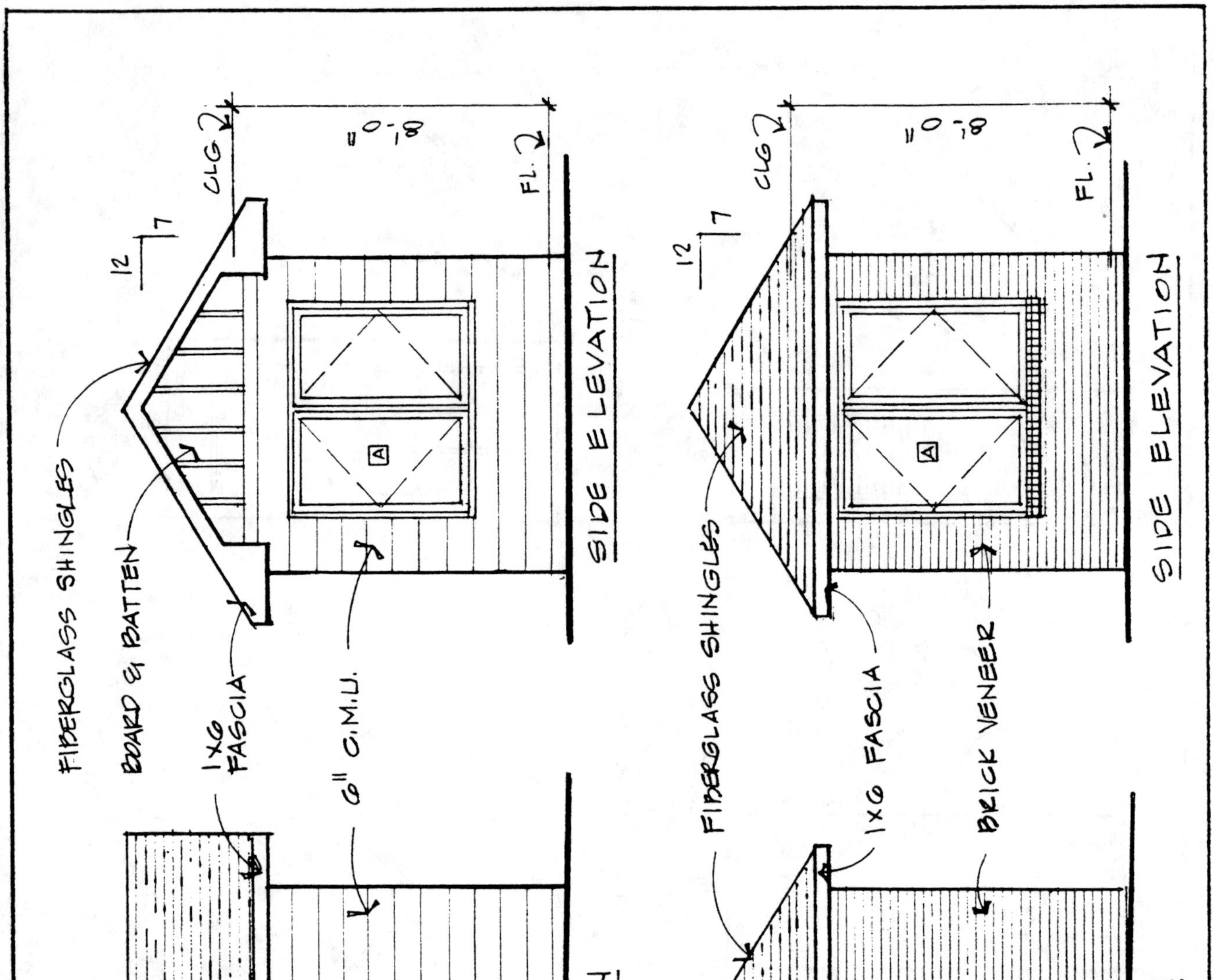

CHAPTER 4, EXERCISE 5

CHAPTER 4
REVIEW QUESTIONS AND ANSWERS

1. What do we mean by contrast in linework?

ans. Contrast in linework is achieved by line width and degree of darkness. Emphasis is placed on an object when the lines forming the objects are drawn dark and bold. Less important lines are drawn narrow and light in value.

2. How may broken lines or dashed lines be varied to represent various features on a drawing?

ans. Broken lines may be varied in length and width to represent various features on a drawing. Short broken lines may represent a hidden surface above or below the surface. Long broken lines may indicate the outline of a footing on a foundation plan or electrical wiring on an electrical plan.

3. What is a typical architectural characteristic of line intersections at corners?

ans. Line intersections should meet at corners, however,a slight overlap of lines at corners is acceptable.

4. From what directions on a drawing are dimensions made to read?

ans. Horizontal dimensions should be placed above the dimension line. Vertical dimensions should be placed to the left of the dimension line.

5. Why is a series of dimensions best placed along a continuous line on a floor plan?

ans. Dimensions are easy to locate and easy to read if they are placed along a continuous line on a floor plan.

6. What is the conventional method of expressing architectural measurement with numbers?

ans. The conventional method of expressing architectural measurement with numbers is to show feet, inches, and fractions of an inch.

7. Why are the basic structural features of a plan the first dimensions to be given consideration?

ans. **The basic structural features of a plan are the first dimensions given consideration because the structure is the basic organizing element of the building. Location of columns and load-bearing walls should be first priority.**

8. Why is it preferable to use only those abbreviations that have been standardized and commonly acceptable?

ans. **Many people working in the construction industry need to read architectural drawings, so it is preferable to use only standard abbreviations which are recognized by the majority of those reading the drawings.**

9. How can pencil smudging be removed from tracings?

ans. **Pencil smudges are difficult to remove from a pencil drawing. They can be erased with a soft eraser using an eraser shield. Care should be taken not to erase important line work.**

10. Describe three techniques used by drafters to keep drawings neat while drafting.

ans. **Using a dry cleaning pad, lifting drafting instruments over the drawing, and covering the finished part of a drawing with tracing paper are three techniques used by drafters to keep drawings neat while drafting.**

11. Draw the proper symbol for expressing a 5:12 roof pitch on a working drawing.

ans.

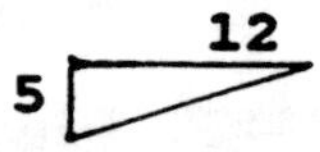

12. What is another term used for symbol hatching?

ans. **Poché is another term used for symbol hatching.**

13. On floor plans of commercial buildings, dimensions are shown from wall to wall. How are the corresponding dimensions shown on residential floor plans?

ans. **Dimensions on residential floor plans are usually shown from the centerline of partition to the centerline of partition.**

14. Why is it necessary to draw a north arrow on floor plans?

ans. **The north arrow is shown on floor plans for orientation of the building.**

15. An arrowhead is used at the ends of dimension lines, what other symbol may be used at the ends of dimension lines?

ans. **A dot is used at the intersection of dimension lines.**

16. Identify two types of schedules used on working drawings and describe how they are organized.

ans. **Room finish schedules used on working drawings are organized in vertical columns showing room numbers, room names, and finishes for walls, ceilings, and floors. Door schedules used on working drawings are organized in vertical columns showing door numbers, types, and sizes.**

17. What is the advantage of using a schedule when considerable information is involved?

ans. **A schedule offers the advantage of consolidating an extensive amount of similar information in a single location on drawings thus making the information easily accessible to estimators and builders.**

CHAPTER 5
REVIEW QUESTIONS AND ANSWERS

1. What is the main unit of length in the metric system?

   ans. **The main unit of length in the metric system is the meter (m).**

2. Define "soft" and "hard" conversion in relation to the use of metrics in construction.

   ans. **"Soft" conversion means relabeling existing dimensions in SI units and "hard" conversion will require changes in modular components to rounded off metric units.**

3. What is the size of the "basic module" used in metric construction?

   ans. **The "basic module" used in metric construction is 100mm.**

4. Describe modular coordination.

   ans. **Modular coordination is a system of dimensioning and developing plans and elevations based on measurements and building units that are designed on a modular grid that is a multiple of 4". Modular drawings are prepared over a reference grid that is based on 4" multiple.**

5. What is the primary unit of measurement for modular dimensioning?

   ans. **The primary unit of measurement for modular dimensioning is 4".**

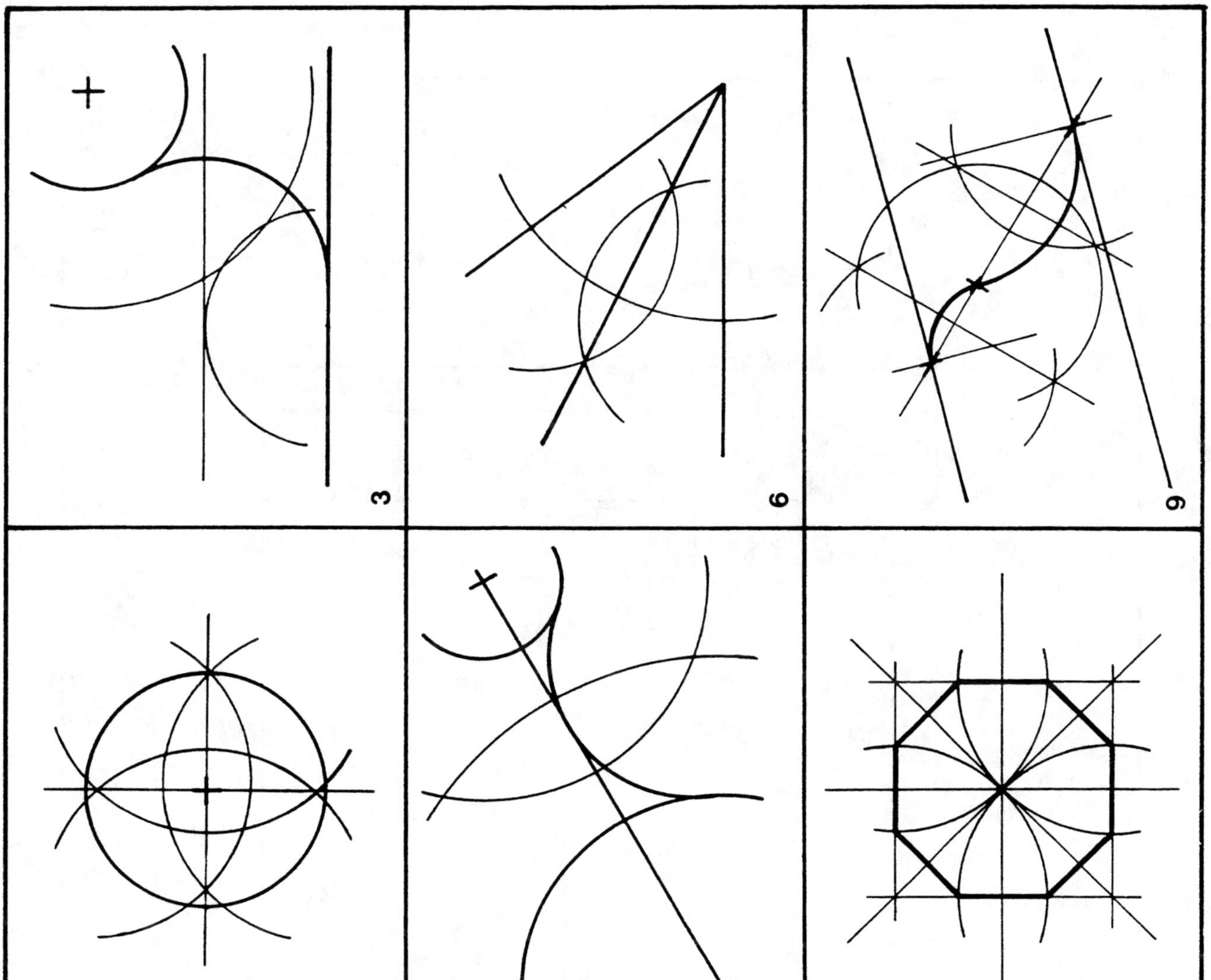

CHAPTER 6, GEOMETRIC CONSTRUCTION, EXERCISE 1-9, FIG. 6-38

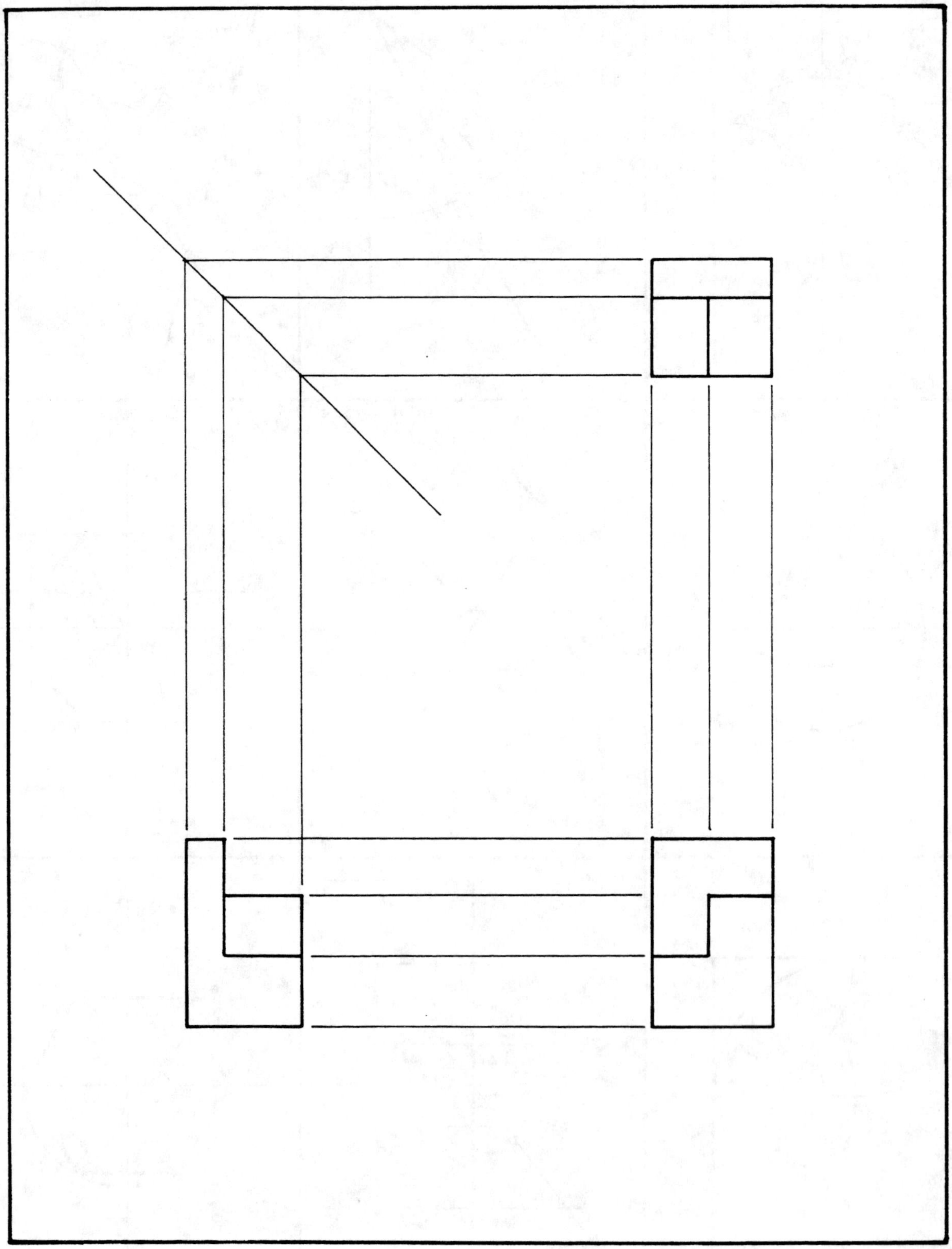

CHAPTER 6, ORTHOGRAPHIC PROJECTION, EXERCISE 1, FIG. 6-39

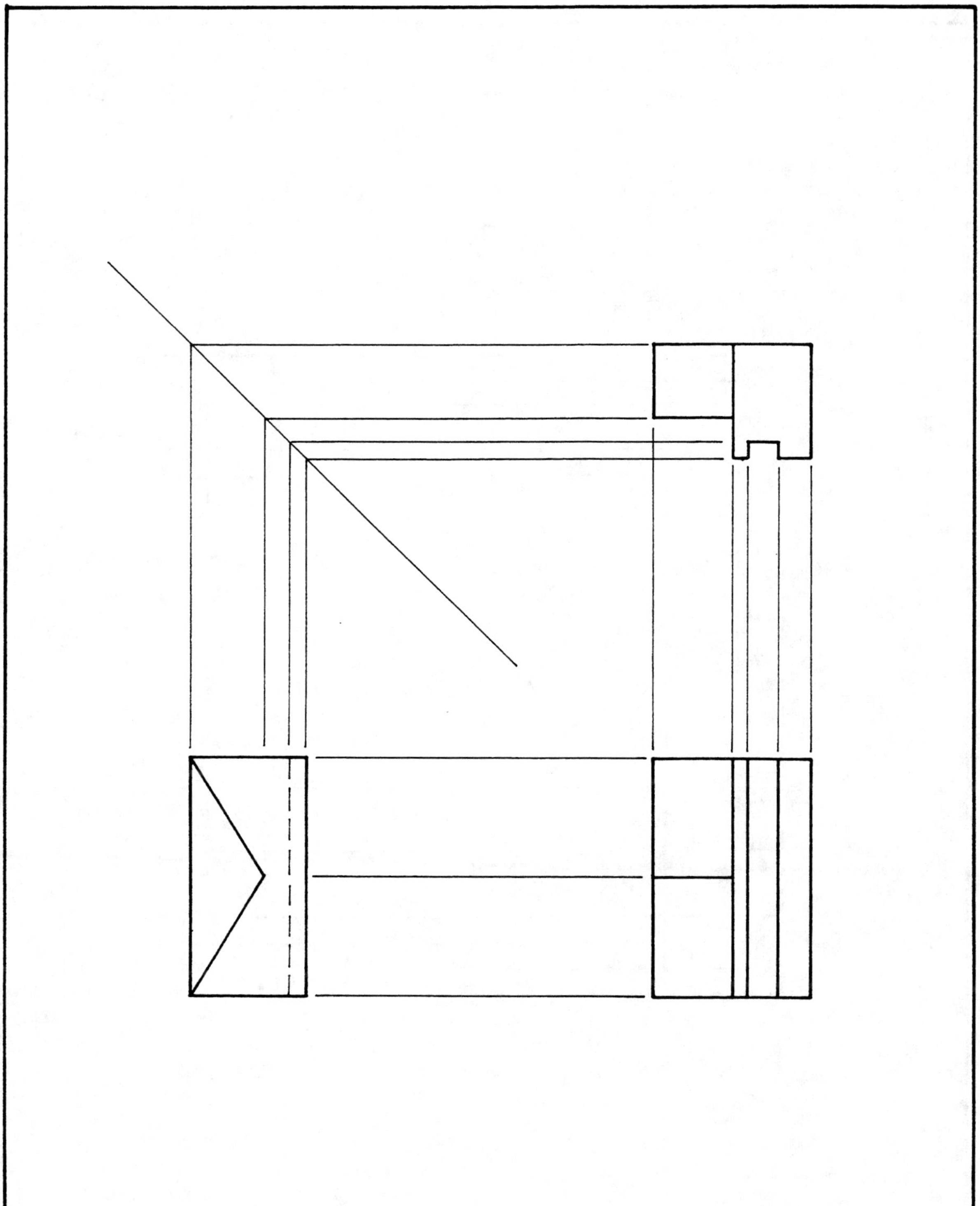

CHAPTER 6, ORTHOGRAPHIC PROJECTION, EXERCISE 2, FIG. 6-39

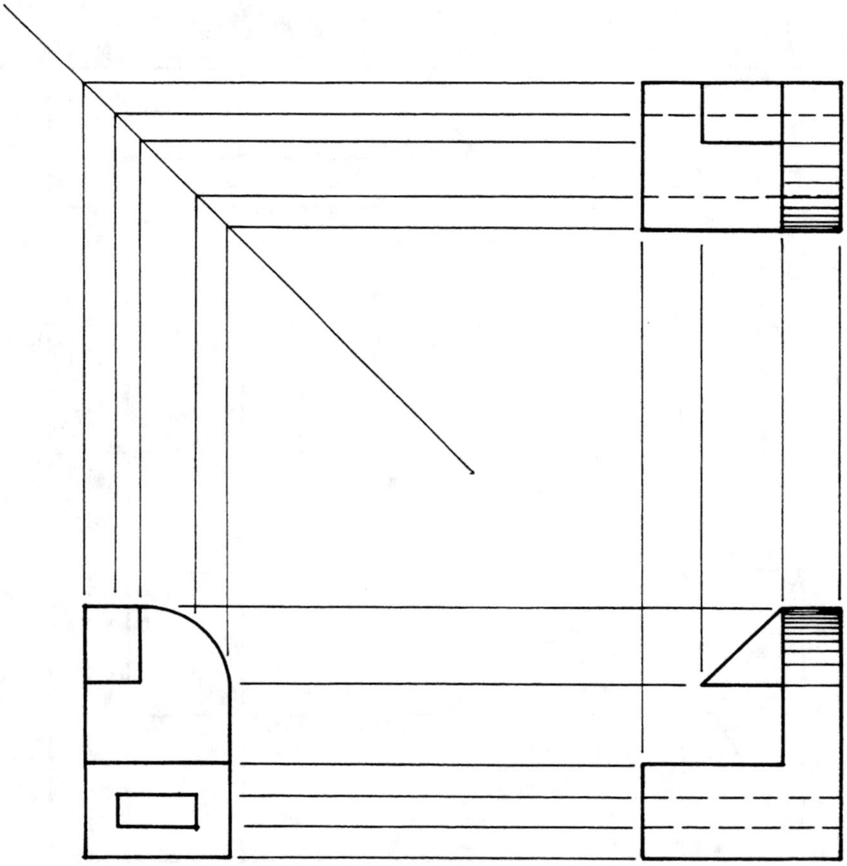

CHAPTER 6, ORTHOGRAPHIC PROJECTION, EXERCISE 3, FIG. 6-39

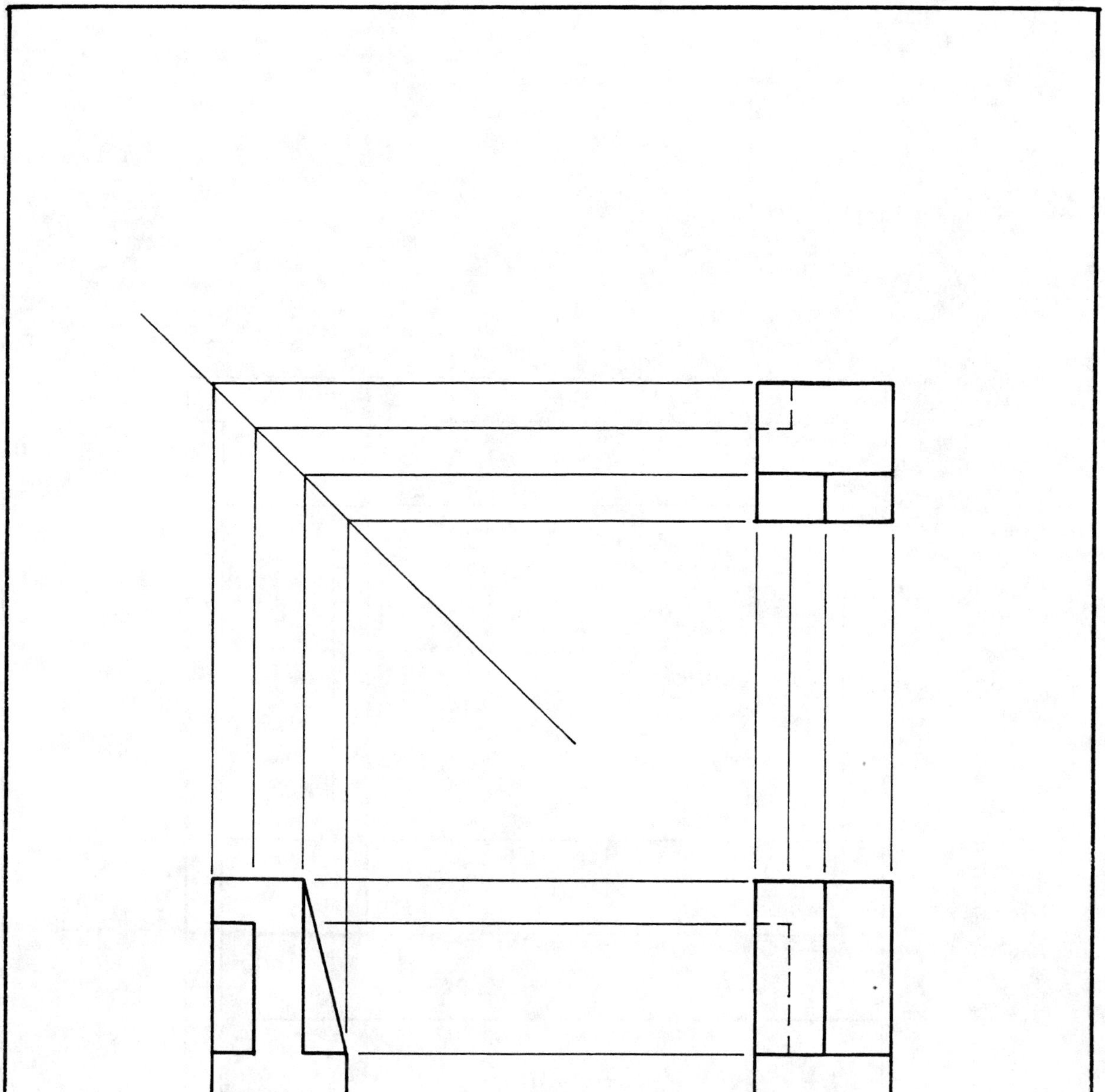

CHAPTER 6, ORTHOGRAPHIC PROJECTION, EXERCISE 4, FIG. 6-39

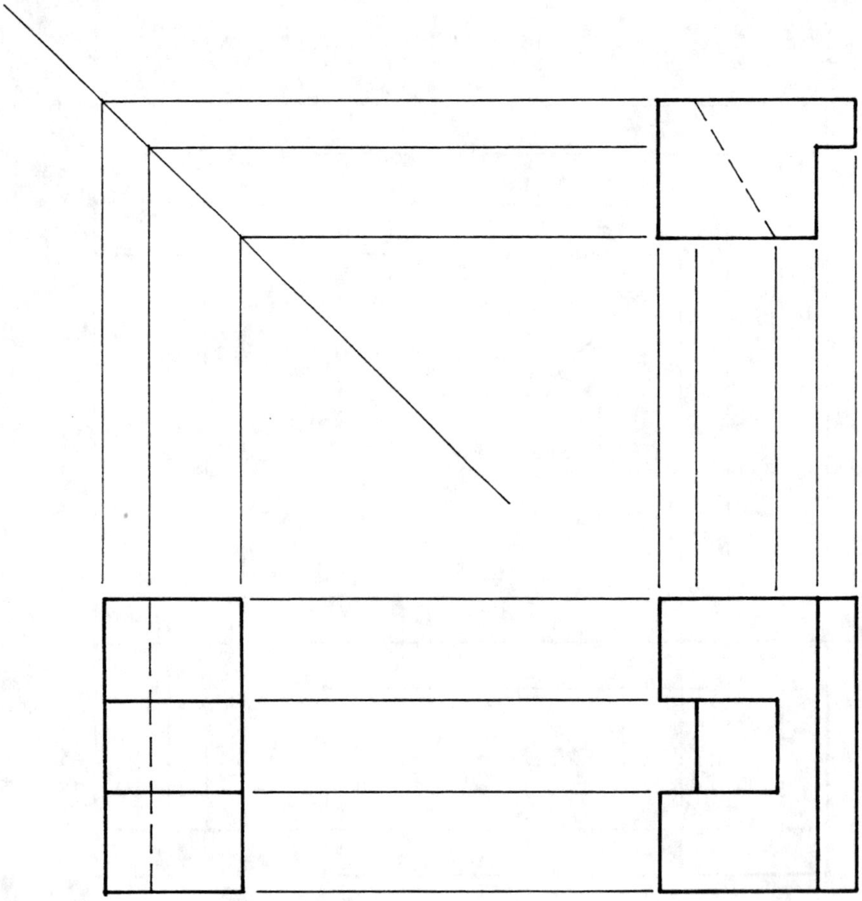

CHAPTER 6, ORTHOGRAPHIC PROJECTION, EXERCISE 5, FIG. 6-39

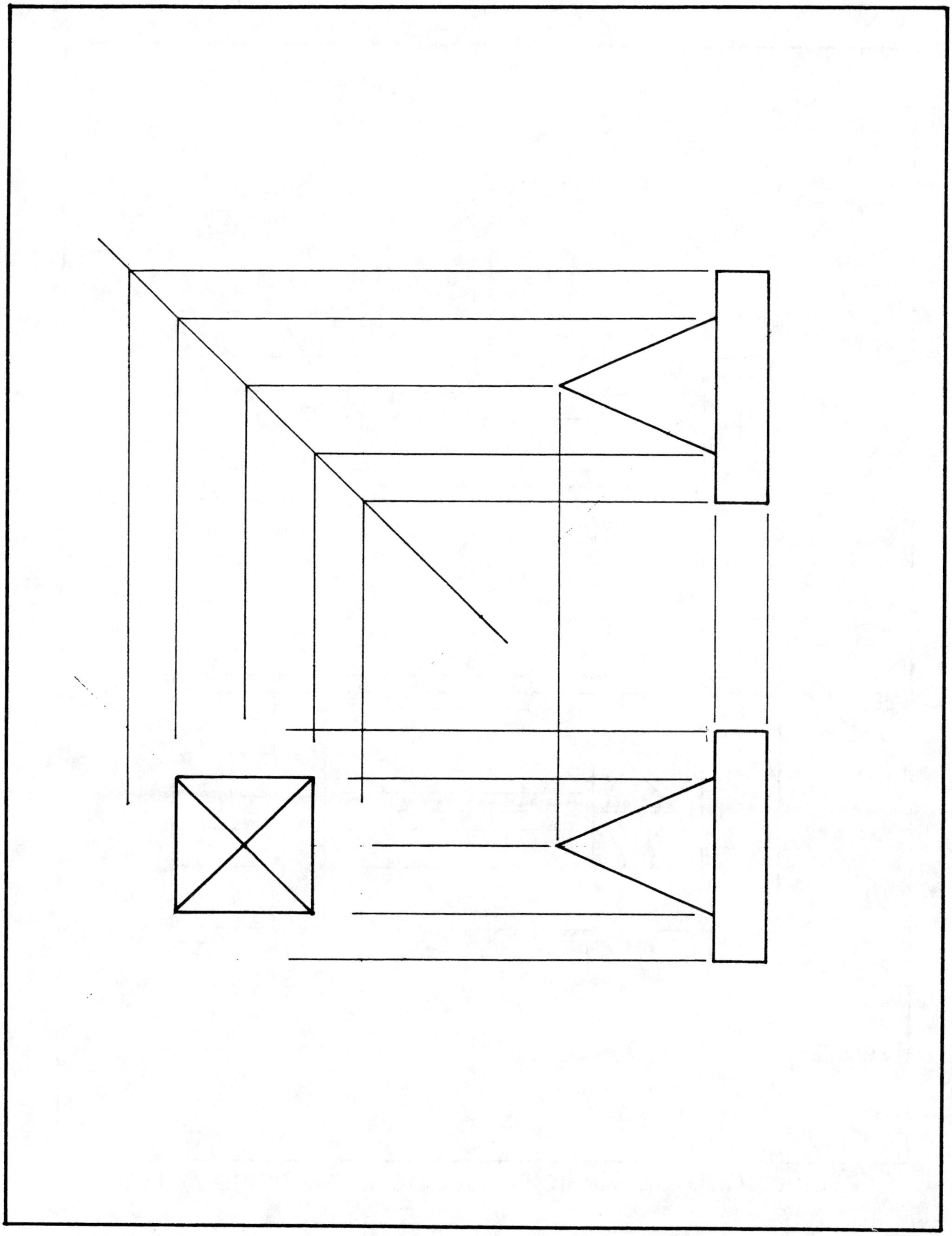

CHAPTER 6, ORTHOGRAPHIC PROJECTION, EXERCISE 6, FIG. 6-39

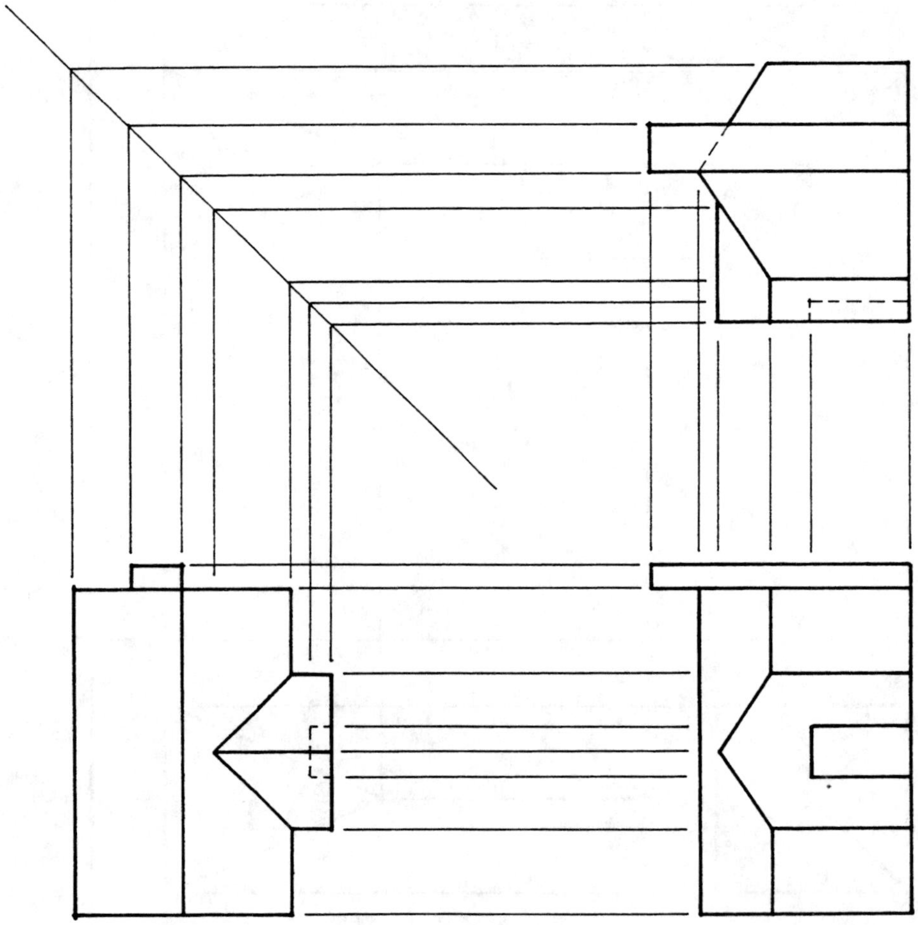

CHAPTER 6, ORTHOGRAPHIC PROJECTION, EXERCISE 7, FIG. 6-39

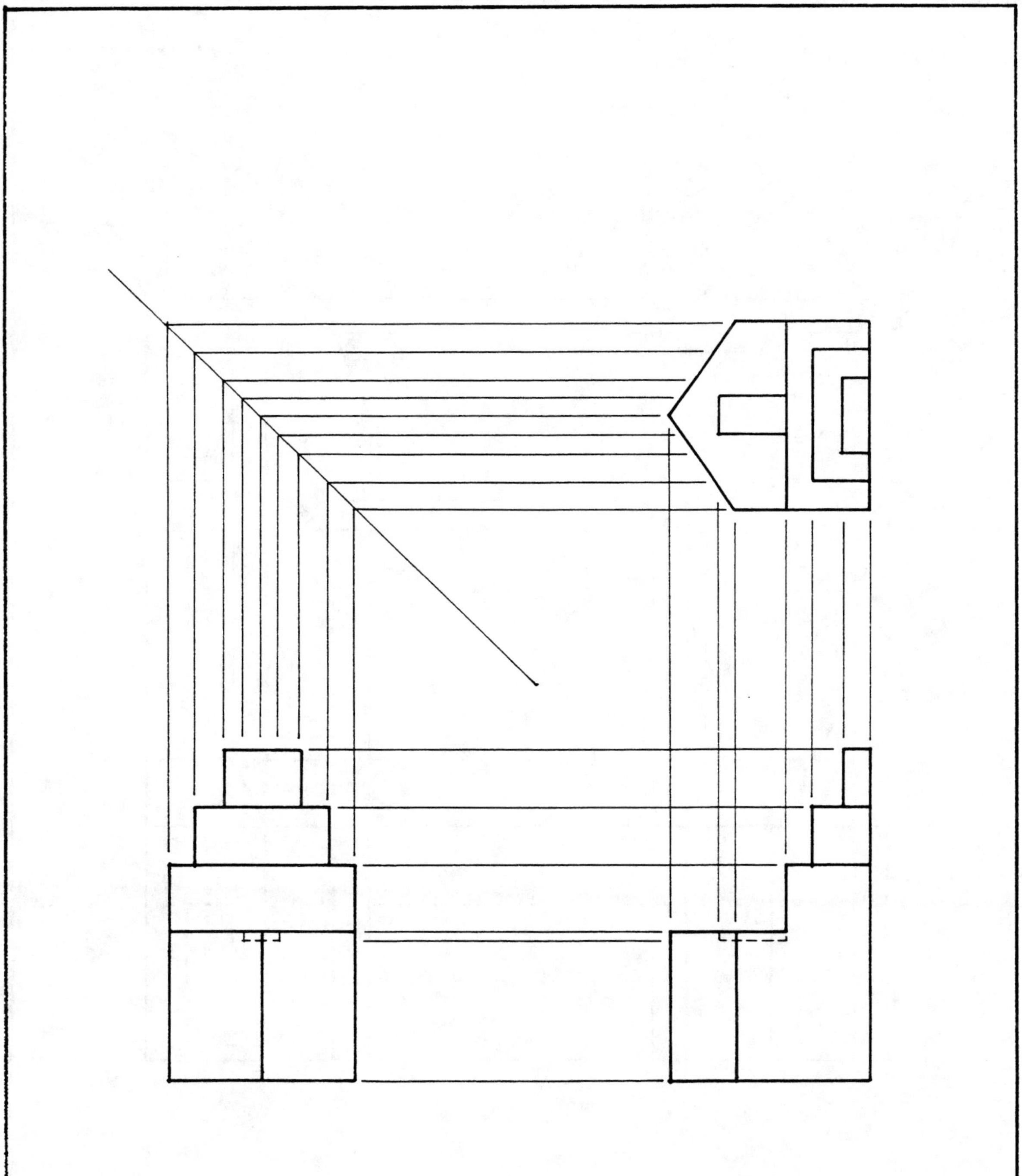

CHAPTER 6, ORTHOGRAPHIC PROJECTION, EXERCISE 8, FIG. 6-39

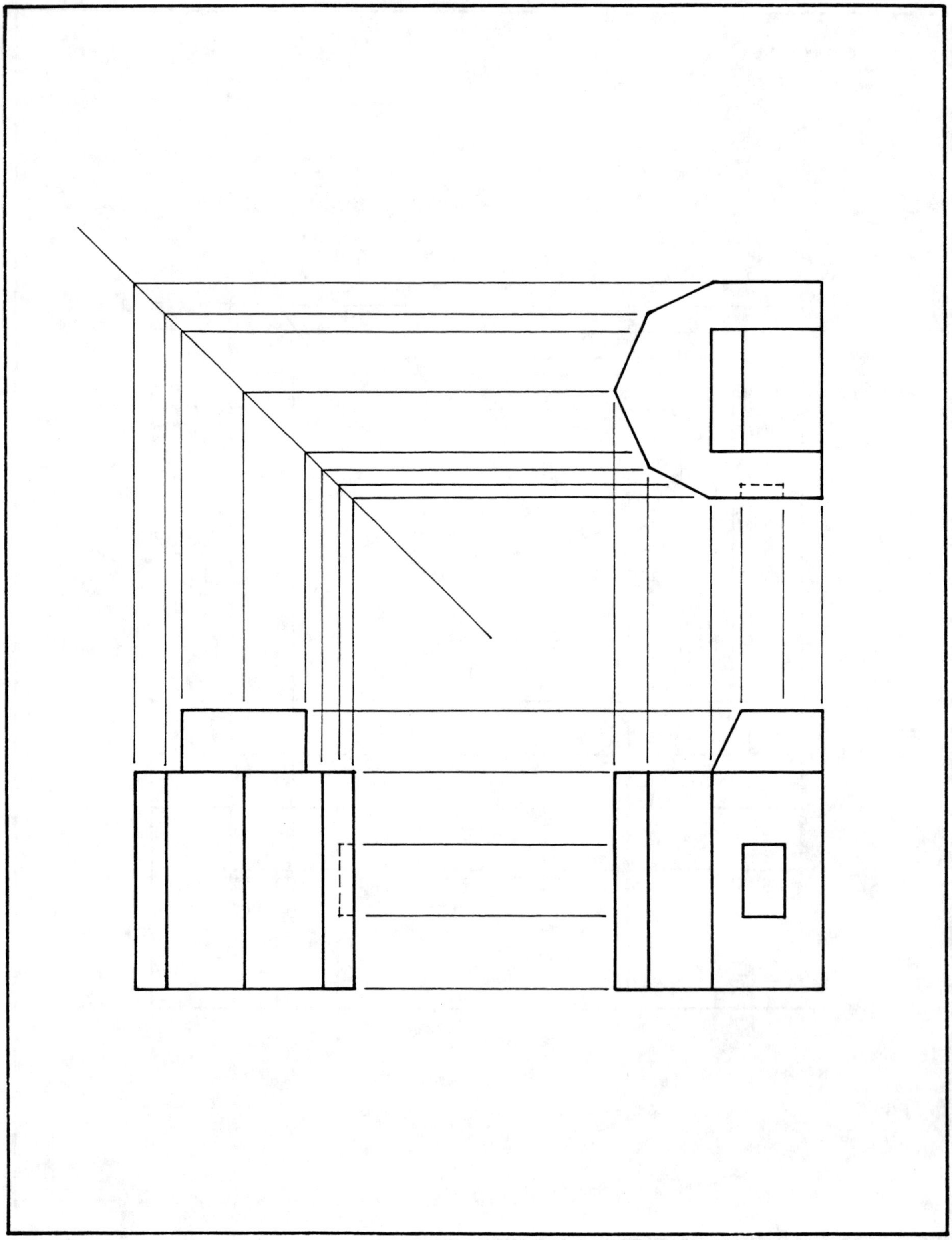

CHAPTER 6, ORTHOGRAPHIC PROJECTION, EXERCISE 9, FIG. 6-39

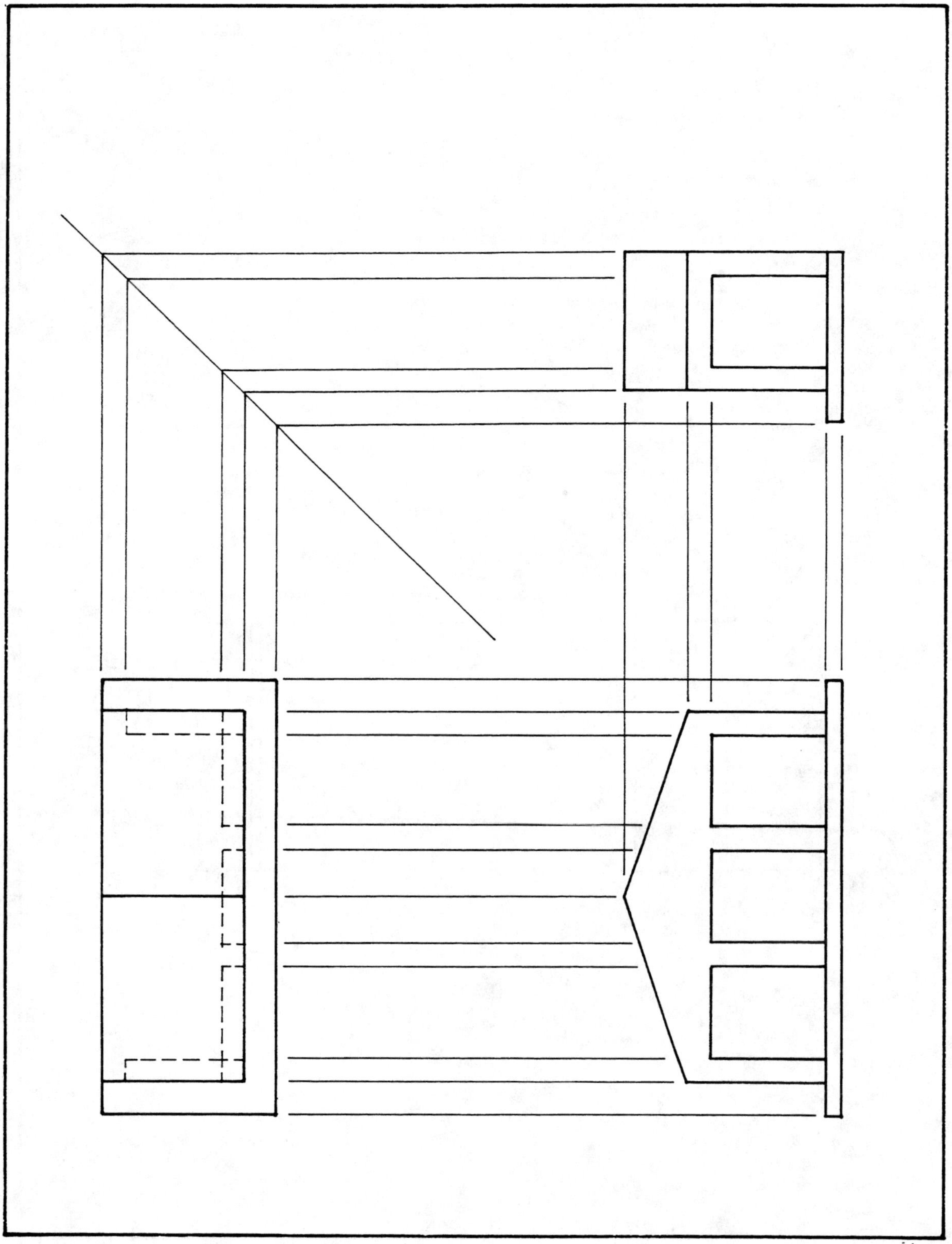

CHAPTER 6, ORTHOGRAPHIC PROJECTION, EXERCISE 10, FIG. 6-39

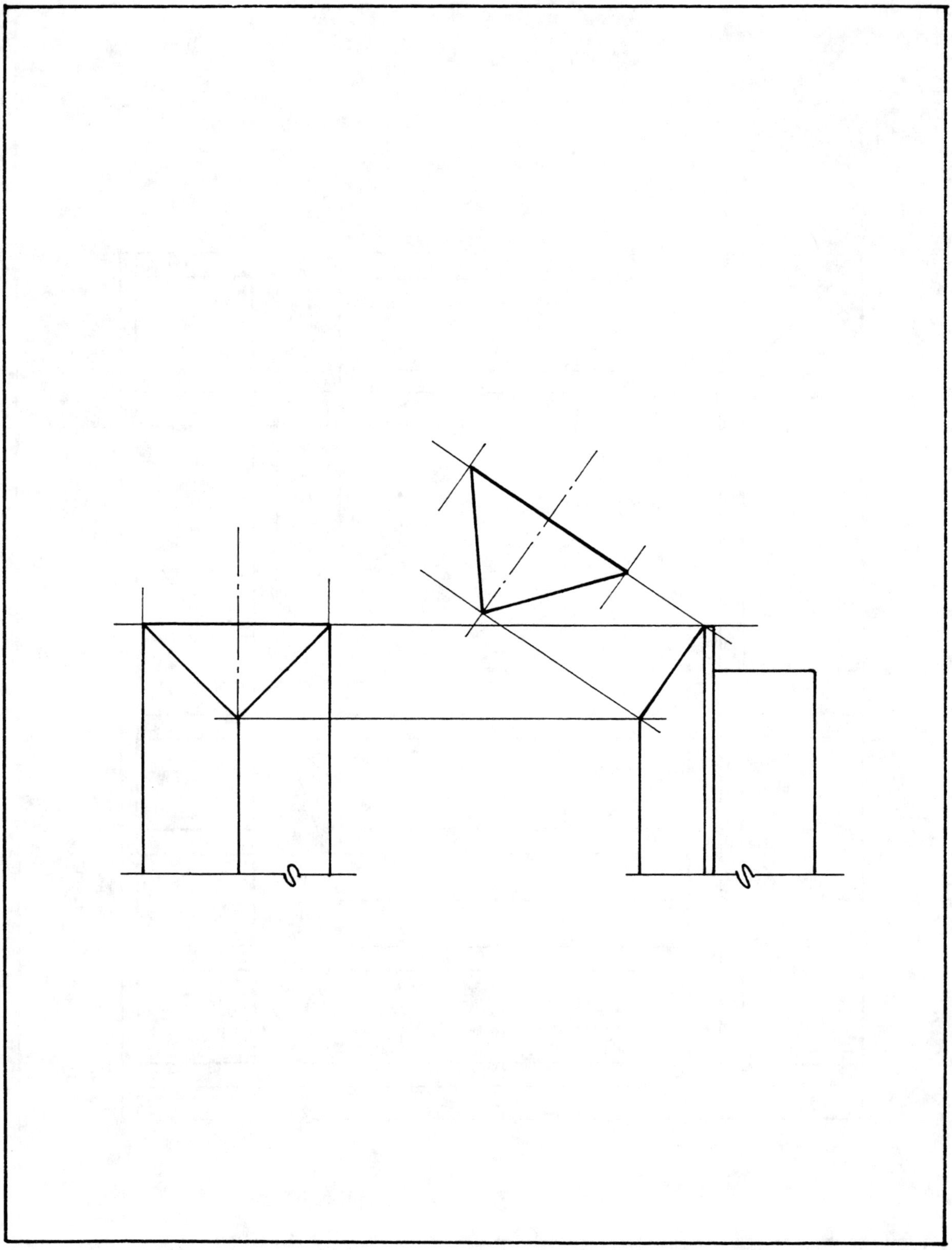

CHAPTER 6, AUXILIARY VIEWS, EXERCISE 1, FIG. 6-17

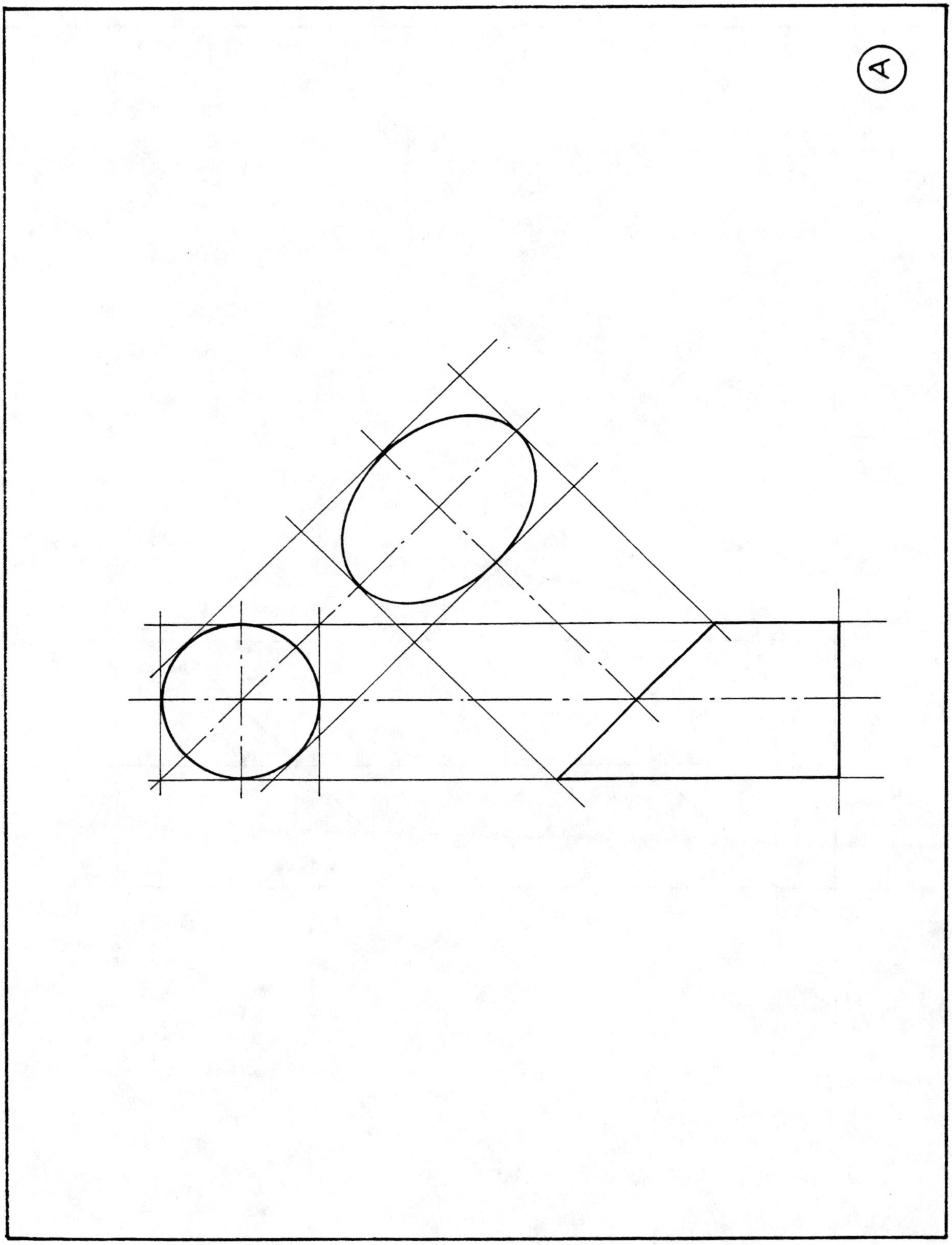

CHAPTER 6, AUXILIARY VIEWS, EXERCISE 2, FIG. 6-40

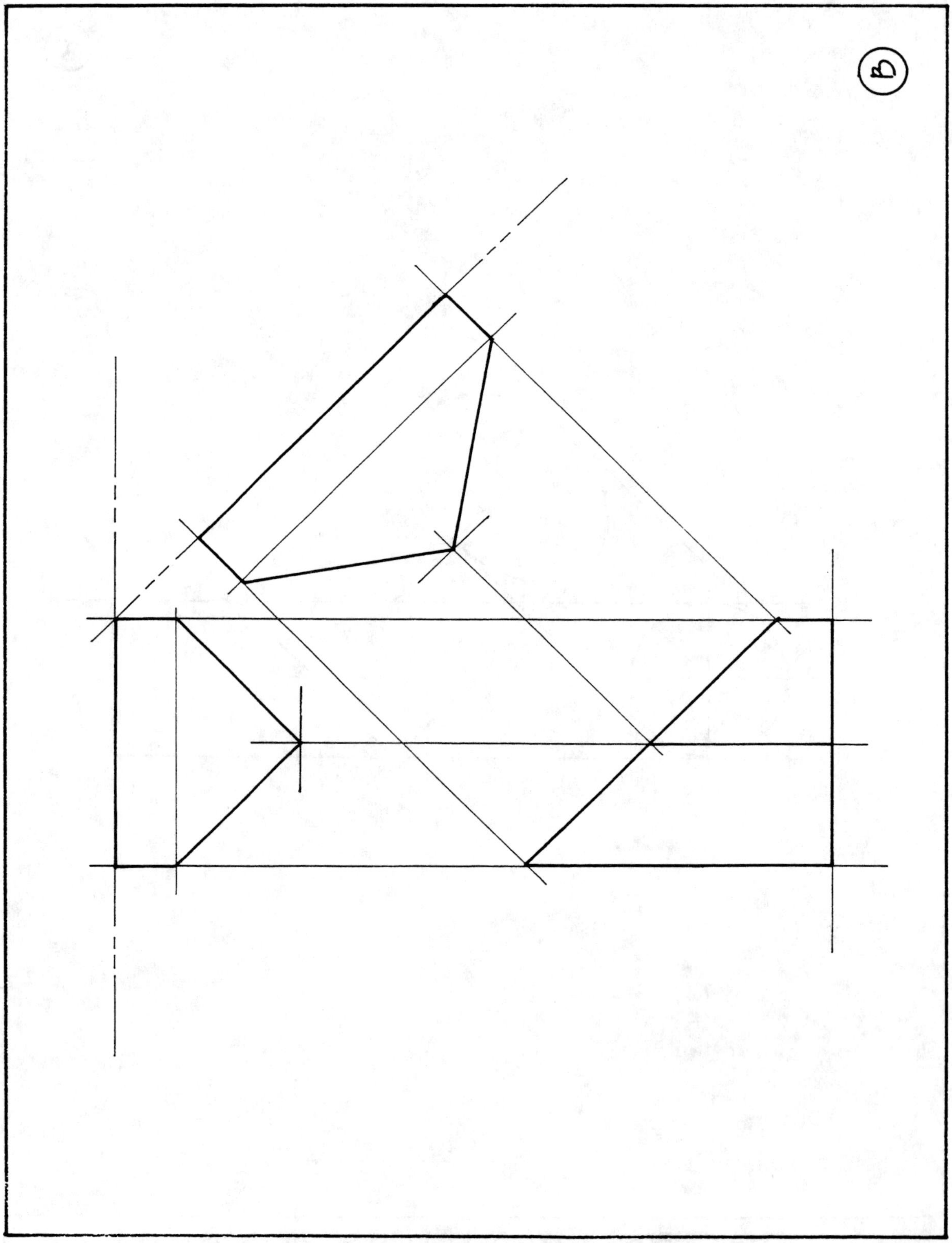

CHAPTER 6, AUXILIARY VIEWS, EXERCISE 2, FIG. 6-40

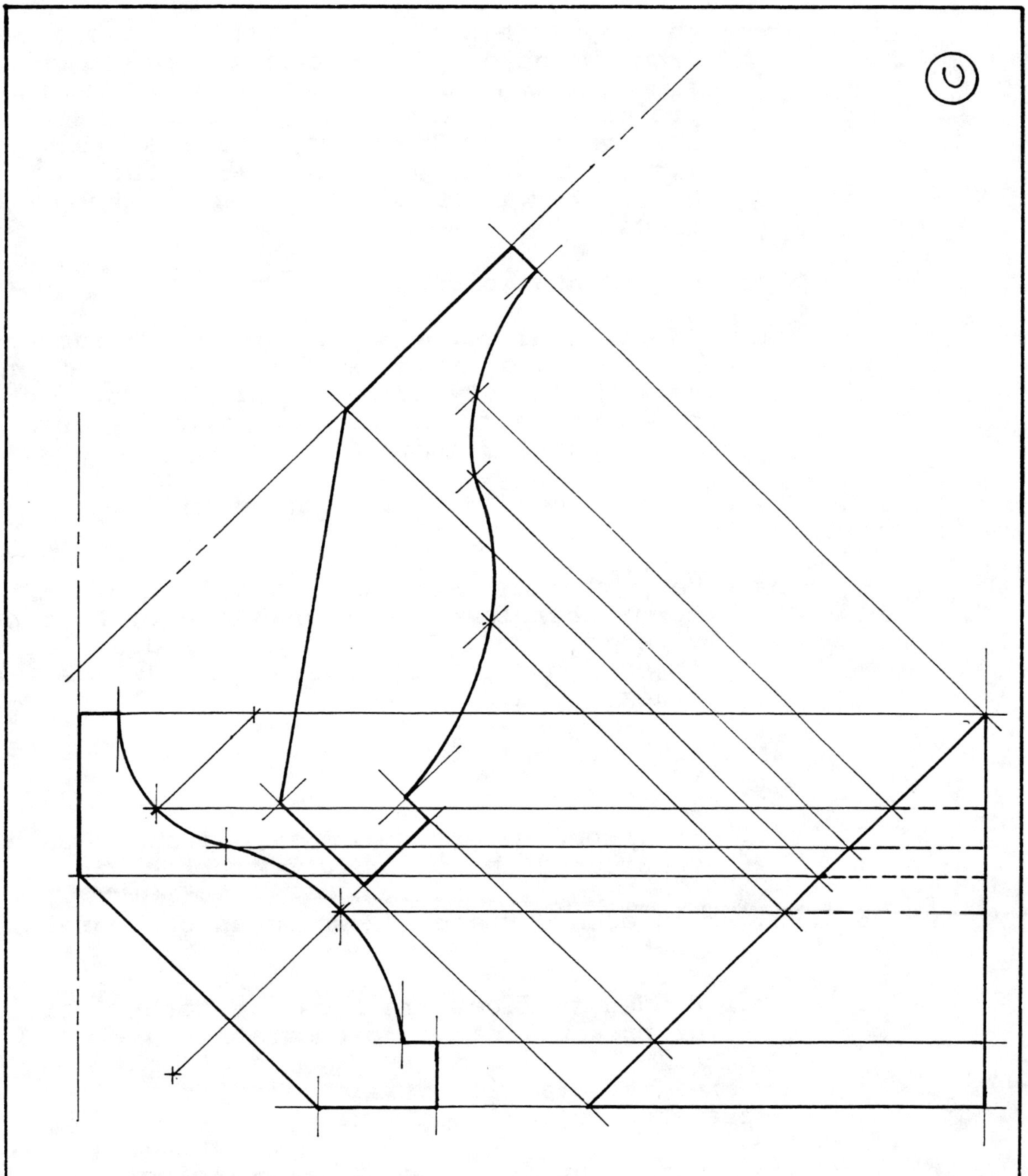

CHAPTER 6, AUXILIARY VIEWS, EXERCISE 2, FIG. 6-40

CHAPTER 6
REVIEW QUESTIONS AND ANSWERS

1. Describe the term orthographic projection.

   ans. **An image created by lines that are projected from an object to a transparent plane out from the object is known as an orthographic projection. Orthographic projections commonly create the front, sides, and rear elevation views of an object; however, the top and bottom views are also considered orthographic views.**

2. What is a frontal plane?

   ans. **The frontal plane is a vertical plane which is positioned out from the front elevation of an object. By the orthographic projection process the front of the object is drawn on the frontal plane.**

3. Why do drawings of many objects require more than one orthographic view?

   ans. **Many objects are complicated in shape and form; therefore, more than one orthographic view is required to adequately describe the object, such as top, bottom, front, rear, and sides.**

4. Which orthographic view is considered the major view?

   ans. **The front elevation of an object is usually considered the major orthographic view.**

5. How are hidden surfaces shown on an orthographic view?

   ans. **Hidden surfaces are shown as dashed (hidden) or broken lines on orthographic views.**

6. Why are orthographic views of a building often drawn in an unrelated position on working drawings?

   ans. **Orthographic views of a building are often drawn in an unrelated position on working drawings so that all the elevation views would have the floor level parallel with the**

bottom of the sheet thus presenting the views as one would see them in reality.

7. What is the cutting plane of a section?

ans. **The cutting plane is an imaginary plane that slices through an object identifying the place at which materials have been removed to reveal a sectional view of the remaining part of the object.**

8. Why are cutting planes sometimes offset rather than straight planes?

ans. **Cutting planes are sometimes offset to show special features about the object that cannot be revealed if the cutting plane passes through the object on a continuous straight plane.**

9. Why are hidden lines seldom used in section views?

ans. **Hidden or dashed lines are seldom shown on section views since these lines may become confusing to the viewer.**

10. What is the advantage of a partial section?

ans. **A partial has the advantage of permitting the viewer to see both the elevation and section view of an object on the same drawing or detail.**

11. Why are auxiliary surfaces projected to planes that are parallel to the surface?

ans. **Auxiliary surfaces are projected to planes parallel to the surfaces to prevent distortion of the surface when drawn.**

12. How are numerous sections identified as to their position on the major view?

ans. **Most sections on the major view will be vertical sections and are identified by a section cut symbol on the front elevation (major view).**

13. Describe a transverse section.

ans. **A vertical section, if completely taken through the narrower width of a building is called a transverse section.**

14. Describe a longitudinal section.

ans. **A vertical section, if completely taken through the long dimension of the building is called a longitudinal section.**

15. Define the term poché.

ans. **Lining a section with the proper symbol to represent a specific building material is called poché.**

16. How many orthographic views can be made from a cube?

ans. **Six orthographic views can be made from a cube: top, bottom, front, rear, right, and left sides.**

17. What two views of a house could be revealed if a horizontal cutting plane passes midway between the floor and ceiling and completely bisects the house?

ans. **The floor plan and the reflected ceiling plan may be revealed if a horizontal cutting plane passes midway between the floor and ceiling and completely bisects the house.**

18. Why is it important to draw a vertical wall section from the footing to the roof of a house?

ans. **It is important to draw a small section from the footing to the roof of a house to show all the materials of construction in detail.**

19. Why are pictorial sections used?

ans. **Sometimes pictorial sections are used because they may be the most effective way to show structural assemblies or other construction features that are awkward to explain with orthographic views.**

20. What is a Golden Section?

ans. **The "golden section" is a Greek method of dividing lines and forms into pleasing proportions. The ratio of one division to the other can be stated as 1 to 1.618.**

The following pages contain an additional set of exercises in three view projection. There is also a solution sheet and a computer generated axonometric view of each solution.

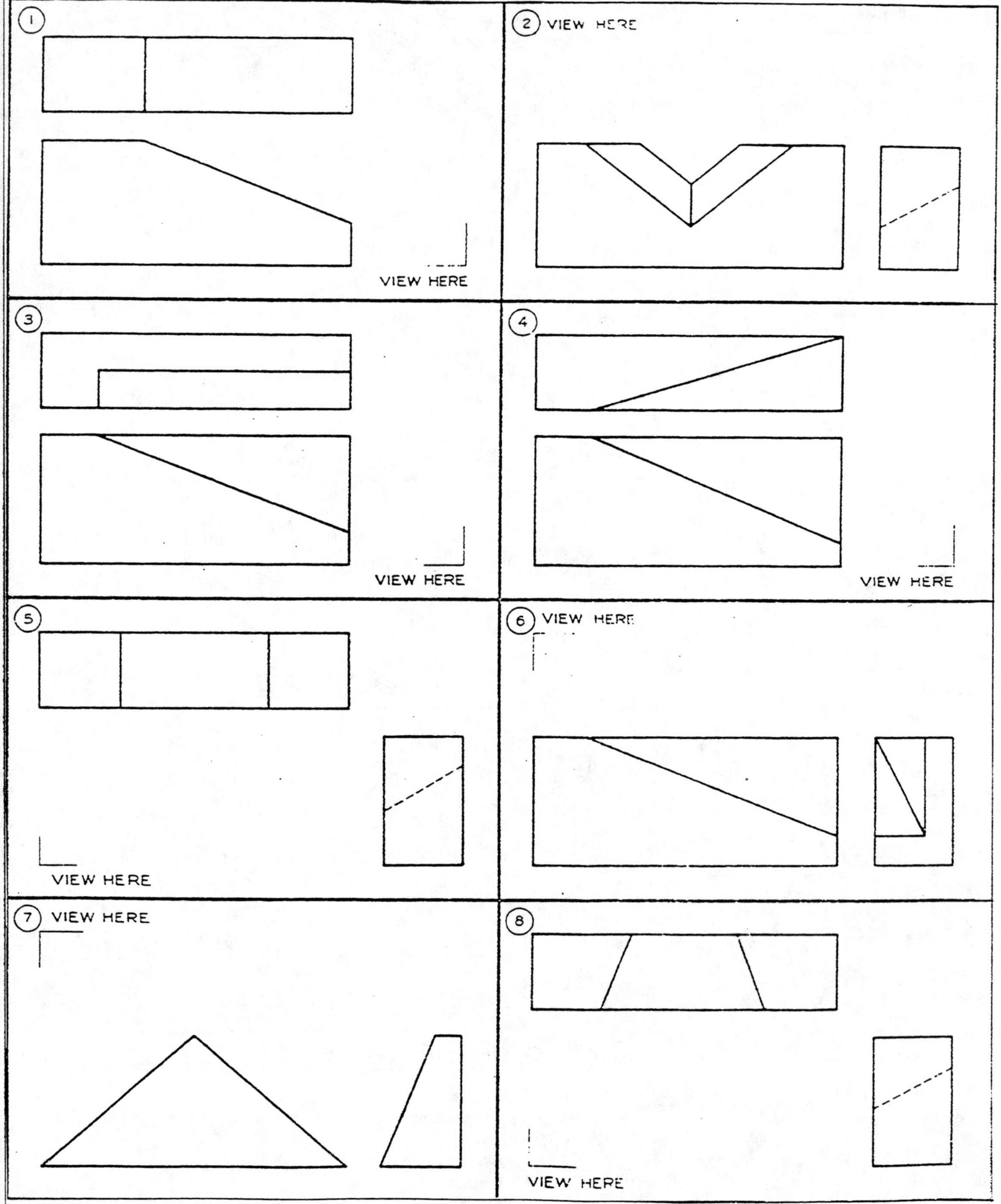
1
VIEW HERE
2 VIEW HERE
3
VIEW HERE
4
VIEW HERE
5
VIEW HERE
6 VIEW HERE
7 VIEW HERE
8
VIEW HERE

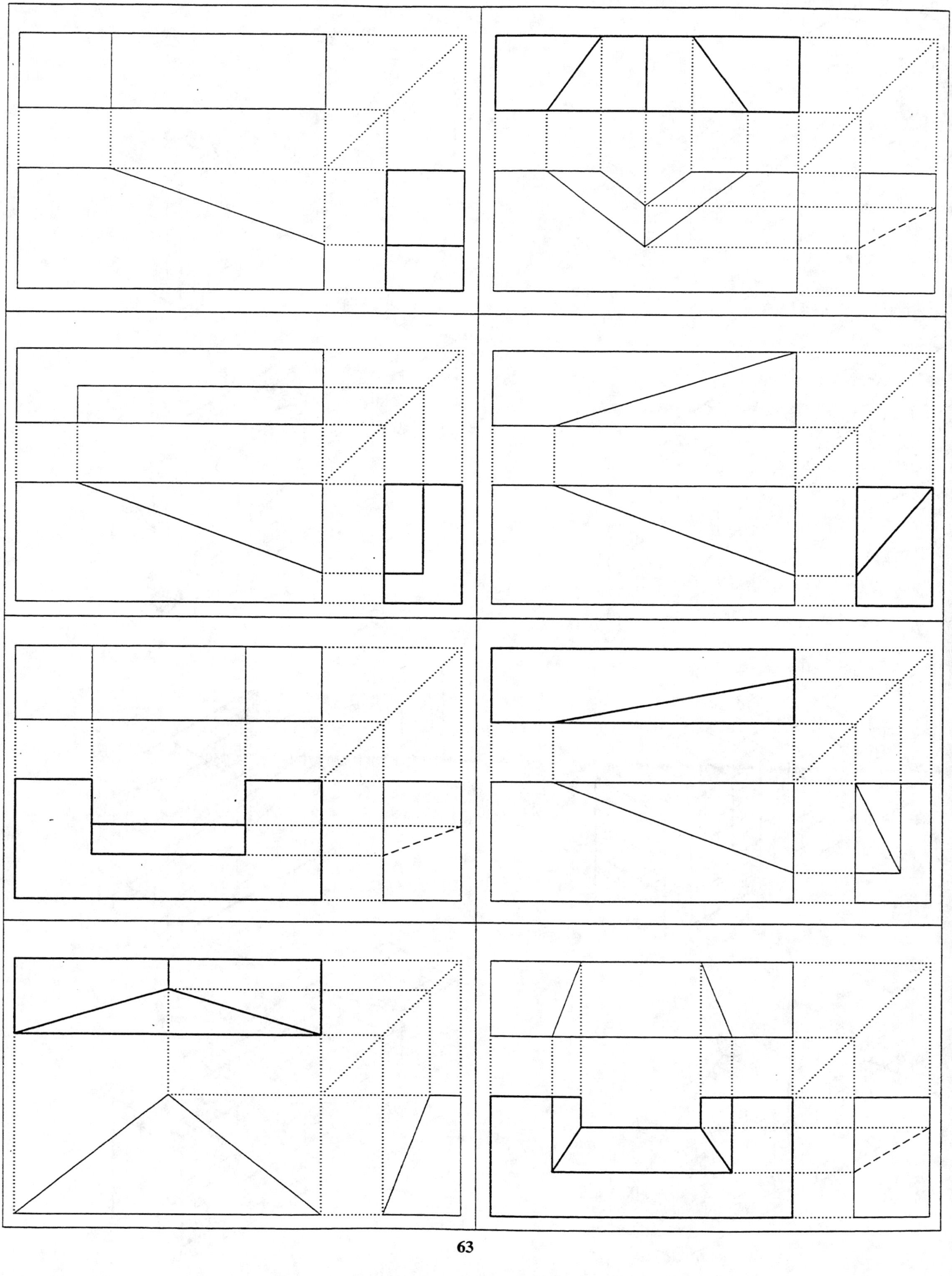

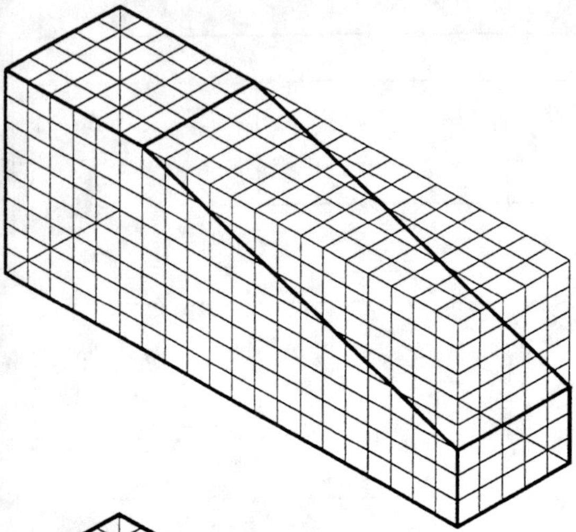
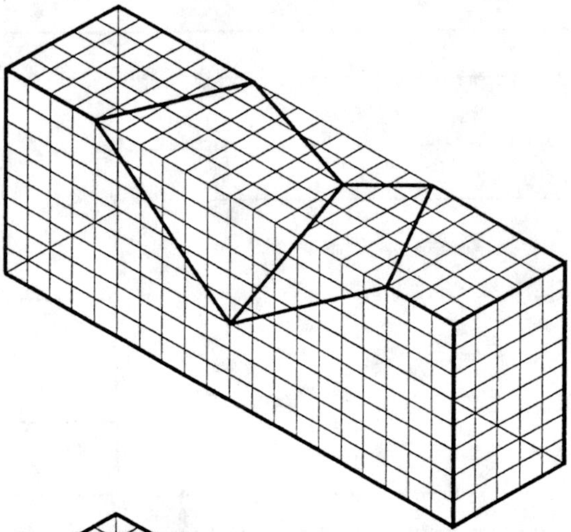
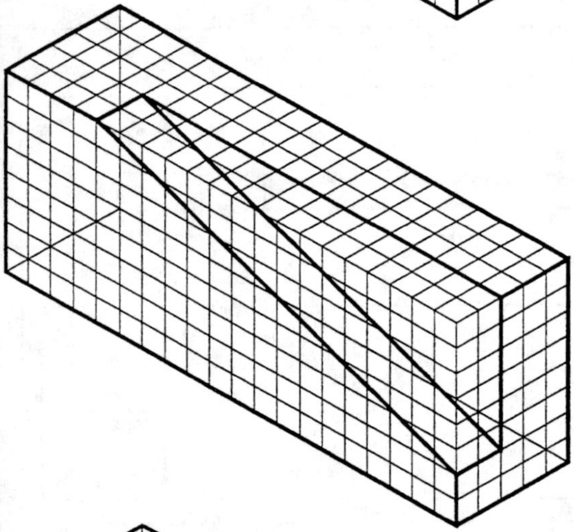
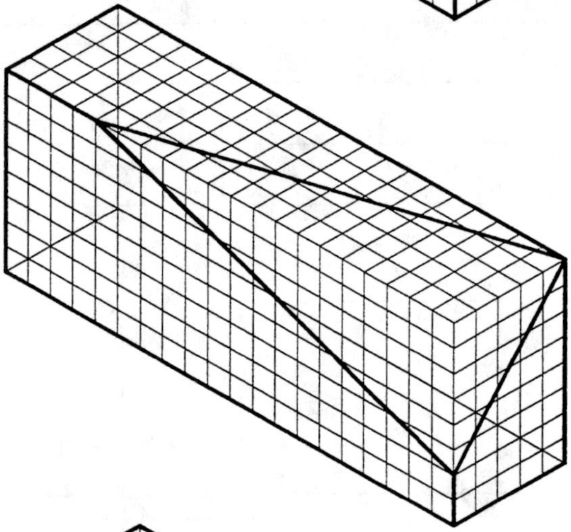
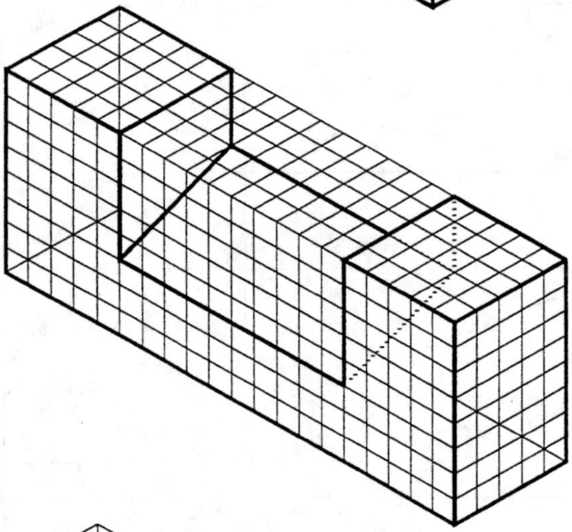
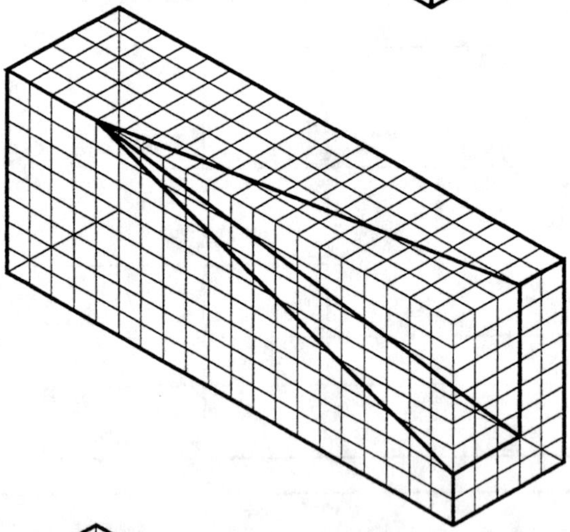
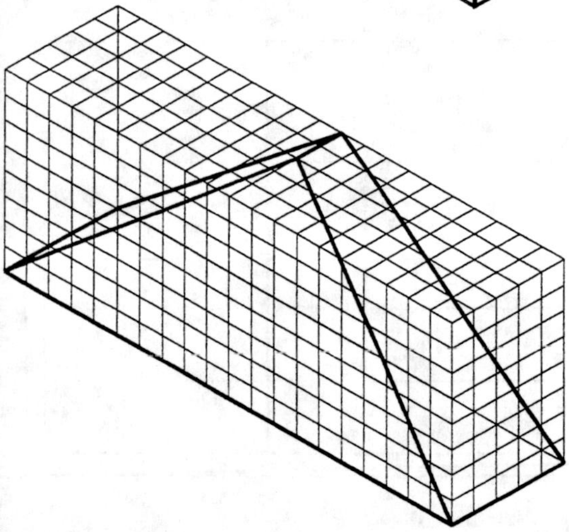
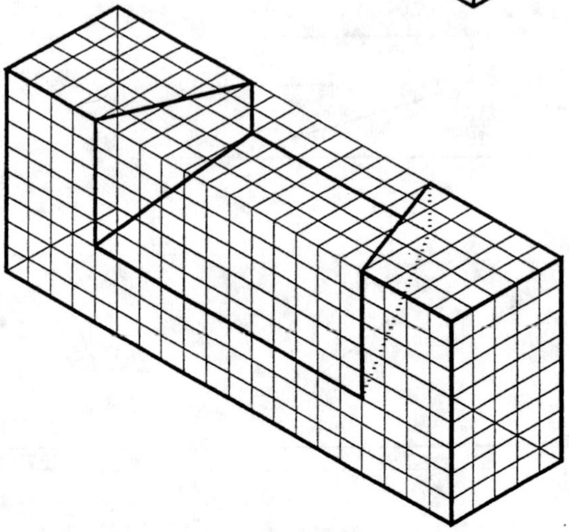

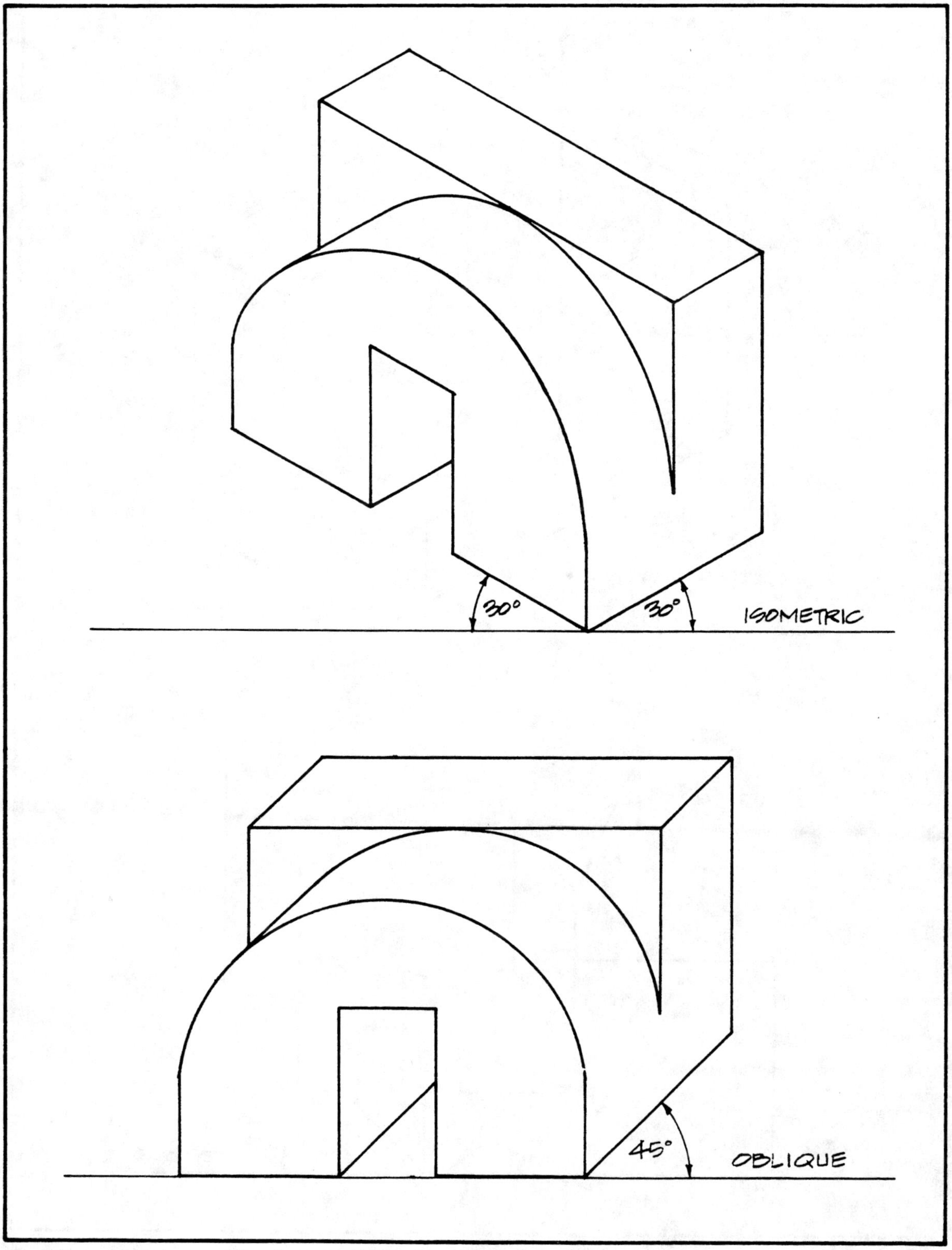

CHAPTER 7, EXERCISE 1, FIG. 7-34

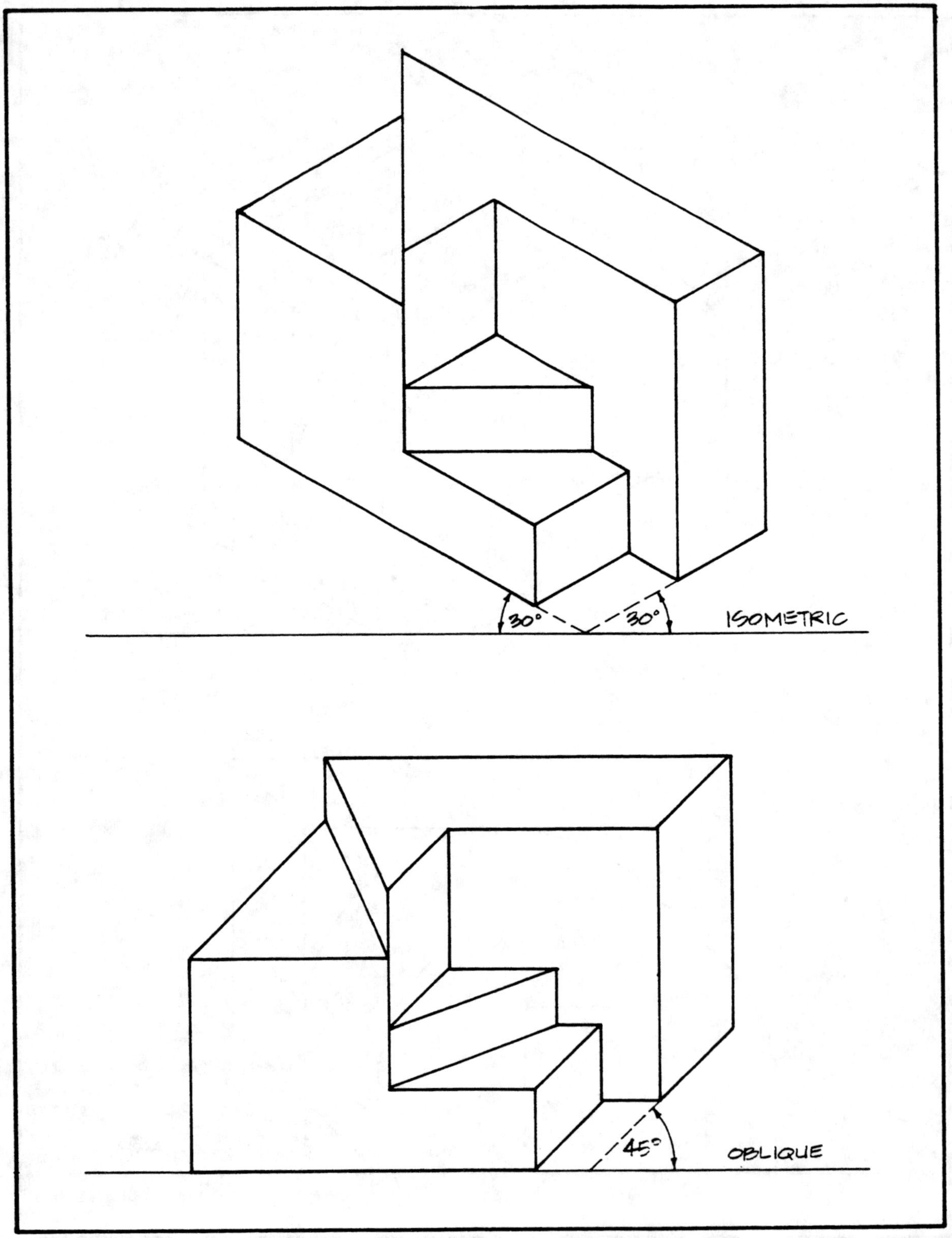

CHAPTER 7, EXERCISE 2, FIG. 7-34

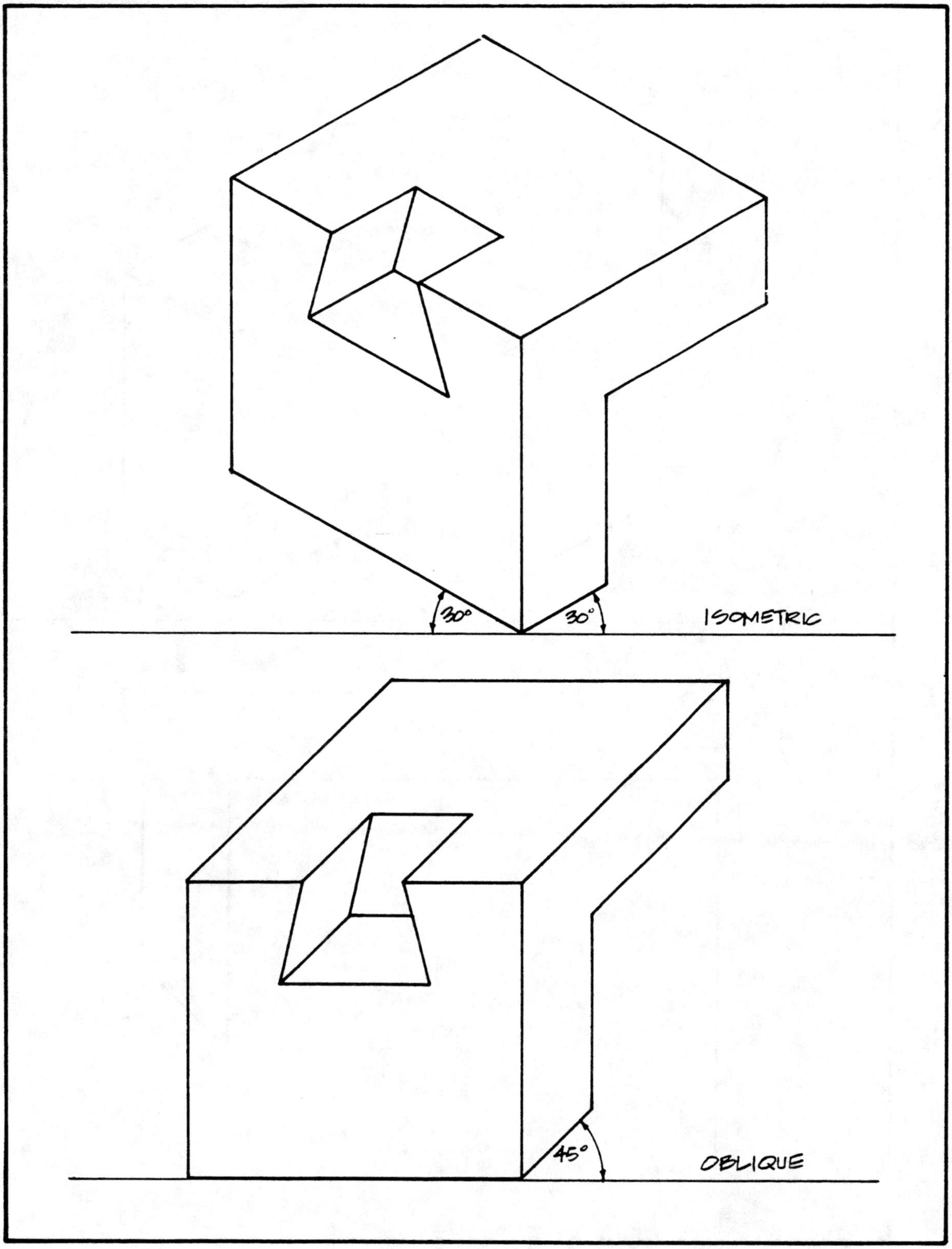

CHAPTER 7, EXERCISE 3, FIG. 7-34

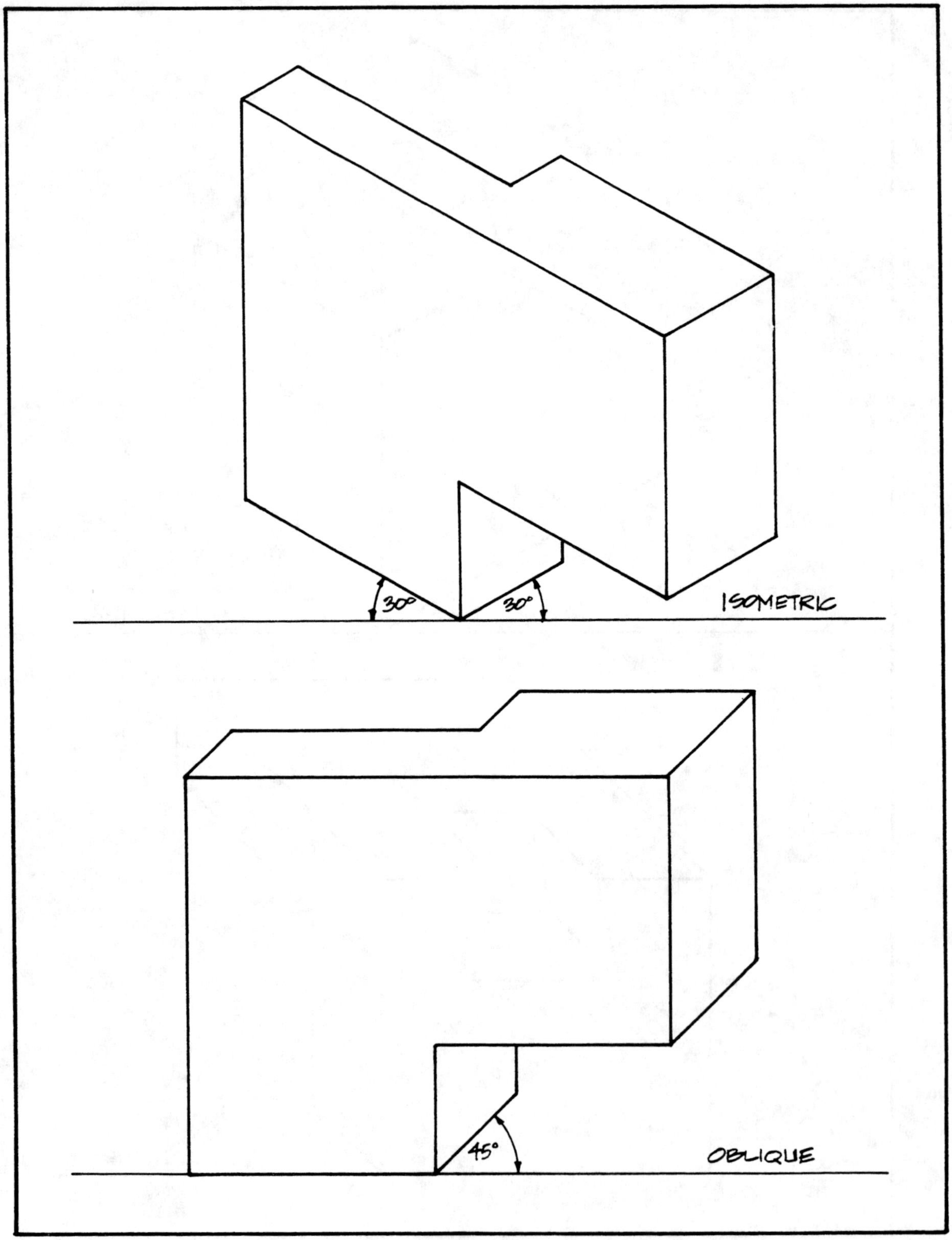

CHAPTER 7, EXERCISE 4, FIG. 7-34

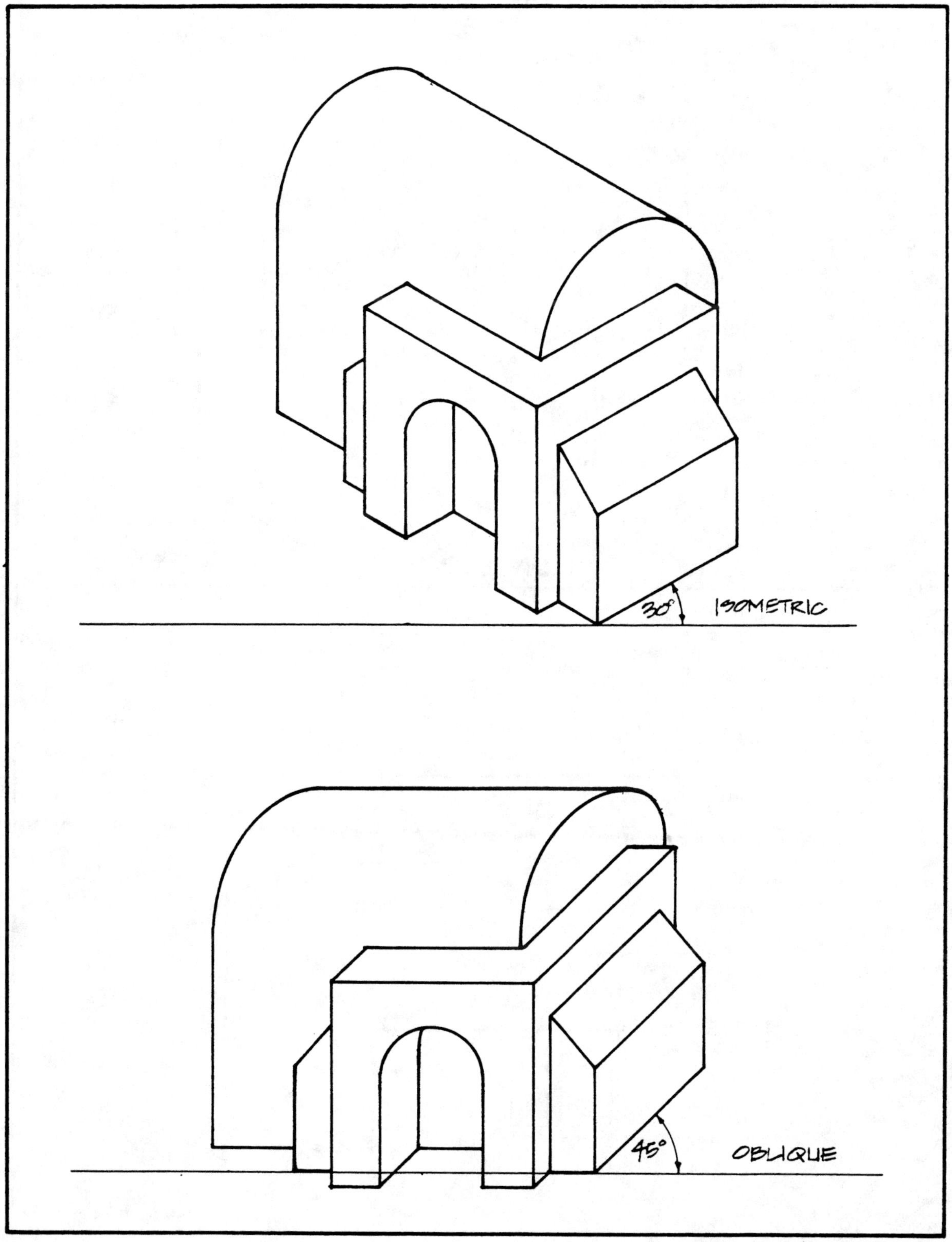

CHAPTER 7, EXERCISE 5, FIG. 7-34

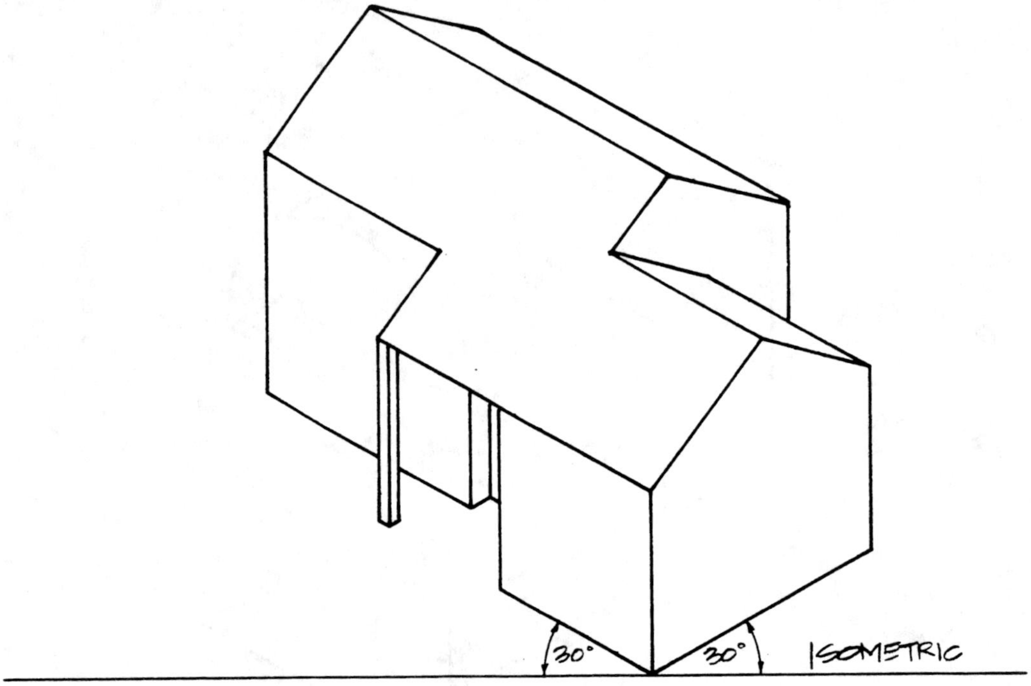

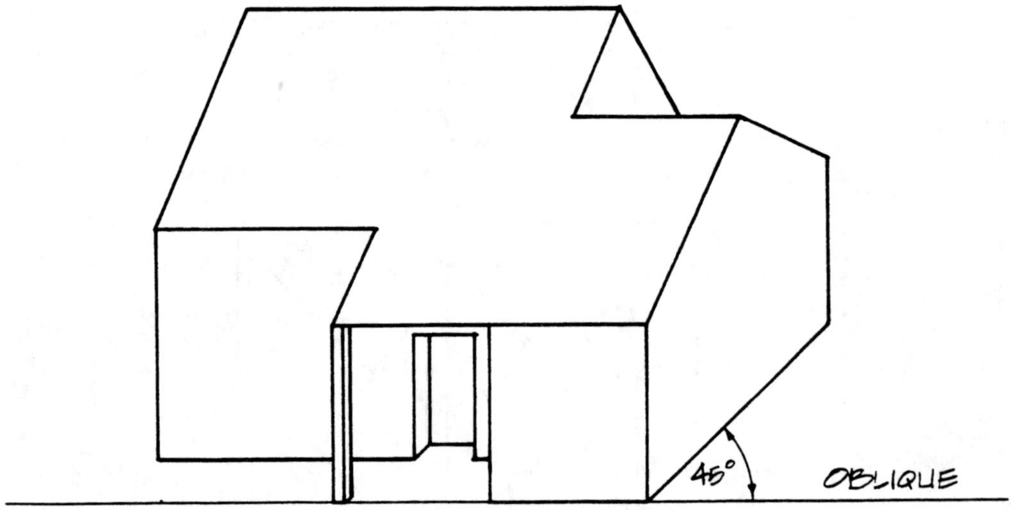

CHAPTER 7, EXERCISE 6, FIG. 7-34

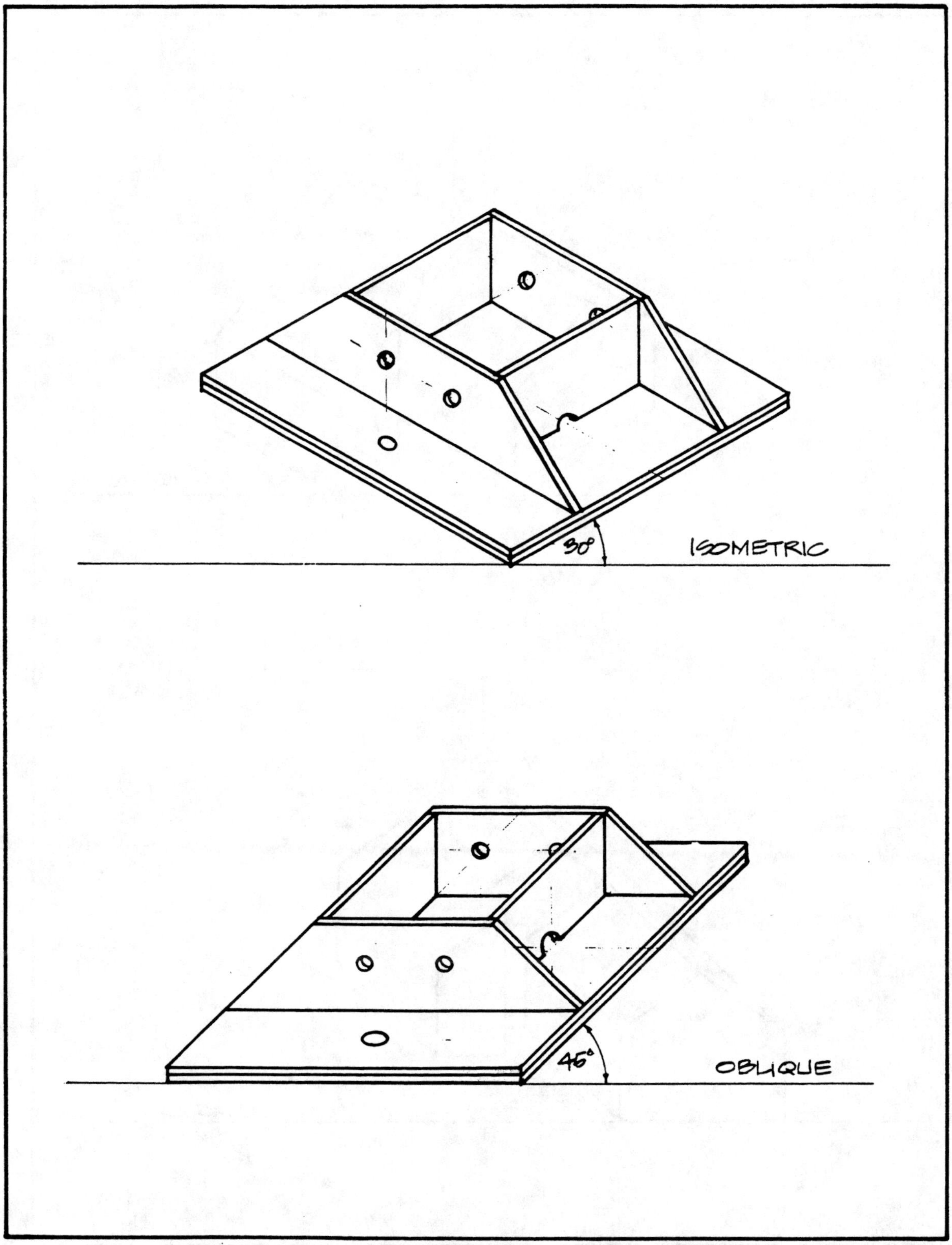

CHAPTER 7, EXERCISE 7, FIG. 7-35

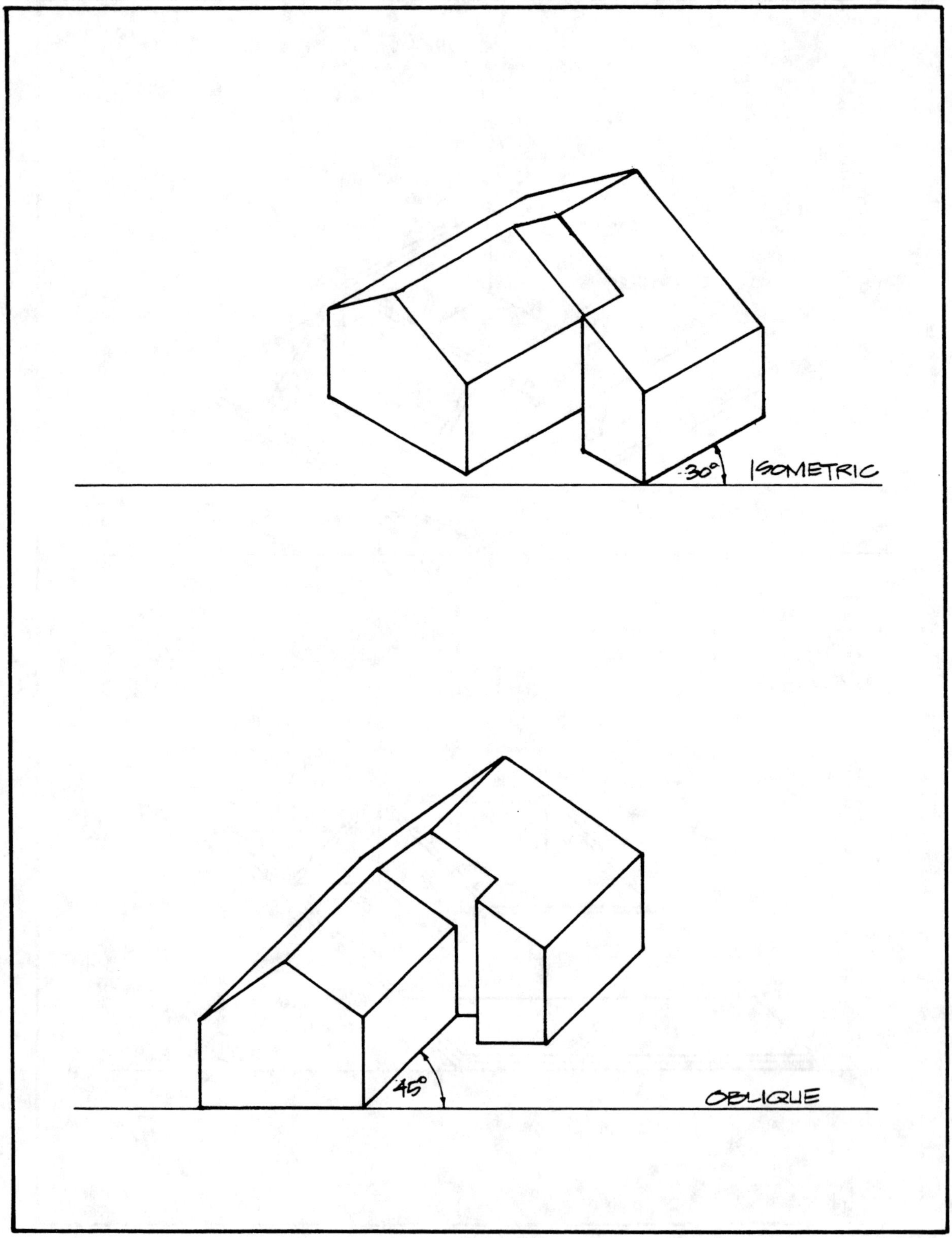

CHAPTER 7, EXERCISE 8, FIG. 7-36

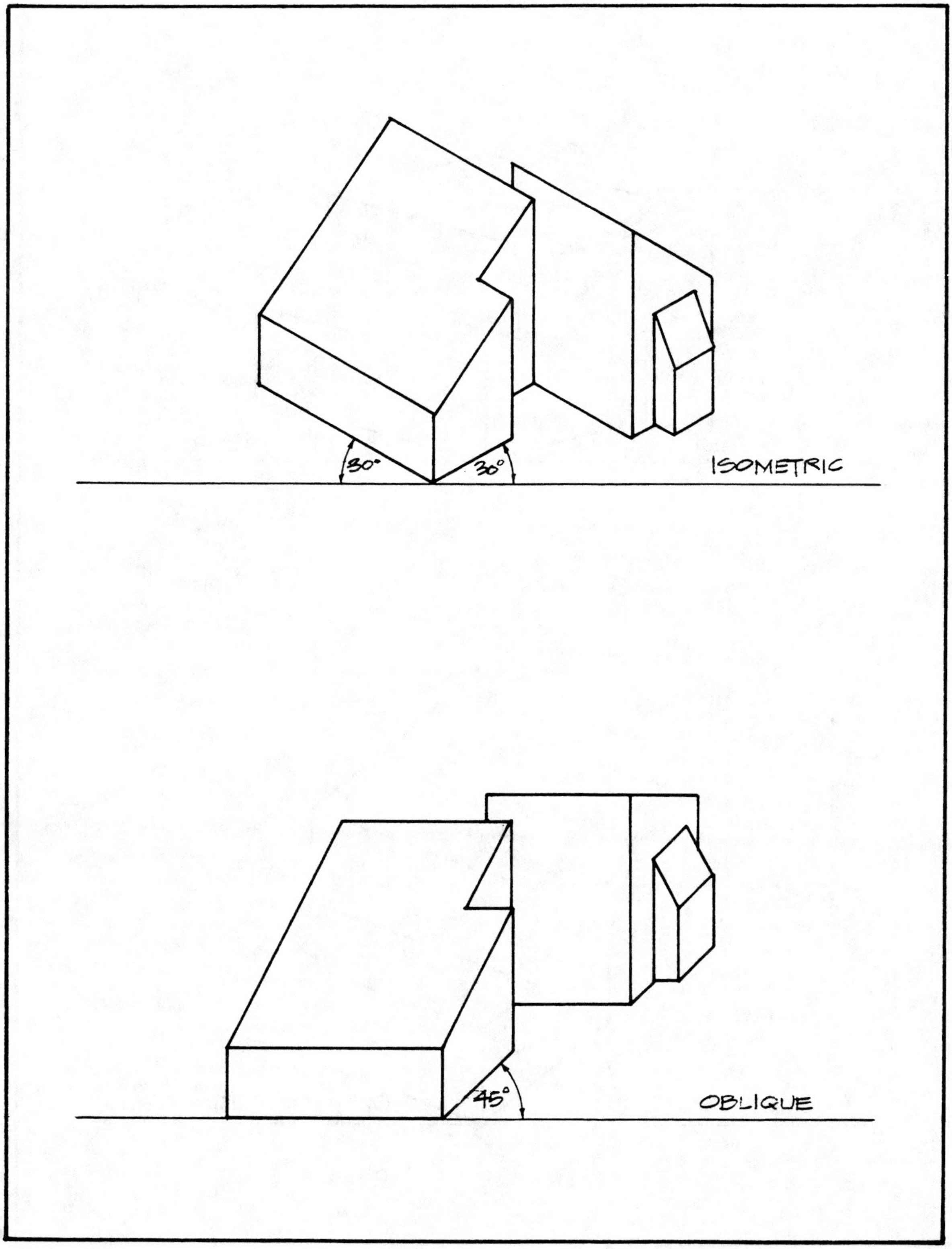

CHAPTER 7, EXERCISE 9, FIG. 7-37

CHAPTER 7, EXERCISE 10, FIG. 7-38

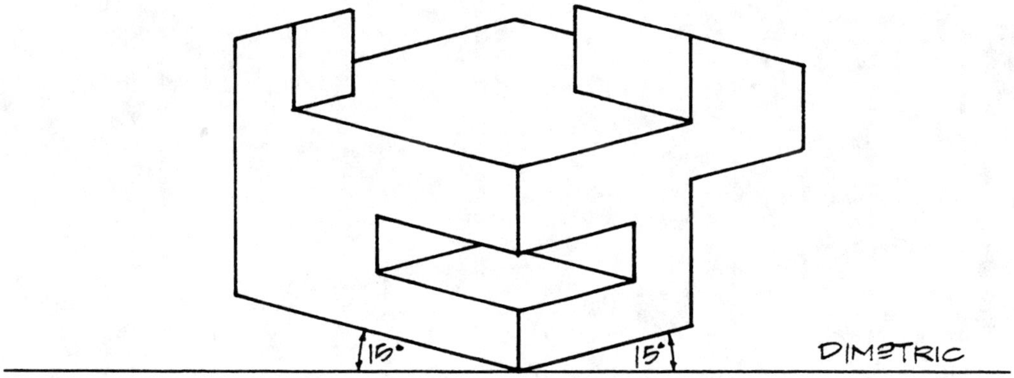

CHAPTER 7, EXERCISE 11, FIG. 7-39

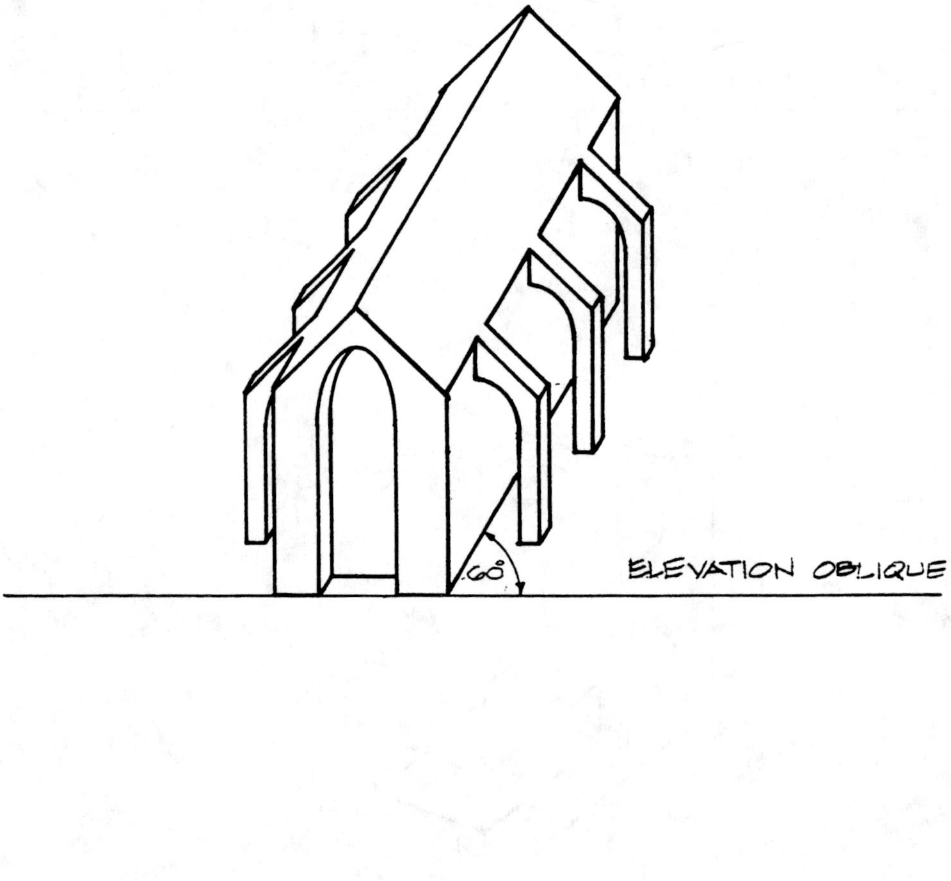

CHAPTER 7, EXERCISE 12, FIG. 7-40

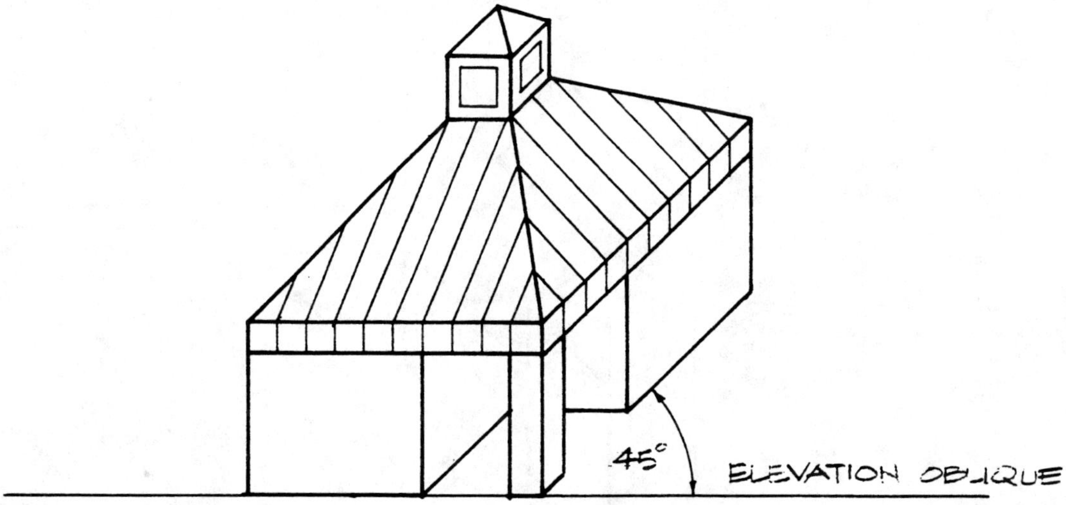

CHAPTER 7, EXERCISE 13, FIG. 7-41

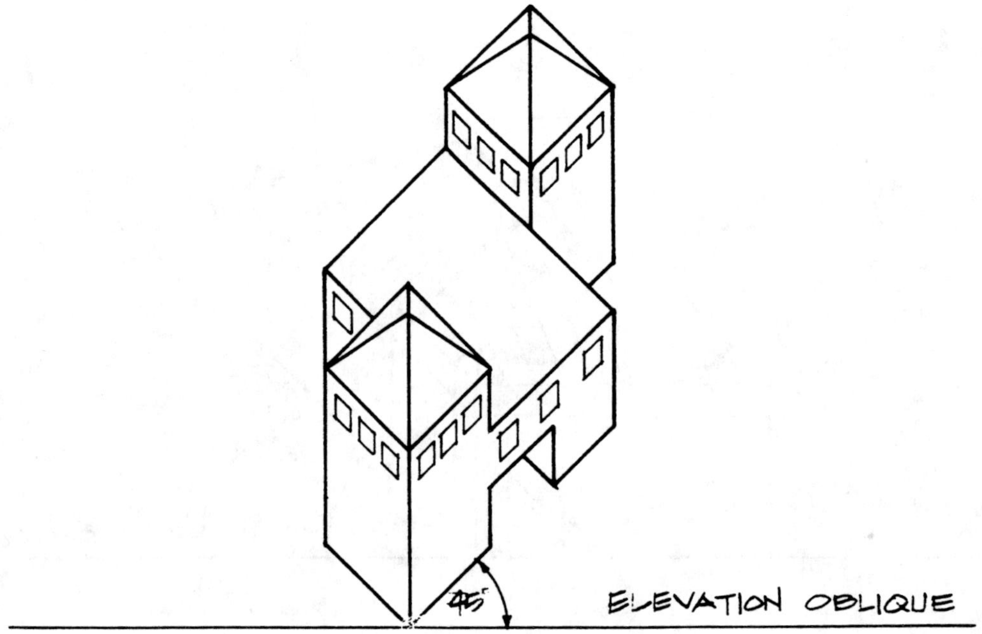

CHAPTER 7, EXERCISE 14, FIG. 7-42

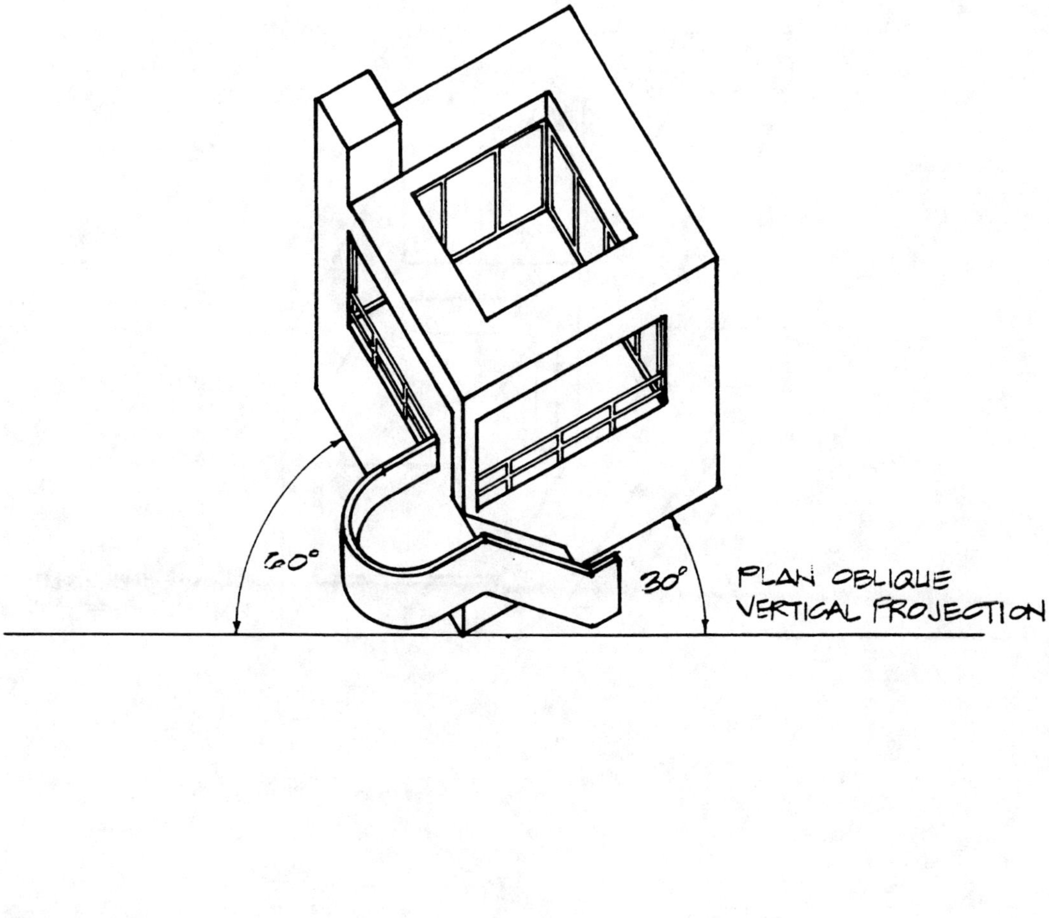

CHAPTER 7, EXERCISE 15, FIG. 7-43

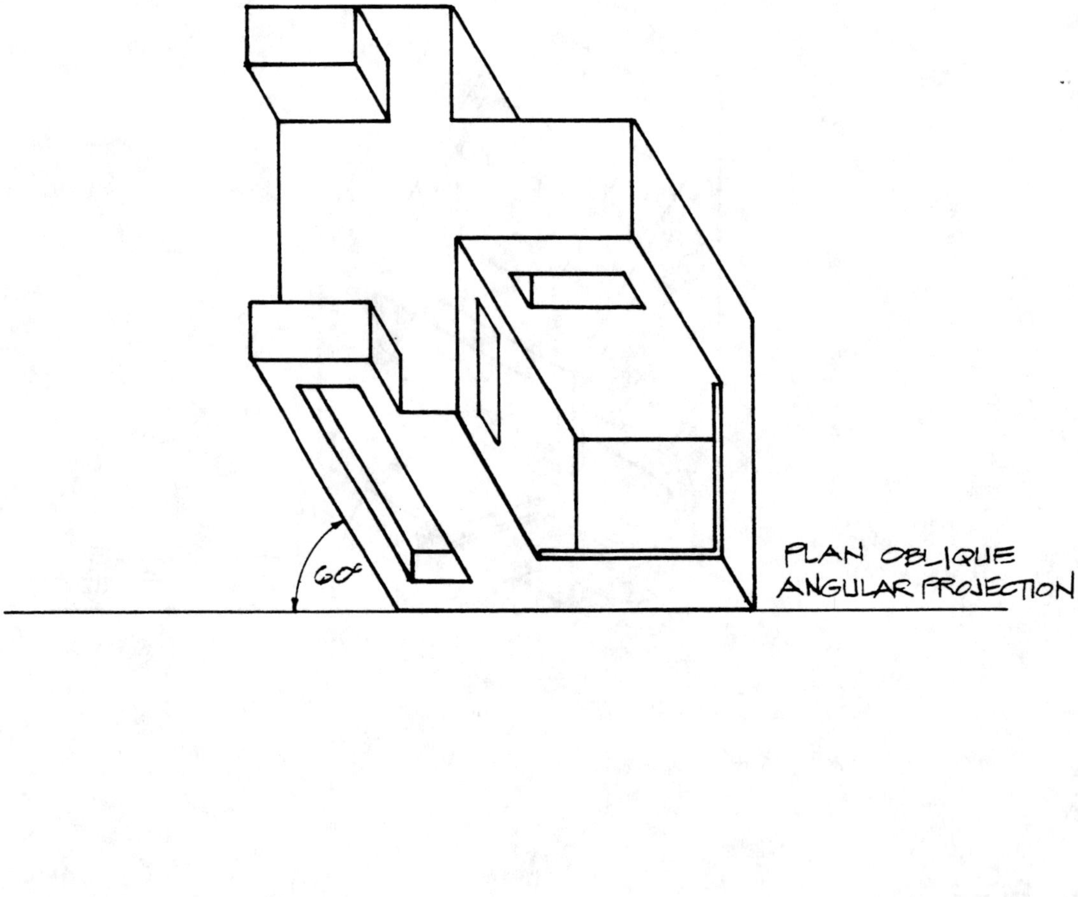

CHAPTER 7, EXERCISE 16, FIG. 7-44

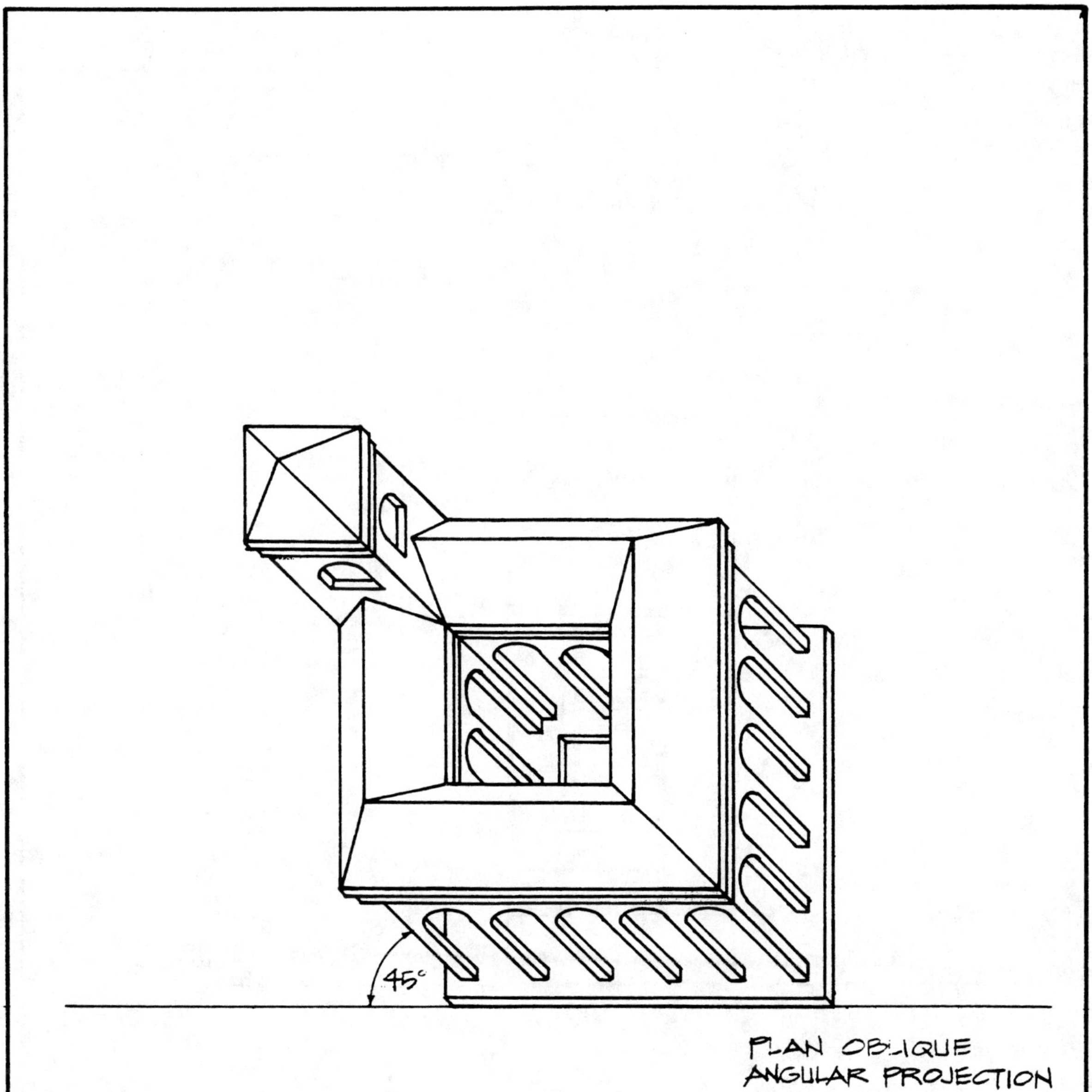

CHAPTER 7, EXERCISE 17, FIG. 7-45

CHAPTER 7, EXERCISE 18, FIG. 7-46

CHAPTER 7
REVIEW QUESTIONS AND ANSWERS

1. What is the advantage of a mechanical pictorial drawing over an orthographic drawing?

ans. **One mechanical pictorial drawing can explain an object in a three dimensional form much better than a series of two dimensional orthographic drawings.**

2. What are the applications of axonometric and oblique drawings on working drawings?

ans. **Axonometric and oblique drawings are easy to construct with instruments and are therefore used to represent some construction details in a three dimensional way on working drawings.**

3. Why does the oblique type of drawing have more versatility than the axonometric?

ans. **Oblique drawings have more versatility than axonometric drawings because one side or plan is shown in orthographic projection and an infinite number of angles may be used to show the receding axes which define the top and side.**

4. What angle from the horizontal give emphasis to the top view in an oblique drawing?

ans. **The 60° angle from the horizontal would place emphasis on the top of an object drawn in oblique.**

5. Describe a cabinet drawing.

ans. **A cabinet drawing is an oblique drawing which has a ratio of 1 to 1/2 and is generally too thin to show most objects other than shallow cabinets.**

6. Why is it advantageous to place the irregular shapes of an object on the frontal plane when making an olbique drawing?

ans. **It is advantageous to place the irregular shapes of an object on the frontal plane when making an oblique drawing because objects**

like circles can be drawn with a compass on the frontal plane in stead of an ellipse which is drawn on the oblique plane.

7. How may a plan view of a building be quickly made into a pictorial drawing?

ans. **A plan drawing can be made into a pictorial drawing by using a "plan oblique" or "elevation oblique" method of pictorial drawing.**

8. In dimensioning pictorial drawings, why are leaders drawn at angles other than those of the principle axes?

ans. **In dimensioning pictorial drawings leaders should be drawn at angles to the principle axes so that they are not confused with dimension lines.**

9. How are dimension numbers made to appear as though they lie on the planes of the drawing?

ans. **Dimension numbers are made to appear as though they lie on the planes of the drawing by using vertical lettering, yet the vertical axis of the lettering is kept parallel with the extension lines of the dimensions.**

10. Are the longest dimensions placed closest to the view or farther from the view, as compared to the shorter dimensions?

ans. **The longest dimensions are placed farthest from the view.**

11. What is the difference between the axonometric drawing and a perspective drawing?

ans. **An axonometric drawing is an accurately scaled pictorial drawing which has been rotated on its axis to give it a three dimensional appearance and appears distorted. A perspective is a three dimensional drawing which is developed with a horizon line, station point and vanishing point or points and results in a pictorial view which is normal to the eye and not distorted.**

12. What is the proper title of a pictorial drawing

that has x, y, and z axes and two of the angles between adjacent axes are equal?

ans. The proper title of a pictorial drawing that has x, y, and z axes and two of the angles between the adjacent axes are equal is a "diametric" drawing.

13. What view of an object is revealed by a reverse axes drawing?

ans. The underside or bottom of an object is revealed by a reverse axes drawing.

14. List the types of pictorial drawings that require a true-shape plan view that can be traced as a basis for the drawing?

ans. Plan-oblique - vertical projection, plan oblique-angular projection, and planometric are drawings which require a true-shape plan view that can be traced as a basis for the drawing.

15. Why are 30°, 45°, and 60° angles used in preparing most pictorial drawings?

ans. The 30°, 45°, and 60° angles are used in preparing most pictorial drawings because these angles are standard angles of drafting triangles.

16. What is the proper title of the pictorial drawing that has equal angles between the x, y, and z axes?

ans. The "isometric" is a pictorial drawing that has equal angles between the x, y, and z axes.

17. Define paraline drawings.

ans. Paraline drawings are pictorial drawings that enable the drafter to create singleview images which represent three dimensional space. Axonometric and oblique drawings are paraline drawing. The sides of the object on the drawing are represented by parallel lines, conveniently executed with the parallel bar and triangles.

18. List the type of pictorial drawings that require

true measurements for all lines making up the drawing.

ans. **Axonometric (isometric, diametric, trimetric, and planometric), and oblique (elevation-oblique and plan-oblique) are pictorial drawings that require true measurements for all lines making up the drawing.**

19. What is the difference between a plan oblique with vertical projection and a plan oblique with angular projection?

ans. **The plan oblique-vertical projection is executed by rotating a true-shape plan 45° or 30°-60° to the horizontal and using a triangle to draw all vertical lines perpendicular to the horizontal; where as, a plan oblique-angular projection is executed by placing a true-shape plan parallel to the picture plane and the vertical lines are projected upward at a 45° or 60° angle to the horizontal.**

20. What characteristic is lost in the planometric drawing that is evident in the plan-oblique drawing?

ans. **The planometric negates all right-angled side planes that are evident in the plan oblique drawing.**

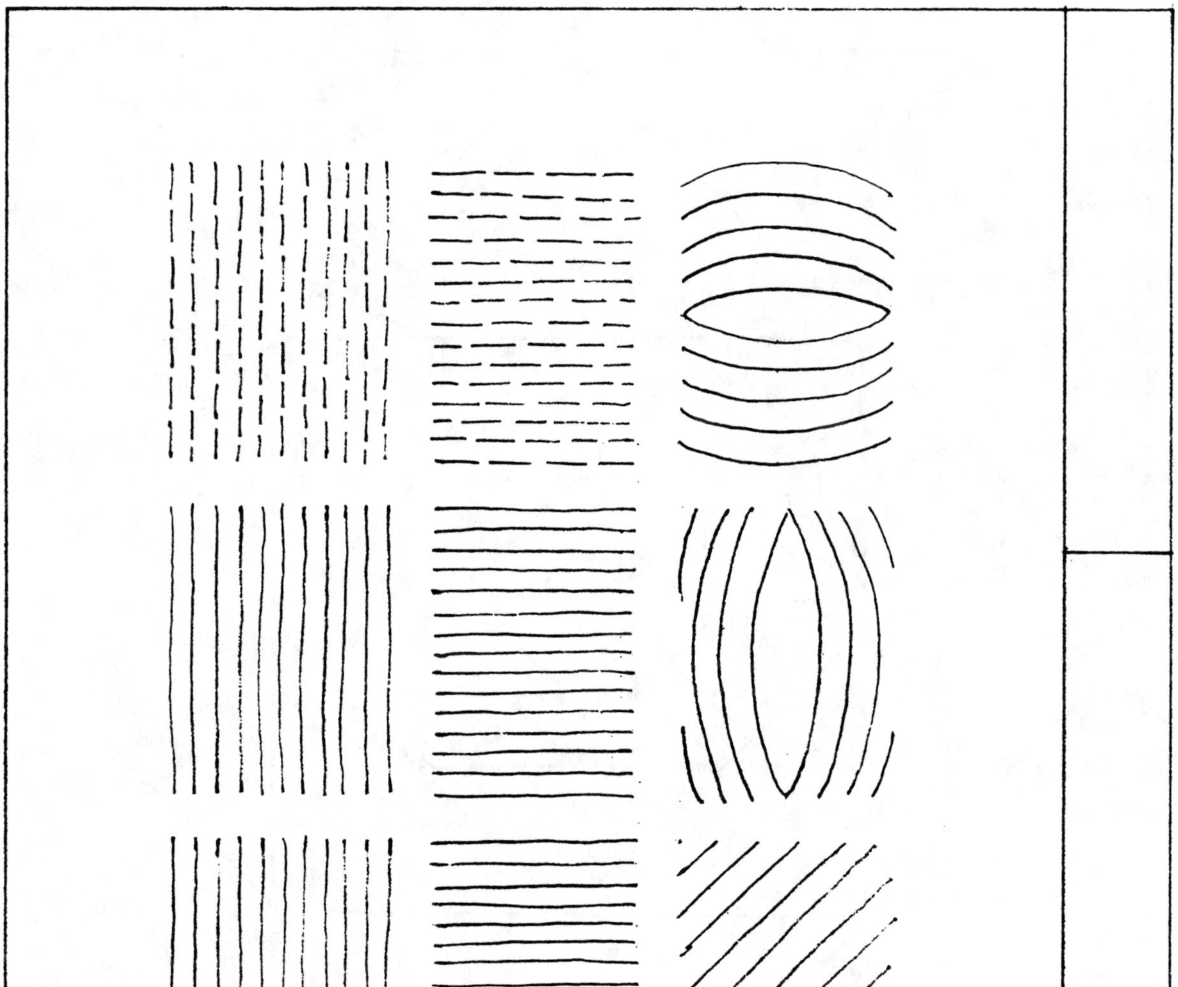

CHAPTER 8, EXERCISE 1, FIG. 8-32

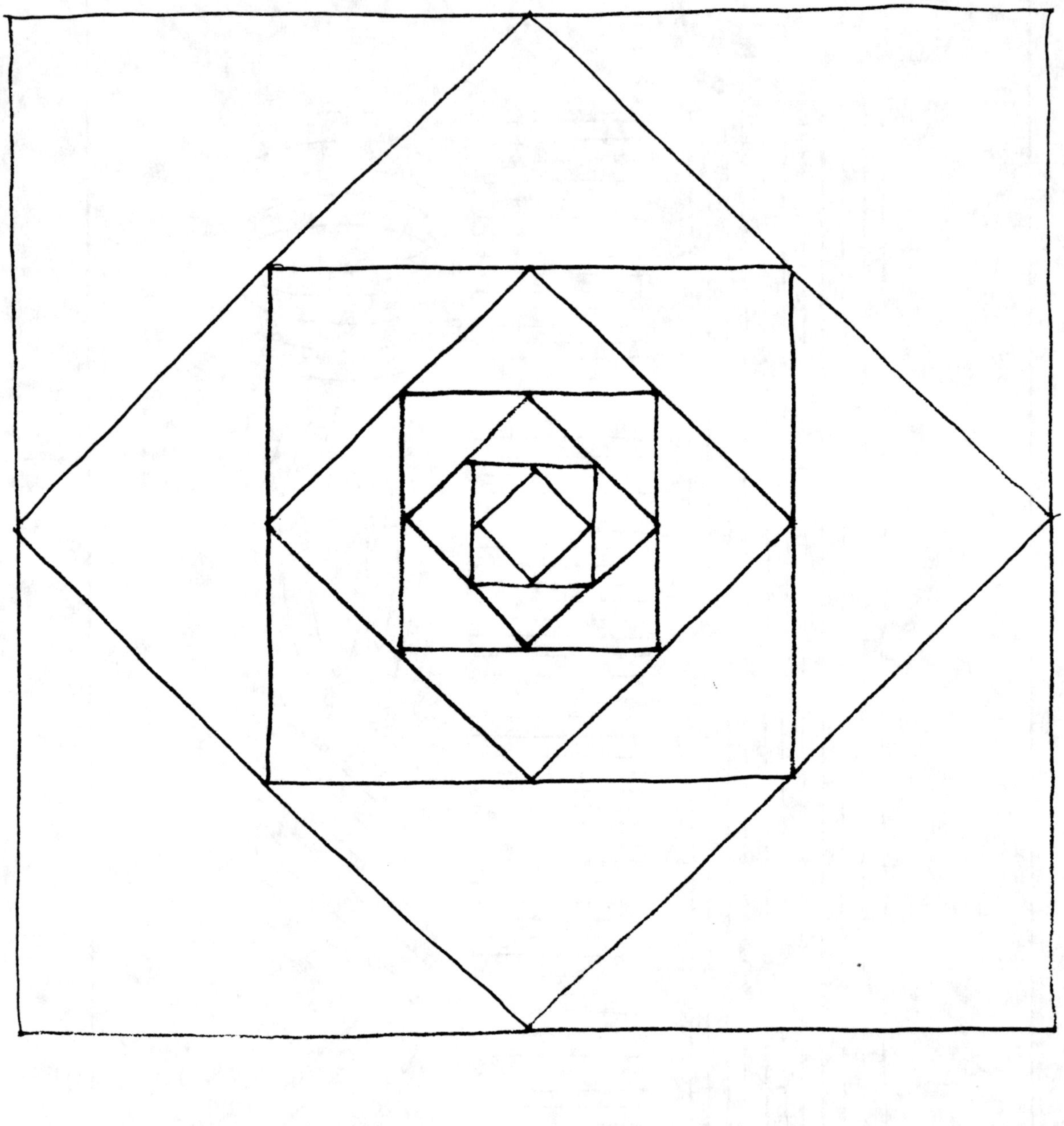

CHAPTER 8, EXERCISE 2, FIG. 8-33

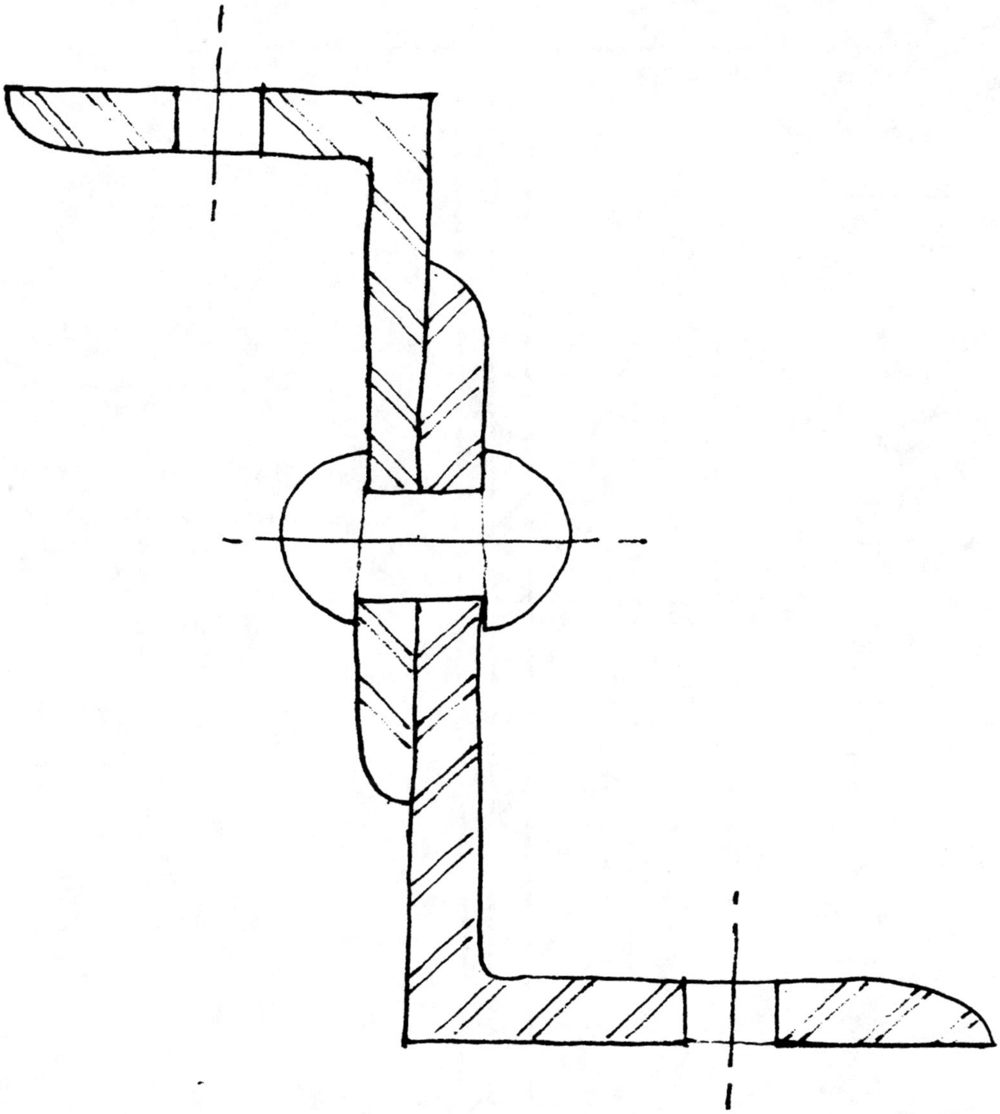

CHAPTER 8, EXERCISE 3, FIG. 8-19

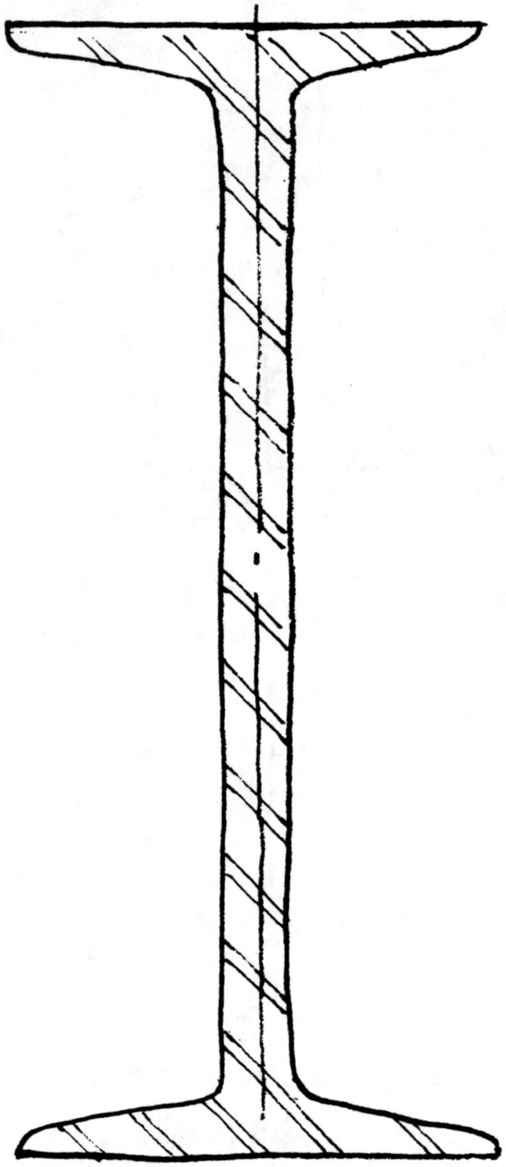

CHAPTER 8, EXERCISE 4, FIG. 8-19

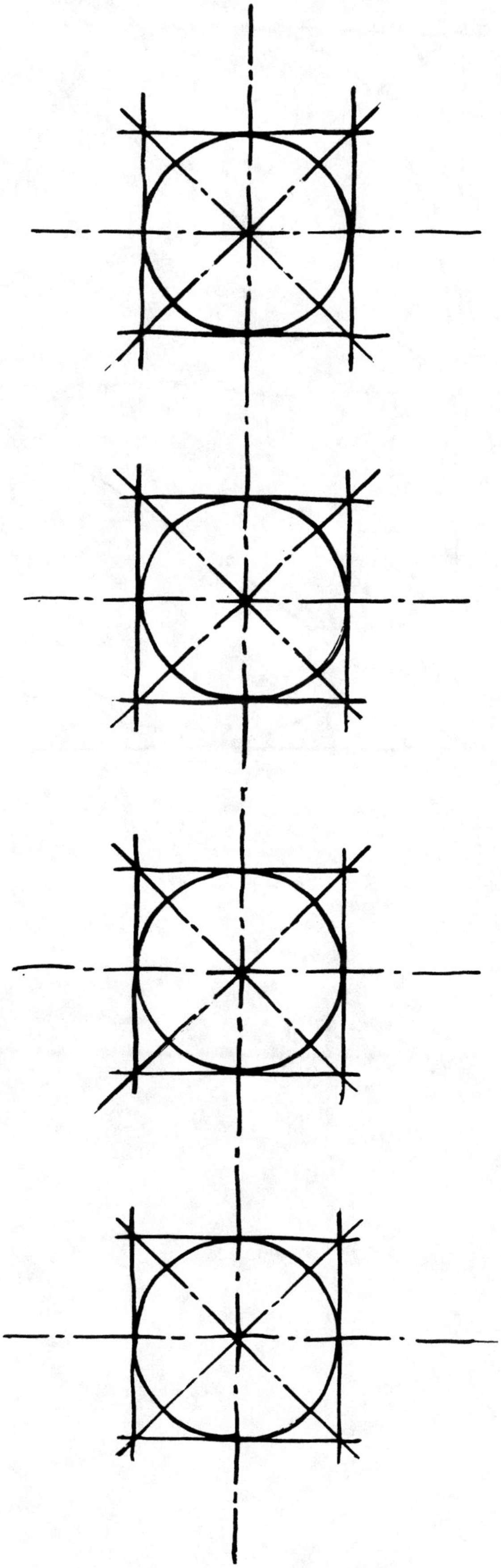

CHAPTER 8, EXERCISE 5, FIG. 8-12

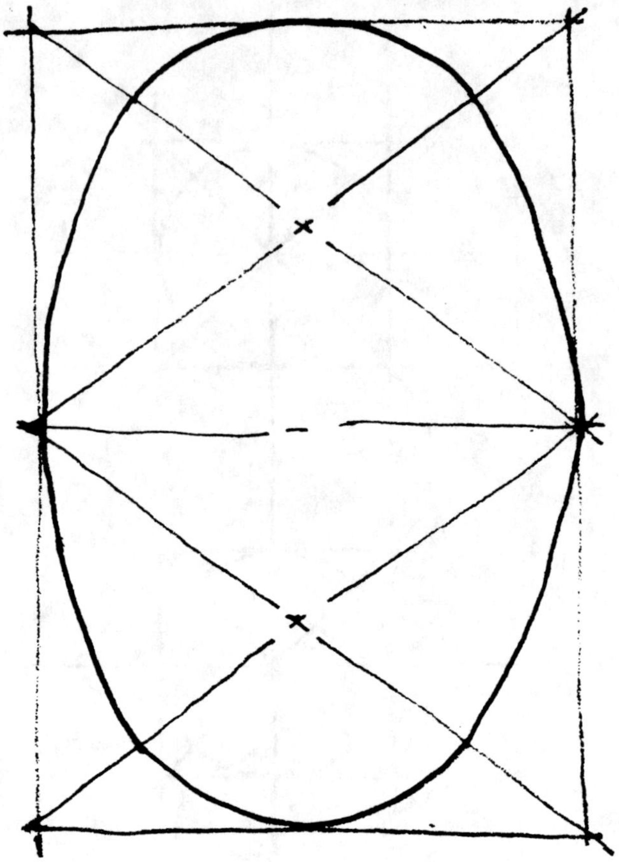

CHAPTER 8, EXERCISE 6, FIG. 8-16

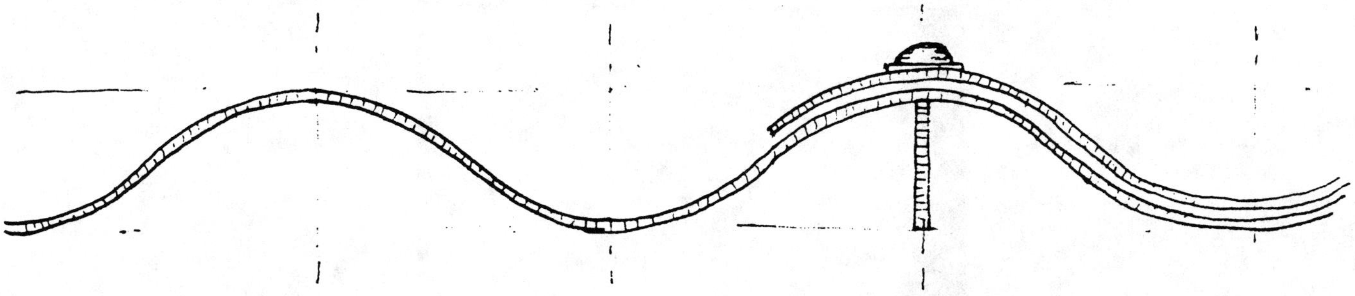

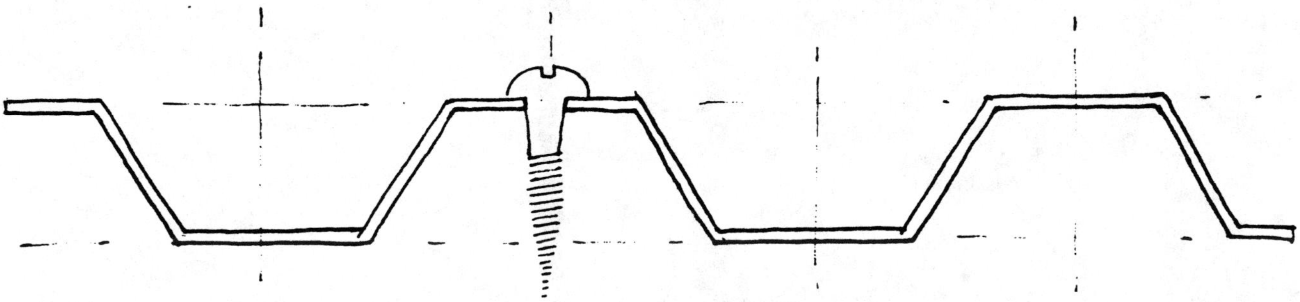

CHAPTER 8, EXERCISE 7, FIG. 8-18

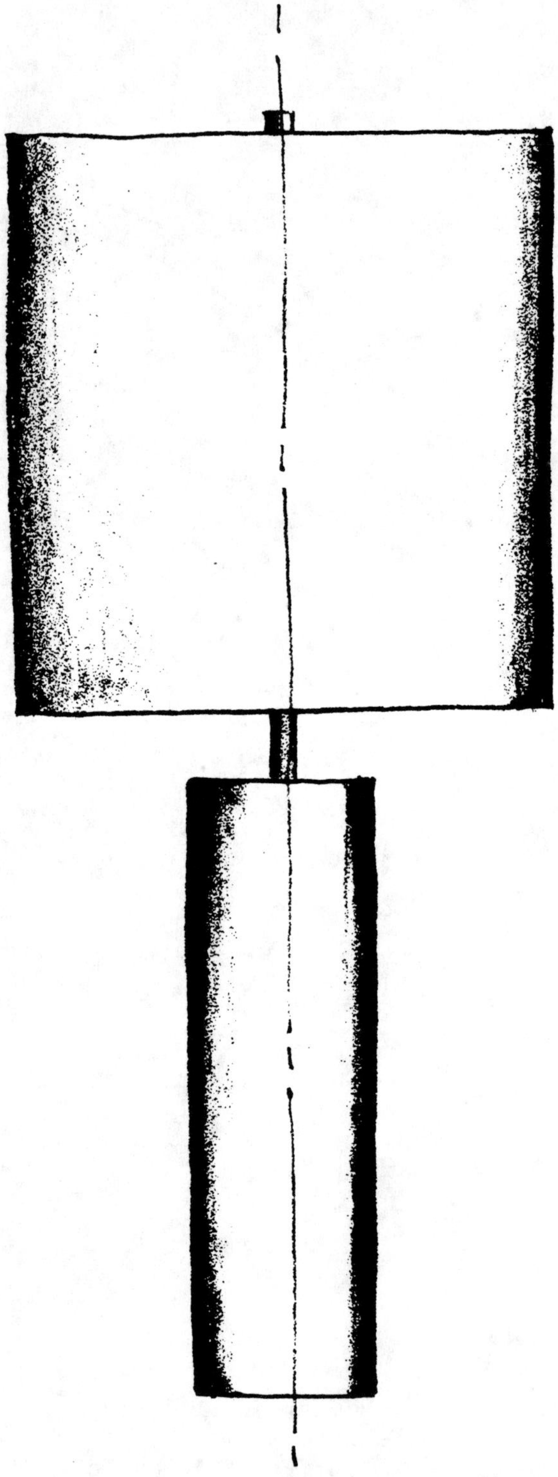

CHAPTER 8, EXERCISE 8, FIG. 8-21

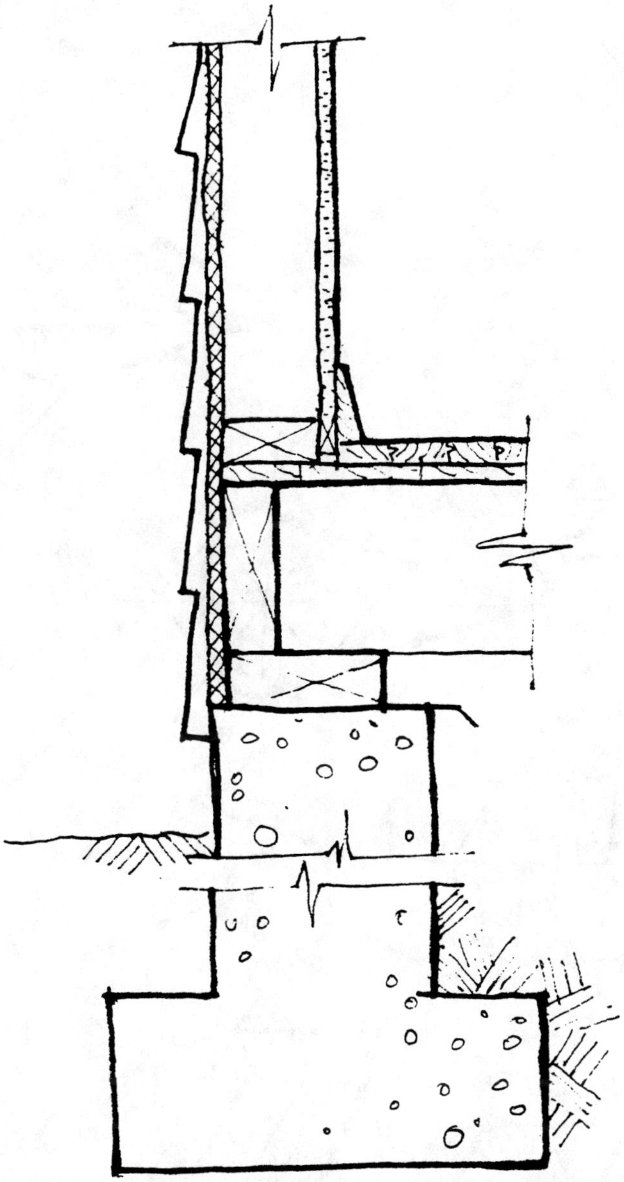

CHAPTER 8, EXERCISE 9, FIG. 8-25A

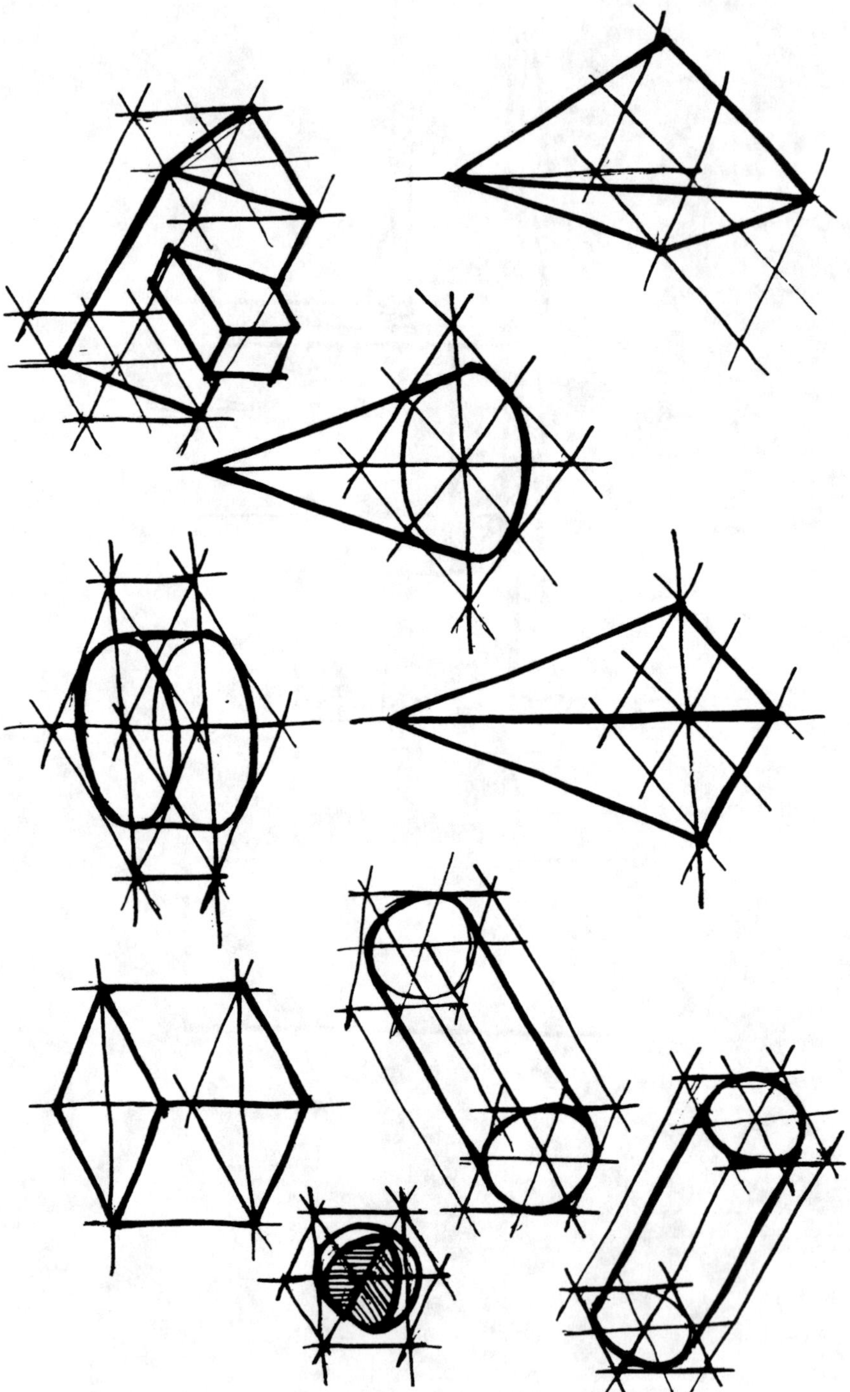

CHAPTER 8, EXERCISE 12, FIG. 8-30

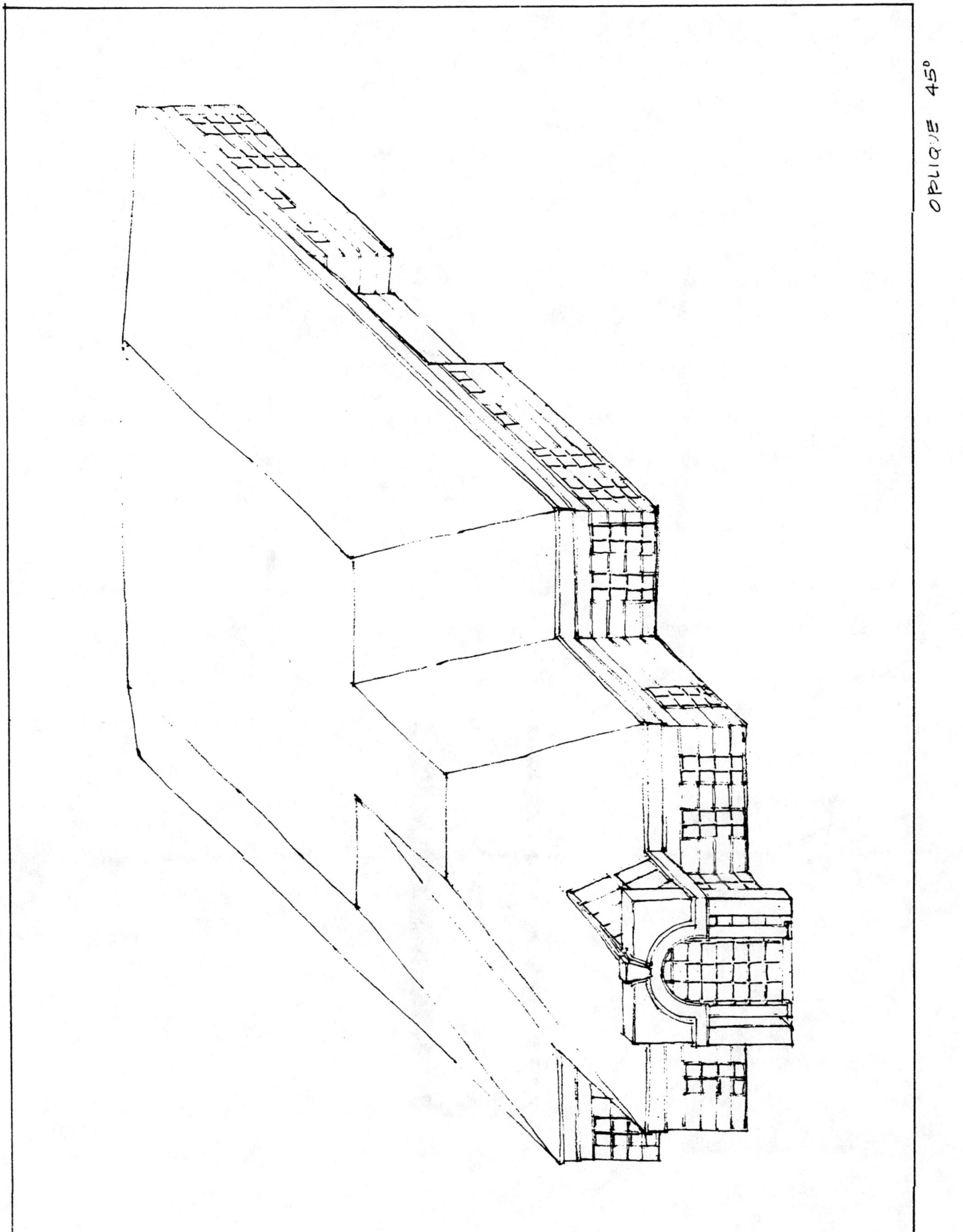

CHAPTER 8, EXERCISE 13, FIG. 8-35

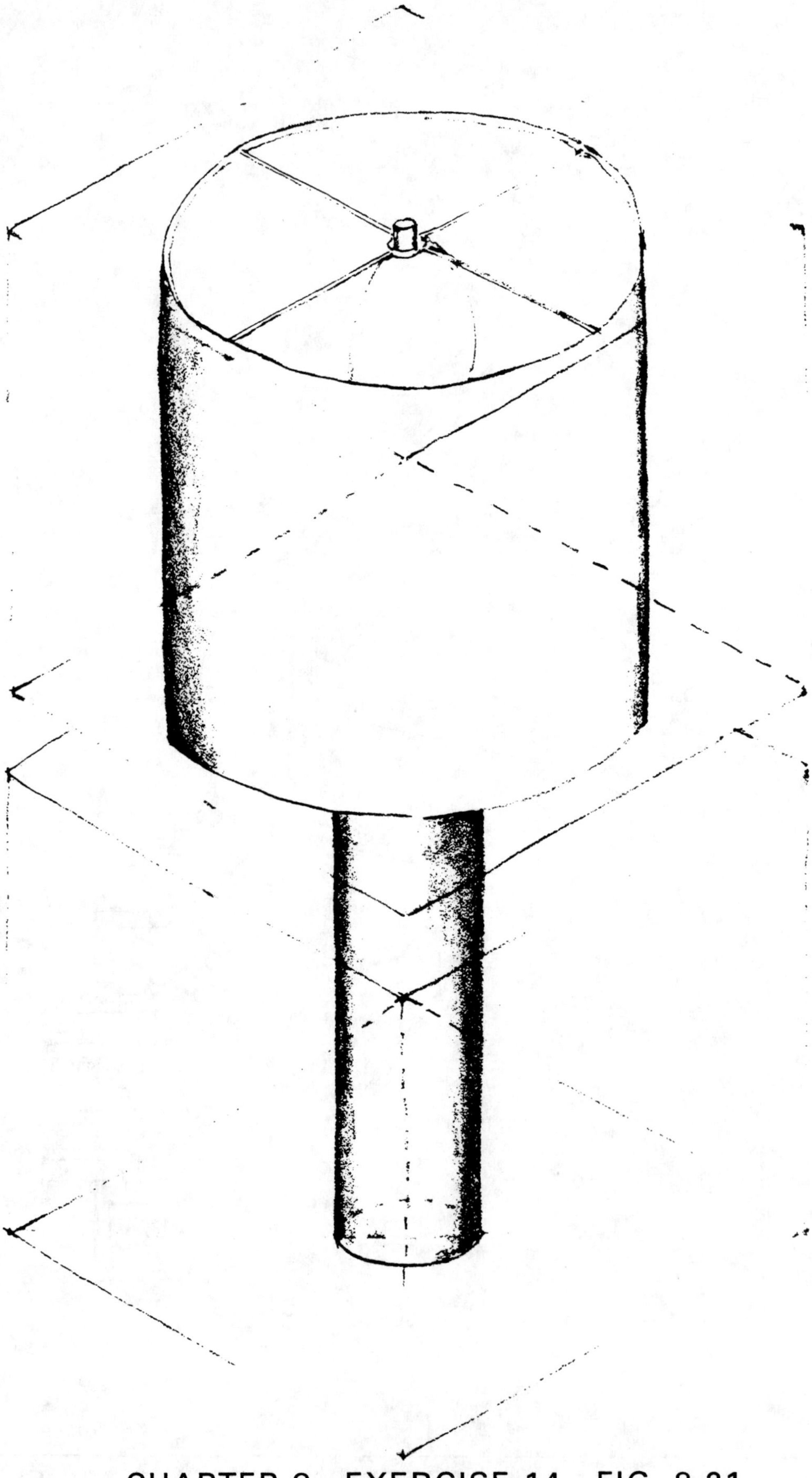

CHAPTER 8, EXERCISE 14, FIG. 8-21

CHAPTER 8
REVIEW QUESTIONS AND ANSWERS

1. Why does ability in sketching require a strong sense of observation?

ans. **Sketching ability requires a strong sense of observation, because the eye must be trained to see the correct proportion of how one part relates to the other.**

2. Explain the structural or skeleton method of developing a sketch.

ans. **Many objects have a basic structural system which should be studied before sketching the object. An example would be the need to study the human skeletal structure before drawing human body figures.**

3. Why is sketching a subject reduced to its simplest geometric forms in organizing the sketch and the details drawn later?

ans. **A sketching subject is reduced to its simplest geometric form in order to distinguish its proportion to scale.**

4. What type of practice sketches should precede pictorial sketches?

ans. **Pictorial sketches should be preceded by practice sketches of lines, angles, circles, and arcs.**

5. Which simple geometric form aids in establishing proportion?

ans. **The simple geometric form of the square aids in establishing proportion.**

6. Why do architectural drafters prefer to do their sketching on inexpensive tracing paper?

ans. **Architectural drafters prefer to do their sketching on inexpensive tracing paper because of the ease with which sketches can be modified or altered simply by placing the transparent paper over previous sketches. Tracing is quicker than reconstructing or**

erasing. Numerous sketches are needed before a final detail is created.

7. For what reason is sketching a necessary part of drafting training?

ans. **Sketching is a necessary part of drafting training in order to generate ideas and to make concepts workable realities.**

8. What is meant by a schematic sketch of a floor plan?

ans. **A schematic sketch of a floor plan is a preliminary plan showing possible room locations.**

9. Why is the use of coordinate paper underlays especially helpful in sketching floor plans?

ans. **Coordinate paper underlays are helpful in sketching floor plans because they give a reference to scale.**

10. In perspective sketching, why may it be necessary to try several basic-block forms before arriving at suitable vanishing points when drawing a building?

ans. **In perspective sketching, it may be necessary to try several basic-block forms before arriving at suitable vanishing points in order to get the proper angle of the building that you want to show on the drawing.**

11. Why is it essential for the beginner to practice sketching basic geometric shapes?

ans. **It is essential for the beginner to practice sketching basic geometric shapes because they are the fundamental forms of architecture.**

12. Describe the method used for drawing a freehand circle using two pencils.

ans. **A freehand circle may be drawn by holding two pencils of the same length rigidly in the hand so that they act much as a compass. One pencil becomes the pivot; the other scribes the circle when the paper is revolved under the pencils.**

13. How is good line technique acquired?

ans. **Good line technique is developed with practice; each successive exercise should be a deliberate effort to improve.**

14. What method is recommended for sketching symmetrical objects?

ans. **To sketch a symmetrical object draw a centerline on the paper and proportion the object equally on either side of the centerline.**

15. Why is it important for the drafter to have the ability to make freehand sketches?

ans. **The drafter needs the ability to sketch so that he or she can communicate ideas quickly. Most detailed drawings are developed from sketches.**

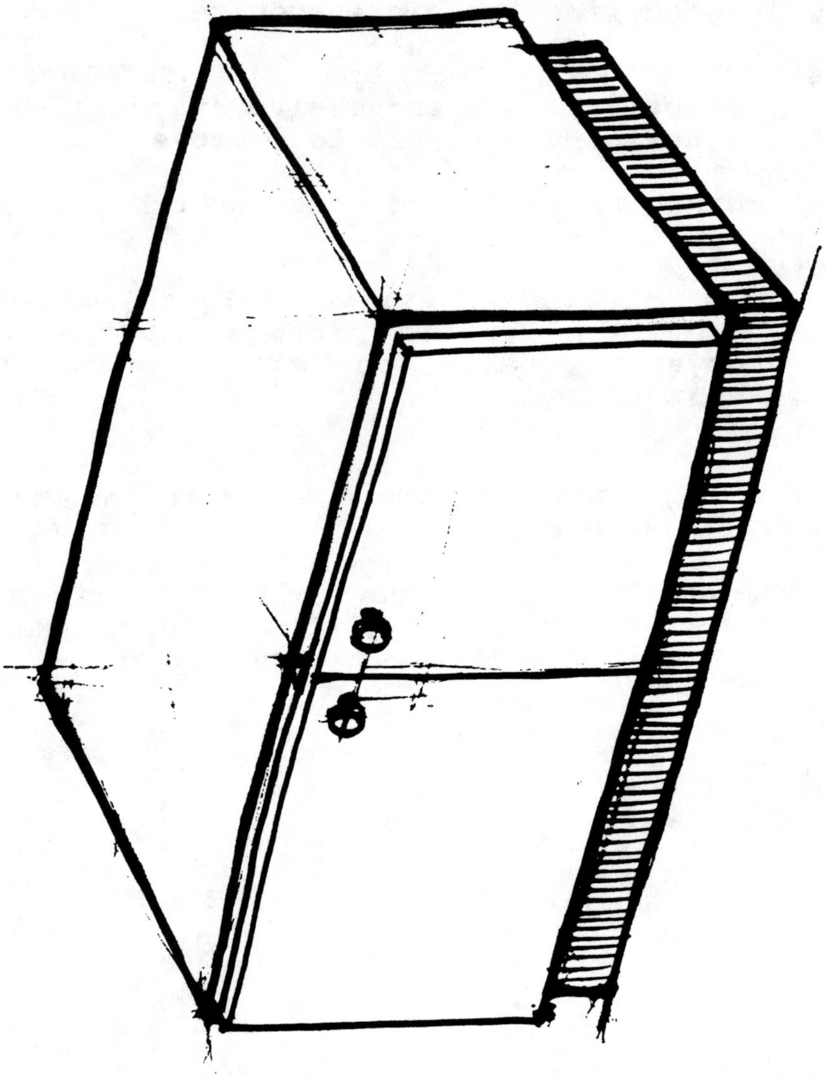

CHAPTER 9, EXERCISE 1, FIG. 8-22

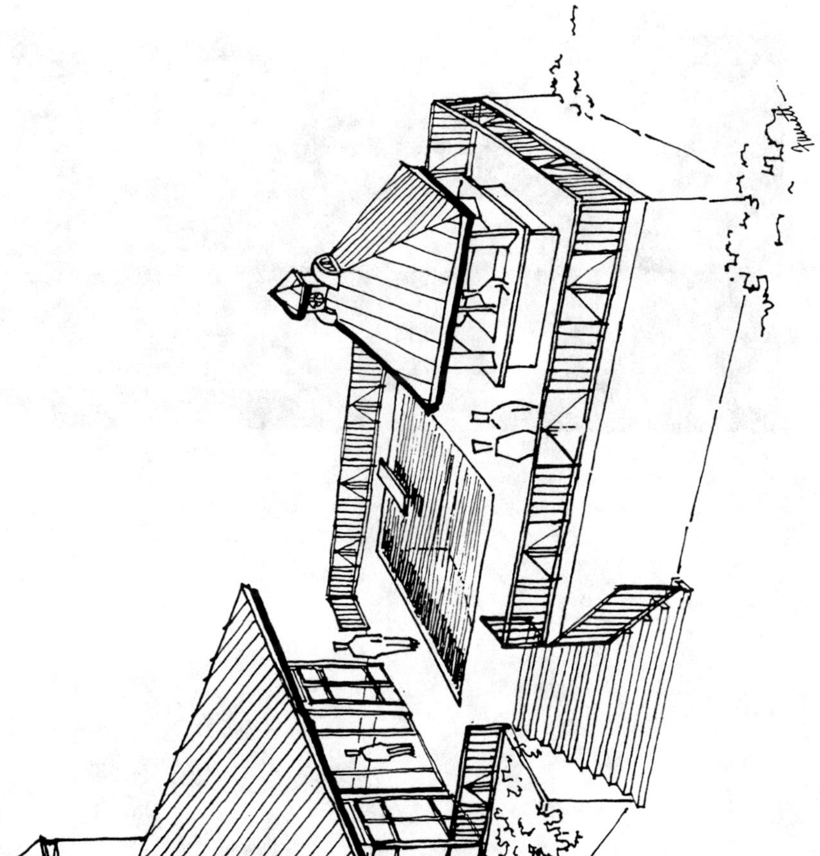

CHAPTER 9, EXERCISE 2, FIG. 8-34

CHAPTER 9, EXERCISE 3

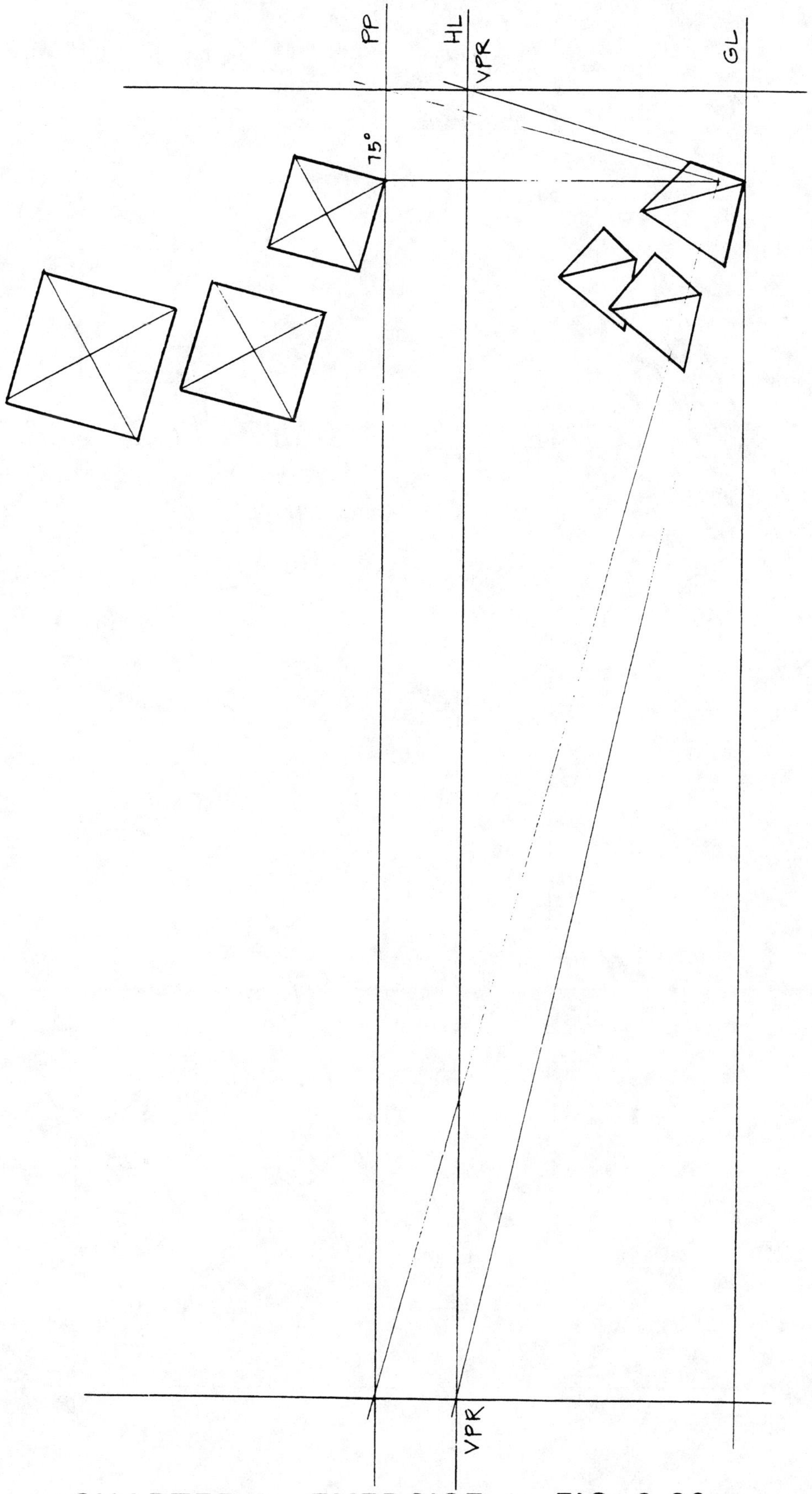

CHAPTER 9, EXERCISE 4, FIG. 9-36

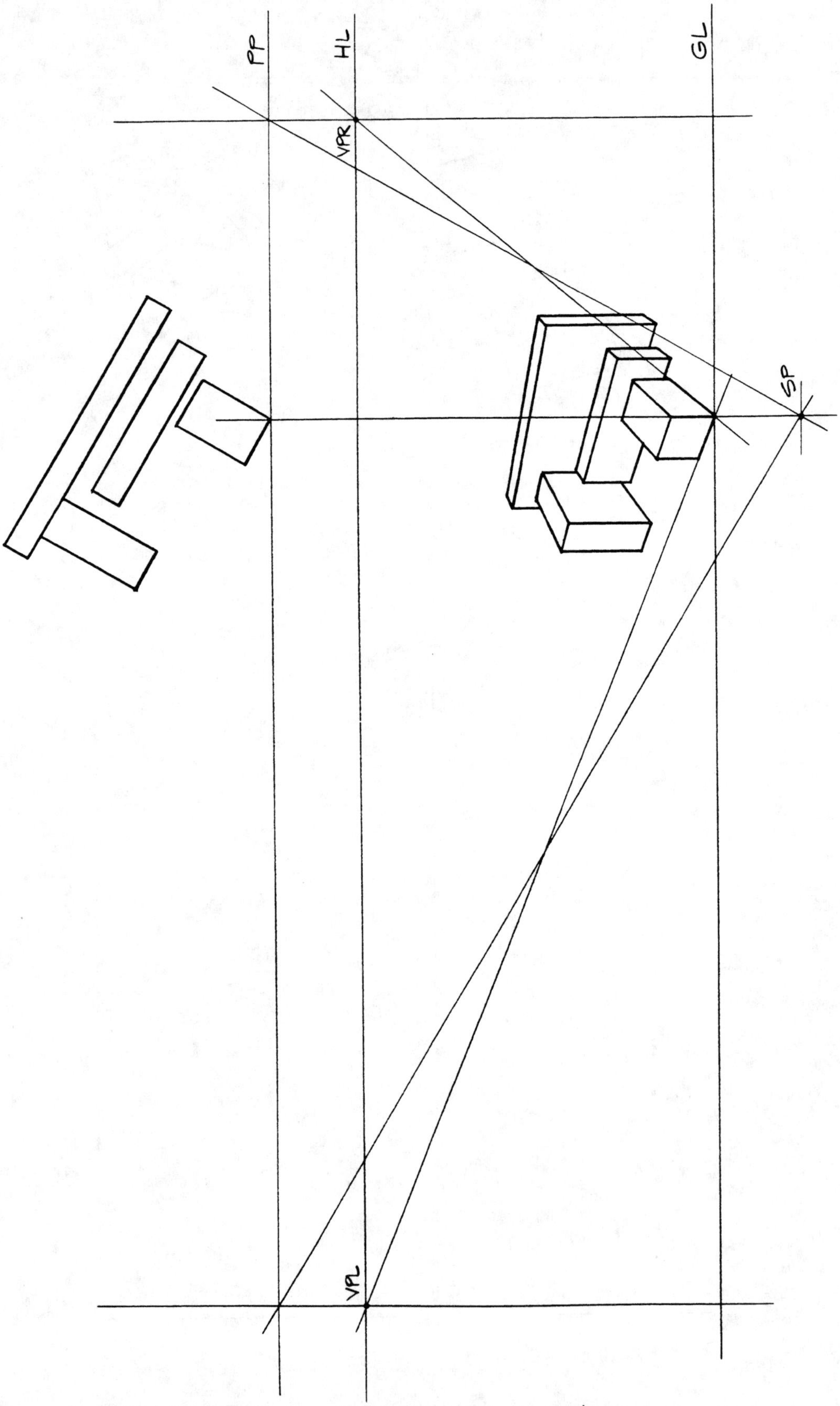

CHAPTER 9, EXERCISE 4, FIG. 9-36

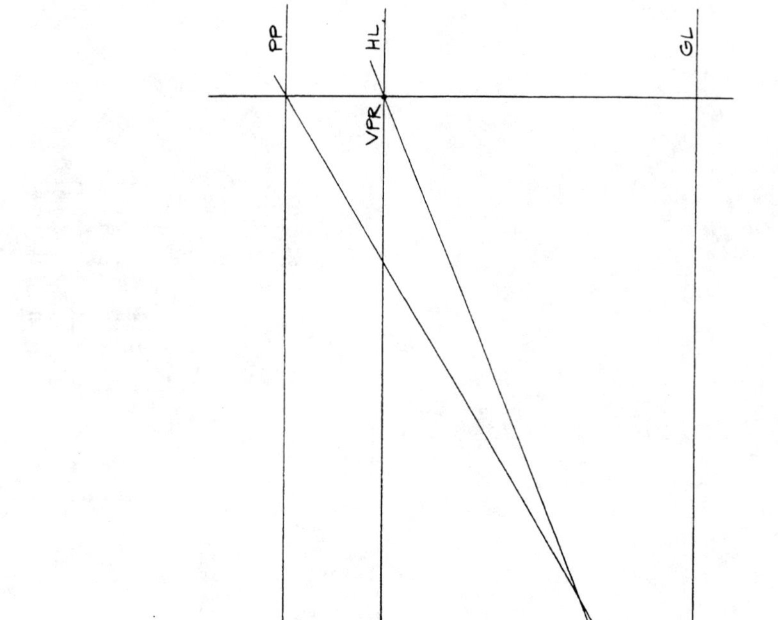

CHAPTER 9, EXERCISE 4, FIG. 9-36

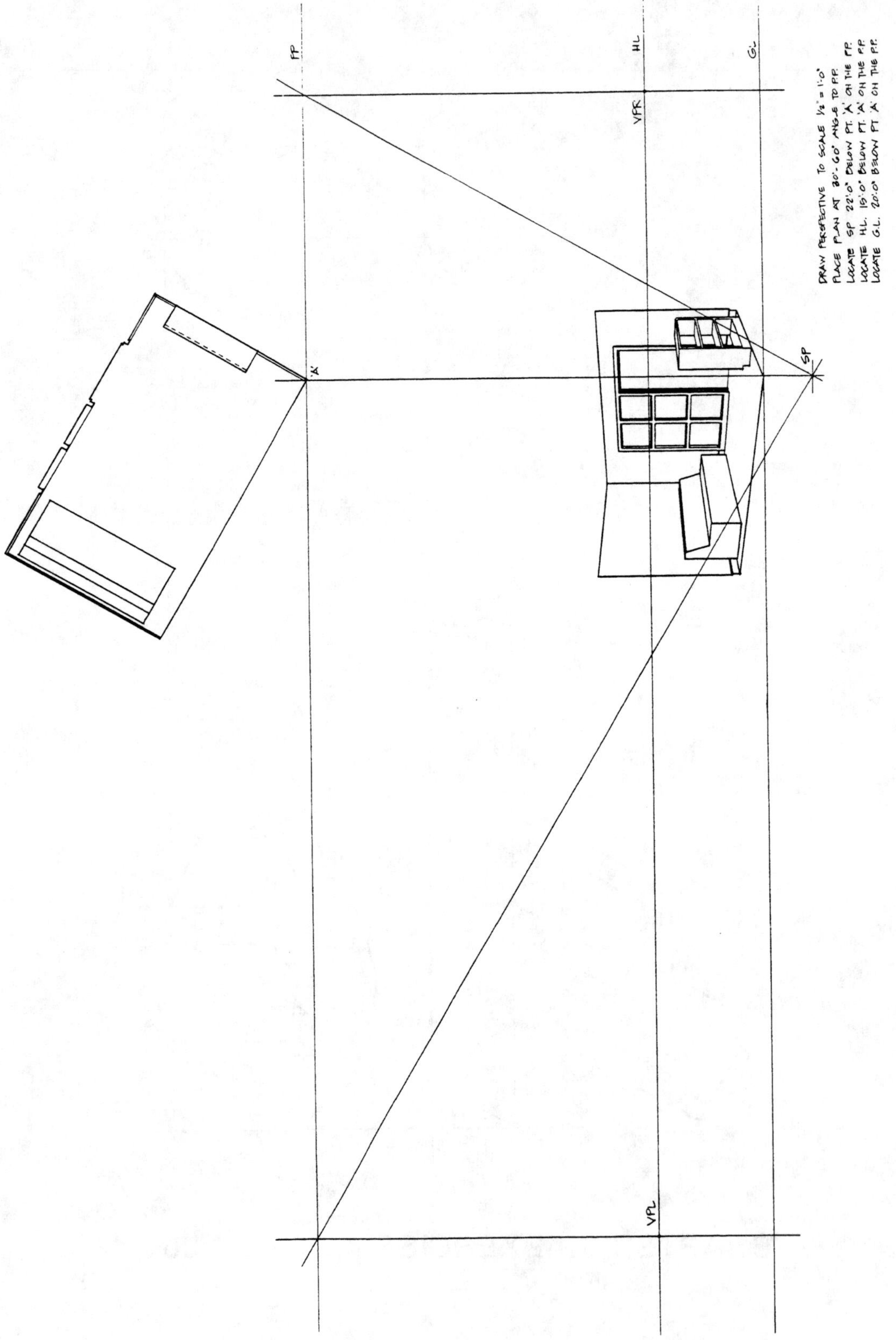

CHAPTER 9, EXERCISE 5, FIG. 9-37

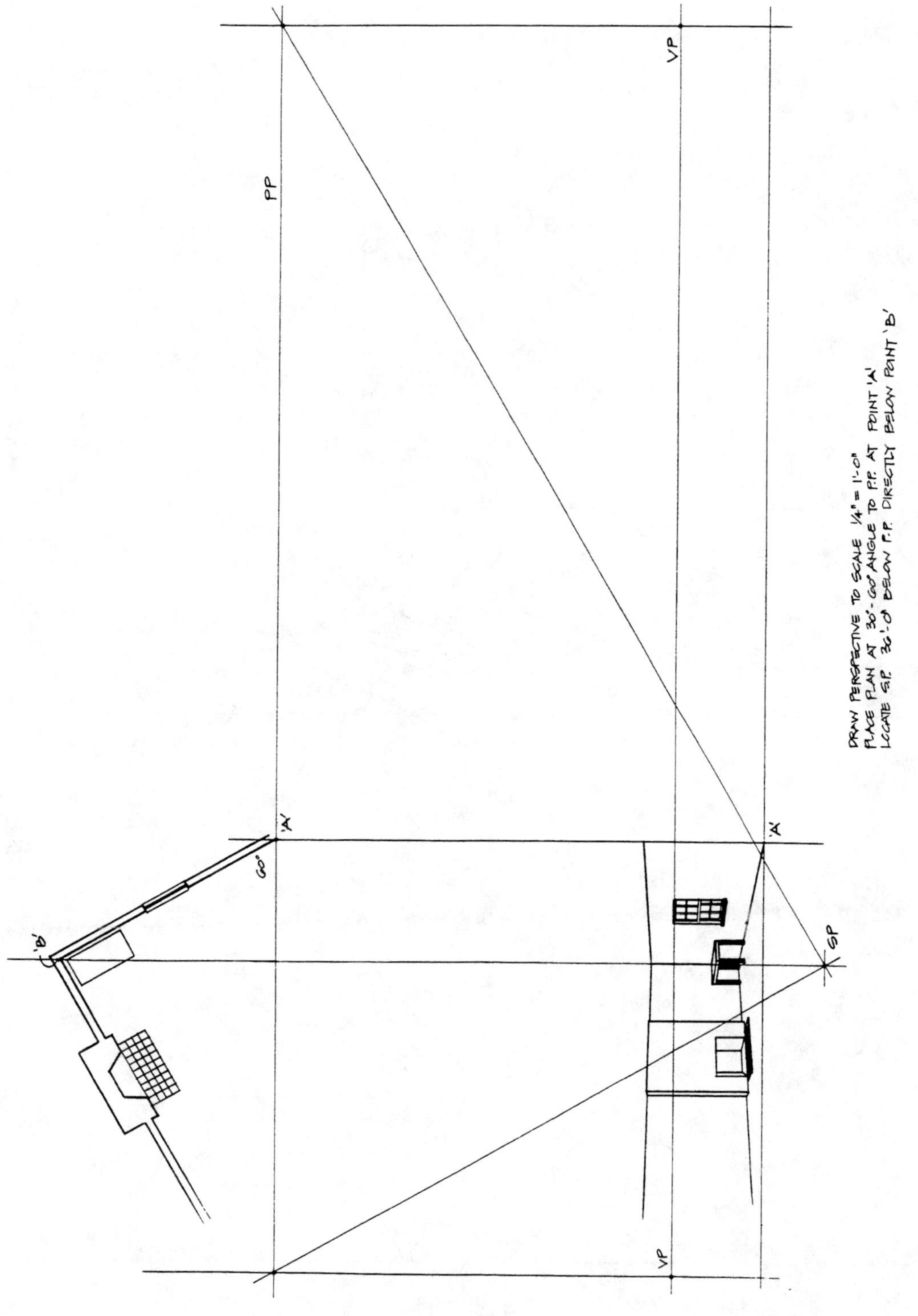

CHAPTER 9, EXERCISE 5, FIG. 9-38

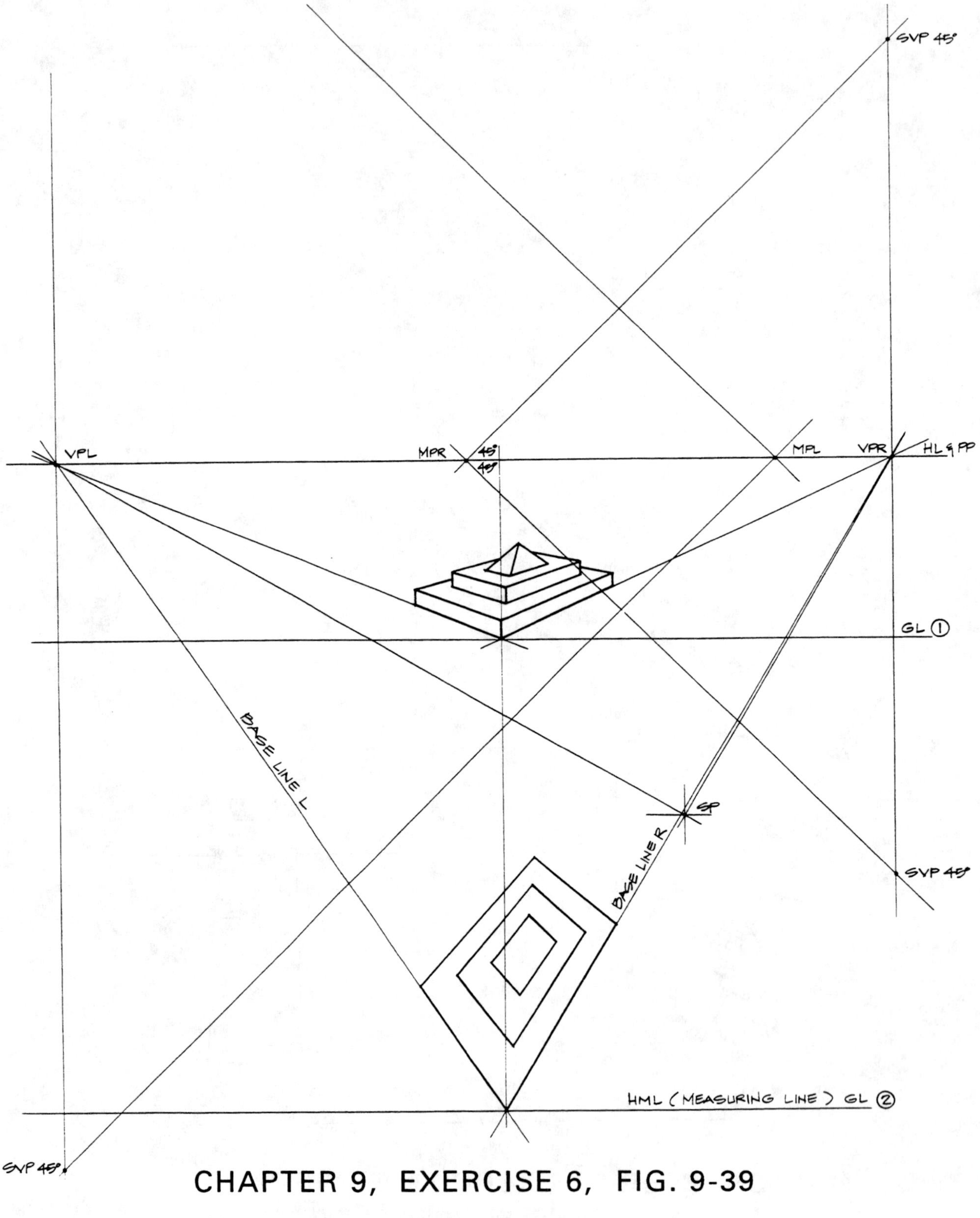

CHAPTER 9, EXERCISE 6, FIG. 9-39

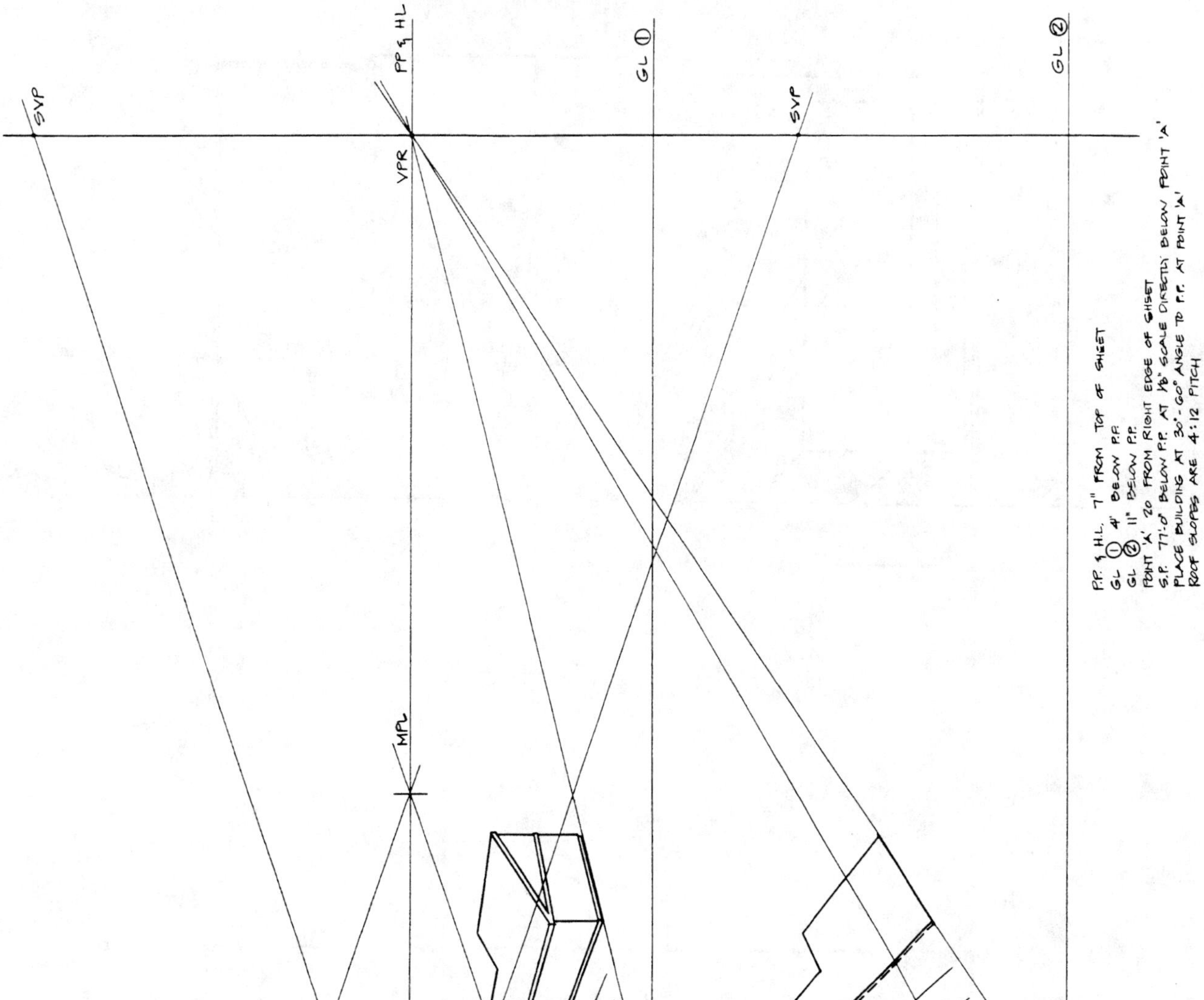

CHAPTER 9, EXERCISE 6, FIG. 9-40

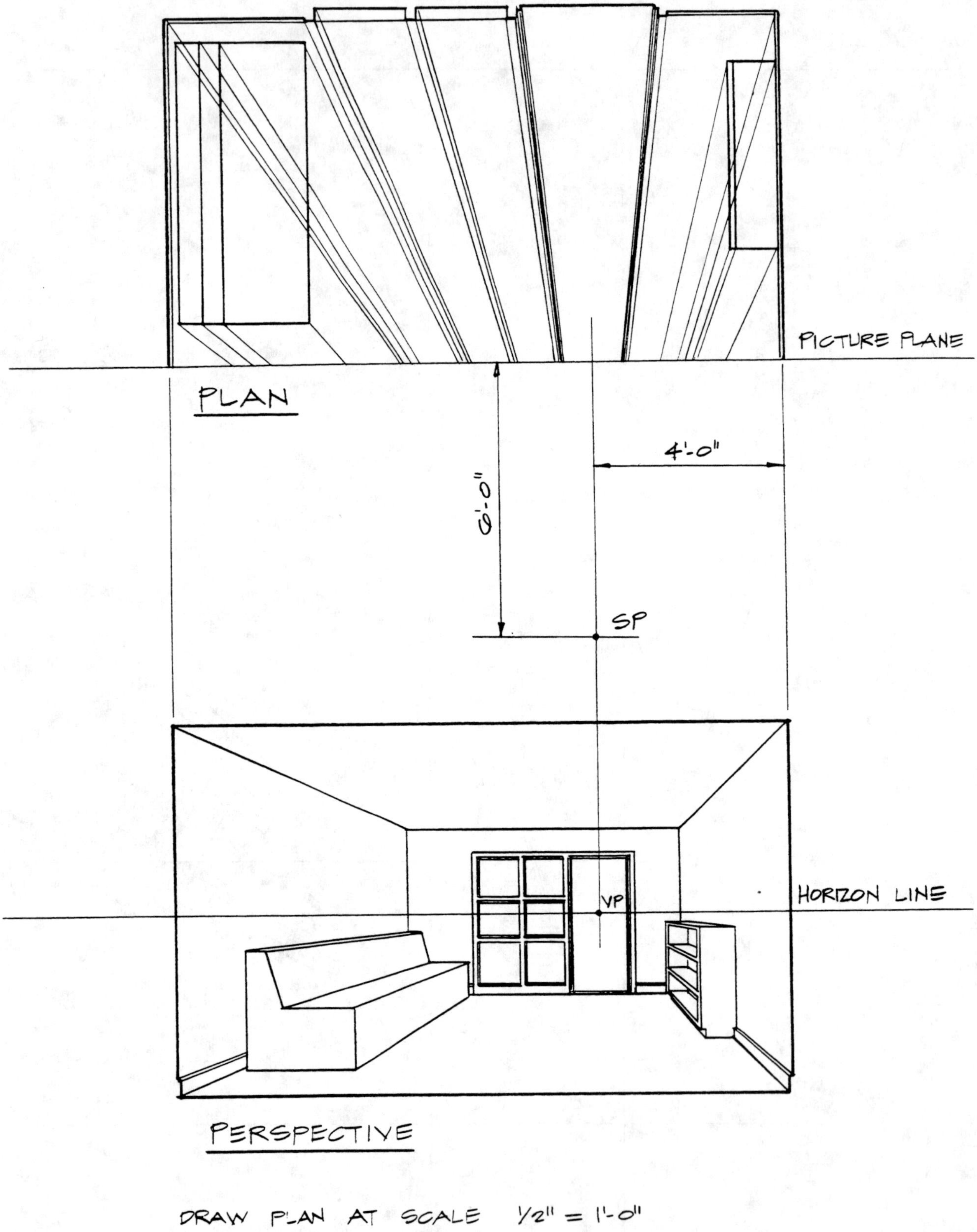

CHAPTER 9, EXERCISE 7, FIG. 9-37

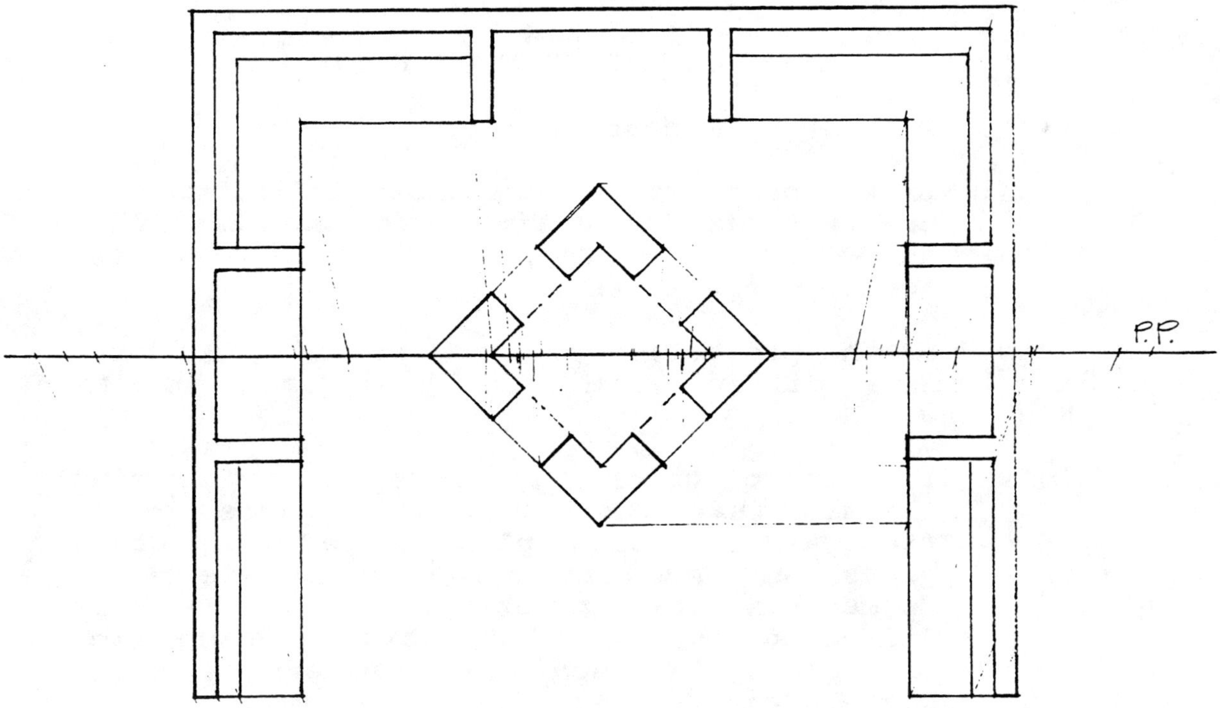

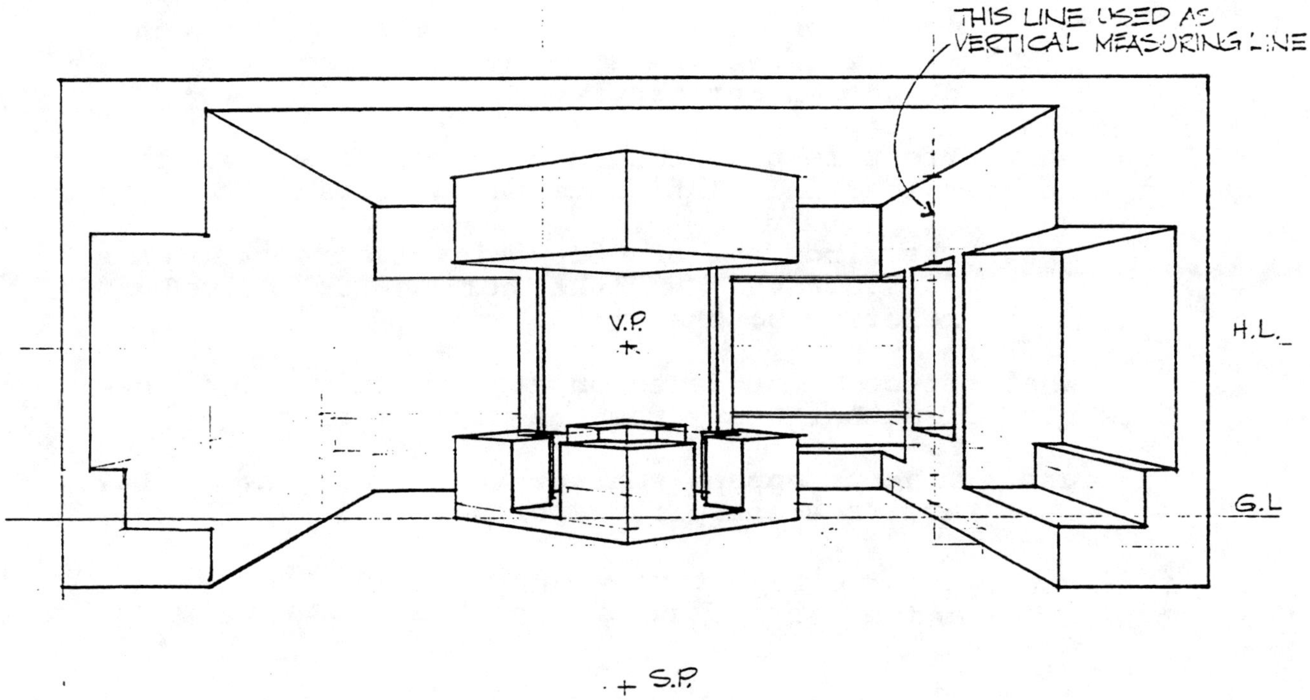

CHAPTER 9, EXERCISE 9, FIG. 9-42

CHAPTER 9
REVIEW QUESTIONS AND ANSWERS

1. What is meant by linear perspective?

ans. **Linear perspectives are those defining outlines used by delineators and classified as either one-point, two-point, or three-point perspectives.**

2. How does the projection of a perspective view of the picture plane differ from the projection of an orthographic view?

ans. **The basic theory in perspective drawing assumes that the image is produced on a transparent vertical plane called the picture plane very much as orthographic views are formed on transparent planes. The only difference is the orthographics have parallel projectors, whereas the perspective views have projectors radiating from a single person's eye.**

3. What is the point called that approximates the eye when a person draws an object in perspective?

ans. **The station point is the point that approximates the eye when a person draws an object in perspective.**

4. What effect is produced on a perspective when the horizon line is raised in relation to the groundline?

ans. **The birds eye or "top" view is produced on a perspective when the horizon is raised in relation to the groundline.**

5. What effect is produced on a perspective when the object is placed farther away from the picture plane?

ans. **Objects appear smaller the farther back they are from the picture plane.**

6. What type of perspective view is established when the ground line and horizon line are placed close to each other?

ans. **The worm's eye view is the perspective view which is established when the ground line and horizon line are placed close to each other.**

7. Describe the step by step procedure used in setting up a freehand 2-point perspective.

ans. **Steps in setting up a 2-point perspective:**

a. Draw a vertical line to represent the closest vertical corner of the building.

b. Sketch a horizontal line across the paper at a point that appears to be about 6′ high from the bottom of the vertical line just drawn.

c. On the horizontal line establish a vanishing point to the right and one to the left of the vertical line well beyond the area intended for the building.

d. From the top and bottom of the vertical line sketch angular lines to each vanishing point. These lines will block-in the building.

e. Develop the irregularities and details once the perspective is blocked-in.

8. Describe in detail the difference between a 1-point perspective and 2-point perspective.

ans. **A 1-point perspective has a single vanishing point located on the horizon line. A 2-point perspective has two vanishing points located on the horizon line. 1-point perspectives are generally used for interior sketches where the lines perpendicular to the viewer vanish to the vanishing point and lines parallel to the viewer are drawn parallel. 2-point perspectives are generally used for exterior sketches where all lines except vertical lines vanish to the vanishing points. Two sides of an object are shown in 2-point perspective sketches.**

9. Why must true heights of an object be established only on the picture plane?

ans. **True heights of an object must be established only at the picture plane, since in perspective drawing, objects beyond the picture plane are smaller than true height and objects in front of it are larger than true height.**

10. If an object is placed in an oblique position in relation to the picture plane, why are two vanishing points necessary?

ans. **When a building is placed in an oblique position on a picture plane, the viewer would see two sides of the building; therefore there must be two vanishing points.**

11. What are the advantages of using the perspective-plan method for drawing a perspective?

ans. **The perspective-plan method has more versatility than the office-method. Drawings can be completed more quickly once the principles have been mastered since measurements can be placed on a measuring line eliminating the need to draw the floor plan above the perspective view and make projections from it.**

12. In a one-point parallel perspective view of an interior, is the single vanishing point used to draw a piece of furniture that is in a diagonal position?

ans. **Yes, there is one vanishing point in a one-point parallel perspective view.**

13. When would it be appropriate to use a three-point perspective?

ans. **It would be appropriate to use a three-point perspective for an aerial view of a very tall building or for a ground view looking up at a very tall building.**

14. Why are most two-point perspectives drawn with the horizon line located about 6′ above the ground plane?

ans. **Most two-point perspectives are drawn with the horizon line located about 6′ above the ground plane; this distance represents the eye level height of the average person standing on level ground.**

15. Why is it important to limit the cone of vision from the station point to the picture plane to an angle of 30° to 45°?

ans. **It is important to limit the cone of vision from the station point to the picture plane to an angle of 30° to 45° to prevent distortion of the perspective.**

16. When would it be appropriate to use a bird's eye view perspective?

ans. **A bird's eye view perspective would be used for a roof-top or aerial view of a building.**

17. Describe a convenient method for drawing a circle in a two-point perspective?

ans. **Draw a square in perspective that has sides of the same dimensions as the diameter of the circle. Find the center points of each side of the square. Construct arcs tangent to center points on the sides of the square. The circle will appear as an ellipse in perspective.**

The following page has a quick quiz that can be copied and given to students prior to starting the perspective exercises. The solution is also included.

IDENTIFY THE INDICATED COMPONENTS OF THE PERSPECTIVE DRAWING BELOW.

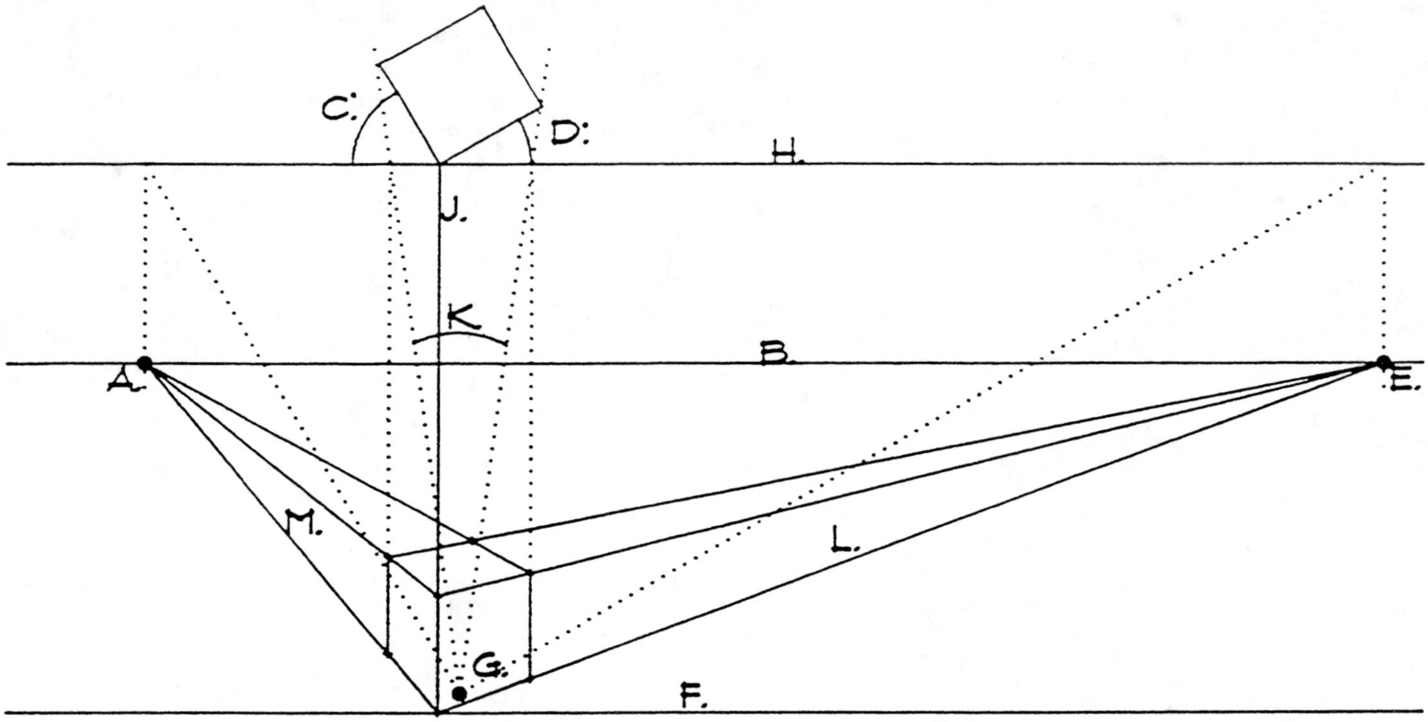

A. ________________________________

B. ________________________________

C. ________________________________

D. ________________________________

E. ________________________________

F. ________________________________

G. ________________________________

H. ________________________________

J. ________________________________

K. ________________________________

L. ________________________________

M. ________________________________

IDENTIFY THE INDICATED COMPONENTS OF THE PERSPECTIVE DRAWING BELOW.

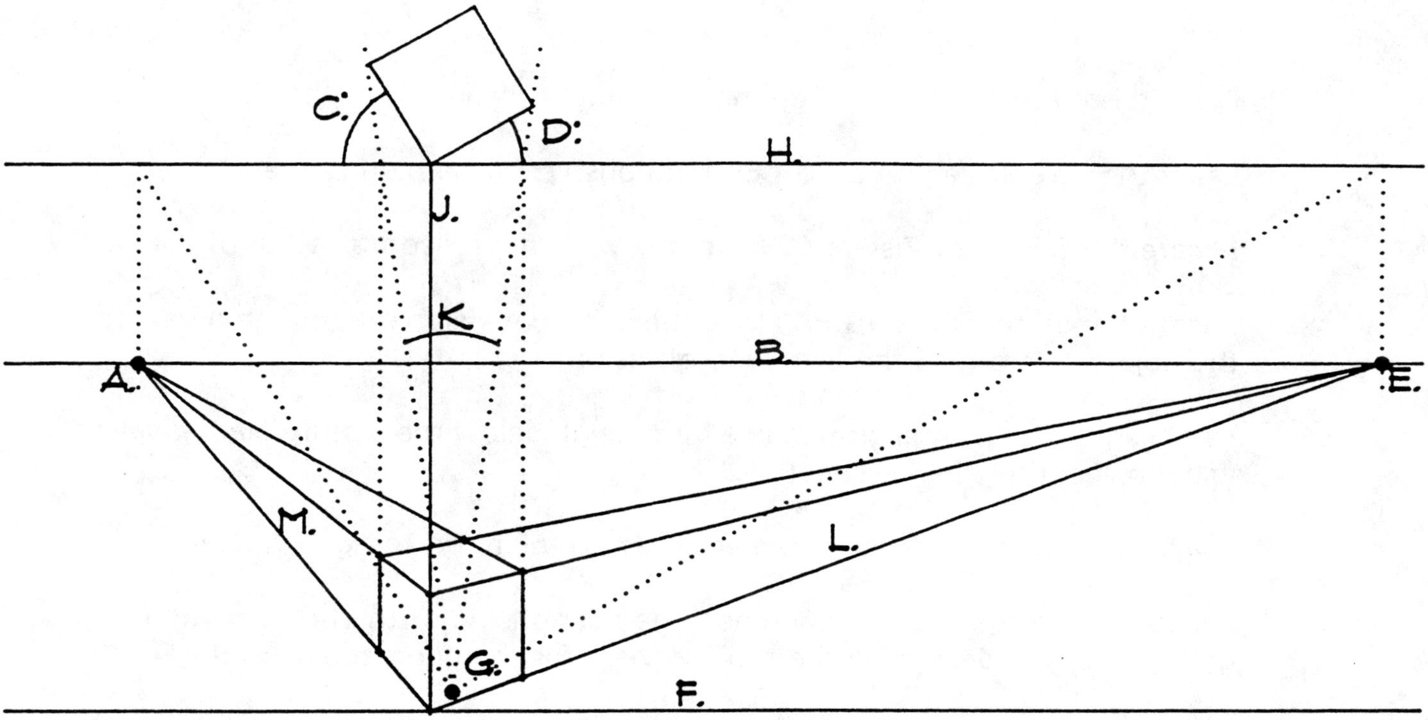

A. V.P.L

B. HORIZON

C. 60° L

D. 30° L

E. V.P.R.

F. GROUND

G. STATION POINT

H. PICTURE PLANE

J. T.H.L.

K. CONE OF VISION

L. VANISHING LINES - RIGHT

M. VANISHING LINES - LEFT

The following pages can be copied and used as overhead transparencies to review the steps involved in the set-up and drawing of a two-point perspective of a simple geometric object using the Office Method. The numbers of the steps listed below correspond to the drawing numbers.

1. Draw a horizontal line representing the picture plane.

2. Draw the object plan on a 30 - 60 relationship to the picture plane.

3. Locate the Center of Vision (C.V.) midway on the horizontal width of the plan.

4. Locate the Station Point (S.P.) along the center of vision far enough away from the object to produce the 30 cone of vision.

5. Establish the horizontal ground line far enough below the picture plane to allow enough room for the perspective.

6. Draw the elevation, at the same scale as the plan, on the ground line.

7. Locate the horizon line. Remember, the relationship of the horizon line to the ground line will determine the type of view for the perspective.

8. From the station point draw a line to the right, parallel to the right side of the object, up to the picture plane.

9. From the station point draw a line to the left, parallel to the left side of the object, up to the picture plane.

10. On the right, where the projected line crosses the picture plane, drop a vertical line to the horizon line. Where these lines cross is the Vanishing Point Right (V.P.R.).

11. On the left, where the projected line crosses the picture plane, drop a vertical line to the horizon line. Where these lines cross is the Vanishing Point Left (V.P.L.).

12. Draw the vertical True Height Line (T.H.L.) from the corner of the object touching the picture plane down to the ground line.

13. Project true heights from the elevation to the vertical true height line.

14. Draw vanishing lines from the 'top' and 'bottom' of the heights projected onto the true height line to the vanishing point right.

15. Draw vanishing lines from the 'top' and 'bottom' of the heights projected onto the true height line to the vanishing point left.

16. Draw lines from the corners of the object in plan down to the station point.

17. Where these lines cross the picture plane draw vertical lines down to the constructed 'top' and 'bottom' vanishing lines.

18. Where the vertical line crosses the top left vanishing line project a line to the vanishing point right.

19. Where the vertical line crosses the top right vanishing line project a line to the vanishing point left.

20. Darken the line segments that outline the object in perspective.

Drawings 21 and 22 show the above process repeated for a condition where the horizon line is located below the ground line.

DRAWING 1

PICTURE PLANE

DRAWING 2

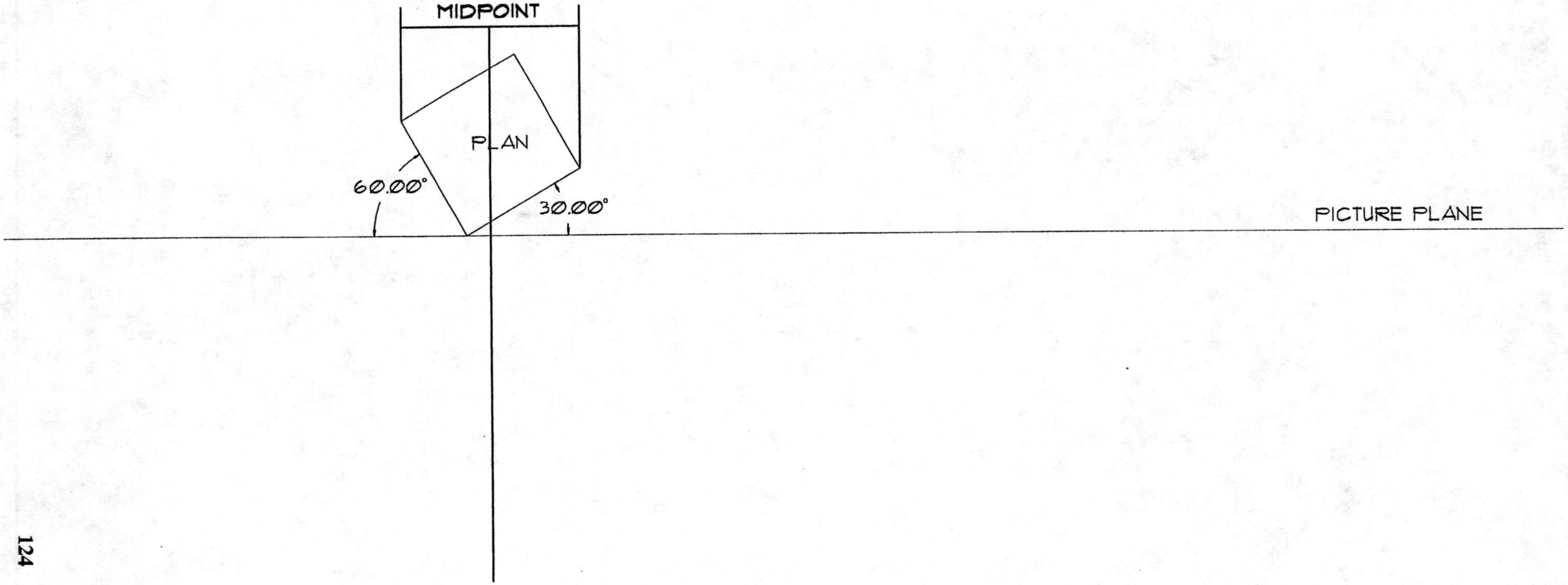

DRAWING 3

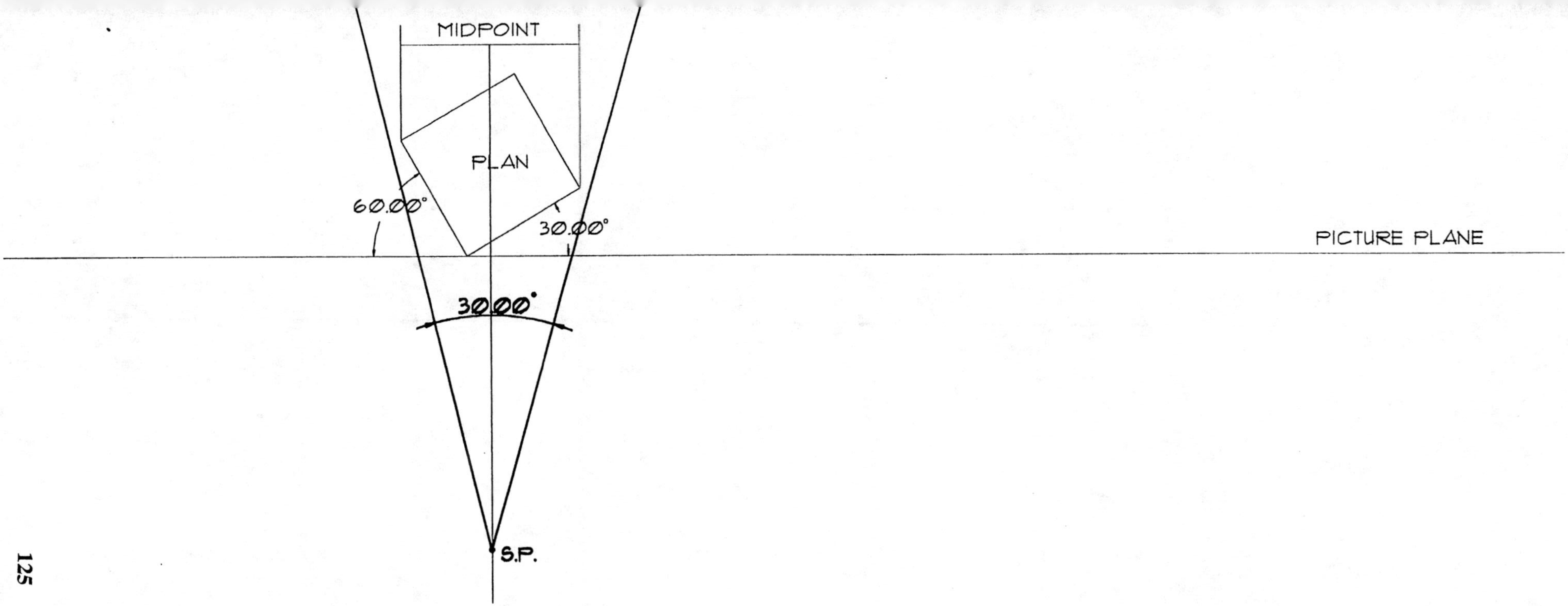

DRAWING 4

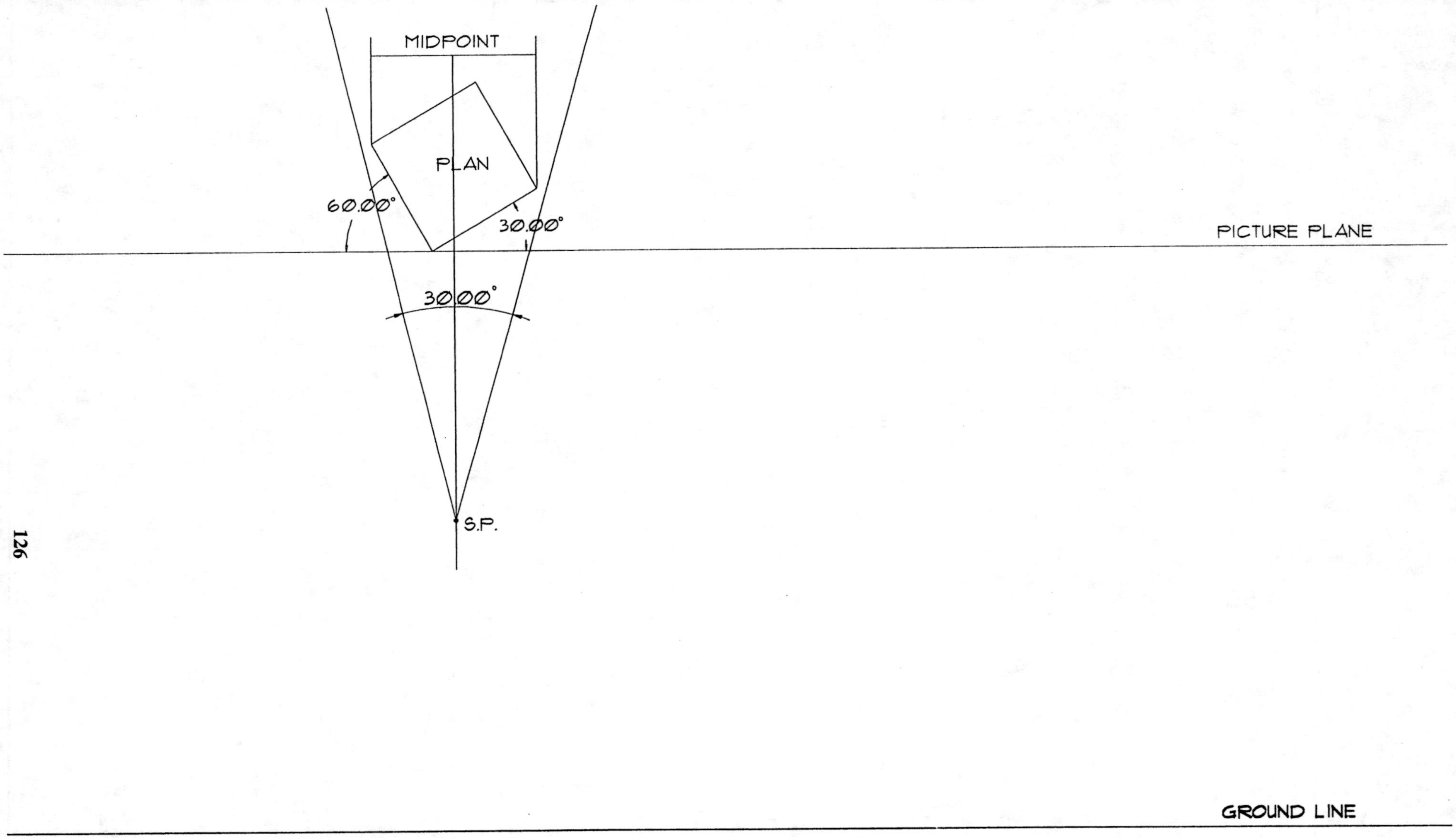

DRAWING 5

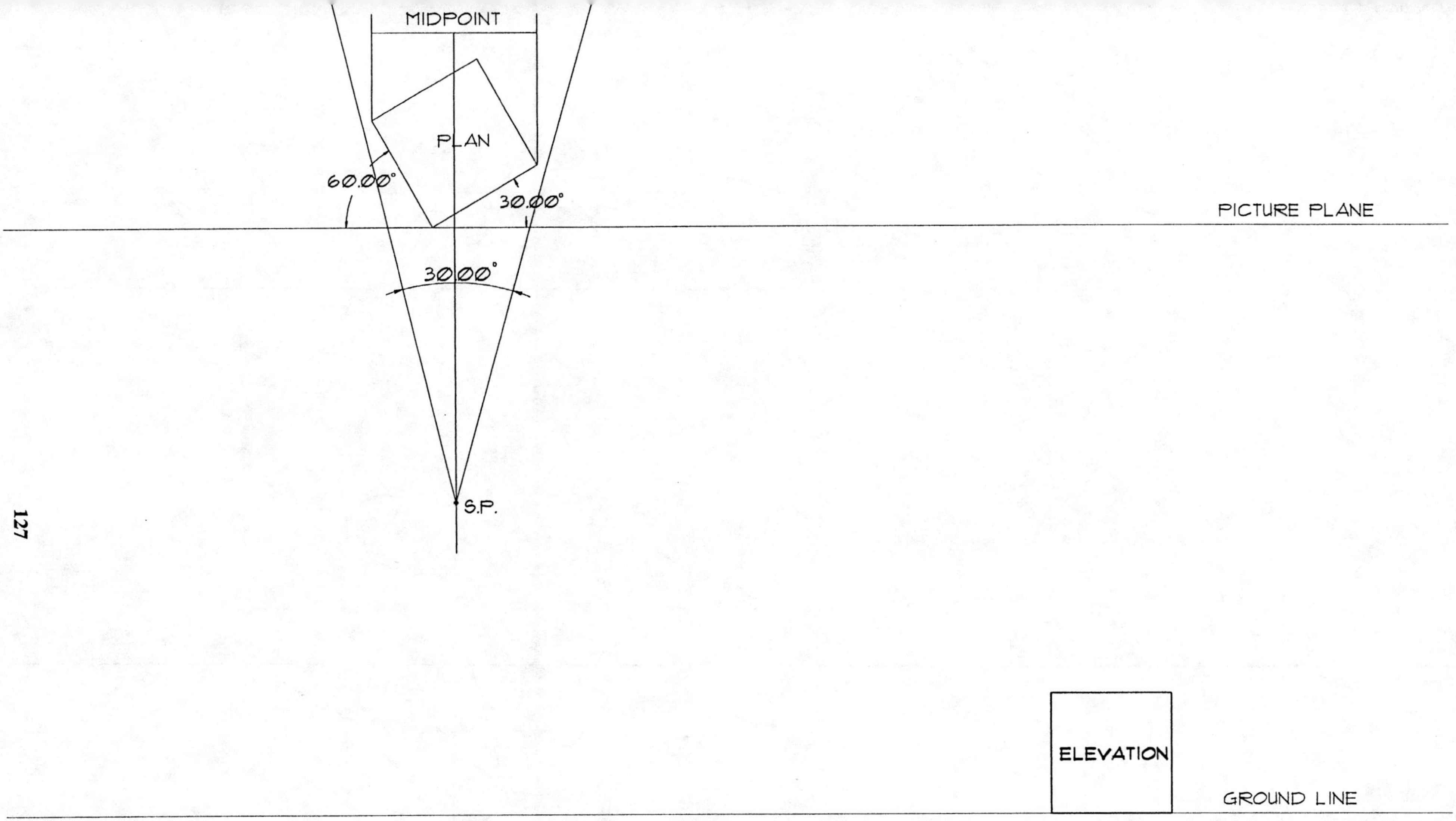
MIDPOINT
PLAN
60.00°
30.00°
PICTURE PLANE
30.00°
S.P.
ELEVATION
GROUND LINE

DRAWING 6

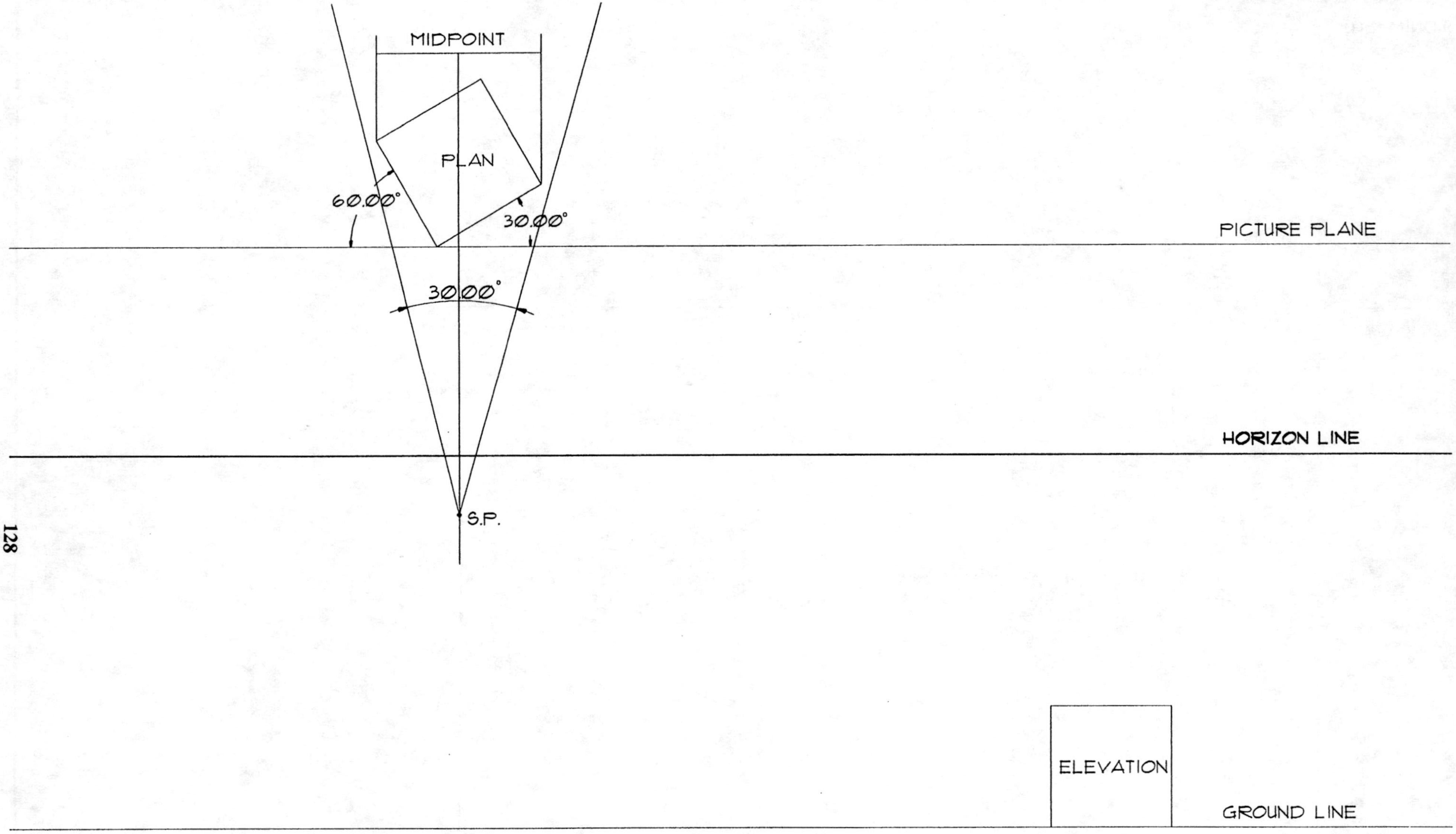
MIDPOINT
PLAN
60.00°
30.00°
PICTURE PLANE
30.00°
HORIZON LINE
S.P.
ELEVATION
GROUND LINE

DRAWING 7

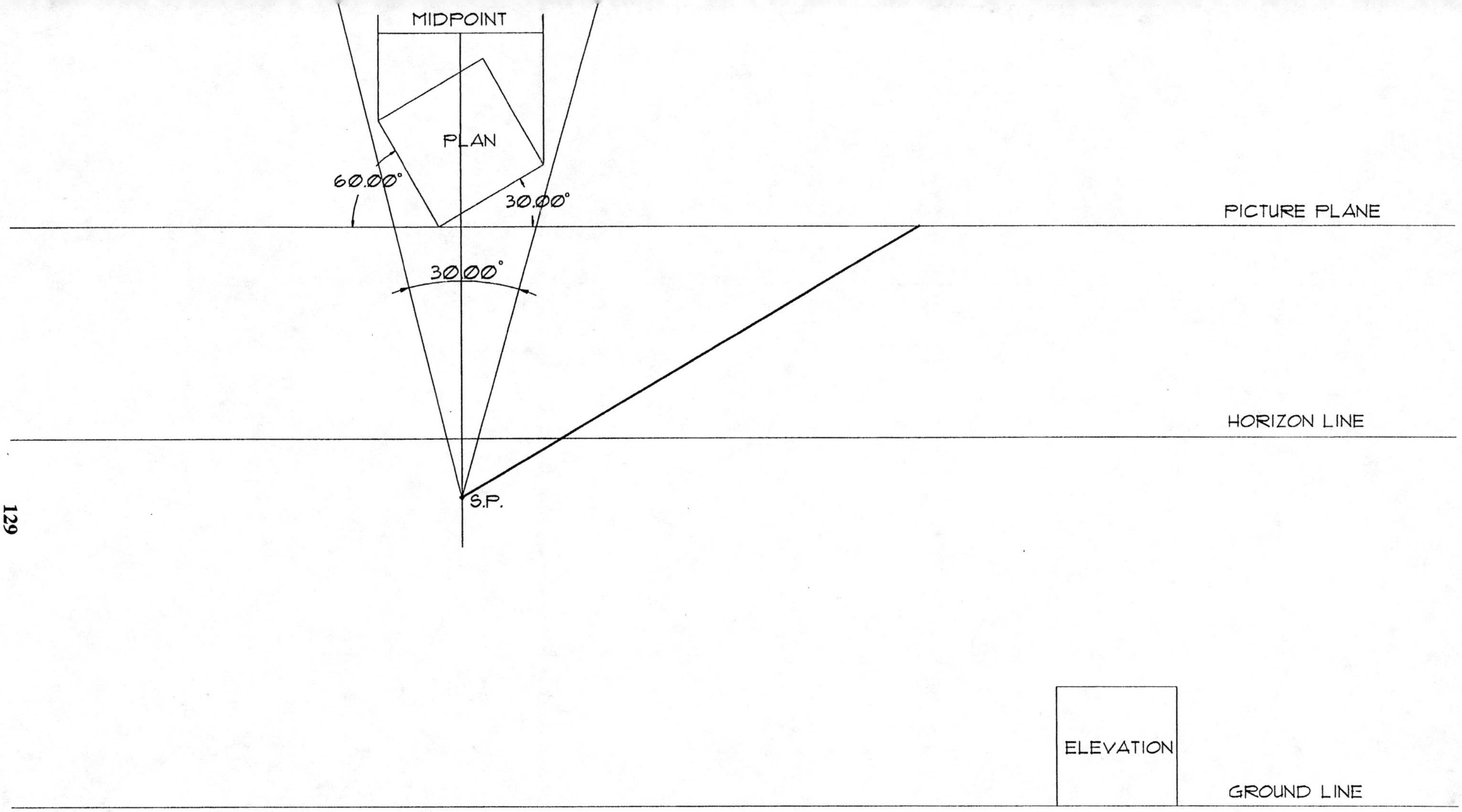
MIDPOINT
PLAN
60.00°
30.00°
30.00°
PICTURE PLANE
HORIZON LINE
S.P.
ELEVATION
GROUND LINE

DRAWING 8

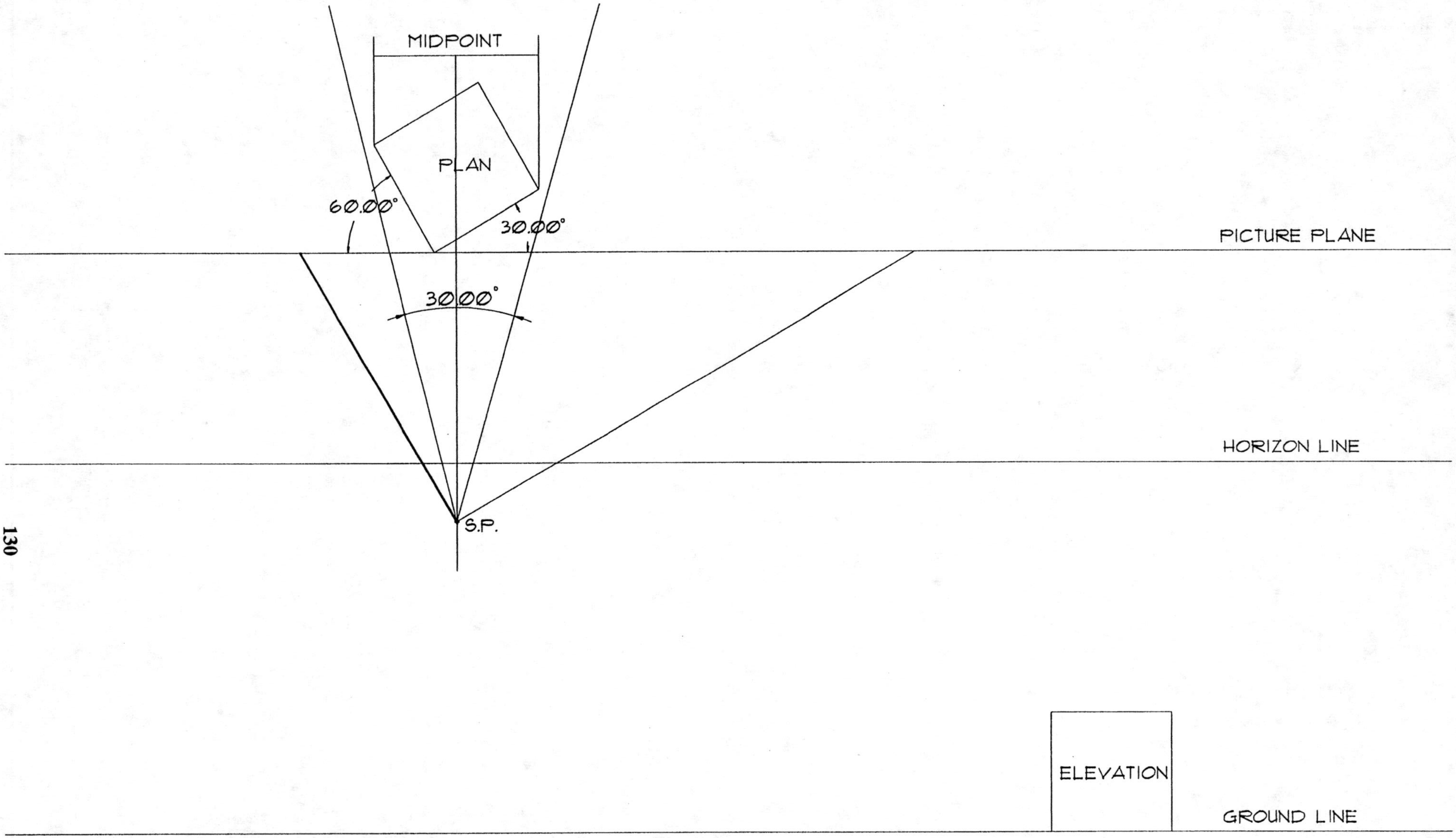
MIDPOINT
PLAN
60.00°
30.00°
30.00°
PICTURE PLANE
HORIZON LINE
S.P.
ELEVATION
GROUND LINE

DRAWING 9

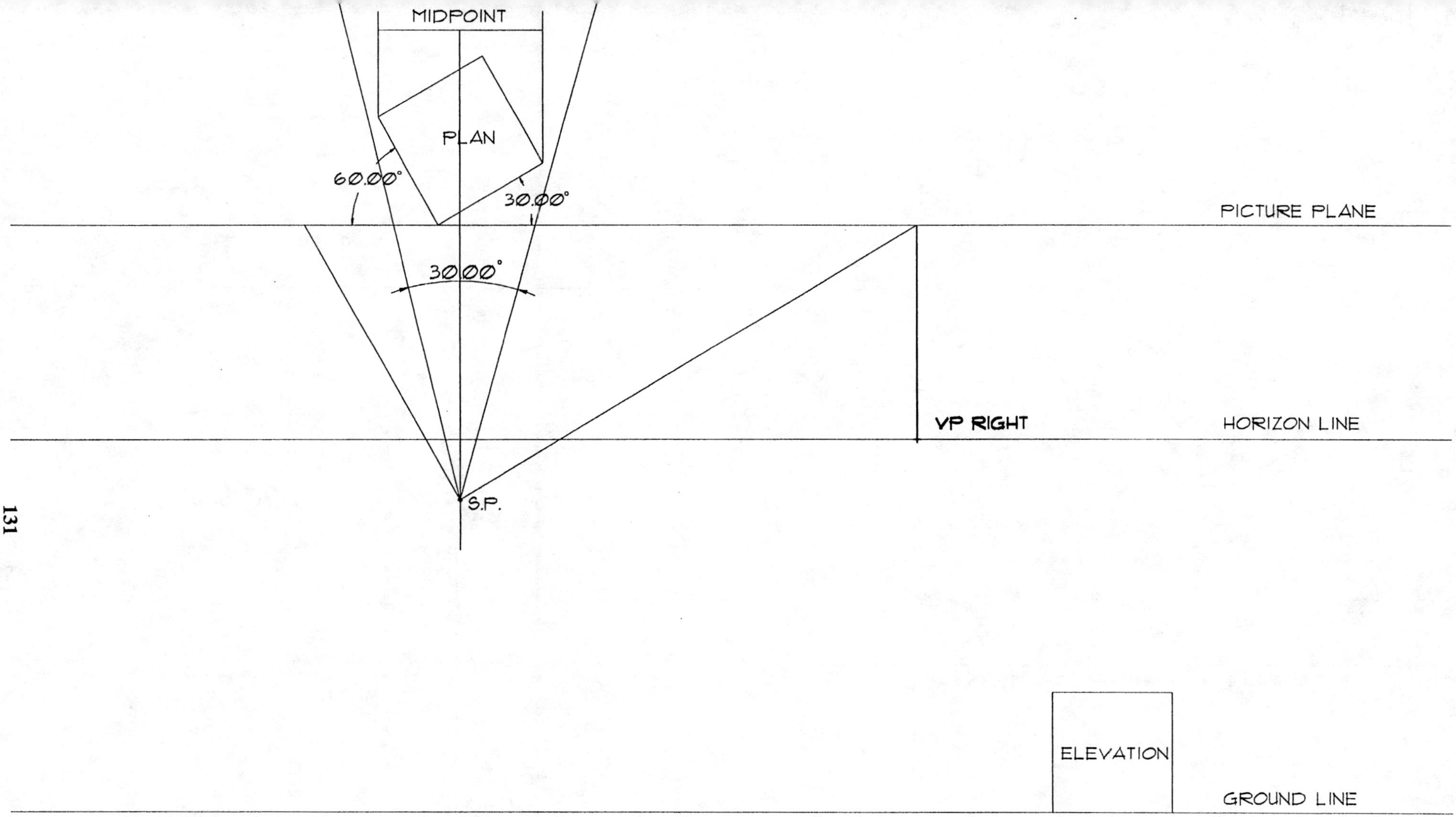
MIDPOINT
PLAN
60.00°
30.00°
30.00°
S.P.
PICTURE PLANE
VP RIGHT
HORIZON LINE
ELEVATION
GROUND LINE

DRAWING 10

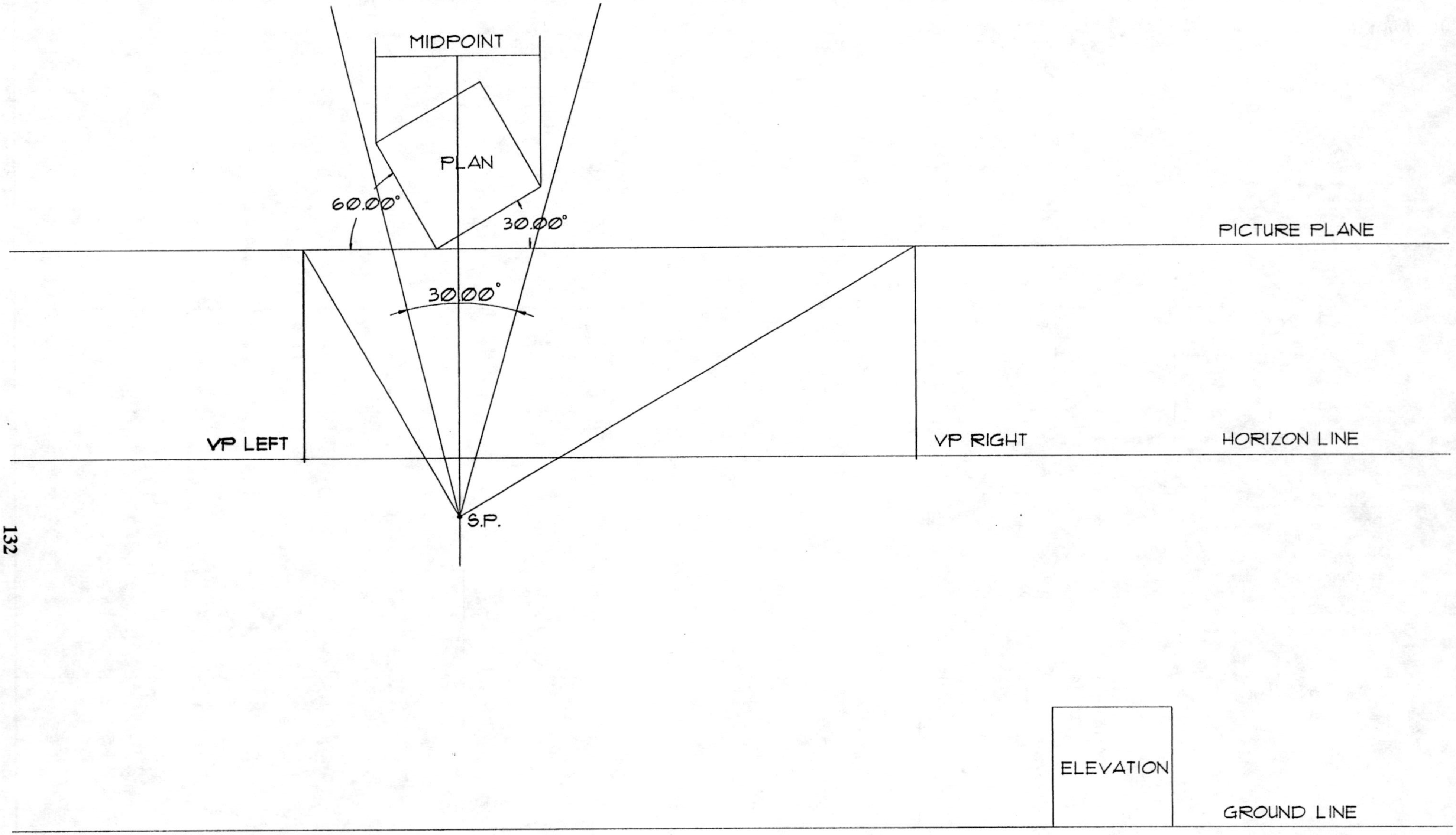
MIDPOINT
PLAN
60.00°
30.00°
PICTURE PLANE
30.00°
VP LEFT
VP RIGHT
HORIZON LINE
S.P.
ELEVATION
GROUND LINE

DRAWING 11

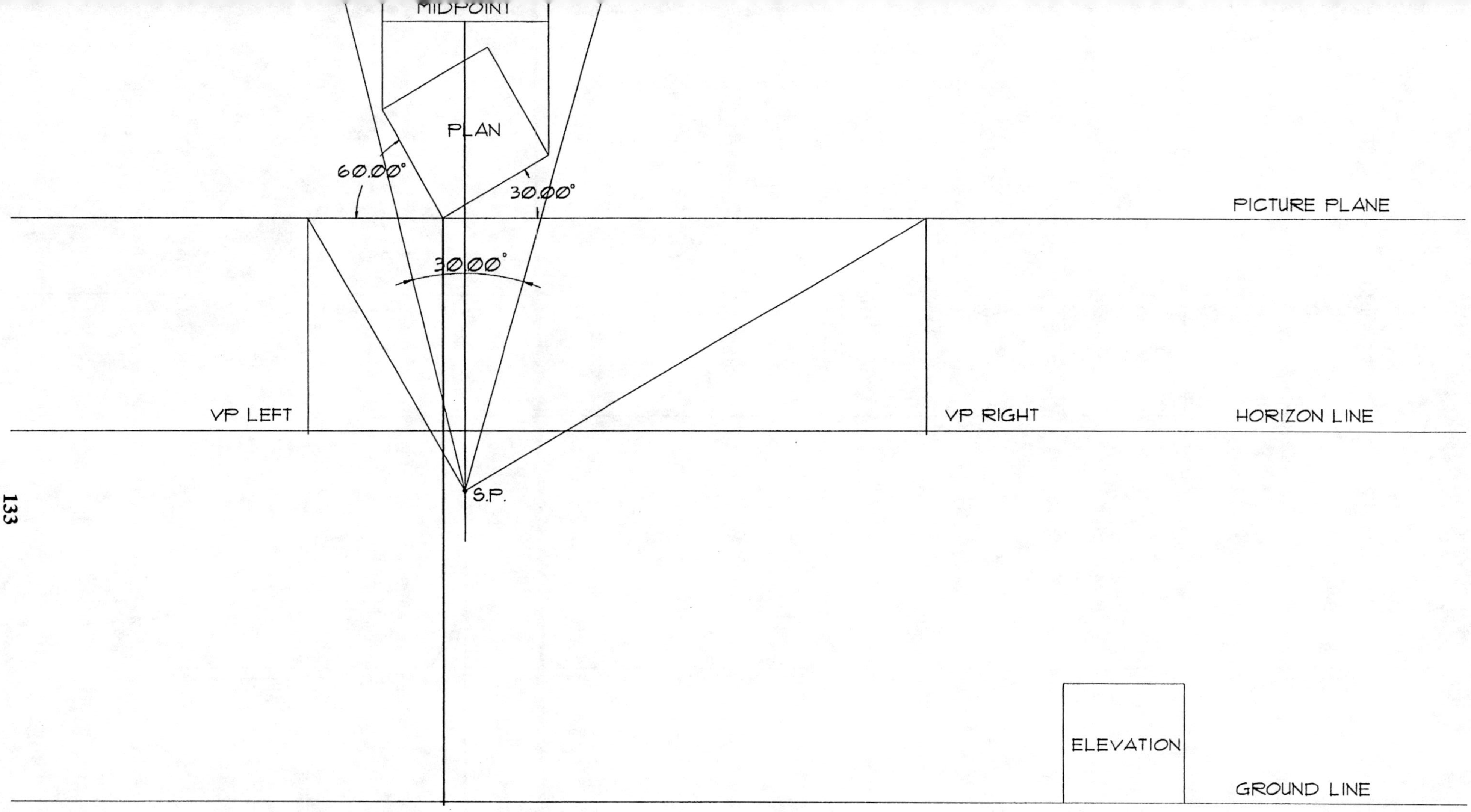
MIDPOINT
PLAN
60.00°
30.00°
PICTURE PLANE
30.00°
VP LEFT
VP RIGHT
HORIZON LINE
S.P.
ELEVATION
GROUND LINE

DRAWING 12

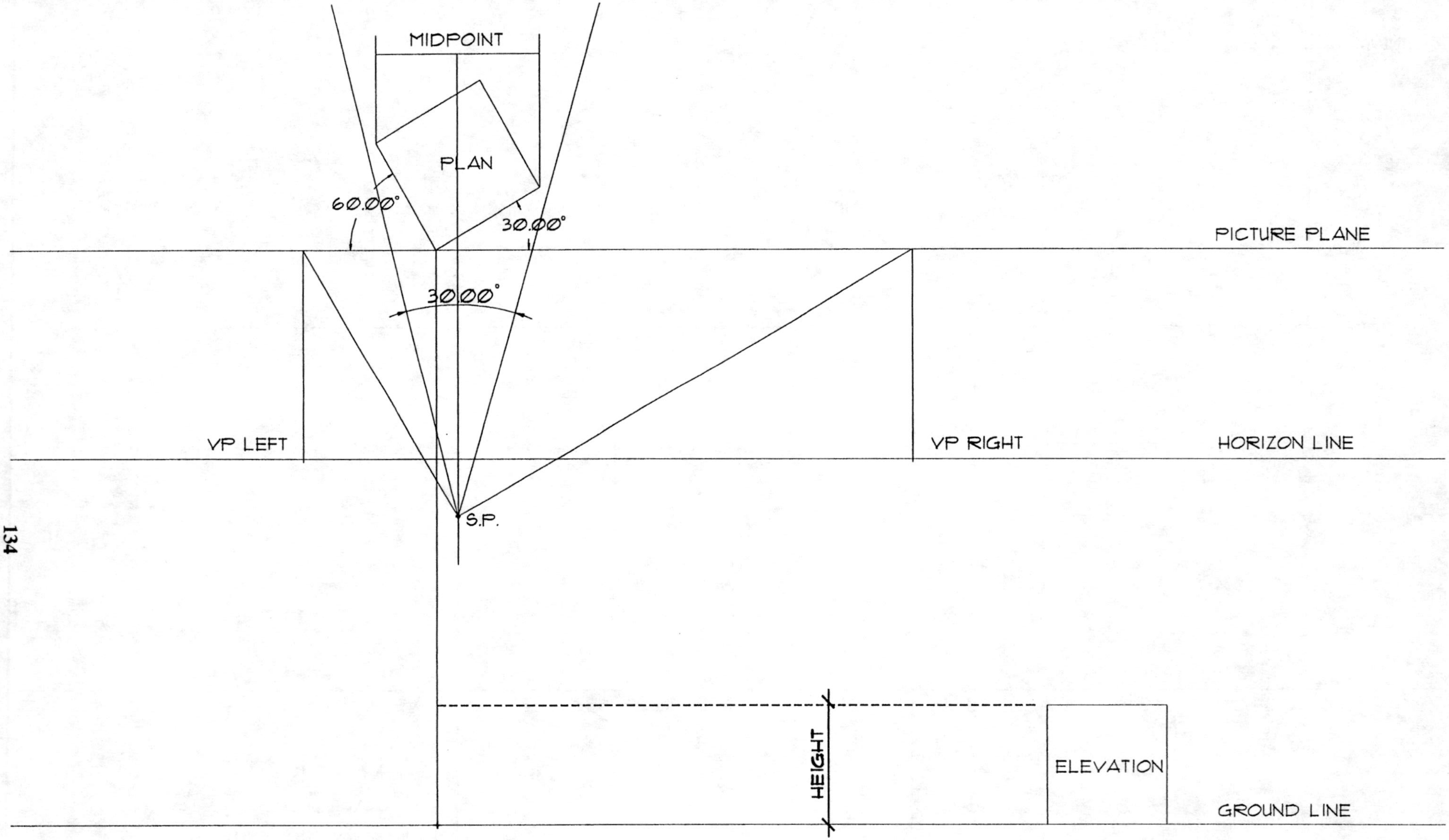
MIDPOINT
PLAN
60.00°
30.00°
PICTURE PLANE
30.00°
VP LEFT
VP RIGHT
HORIZON LINE
S.P.
HEIGHT
ELEVATION
GROUND LINE

DRAWING 13

DRAWING 14

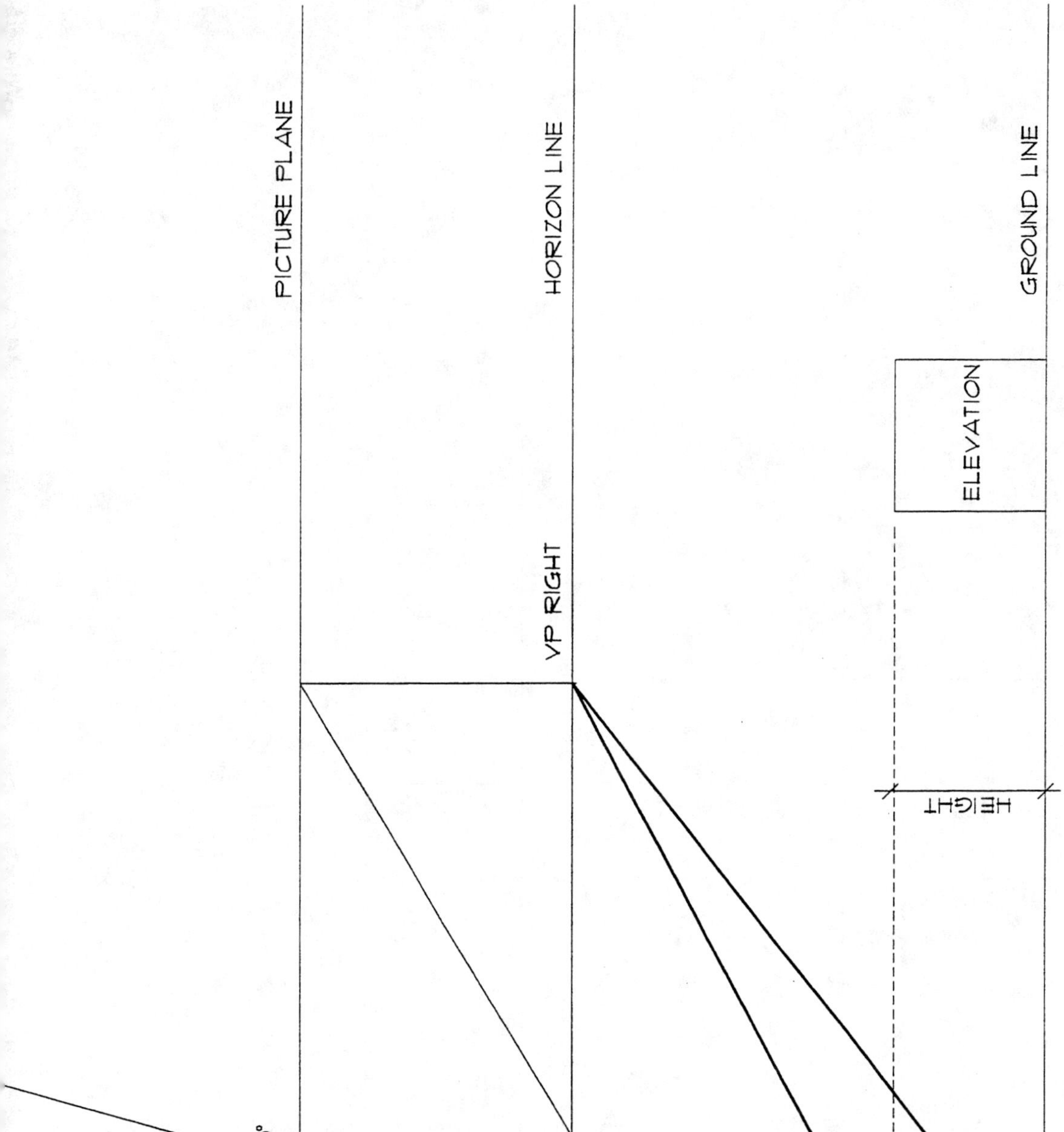
PICTURE PLANE
HORIZON LINE
GROUND LINE
ELEVATION
VP RIGHT
HEIGHT
MIDPOINT
PLAN
30.00°
30.00°
60.00°
S.P.
VP LEFT

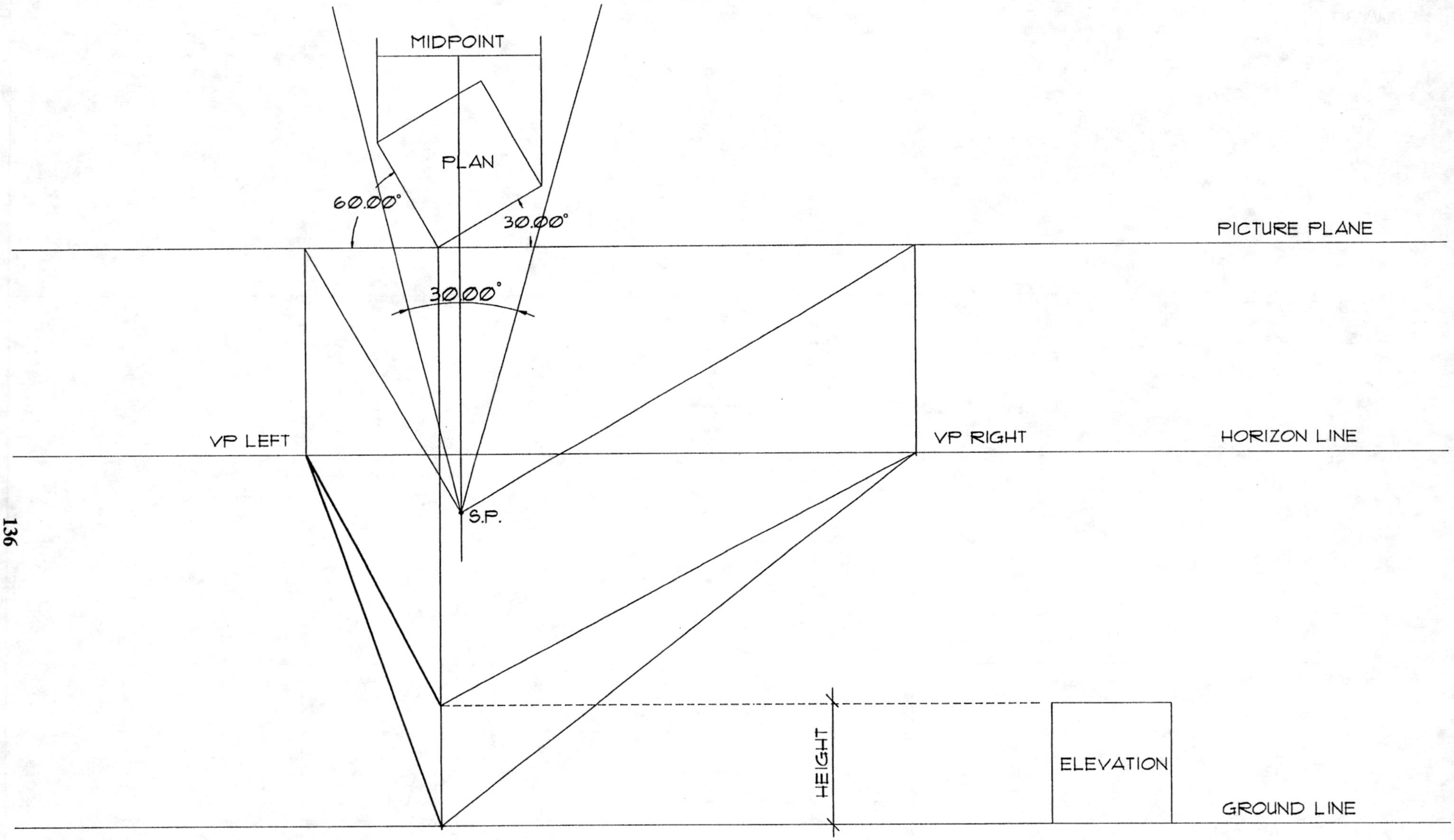
MIDPOINT
PLAN
60.00°
30.00°
PICTURE PLANE
30.00°
VP LEFT
VP RIGHT
HORIZON LINE
S.P.
HEIGHT
ELEVATION
GROUND LINE

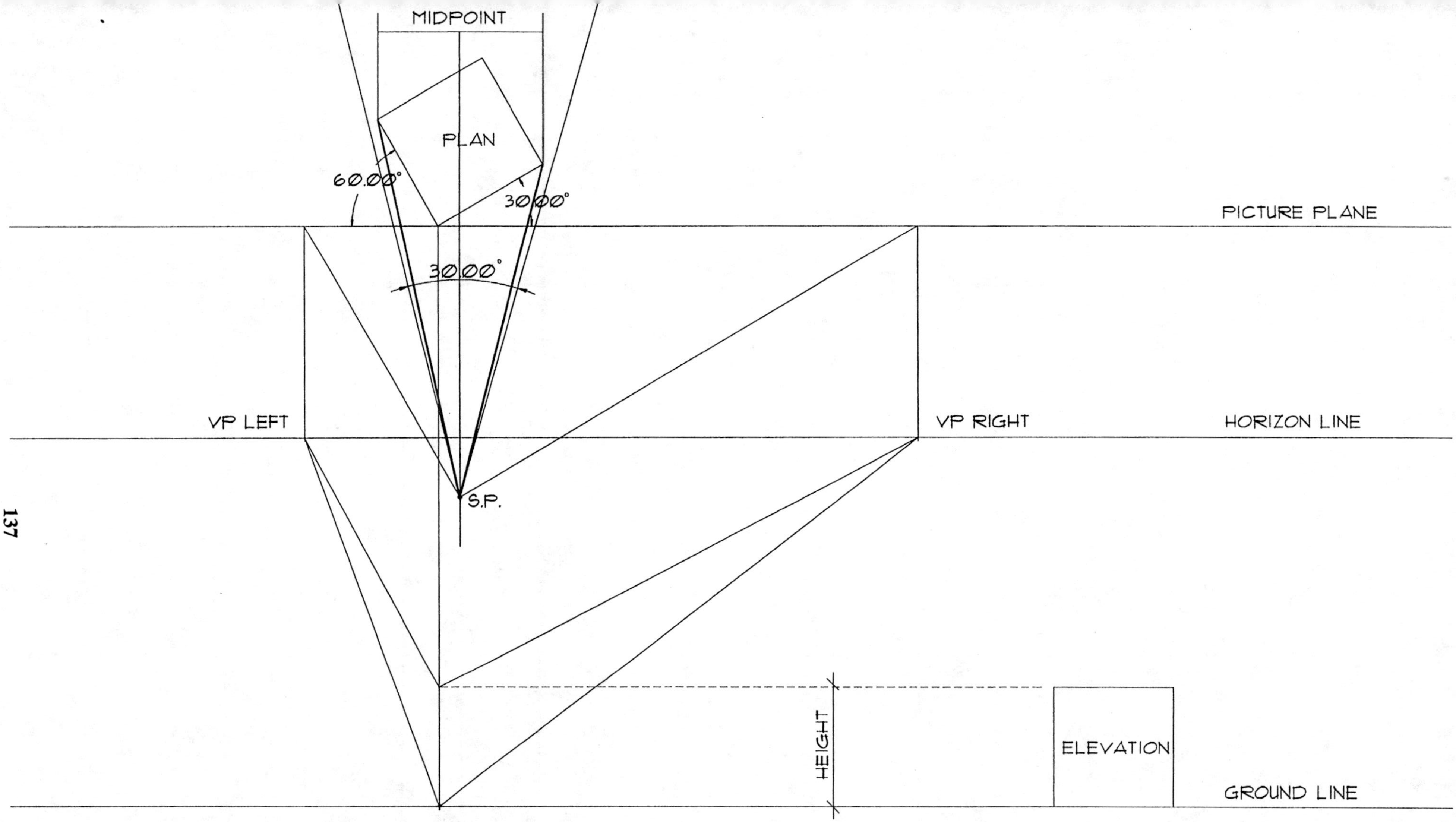
MIDPOINT
PLAN
60.00°
30.00°
30.00°
PICTURE PLANE
VP LEFT
VP RIGHT
HORIZON LINE
S.P.
HEIGHT
ELEVATION
GROUND LINE

DRAWING 16

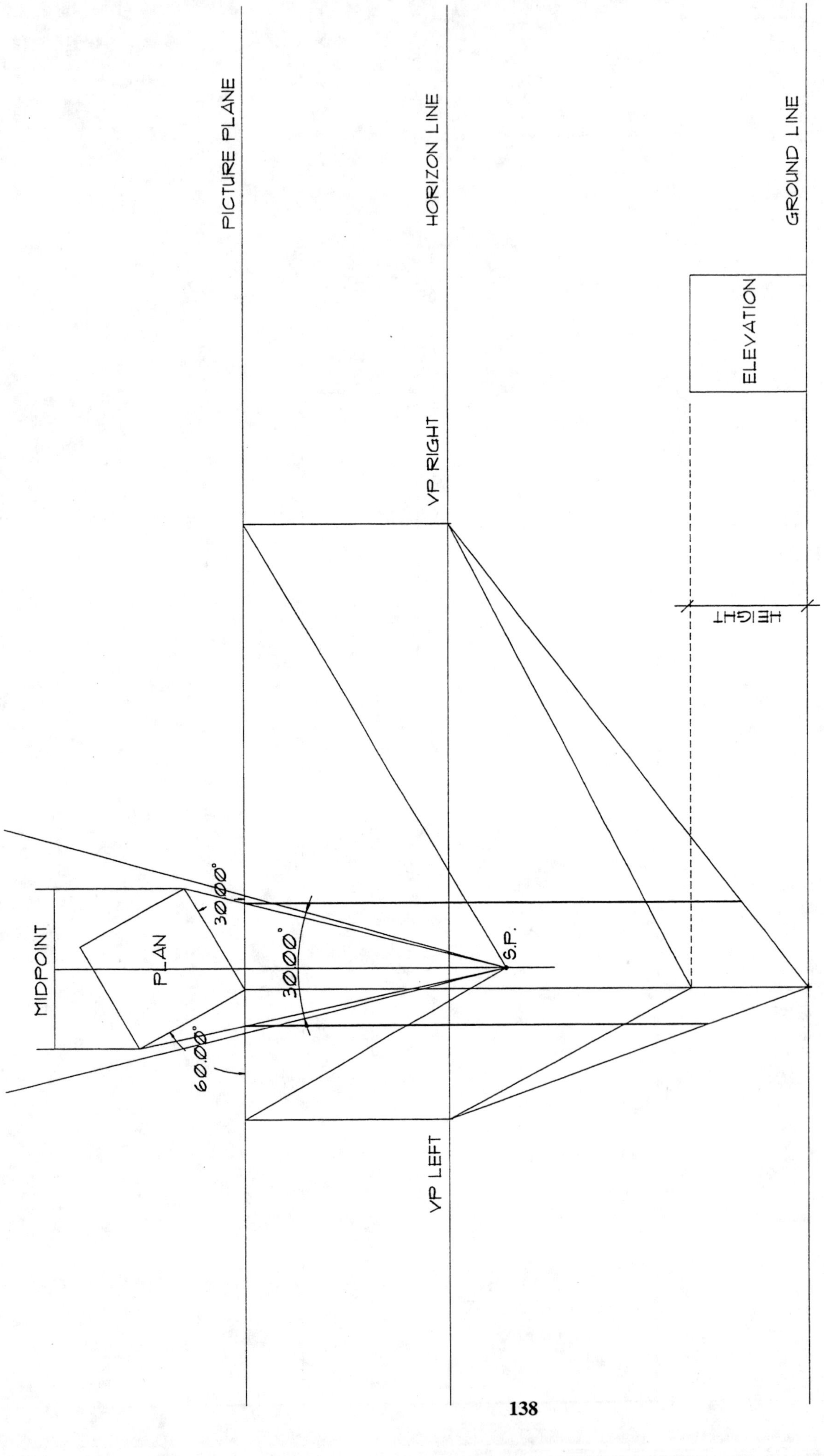
PICTURE PLANE
HORIZON LINE
GROUND LINE
ELEVATION
VP RIGHT
HEIGHT
MIDPOINT
PLAN
30.00°
30.00°
60.00°
S.P.
VP LEFT

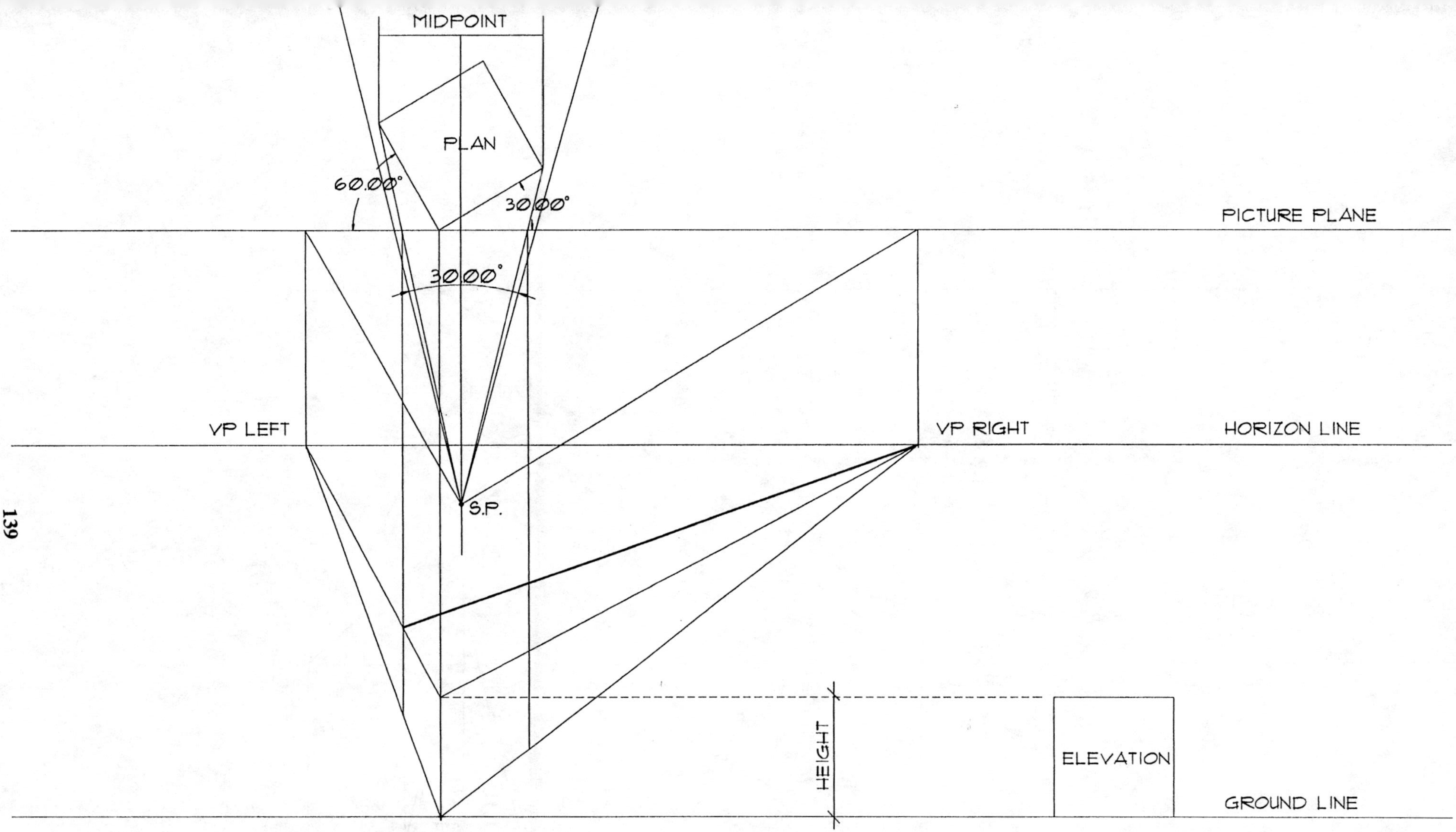

MIDPOINT
PLAN
60.00°
30.00°
PICTURE PLANE
30.00°
VP LEFT
VP RIGHT
HORIZON LINE
S.P.
HEIGHT
ELEVATION
GROUND LINE

DRAWING 18

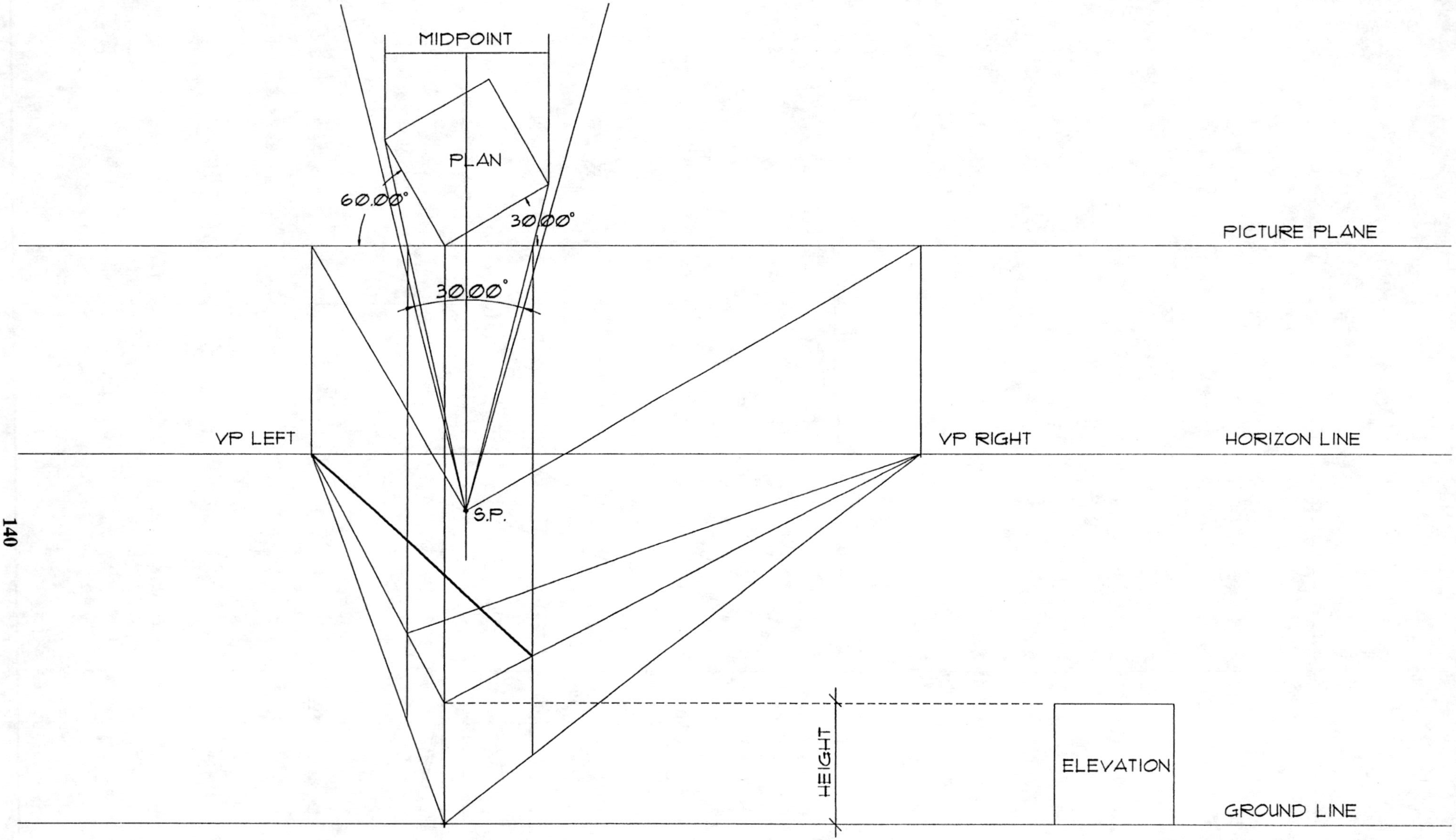
MIDPOINT
PLAN
60.00°
30.00°
30.00°
PICTURE PLANE
VP LEFT
VP RIGHT
HORIZON LINE
S.P.
HEIGHT
ELEVATION
GROUND LINE

DRAWING 19

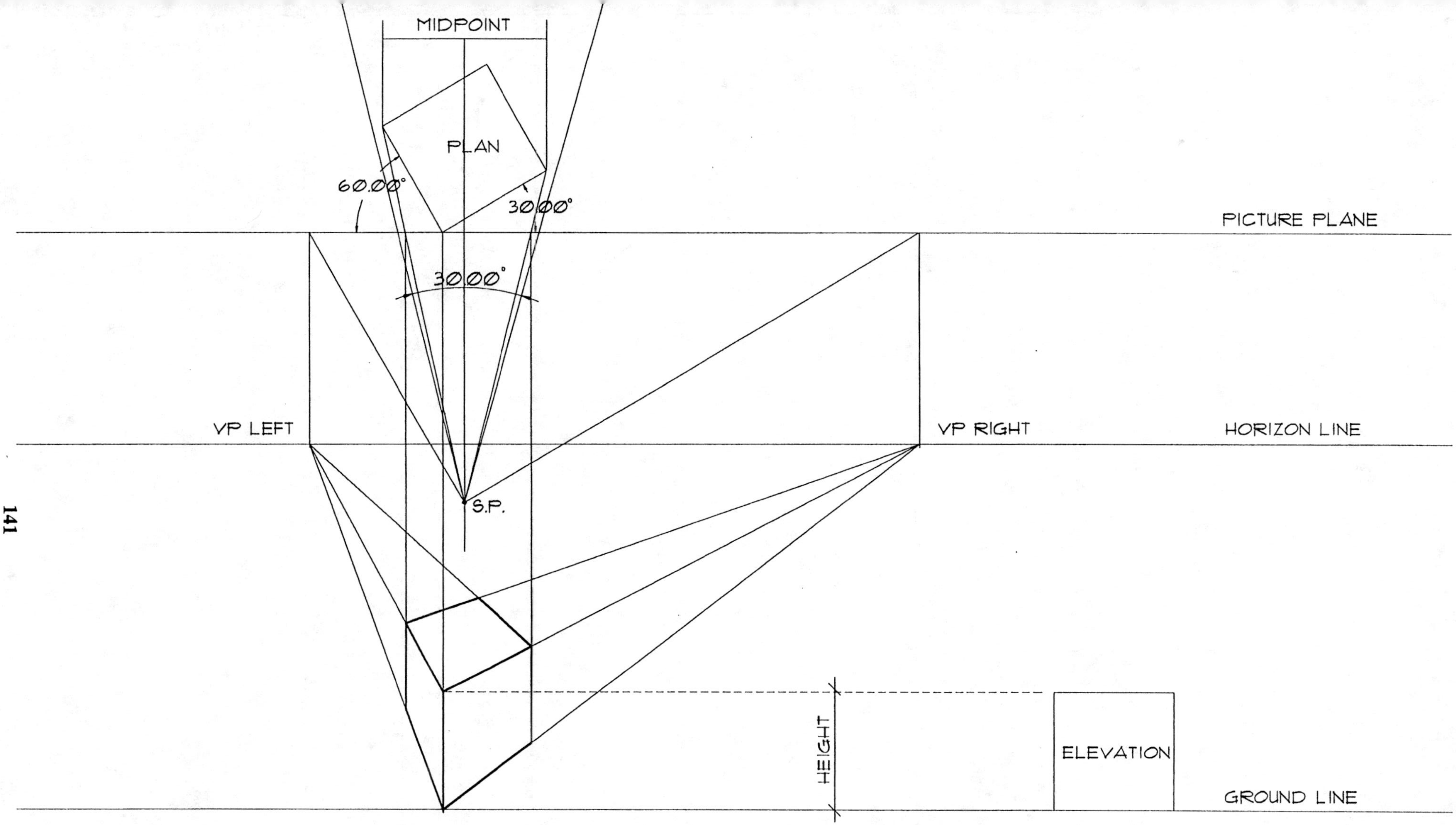
MIDPOINT
PLAN
60.00°
30.00°
PICTURE PLANE
30.00°
VP LEFT
VP RIGHT
HORIZON LINE
S.P.
HEIGHT
ELEVATION
GROUND LINE

DRAWING 20

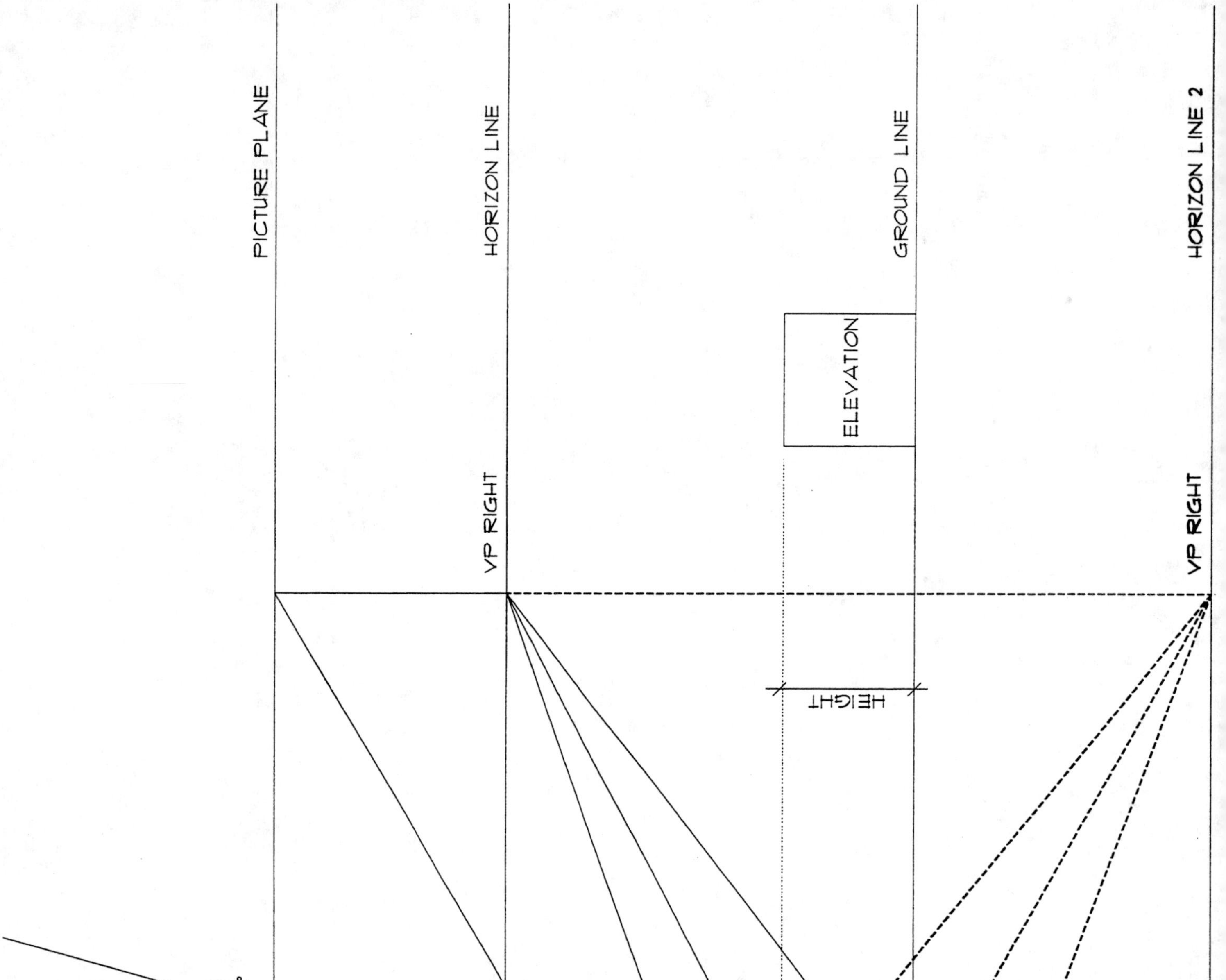
PICTURE PLANE
HORIZON LINE
GROUND LINE
HORIZON LINE 2
ELEVATION
VP RIGHT
VP RIGHT
HEIGHT
MIDPOINT
PLAN
S.P.
30.00°
30.00°
60.00°
VP LEFT
VP LEFT

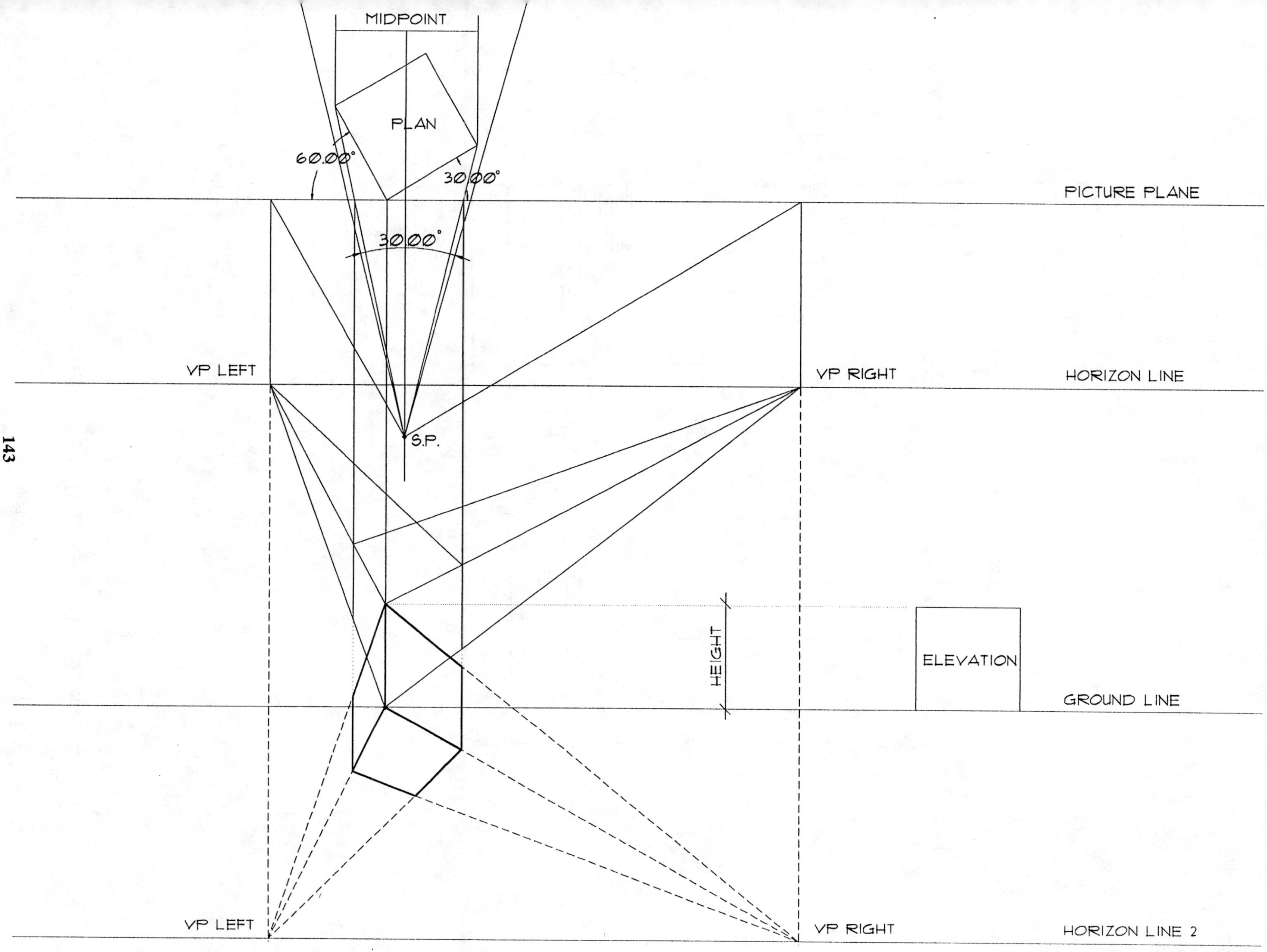
MIDPOINT
PLAN
60.00°
30.00°
30.00°
PICTURE PLANE
VP LEFT
VP RIGHT
HORIZON LINE
S.P.
HEIGHT
ELEVATION
GROUND LINE
VP LEFT
VP RIGHT
HORIZON LINE 2

DRAWING 22

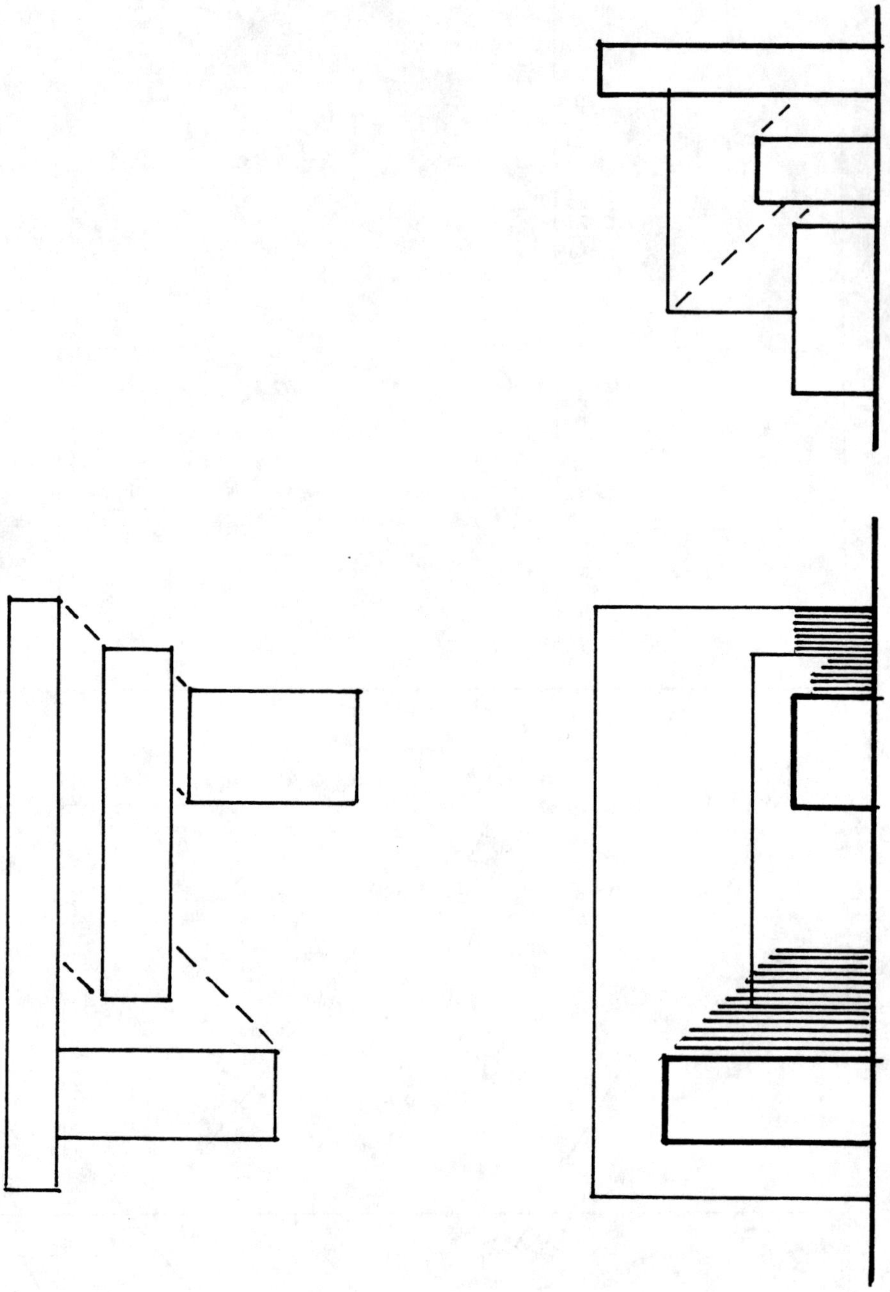

CHAPTER 10, EXERCISE 1, FIG. 10-20B

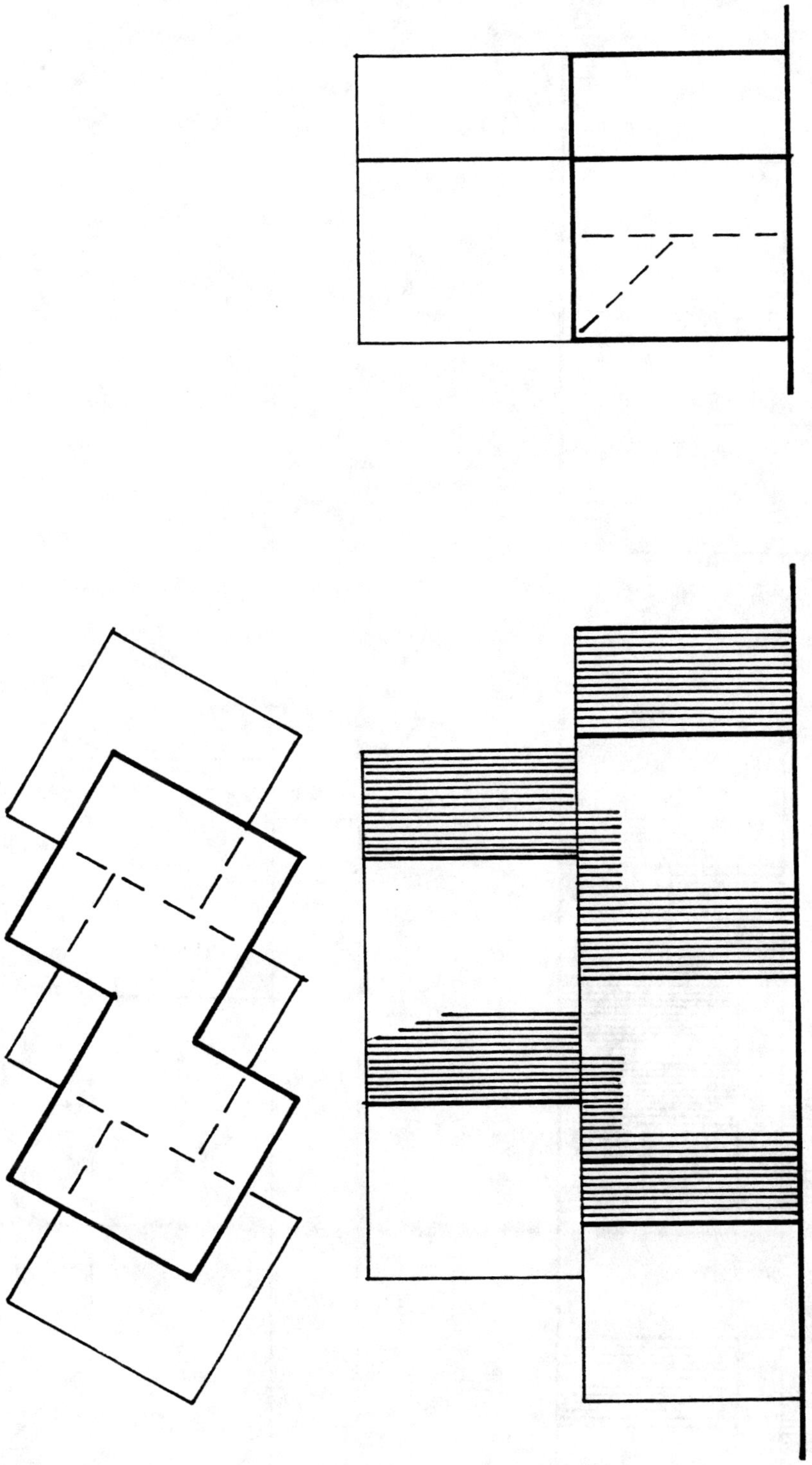

CHAPTER 10, EXERCISE 1, FIG. 10-20C

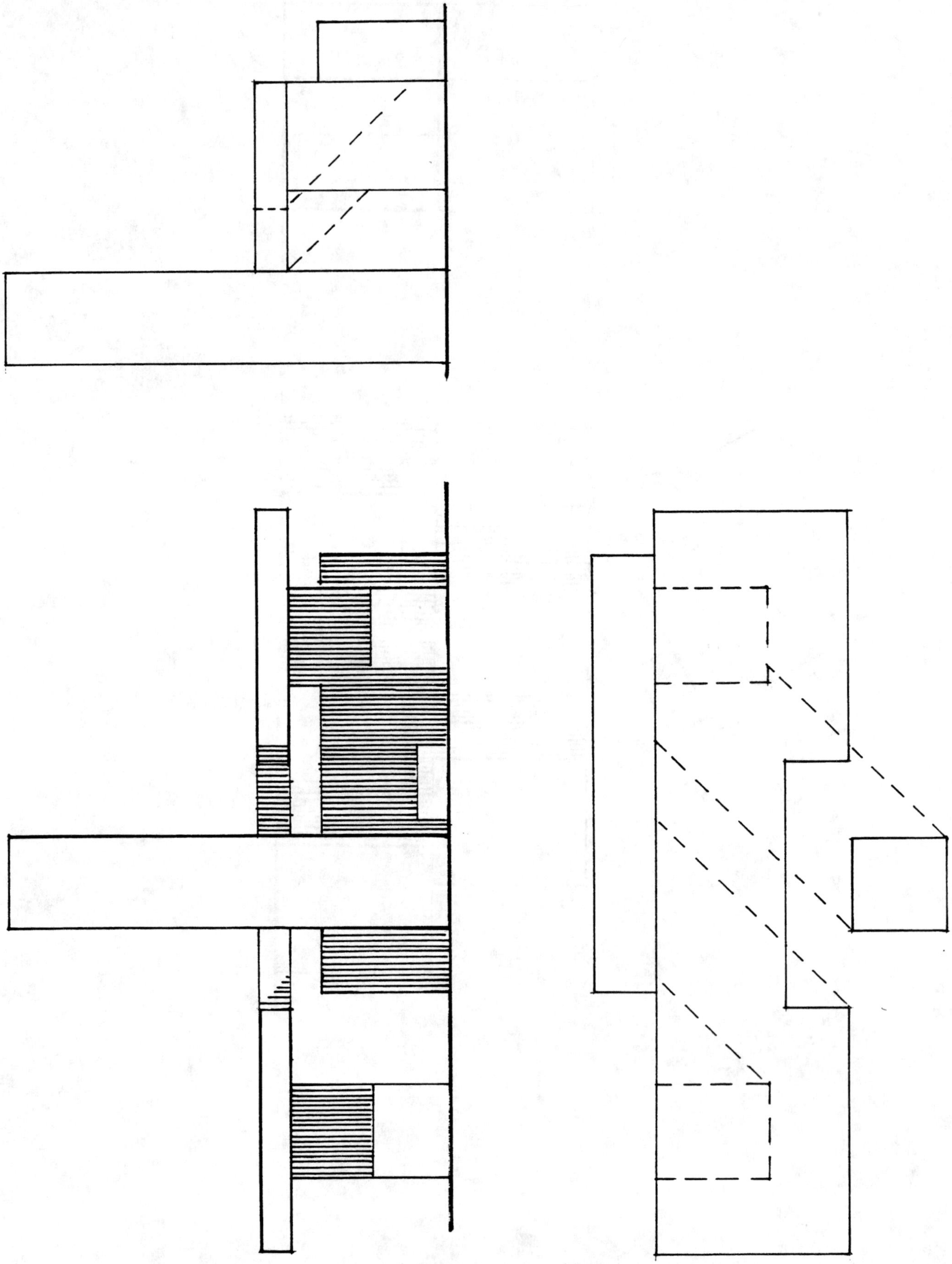

CHAPTER 10, EXERCISE 1, FIG. 10-21

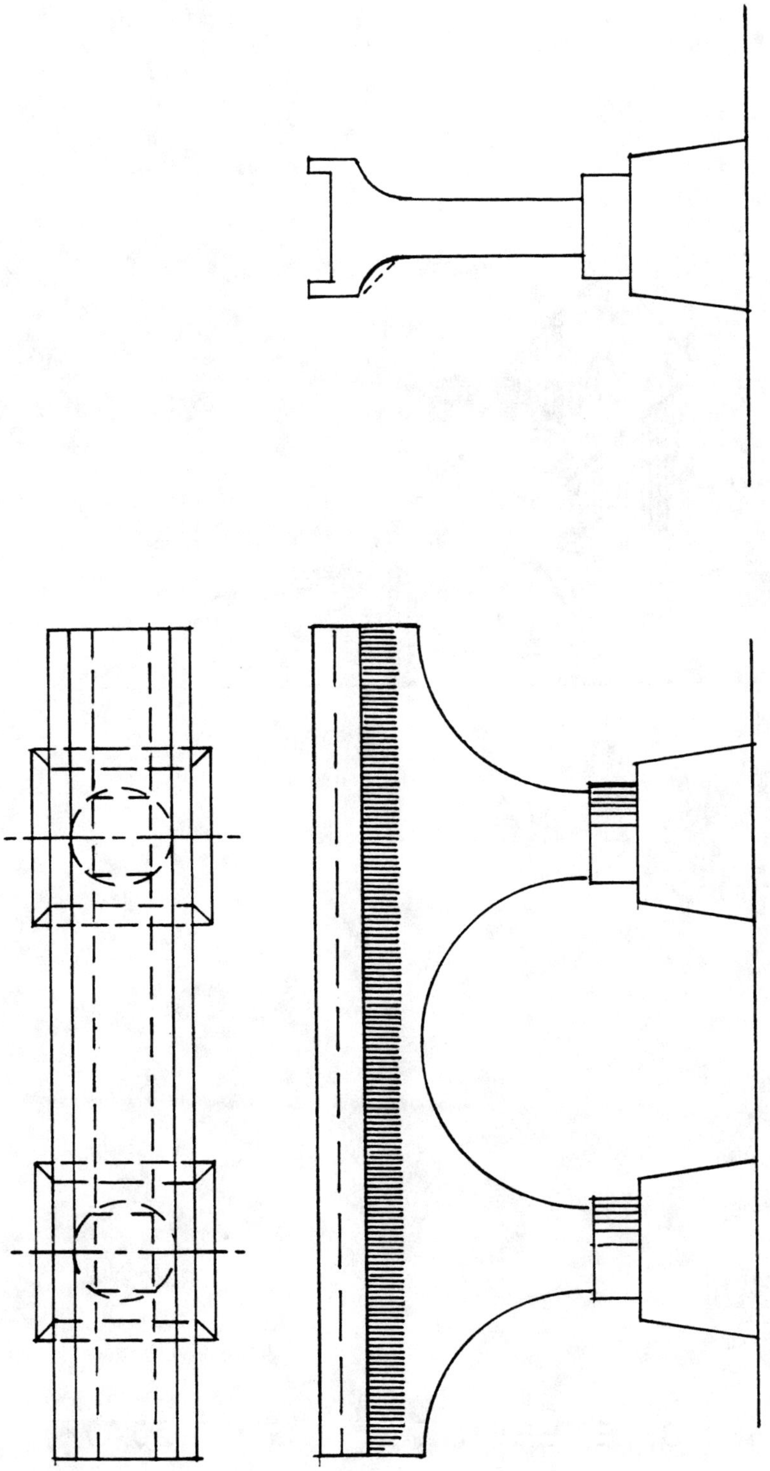

CHAPTER 10, EXERCISE 1, FIG. 10-22

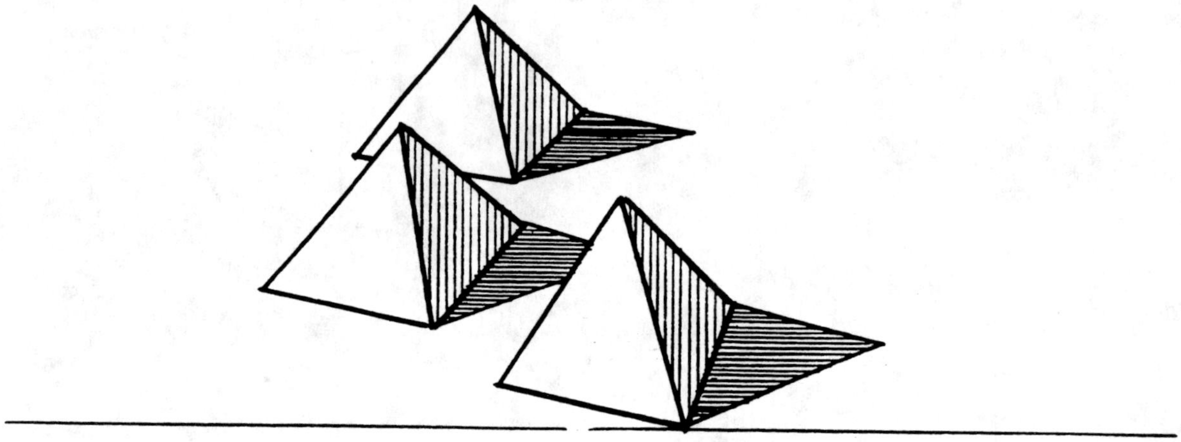

CHAPTER 10, EXERCISE 2, FIG. 10-20A

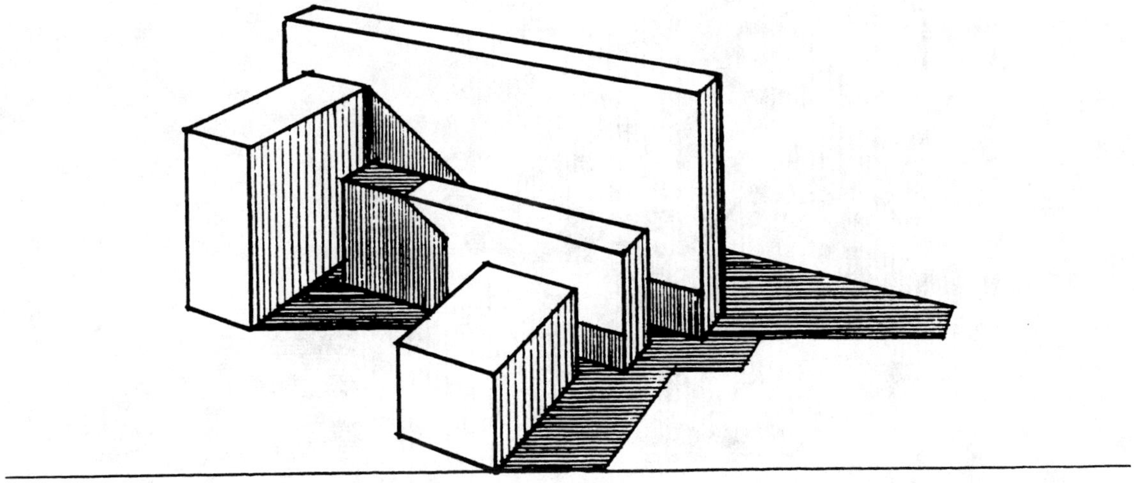

CHAPTER 10, EXERCISE 2, FIG. 10-20B

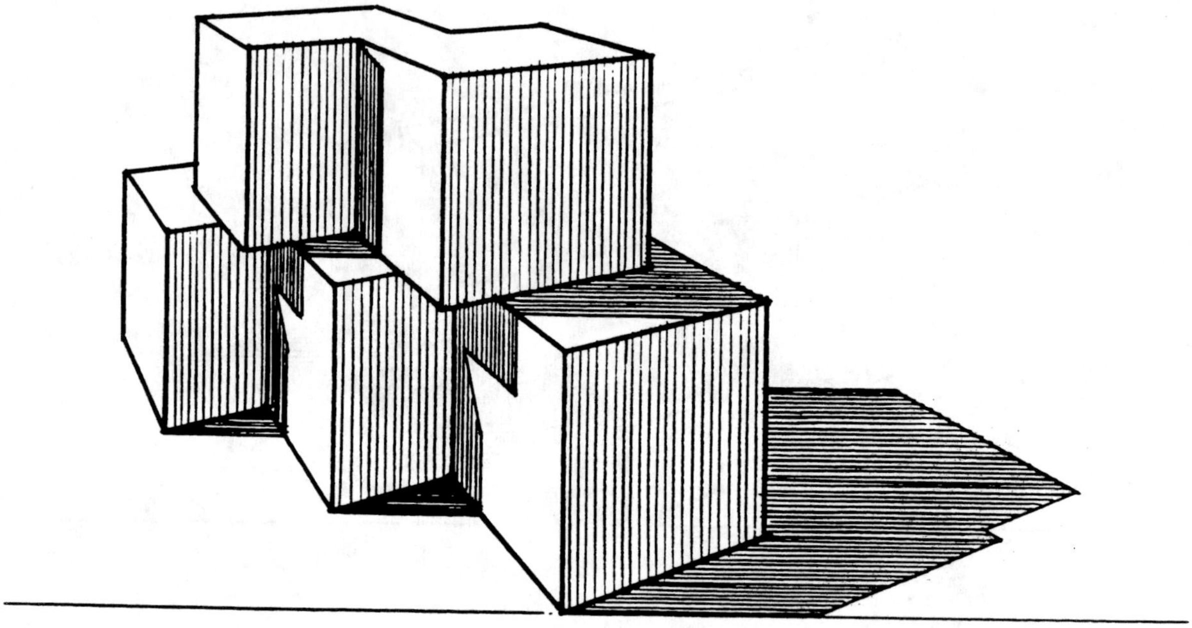

CHAPTER 10, EXERCISE 2, FIG. 10-20C

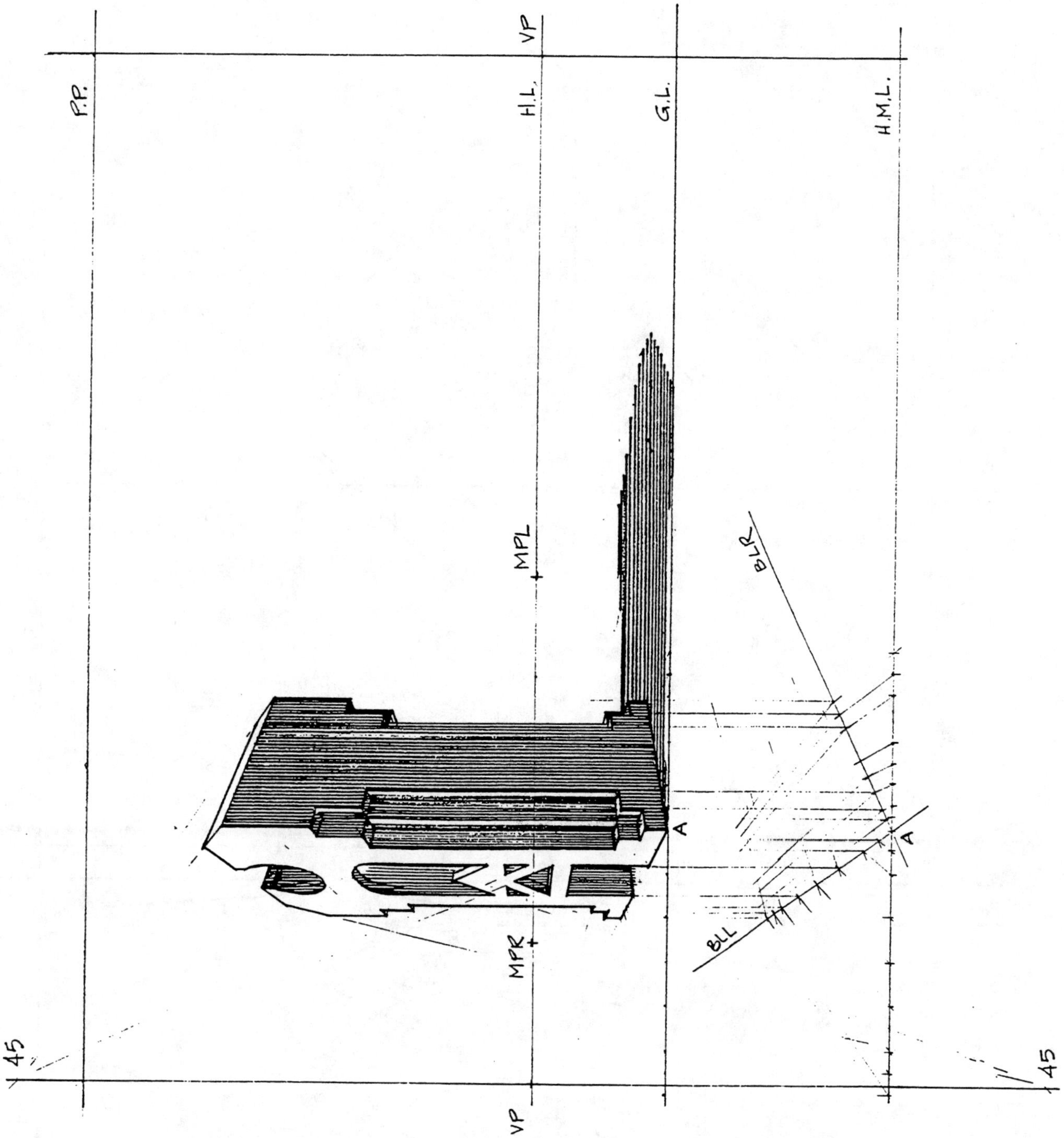

CHAPTER 10, EXERCISE 3, FIG. 10-23

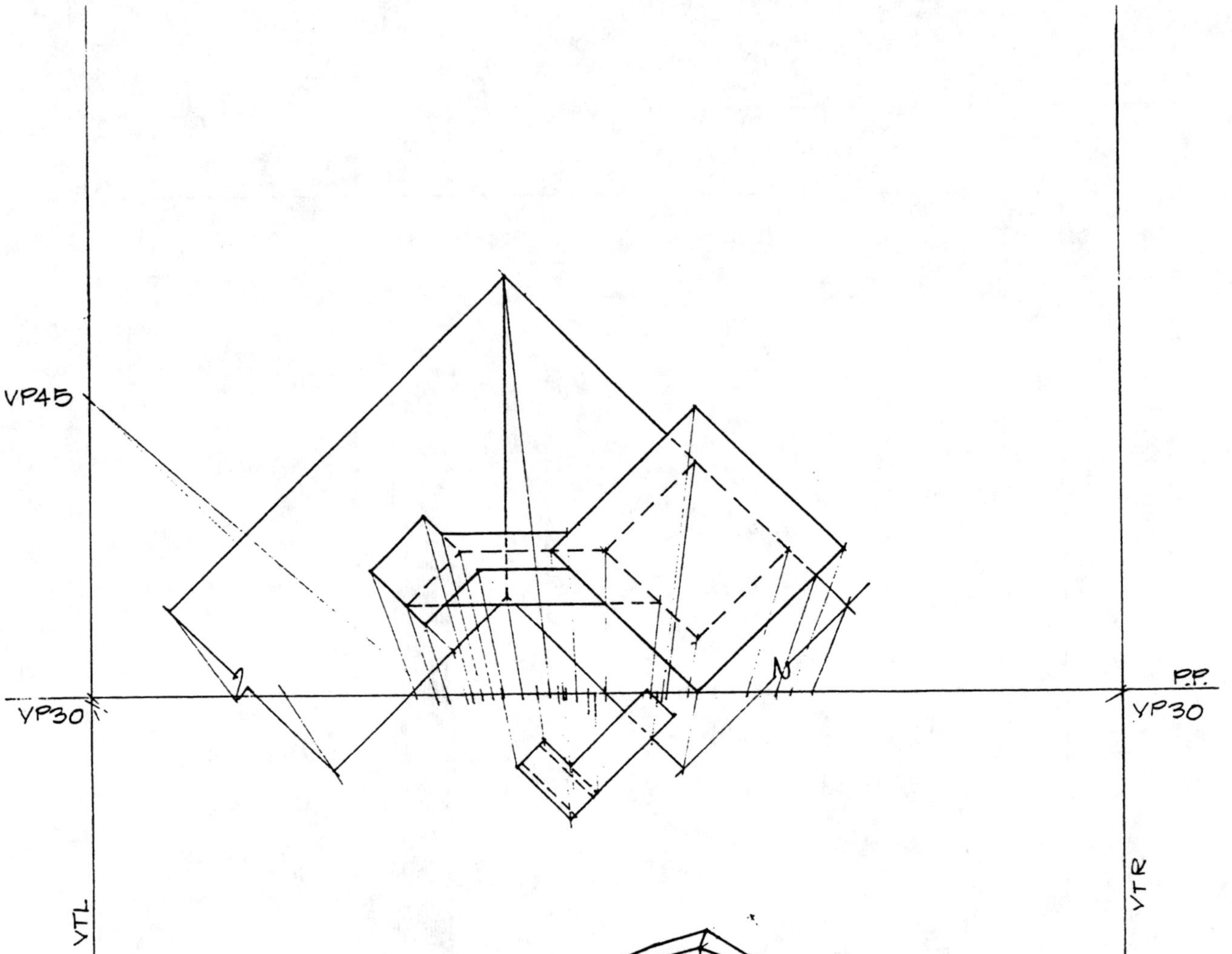

CHAPTER 10, EXERCISE 4, FIG. 10-24

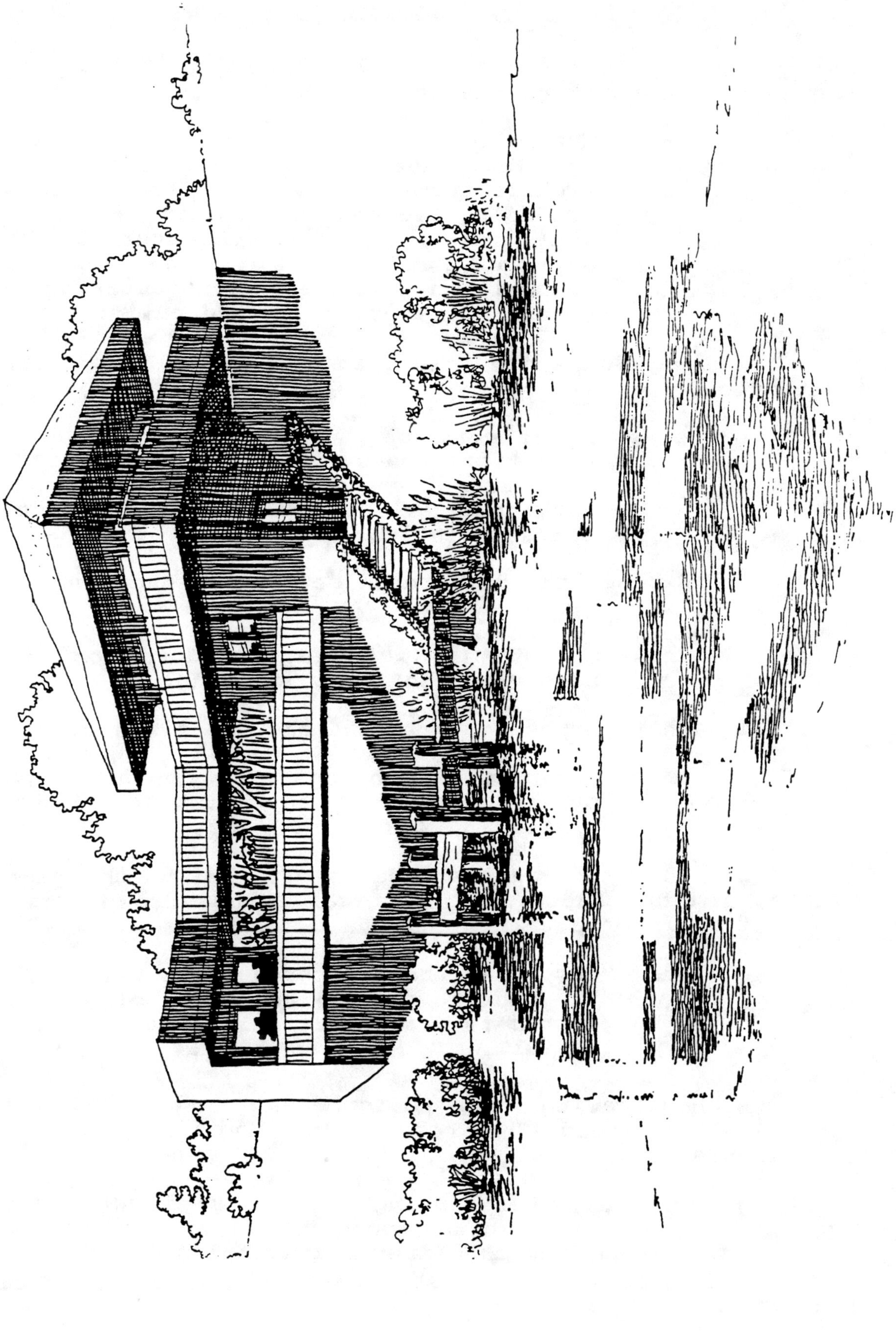

CHAPTER 10, EXERCISE 4, FIG. 10-24

CHAPTER 10
REVIEW QUESTIONS AND ANSWERS

1. Why is the action of light on architectural subjects important to the designer?

ans. The action of light on architectural subjects is important to the designer. Good architectural forms have the property of producing pleasing shadows regardless of the sun's position. To the observer, shadows are an integral part of an architectural composition, and their representation becomes almost as important as the building itself.

2. Why is it convenient to use a 45° light source direction?

ans. It is convenient to use a 45° light source direction because it can be easily drawn with a triangle. Another advantage is that it conveniently reveals depth-dimensional characteristics.

3. Explain the difference between a shade and a shadow.

ans. Objects in light cast shadows; objects not receiving light are in shade.

4. What purpose do orthographic shadows serve?

ans. Orthographic shadows show depth information by association with related orthographic views.

5. When the light source is parallel to the picture plane, is the shadow of a vertical corner drawn vertically when it falls on a wall?

ans. Yes, when the light source is parallel to the picture plane, the shadow of a vertical corner is drawn vertically when it falls on a wall.

6. When drawing lines to represent shadows falling on a ground plane, would it be best to draw the lines vertically or horizontally?

ans. Yes, when drawing lines to represent shadows falling on a ground plane, it would be best to draw the lines horizontally.

7. Why are shades and shadows essential elements of the sketch?

ans. Shades and shadows are essential elements of the sketch to show realism.

8. What advantage does the felt-tip pen sketch have over the pencil sketch when reproduction of the sketch is important?

ans. The reproduction of the felt-tip pen sketch is sharper and darker than the pencil sketch.

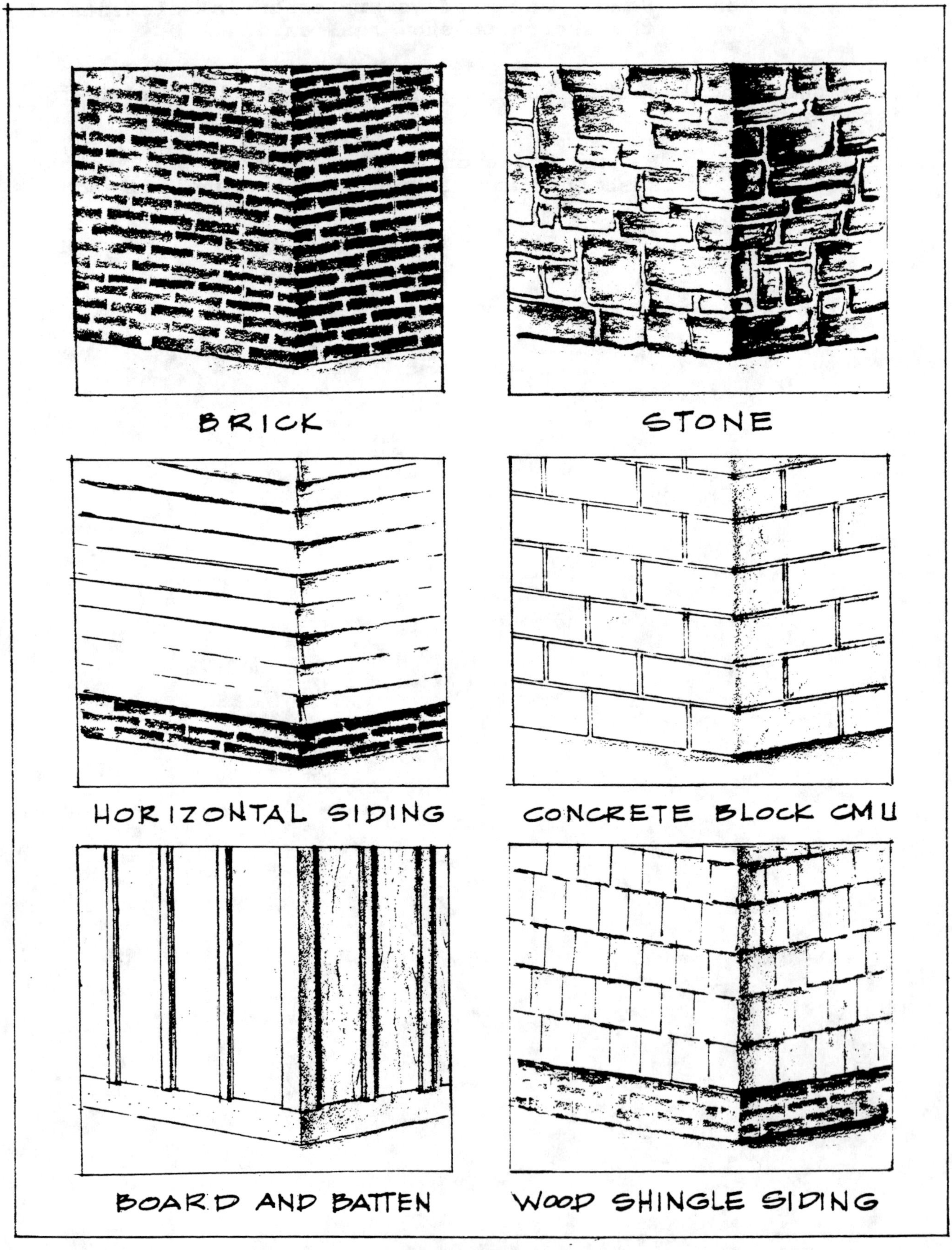

CHAPTER 11, EXERCISE 1, FIG. 11-16

CHAPTER 11, EXERCISE 2

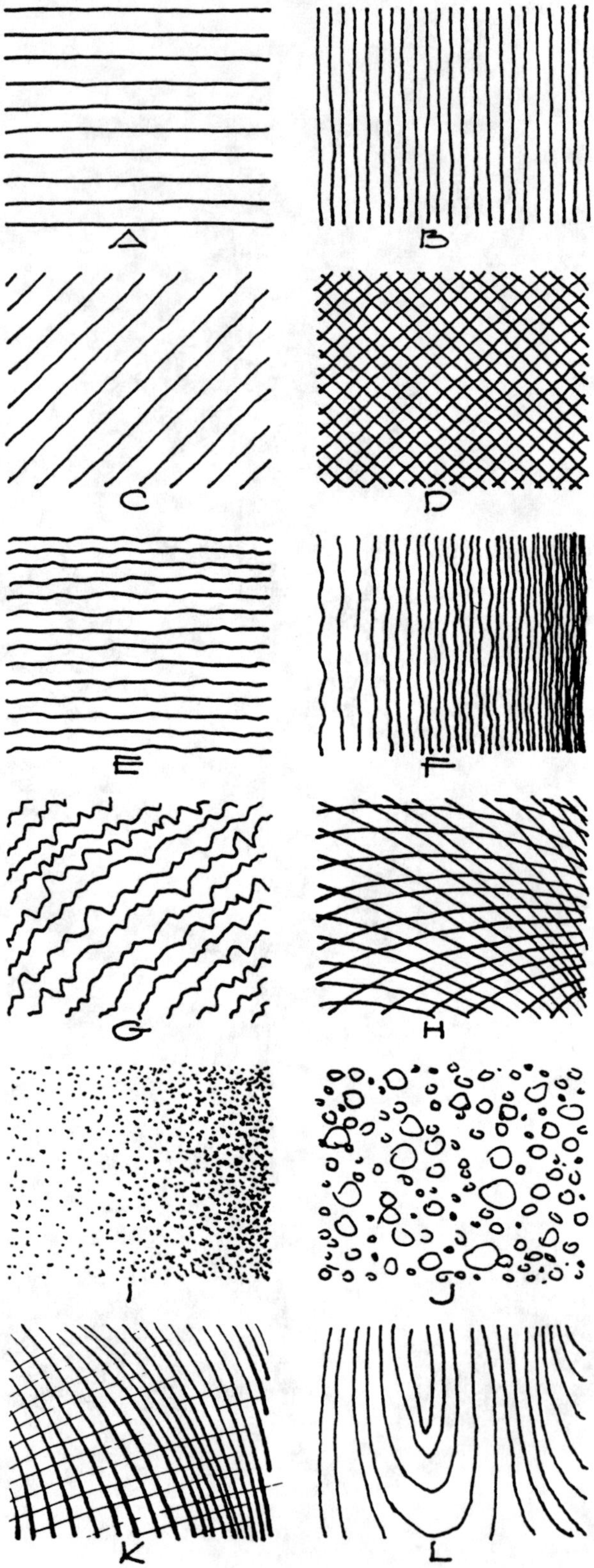

CHAPTER 11, EXERCISE 4, FIG. 11-26

LAKE VIEW ELEVATION 1/4" = 1'-0"

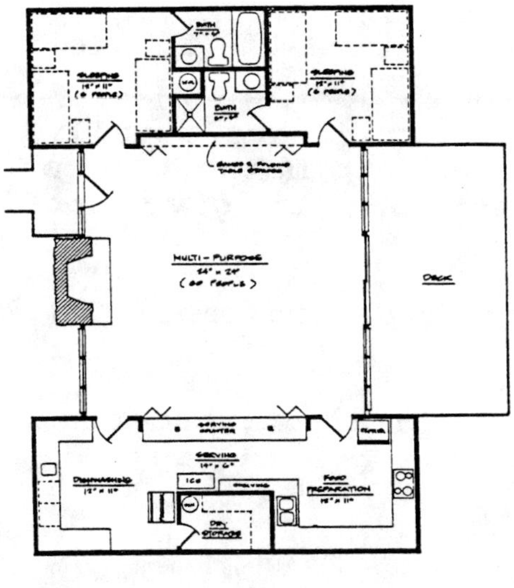

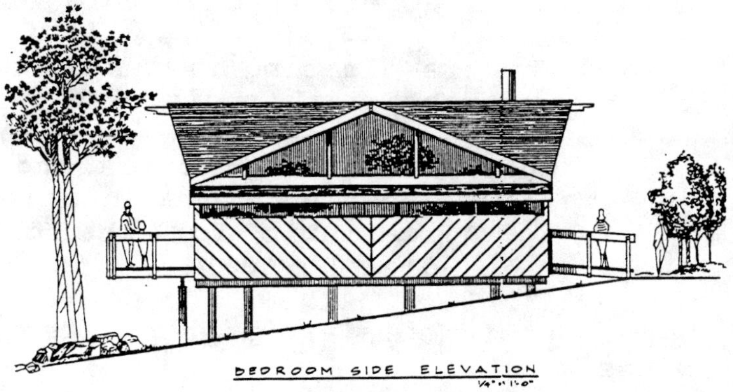

BEDROOM SIDE ELEVATION 1/4" = 1'-0"

FLOOR PLAN 1/4" = 1'-0"

A LAKESIDE LODGE

CHAPTER 11, EXERCISE 5

CHAPTER 11
REVIEW QUESTIONS AND ANSWERS

1. What are the advantages for clients and architects, of preparing a presentation drawing of an architectural proposal?

ans. **There are several advantages for a client and an architect to preparing a presentation drawing of an architectural proposal. These include providing the client with both a tangible proposal for approval and also a marketing instrument. It also offers a means for careful study of the structure's appearance so that any changes and improvements may be made.**

2. For what reason are perspective views generally effective in presentation work?

ans. **Prospective views are generally effective because they present the building in its natural setting in an honest, realistic, artistic manner which is easily understood by the layperson.**

3. What is meant by optical balance?

ans. **Optical balance means arranging the composition so its graphic weights are pleasing and it does not appear bottom heavy. Larger elements have more weight than smaller, darker elements appear to have more weight than lighter, and intense colors appear to have more effect than pale colors.**

4. Why are plumbing fixtures and furniture usually shown on presentation plan views?

ans. **Plumbing fixtures and furniture are usually shown on a presentation plan to make it more realistic for the client and to give the drawing scale.**

5. What media are appropriate for rendering small drawings?

ans. **The most frequently used media for rendering small drawings are pencil or pen and ink.**

6. On perspective renderings, why should the details nearest the observer be made more prominent than those in the distance?

ans. In reality near objects are sharper and closer to the eye than those in the distance.

7. What methods can the renderer employ to produce emphasis?

ans. Emphasis may be obtained by the renderer by the use of contrast in value, size, shape, texture, or a combination of either.

8. What do landscaping indications contribute to a perspective?

ans. Landscaping indications in a perspective tie elements together. They tend to keep strong, isolated elements from falling away from the layout. They also give the drawing realism.

9. What is meant by a value study?

ans. The value study is achieved by tracing over the completed perspective and establishing the general value patterns rather roughly, using a soft pencil or charcoal. Avoid details in this study, but strive for pleasing value patterns that can be created by contrasts of light and shade and from the landscaping composition. This becomes your guide for choosing line technique, value, and landscaping on the final ink drawing.

10. How are analogous colors related to each other on the color wheel?

ans. Analogous colors are adjacent to each other on the color wheel.

11. When rendering sky, should the sky appear darker near the building or near the top edge of the rendering.

ans. When rendering sky, the sky should appear darker near the edge of the rendering.

12. What is the most effective method for rendering glass?

ans. The most effective method of rendering glass

is to have it appear dark unless there are drapes, or shades directly in back of it to receive the sunlight. Highlights on glass appear white. Reflections of trees and buildings also add realism to rendered glass.

13. What is the first step you should take in drawing a tree?

ans. The first step that should be taken in drawing a tree is direct and careful observation from nature. Draw the structure of the tree by drawing the trunk and the branches before adding foliage.

14. List three types of water-based paints frequently used in renderings.

ans. Three types of water-based paints frequently used in rendering are: tempera, acrylic, or casein.

15. Why is it important to draw people on a rendering of a building?

ans. People drawn on a rendering help the viewer to gauge size by comparing the height of the person to the building.

16. What drawing medium would be appropriate if a rendering must be prepared very quickly?

ans. When a rendering must be done very quickly, the most appropriate medium would be felt tip pens.

17. What is the best way to achieve contrast in a rendering?

ans. The variation of lightness or darkness of color or gray is known as value. Before starting a drawing, develop a value scale that ranges from black to white. Plan the drawing so that important features are accented with extreme contrasts and less important features or outlines have lesser amounts of contrast. Plan a definite arrangement of the values.

18. Why are colored pencils a good media for the beginner?

ans. Colored pencils are a good media for the beginner because they are one of the simpler methods. Many colors are available and some are water soluble and can be blended with a wet brush to give a watercolor effect. Renderings done by colored pencils can be completed quickly.

19. Why is waterproof ink essential when it is combined with a wet medium?

ans. Waterproof ink is essential when combined with a wet medium to prevent smearing, running and smudging.

20. What would be the advantage of preparing a pencil or ink rendering on vellum or Mylar instead of illustration board?

ans. The advantage of preparing a pencil or ink rendering on vellum or Mylar instead of illustration board would be the ability to reproduce copies from the original vellum or Mylar by the diazo process.

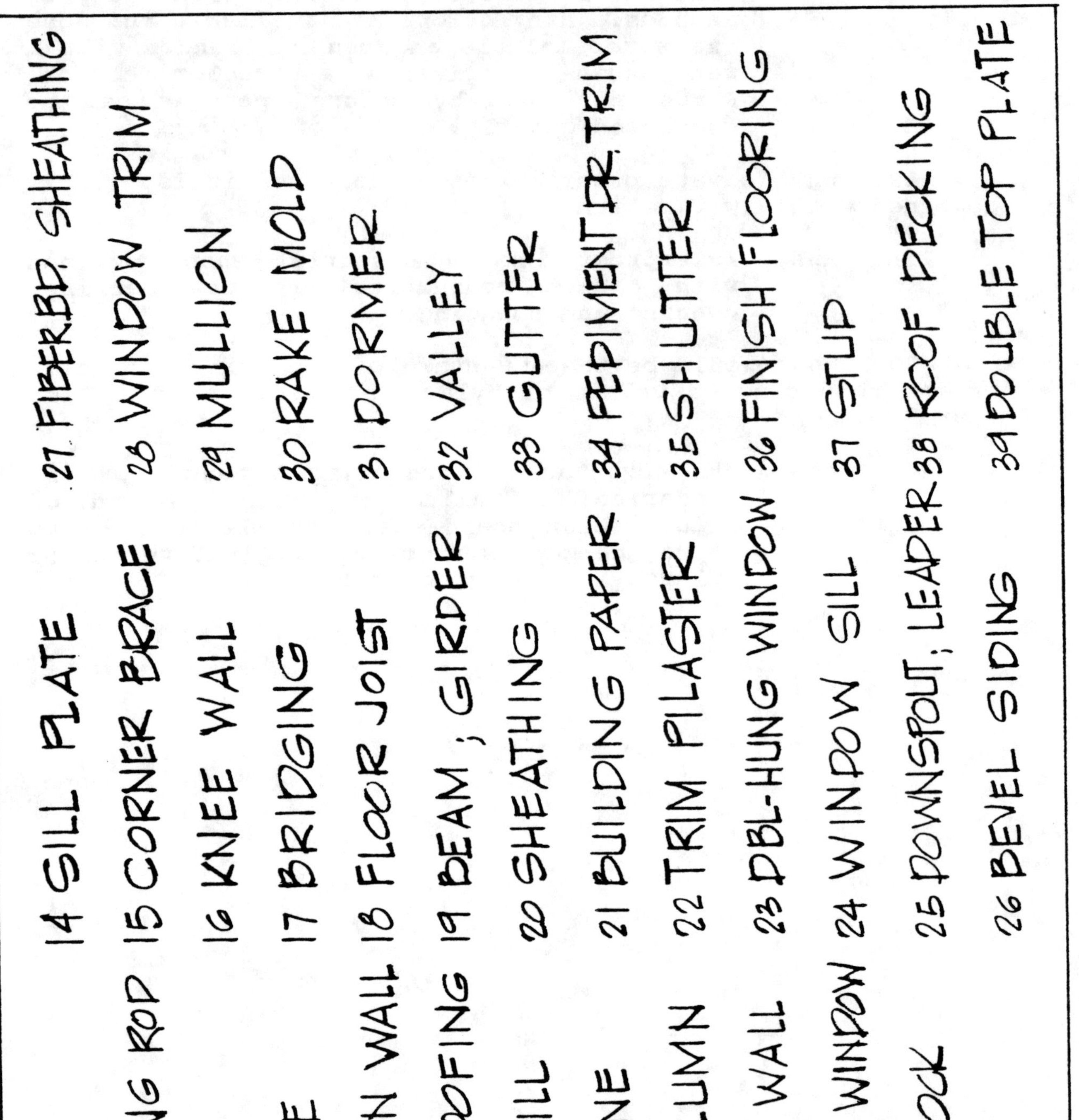

CHAPTER 12, EXERCISE 1, FIG. 12-1

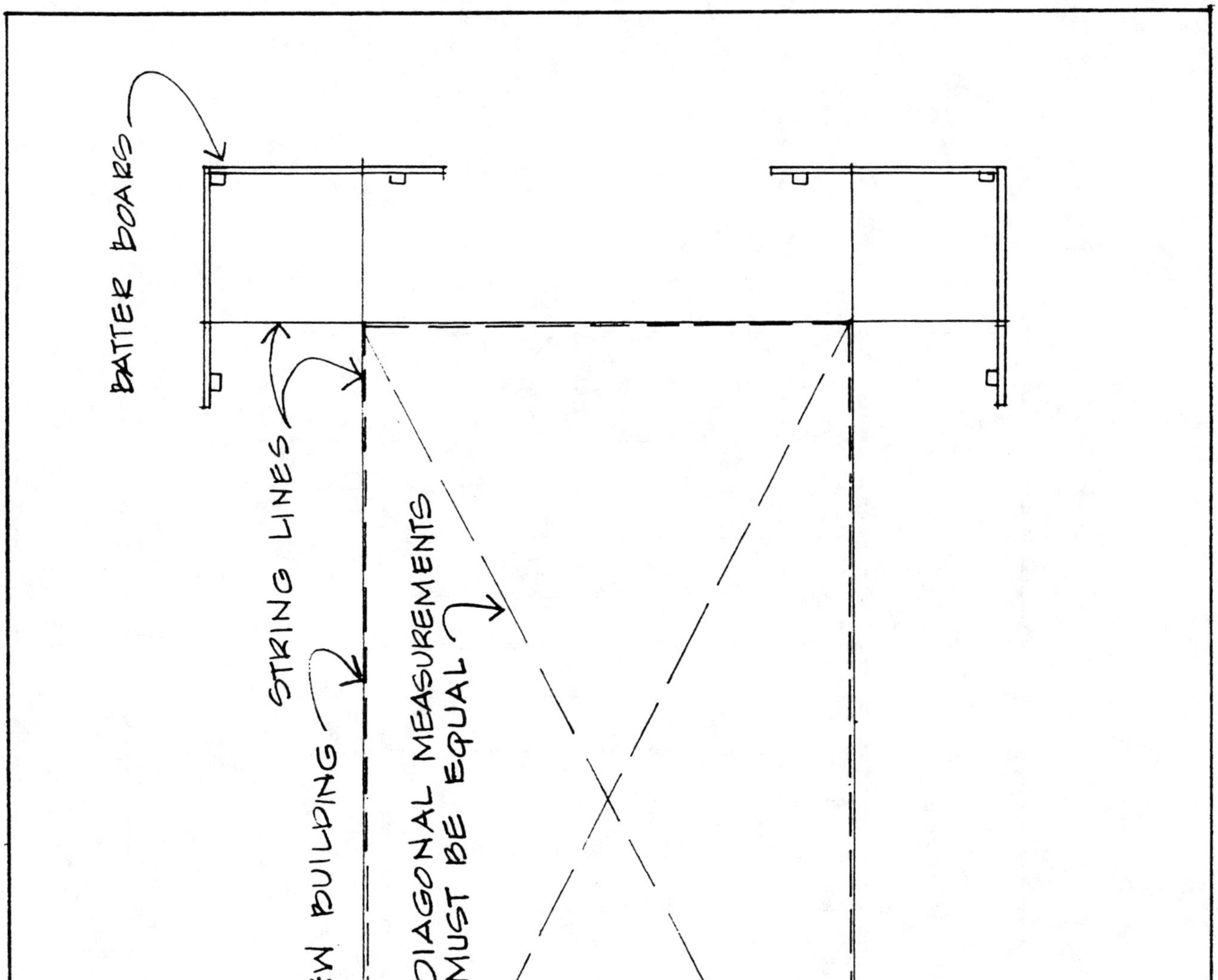

CHAPTER 12, EXERCISE 2

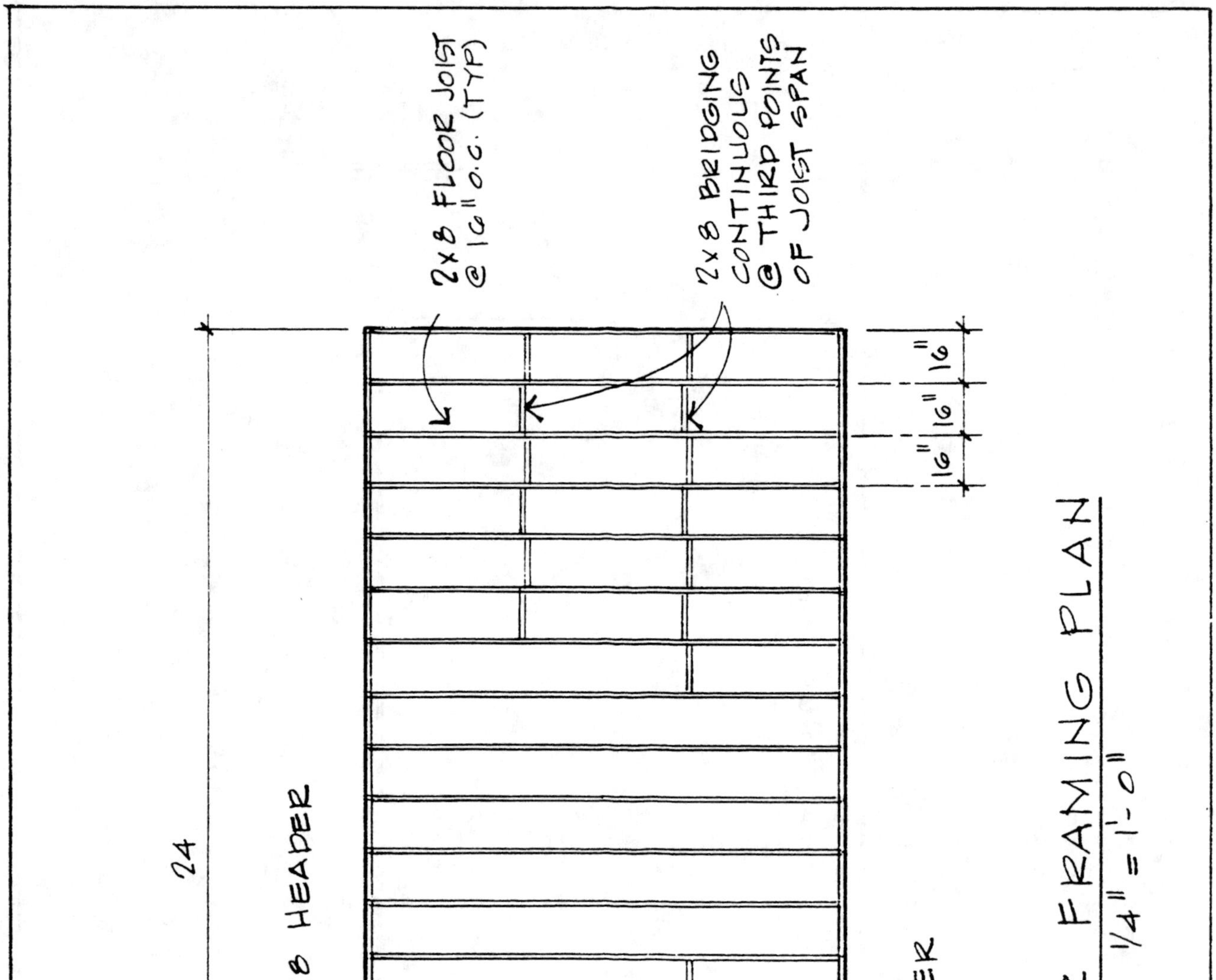

CHAPTER 12, EXERCISE 3

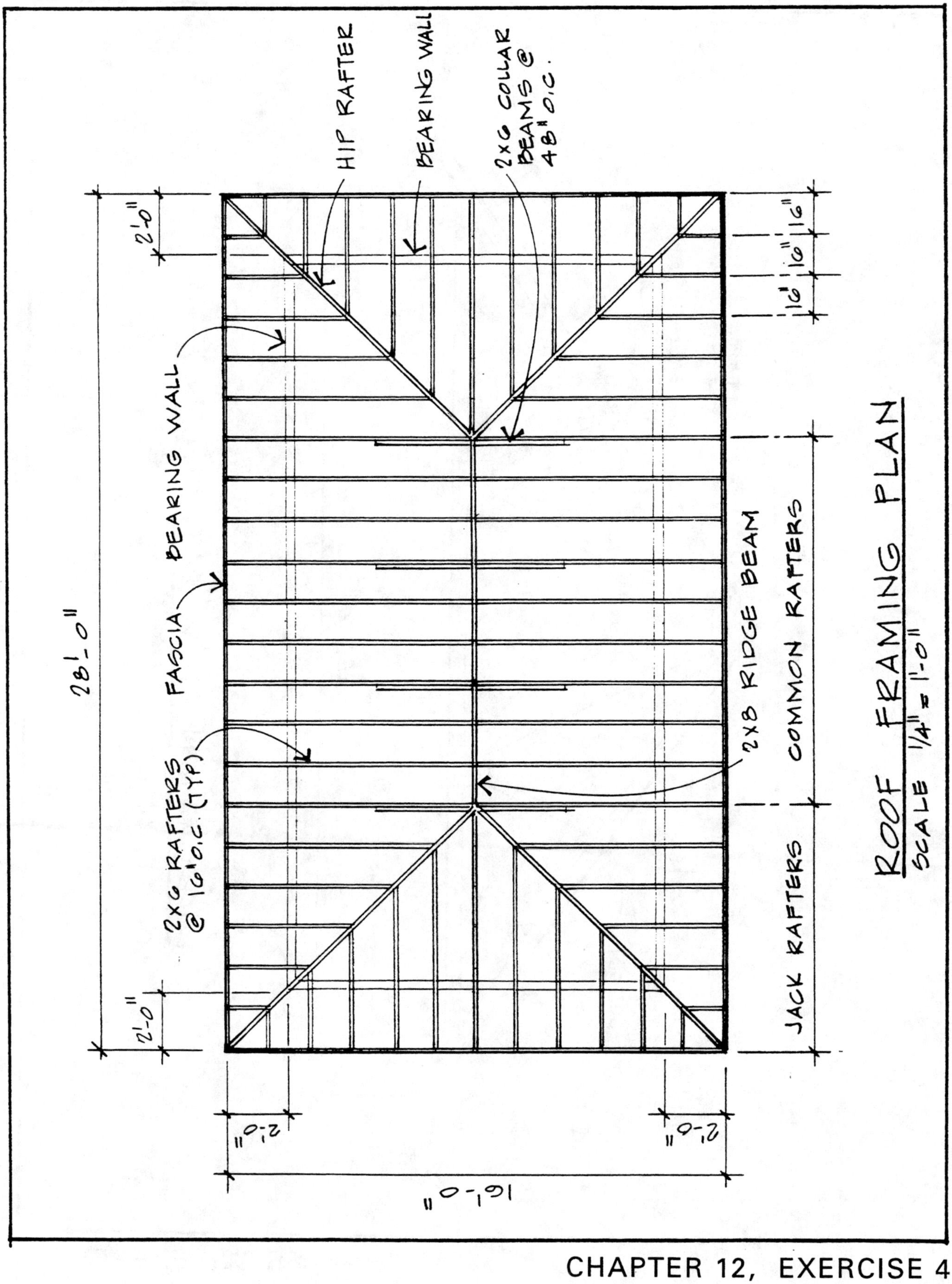

CHAPTER 12, EXERCISE 4

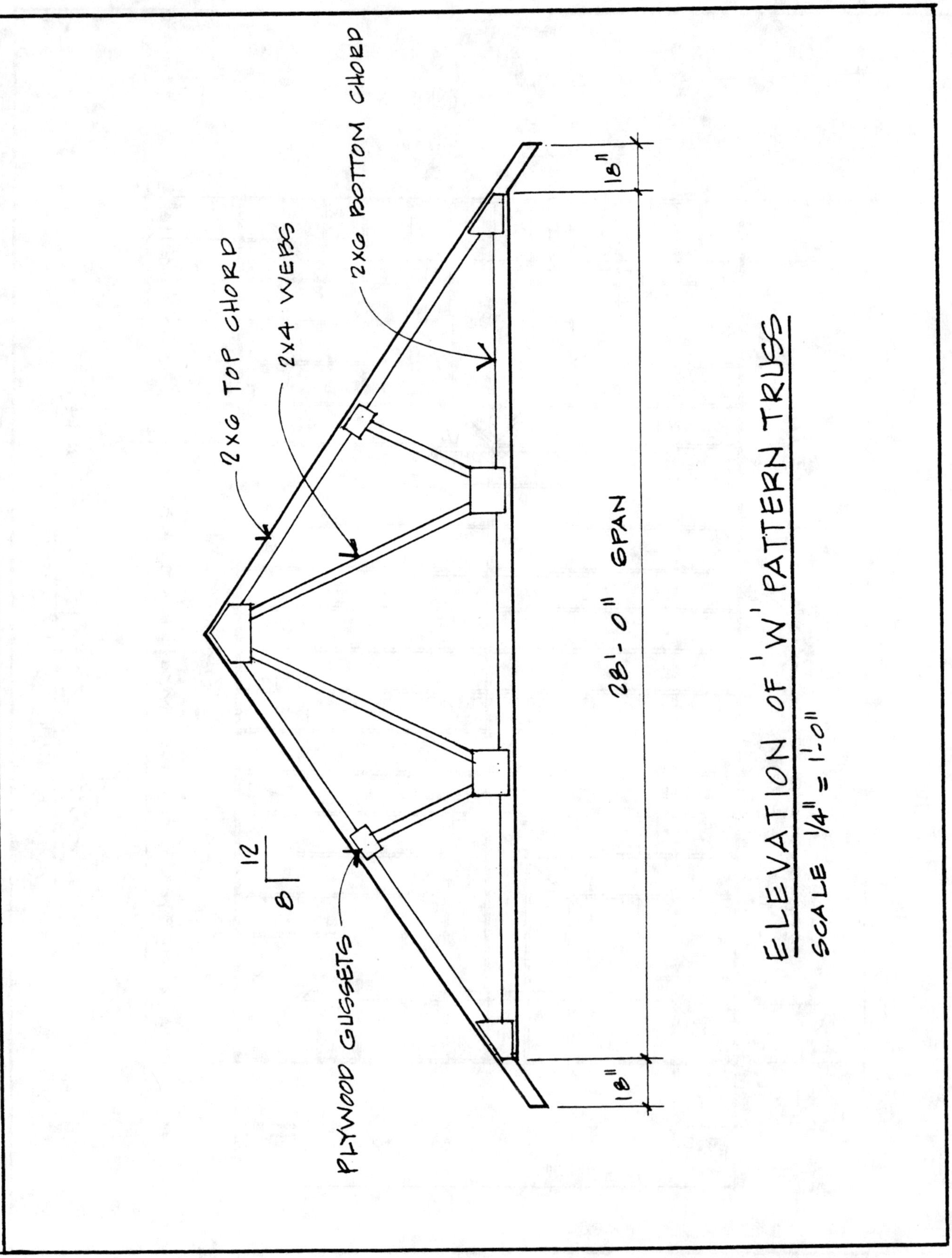

CHAPTER 12, EXERCISE 5

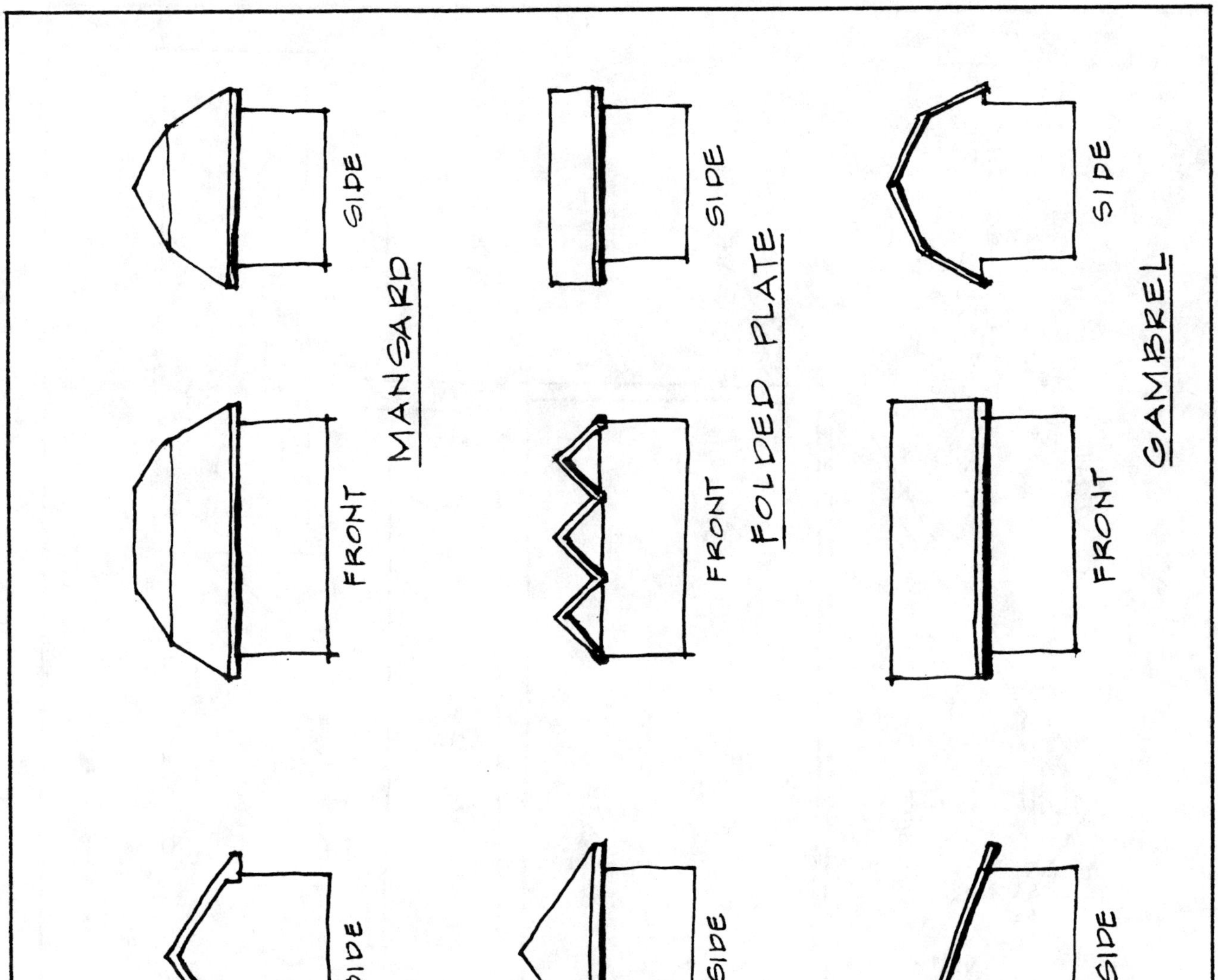

CHAPTER 12, EXERCISE 6

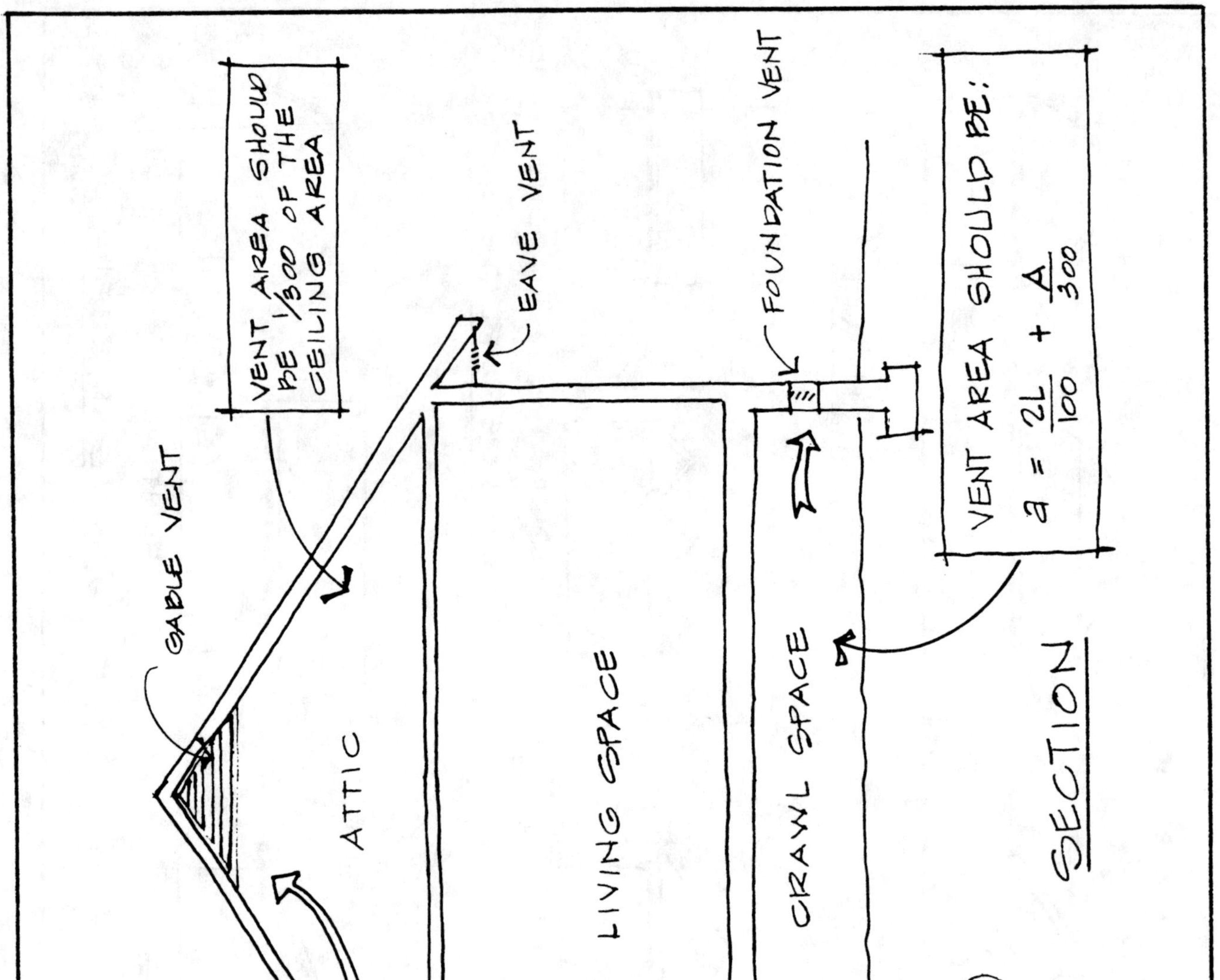

CHAPTER 12, EXERCISE 7

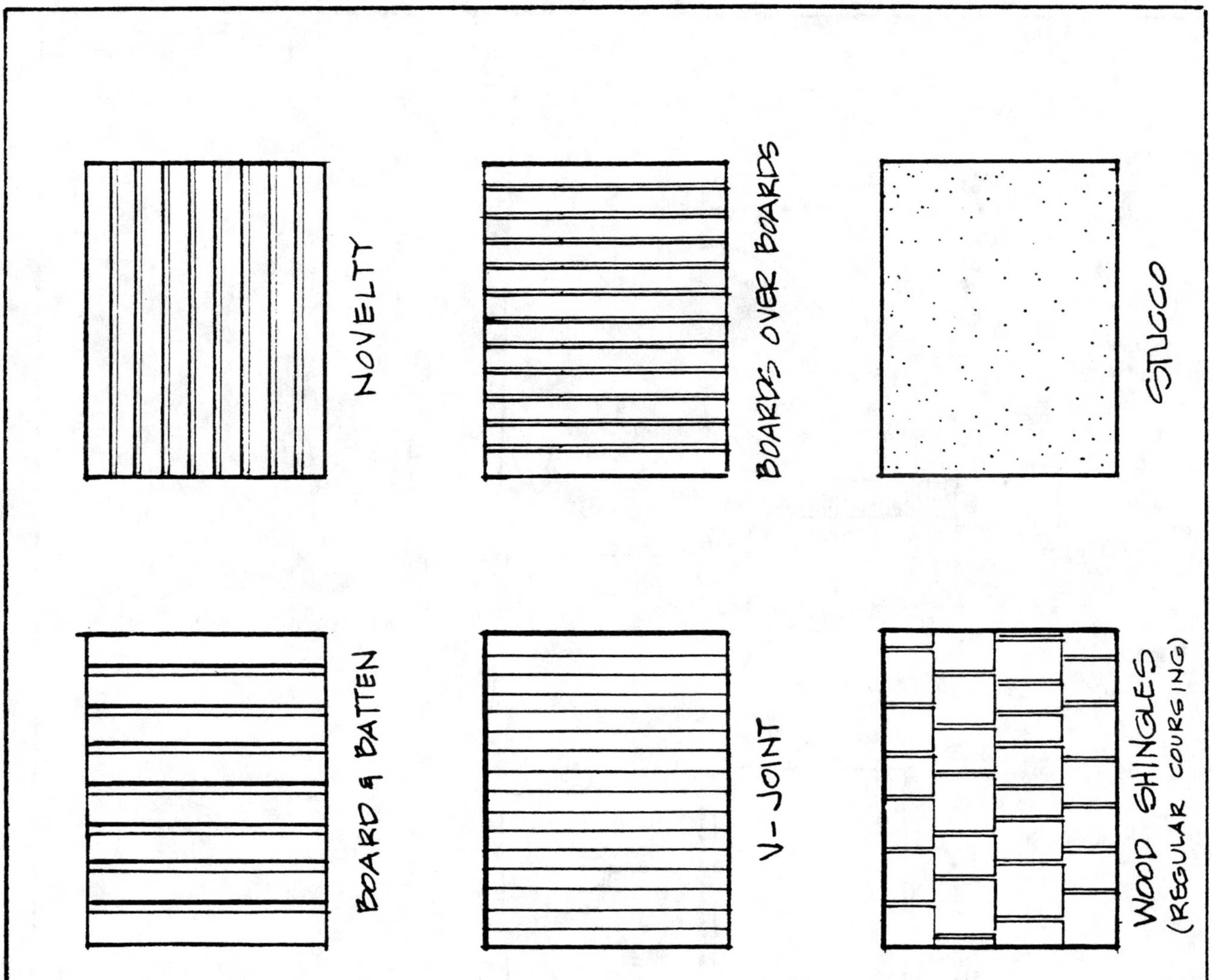

CHAPTER 12, EXERCISE 8

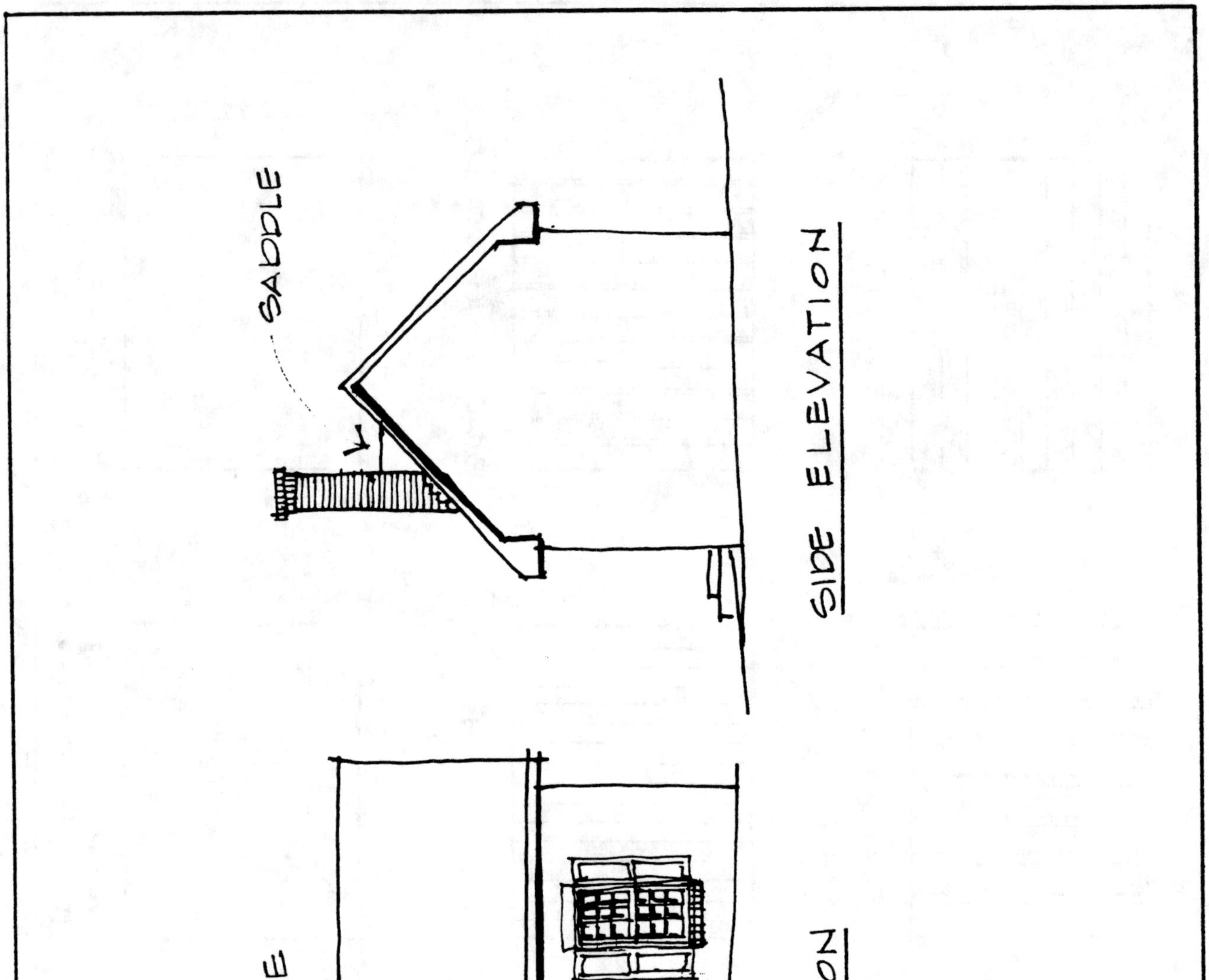

CHAPTER 12, EXERCISE 9

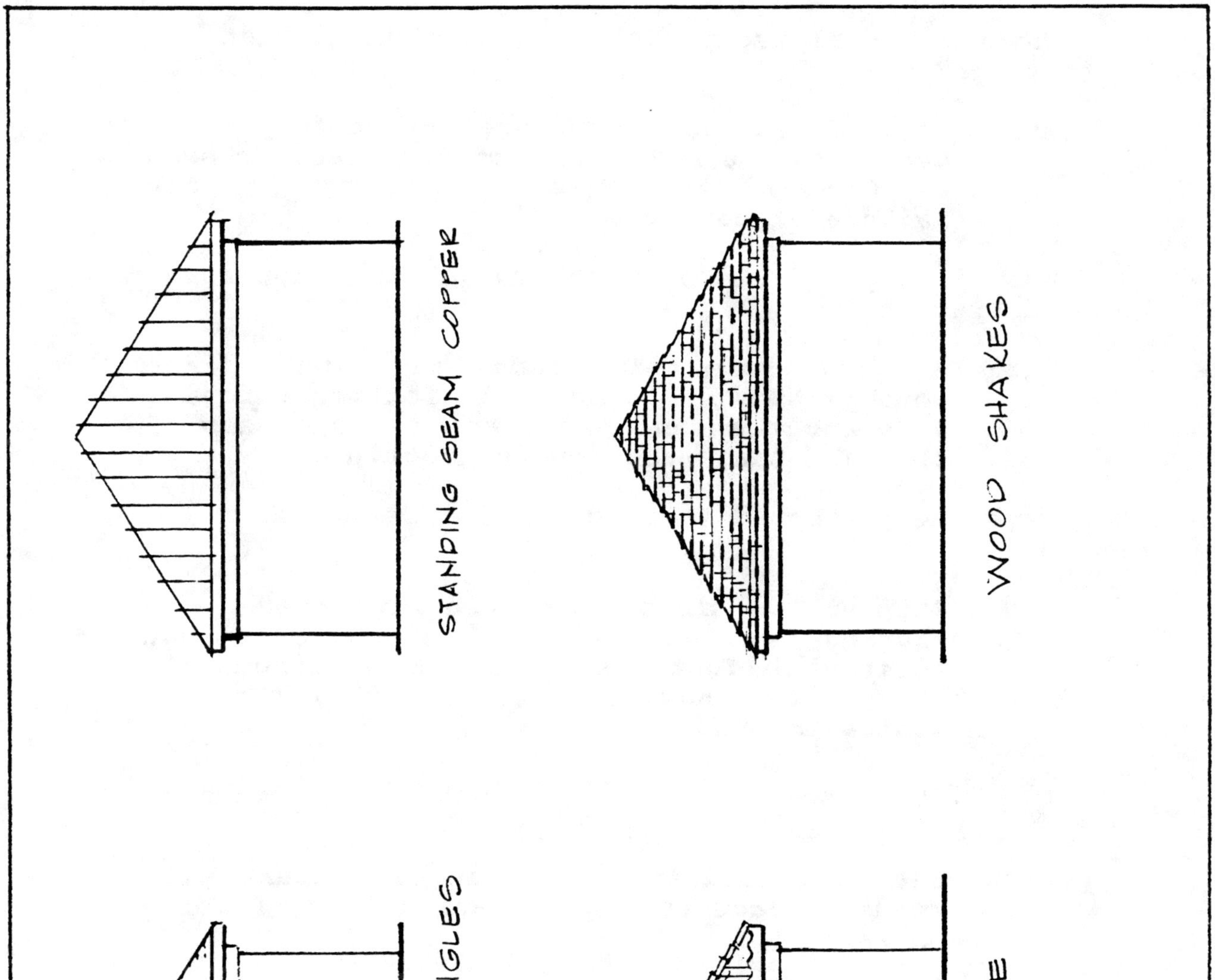

CHAPTER 12, EXERCISE 10

CHAPTER 12
REVIEW QUESTIONS AND ANSWERS

1. Why must local frost depths be considered when drawing footings?

ans. **Local frost depths are prescribed to prevent damage to the footings from frost action such as freezing and thawing that could cause failure of concrete.**

2. What is a good rule of thumb for sizing footings in light construction?

ans. **A good rule of thumb in light frame construction is to make the footing twice as wide and the same depth as the thickness of the wall that rests on the footing.**

3. Describe a stepped footing and indicate its application.

ans. **Stepped footings are usually needed on sloping or steep lots where straight horizontal footings would be uneconomical. Stepped footings change planes to follow the contour of the site.**

4. What condition may require accurate calculation of footing size?

ans. **The soil quality and moisture content will require accurate calculations of footing sizes.**

5. List three materials that are commonly used for foundation walls?

ans. **Three commonly used materials for foundation walls are poured concrete, C.M.U. and brick.**

6. What is a pier?

ans. **A pier is a freestanding post usually constructed of masonry, concrete or pressure treated wood and is used to support a floor beam.**

7. Indicate the logical application of grade beam foundation construction.

ans. **Grade beam foundation construction is used to support light frame structures in areas where poor soil is encountered.**

8. What are the advantages of a slab-on-ground floor construction in comparison to crawl space construction?

ans. **The advantages of slab on-ground construction over crawl space construction are outdoor surfaces become more accessible from the interior of the house, a lower silhouette in the overall appearance of the house is possible and the concrete slab may be more cost effective than wood floor framing in some areas.**

9. What are the identifying characteristics of platform (western) frame construction?

ans. **The characteristics that identify platform frame construction are one floor level is built at a time, thus permitting the completed floor surface to serve as a platform on which walls and the like can be constructed.**

10. Why are trussed rafters widely used in small home construction?

ans. **Trussed rafters are widely used because they are strong and are designated to clear span a residence eliminating the need for interior bearing walls. They are usually pre-fabricated and quickly installed.**

11. In plank and beam framing, how is the load on a roof beam transmitted to the foundation?

ans. **The load on roof beams is transferred directly to the foundation by the use of posts or columns.**

12. Why should the location of beams in plank and beam framing be shown on the working drawings?

ans. **The location of beams on working drawings and beam framing is critical so that the beam might be precisely placed during the construction thus allowing the beam to transmit loads properly.**

13. What part of the construction limits the spacing of beams in plank and beam framing?

ans. **Floor and roof loads limit the spacing of beams in plank and beam framing. The allowable span of wood planks may also limit the spacing of beams that support the planks.**

14. What is a transverse beam?

ans. **A transverse beam is a beam that spans from the ridge beam to the exterior wall and rests on a post or column. A transverse beam is usually shorter in length than a longitudinal beam.**

15. List the good points of brick veneer construction.

ans. **The good points of brick veneer construction are: durability, low maintenance, long-range economy, and availability in a wide variety of colors.**

16. Explain modular sizing of concrete block walls.

ans. **Modular sizing is based on measurements that are multiples of 4". The joint centerline between concrete blocks is an even 16" wide and 8" high; thus, it is easy to construct concrete block walls in modular sizes.**

17. What are the important factors in the selection of a roofing material?

ans. **Some important factors in selecting roofing materials are the environment, structural integrity of the roof, appearance, durability, and cost.**

18. What is the purpose of a vapor barrier in a wood wall and why should it be placed facing the interior side?

ans. **Vapor barriers are used in wood walls to keep condensation out of the wall. They are placed next to the warm humid side of the wall for the purpose of preventing vapor-laden warm air from reaching the insulation in the wall and condensing.**

19. What are metal framing anchors and where are they used in construction?

ans. Metal framing anchors are specially fabricated connectors such as hurricane ties, joist hangers and the like. They are used to tie rafters to a wall, joists to a beam, and a column to a slab or girder.

20. What is flashing and identify two places where flashing is used?

ans. Flashing is usually thin metal that is used to shed moisture away from a joist or the intersection of dissimilar materials. Flashing is placed between a chimney and a roof, above a window or door, and through a cavity wall to divert water to the exterior.

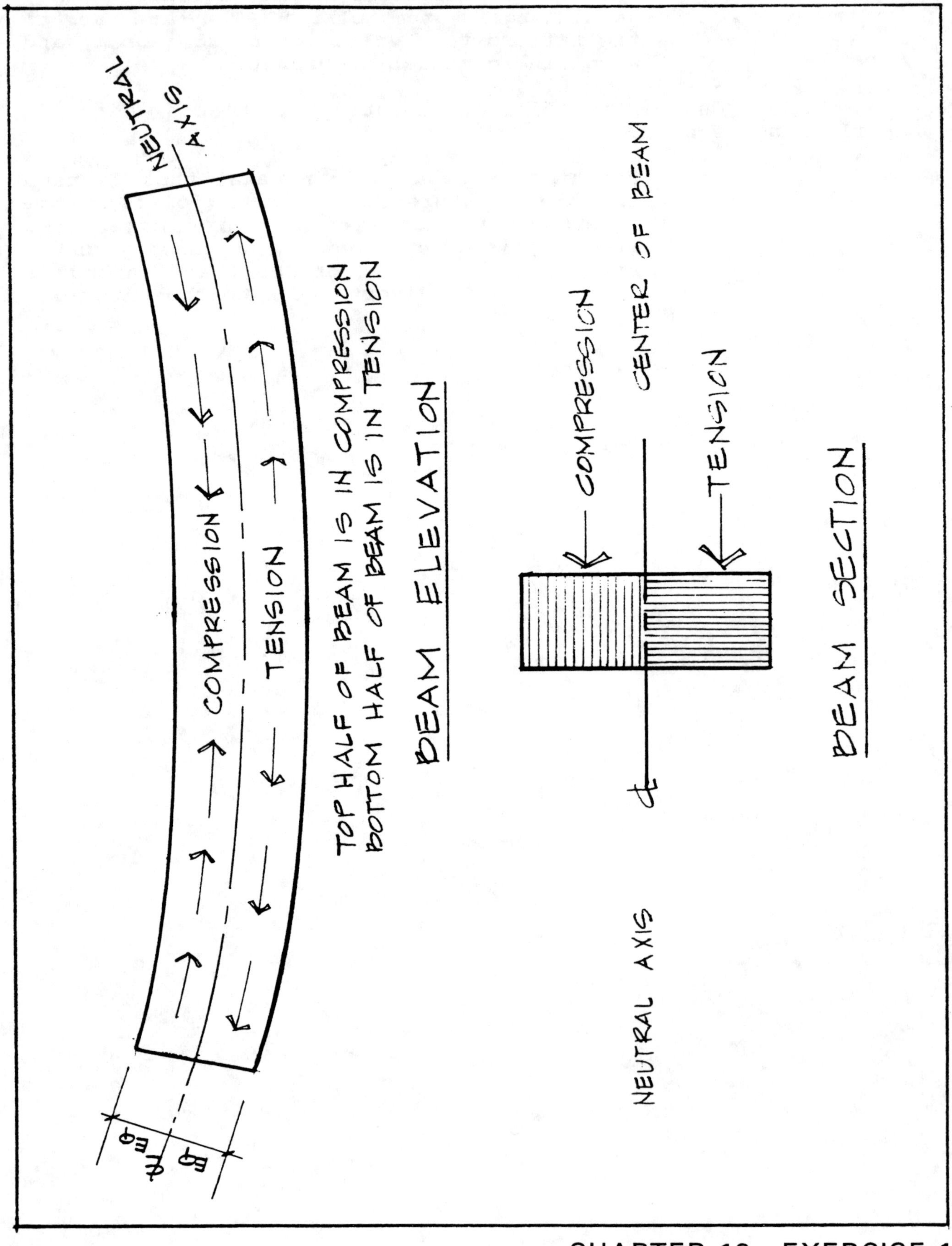

CHAPTER 13, EXERCISE 1

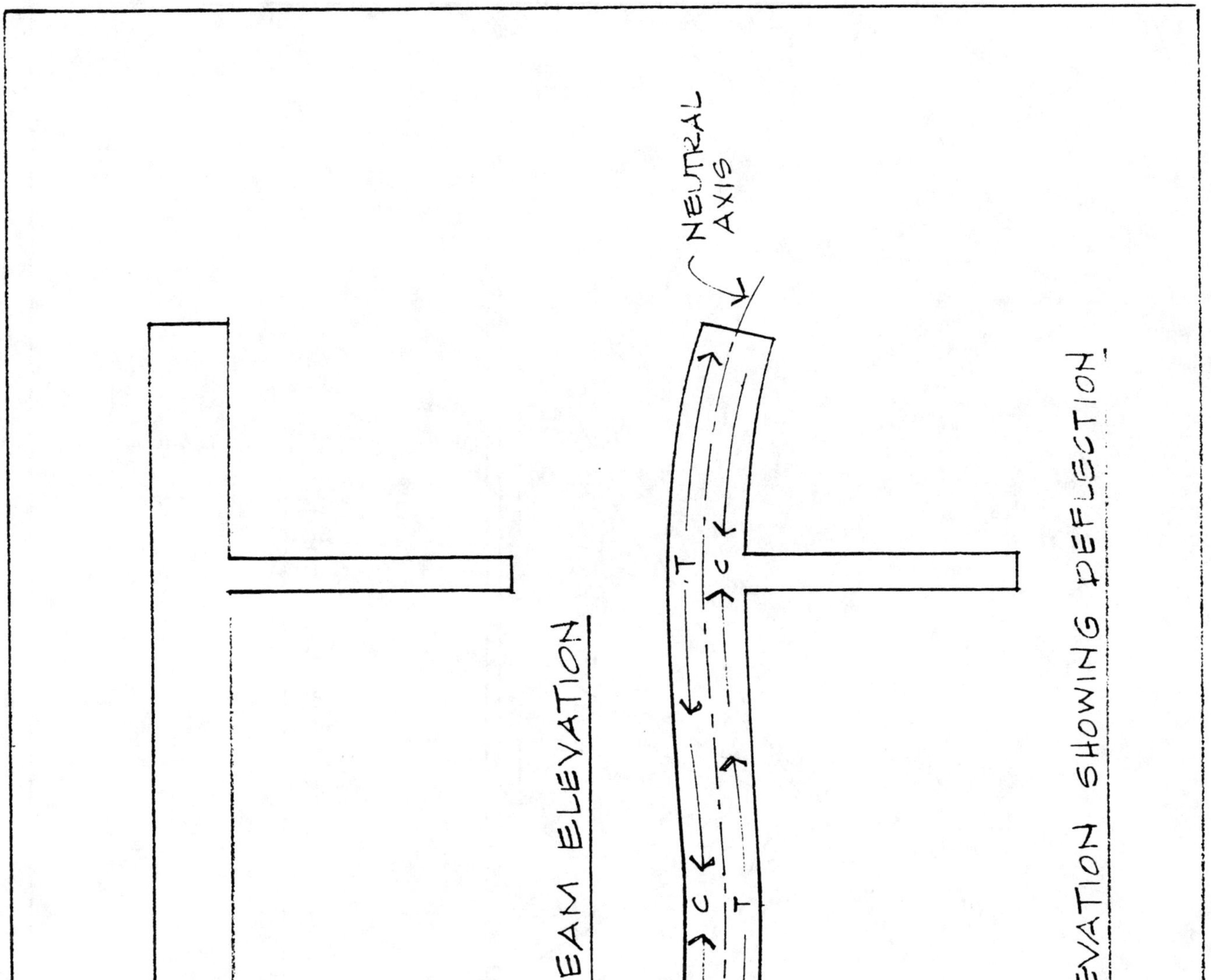

CHAPTER 13, EXERCISE 2

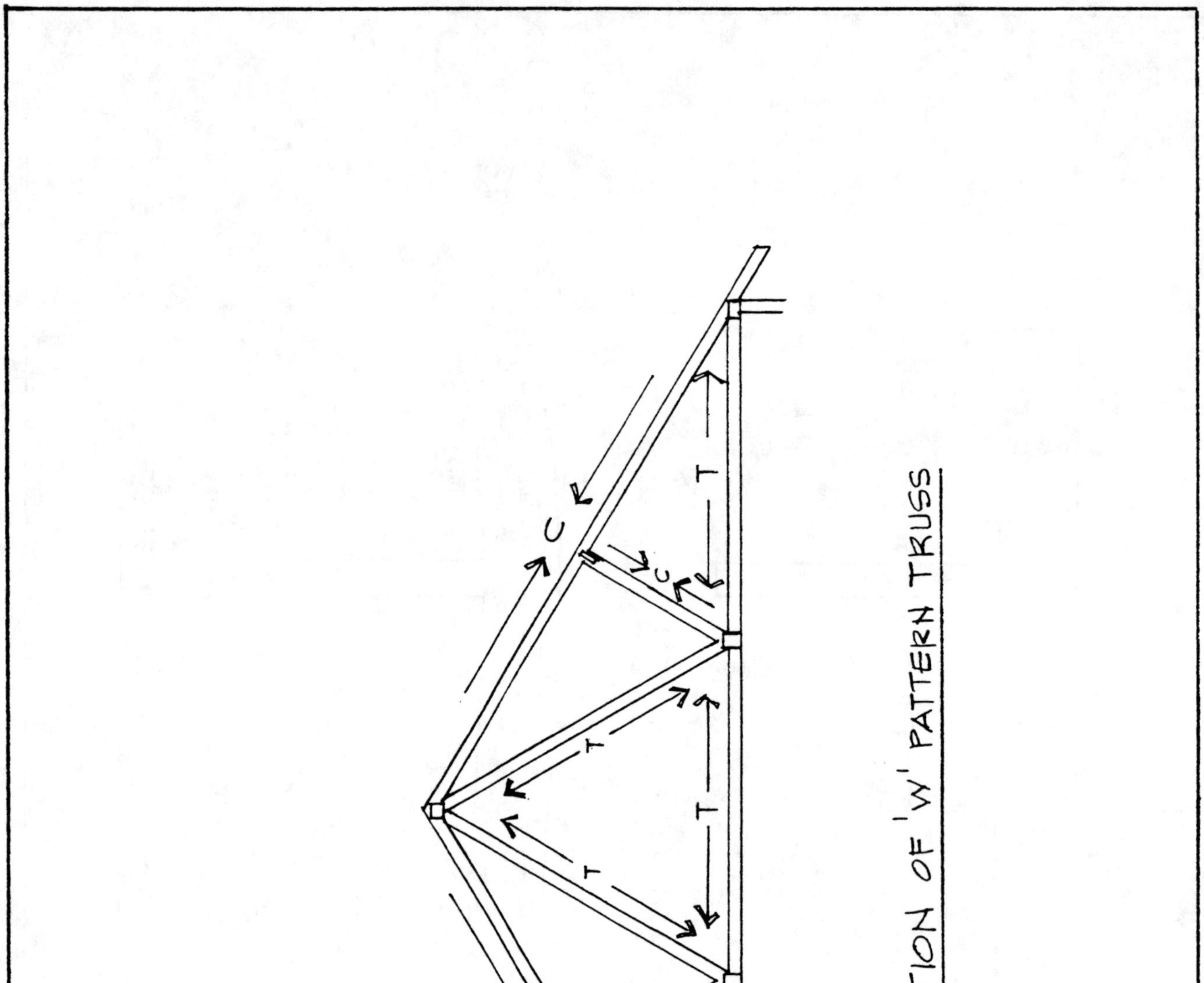

CHAPTER 13, EXERCISE 3

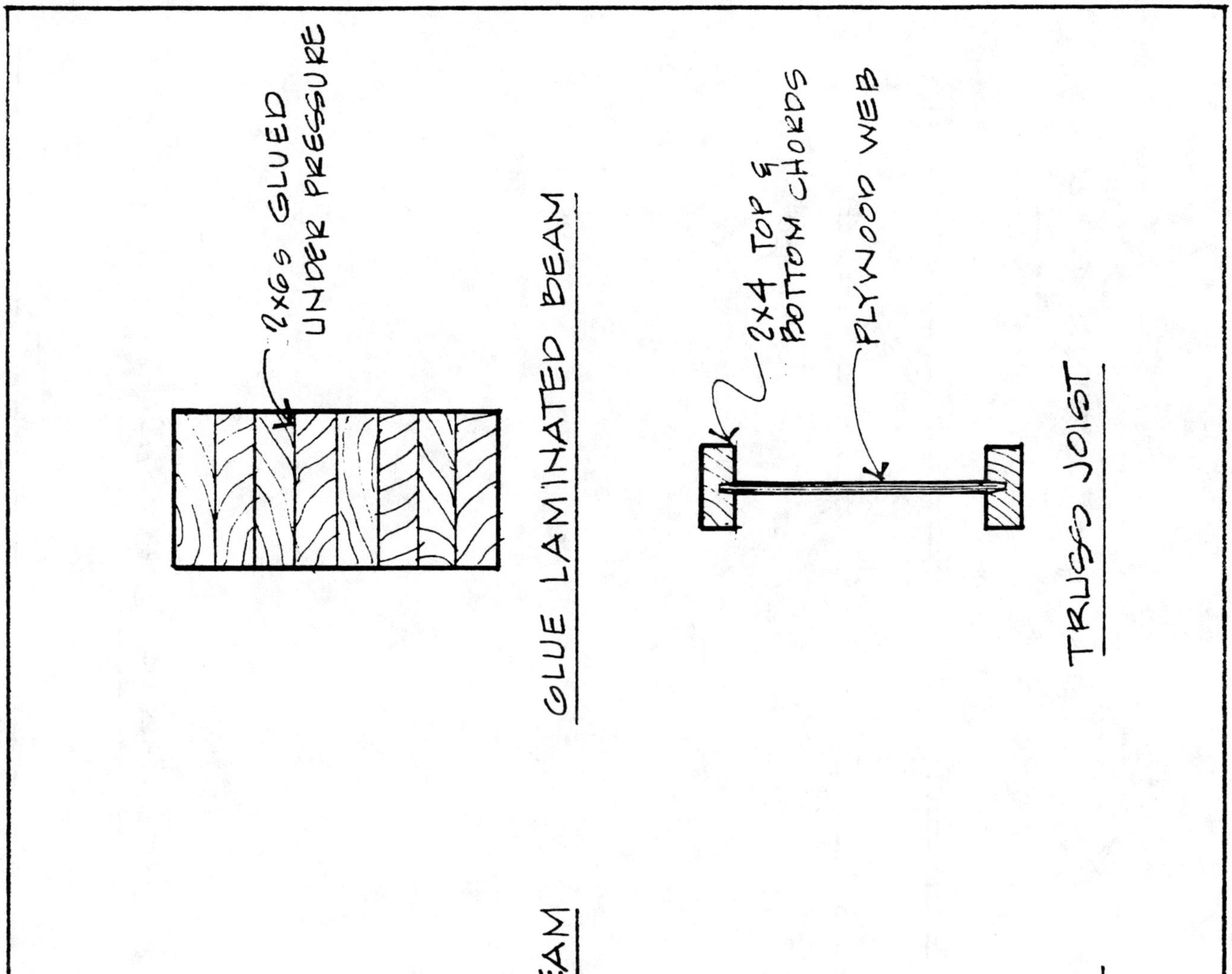

CHAPTER 13, EXERCISE 4

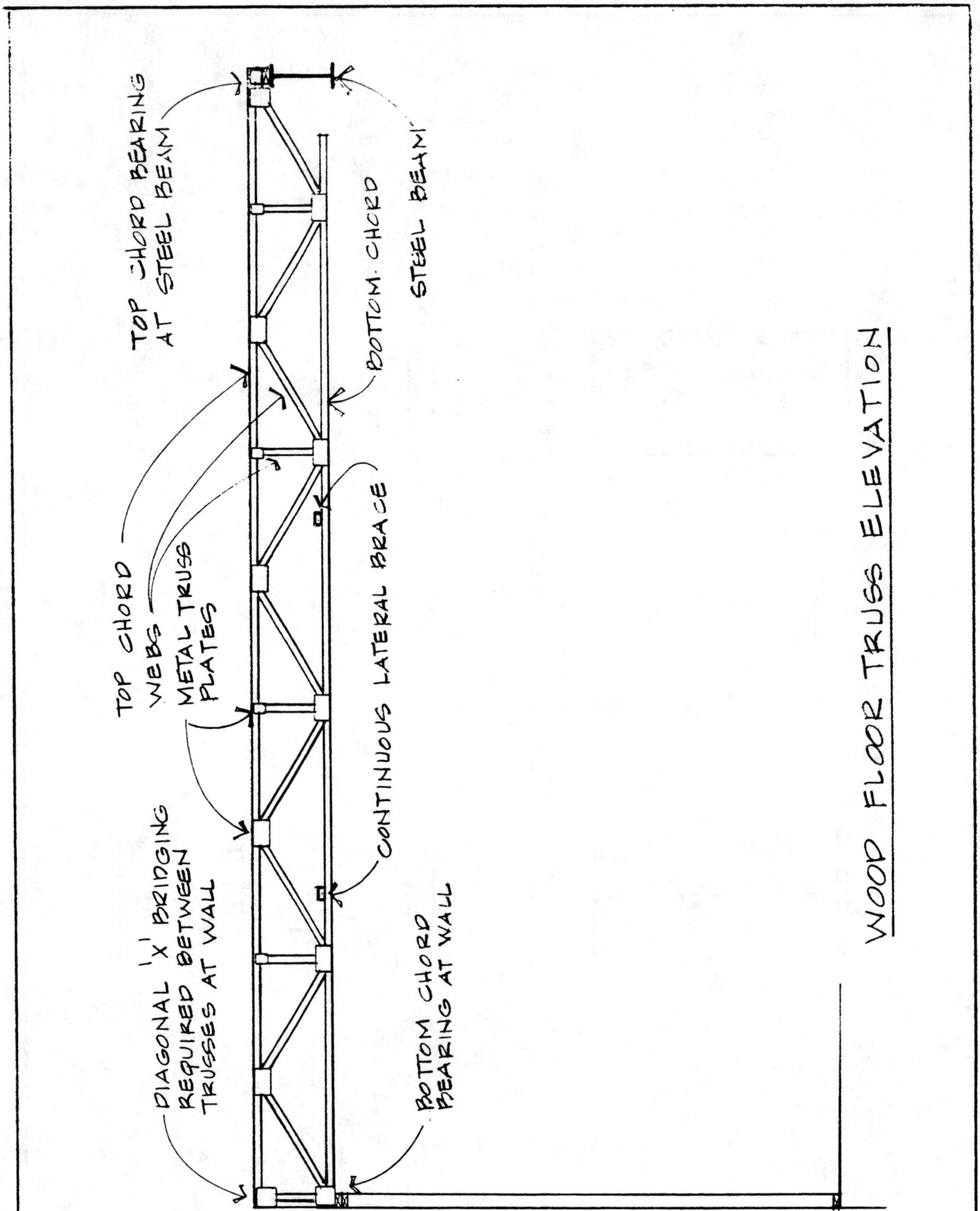

CHAPTER 13, EXERCISE 5

CHAPTER 13
REVIEW QUESTIONS AND ANSWERS

1. What lumber grades are generally used for the major amount of residential framing throughout the country?

ans. **Select structural No.1, No.2, No.3, as well as appearance and stud grade lumber is generally used for the major amount of residential framing throughout the country.**

2. What physical characteristics must structural lumber possess?

ans. **Structural lumber should have few physical defects, and have a large modulus of elasticity which produces stiffness and resistance to deflection.**

3. List the two major species of wood that are now used for framing houses.

ans. **The two major species of wood used for framing houses are Southern pine and Douglas fir.**

4. What is the main use in home construction for oak lumber?

ans. **Oak lumber in home construction is primarily used in high traffic areas like threshholds and floors.**

5. Explain the word deflection as used in structural terminology.

ans. **Deflection in structural terminology describes wood's tendencies to move or sag when put under stress such as supporting a load.**

6. Wood columns used to support a girder in a structure would be subjected to what type of stresses?

ans. **Wood columns used to support a girder in a structure would be subjected to the forces of compression.**

7. What is the maximum amount of moisture allowed in seasoned framing lumber?

ans. **The maximum amount of moisture allowed in seasoned framing lumber is 19% where as some structural lumber has 15% moisture content for critical design loads.**

8. Local building codes require what minimum live load on living room floors?

ans. **Local building codes require a minimum live load on living room floors of 40 psf.**

9. Why must both the live load and the dead load be considered when determining the size of a structural framing member?

ans. **Both the live load and the dead load must be considered when determining the size of a structural framing member for most structural framing lumber will be subjected to both dead loads and live loads.**

10. If using No. 2 Douglas fir for framing a kitchen floor, what size joists would be necessary if they are spaced 16"o.c. and span 11'-6"?

ans. **When framing a kitchen floor with No. 2 Douglas fir spaced 16" o.c. and spanning 11'-6", use 2"X 8" joists.**

11. Specify the ceiling joist size for the following situations: no attic storage, No.2 southern yellow pine, 16"o.c. spacing, and 13'-0" span.

ans. **To span 13'-0" in an attic with No.2 southern yellow pine at 16" o.c., it would take a 2 x 6 joist.**

12. Define the term safety factor.

ans. **All structural framing charts list the maximum allowable loads that a structural member can safely support. Codes require that a safety factor be included in the allowable span tables. Designers who have doubts about a member's capability should up size the member.**

13. Differentiate between light roofing and heavy roofing when sizing rafters.

ans. **When sizing rafters, one must differentiate**

between light roofing and heavy roofing materials. Fiberglass or wood shingles are considered light roofing materials. Slate or mission tile are considered heavy roofing materials.

14. Why is it important in conventional roof framing to have ceiling joists parallel to the rafters?

ans. **Ceiling joists need to run parallel to the rafters in conventional roof framing to counter act the forces of lateral thrust. The ceiling joists help to stabilize the walls and rafters.**

15. In planning a plank and beam roof with wide spacing of the beams, why is the stiffness of the planking an important consideration?

ans. **The planking provides lateral stiffness to a plank and beam roof with wide spacing on the beam.**

16. Is the rafter length or the rafter span used in selecting a proper size for a rafter from Table 8-6?

ans. **The rafter span (horizontal distance not the diagonal distance) is used in selecting a proper size rafter from Table 8-6.**

17. What is the maximum allowable span for 2 x 10 Douglas fir floor joists spaced at 16" o.c. if the live load is 30 lbs/sq/ ft.?

ans. **The maximum allowable span for 2 x 10 Douglas fir floor joists spaced at 16" o.c. with live loads expected to be 30 lbs/sq. ft. is 18'-5".**

18. What will be the length of a rafter if the roof slope is 9:12 and the horizontal span is 16'-0"?

ans. **If a roof slope is 9:12 and the horizontal span is 16'=0", the rafter is 20'-0".**

19. What advantage is gained by the use of a flitch beam?

ans. **The advantage of using a flitch beam insures greater span distances and allows joists to be attached to the beam.**

20. What size of standard steel pipe column is required to support 50 kips if the unsupported length is 10′-0"?

ans. A steel pipe needed to support 50 kips and 10′-0" of unsupported length would have to be 5" in diameter.

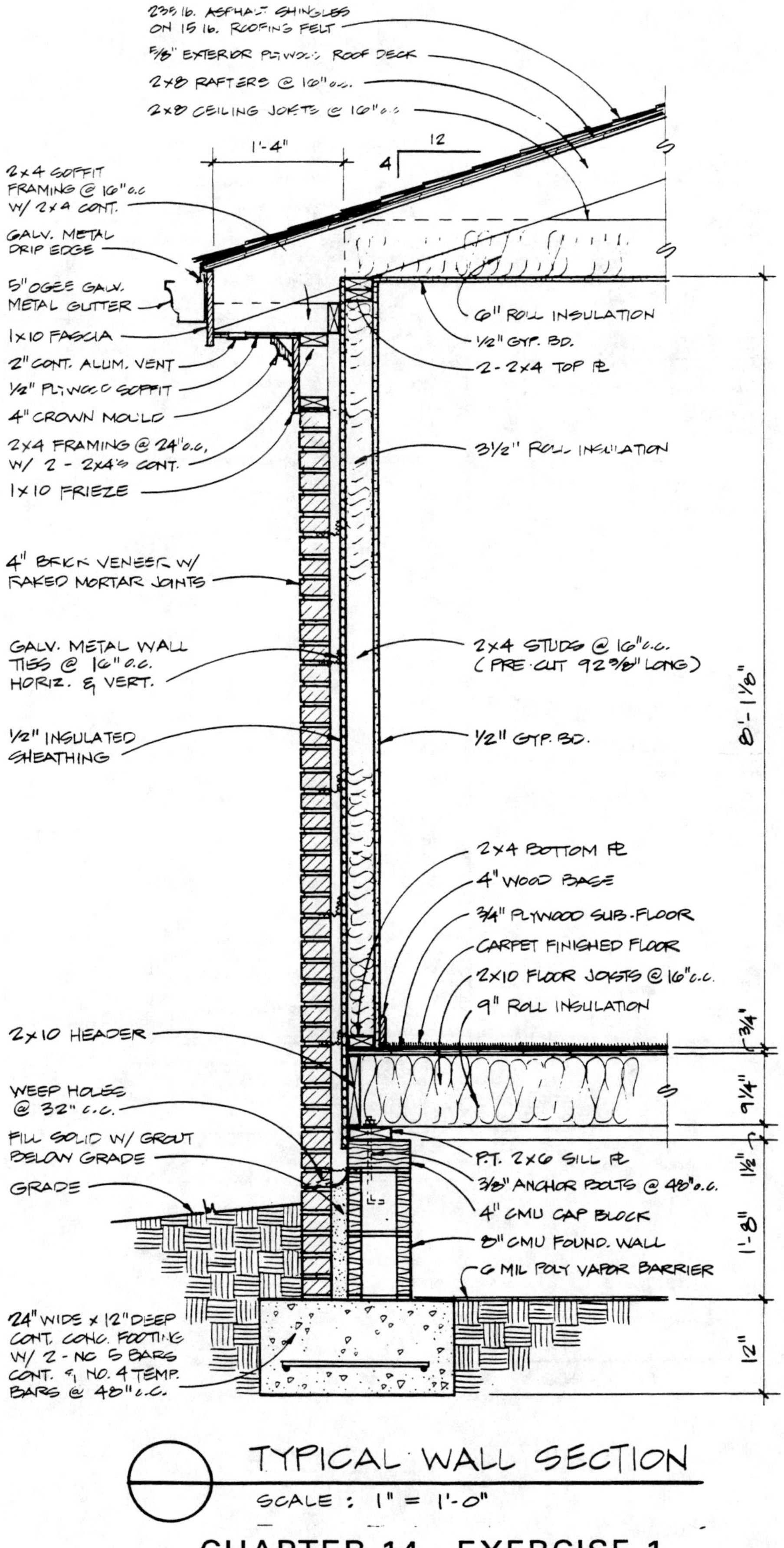

CHAPTER 14, EXERCISE 1

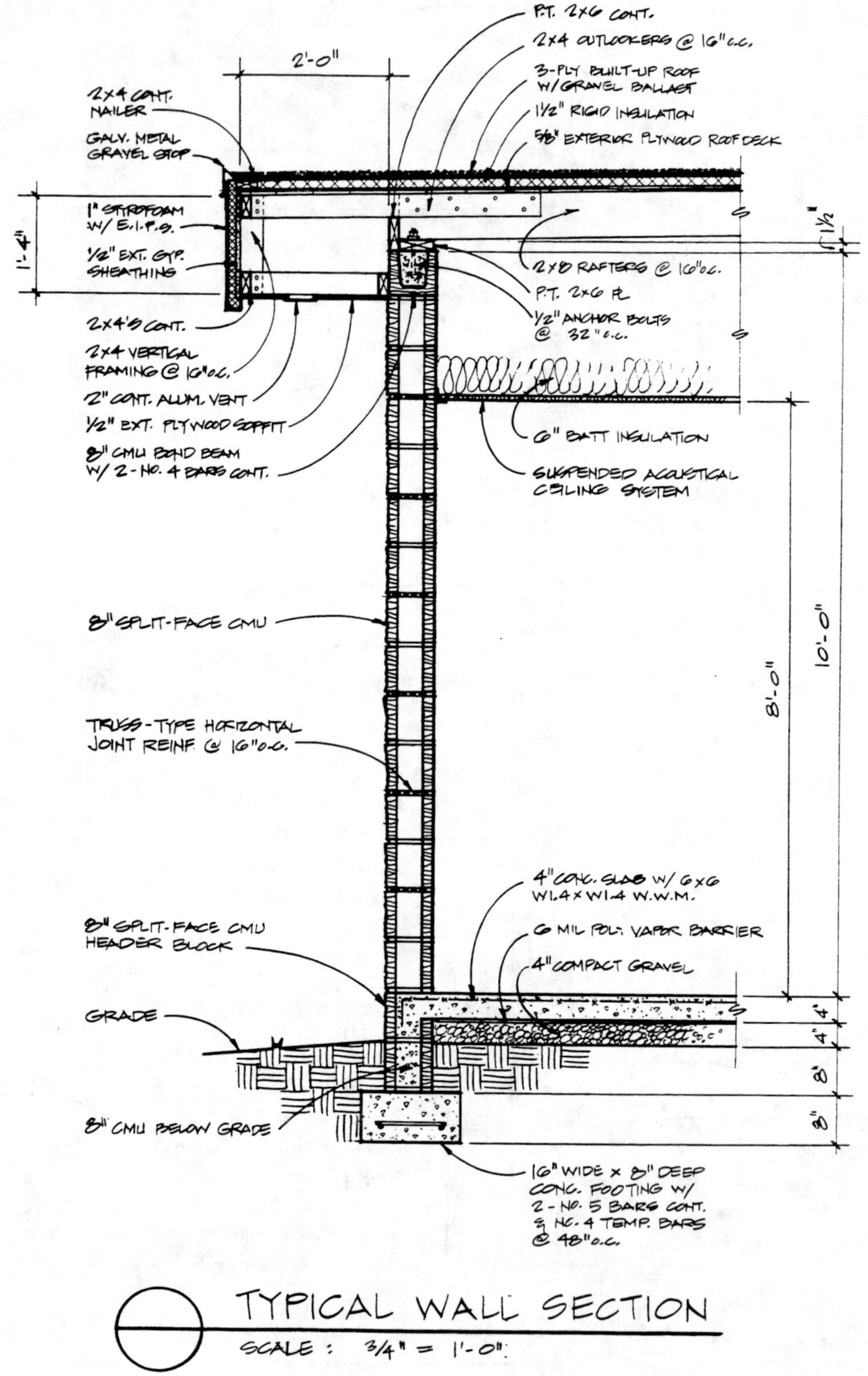

CHAPTER 14, EXERCISE 2

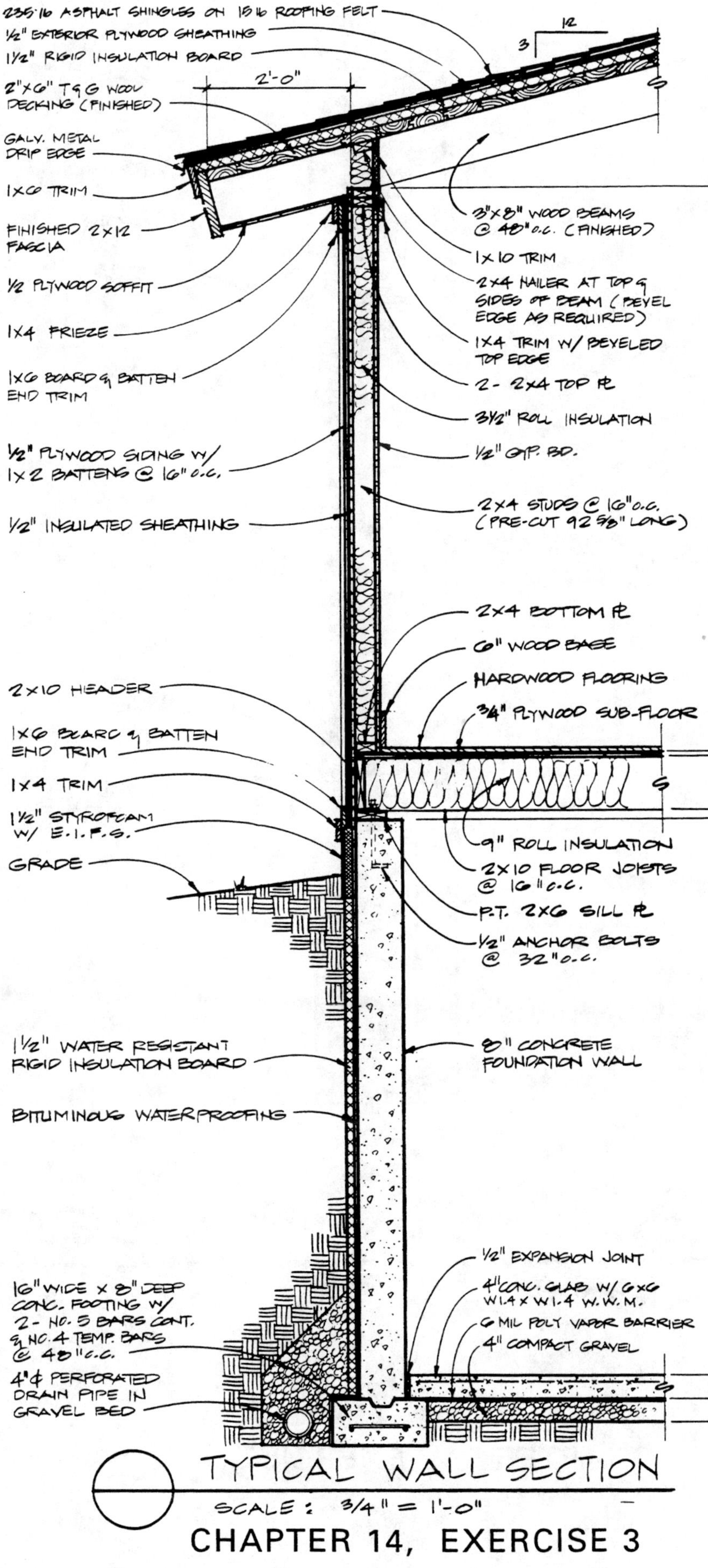

CHAPTER 14, EXERCISE 3

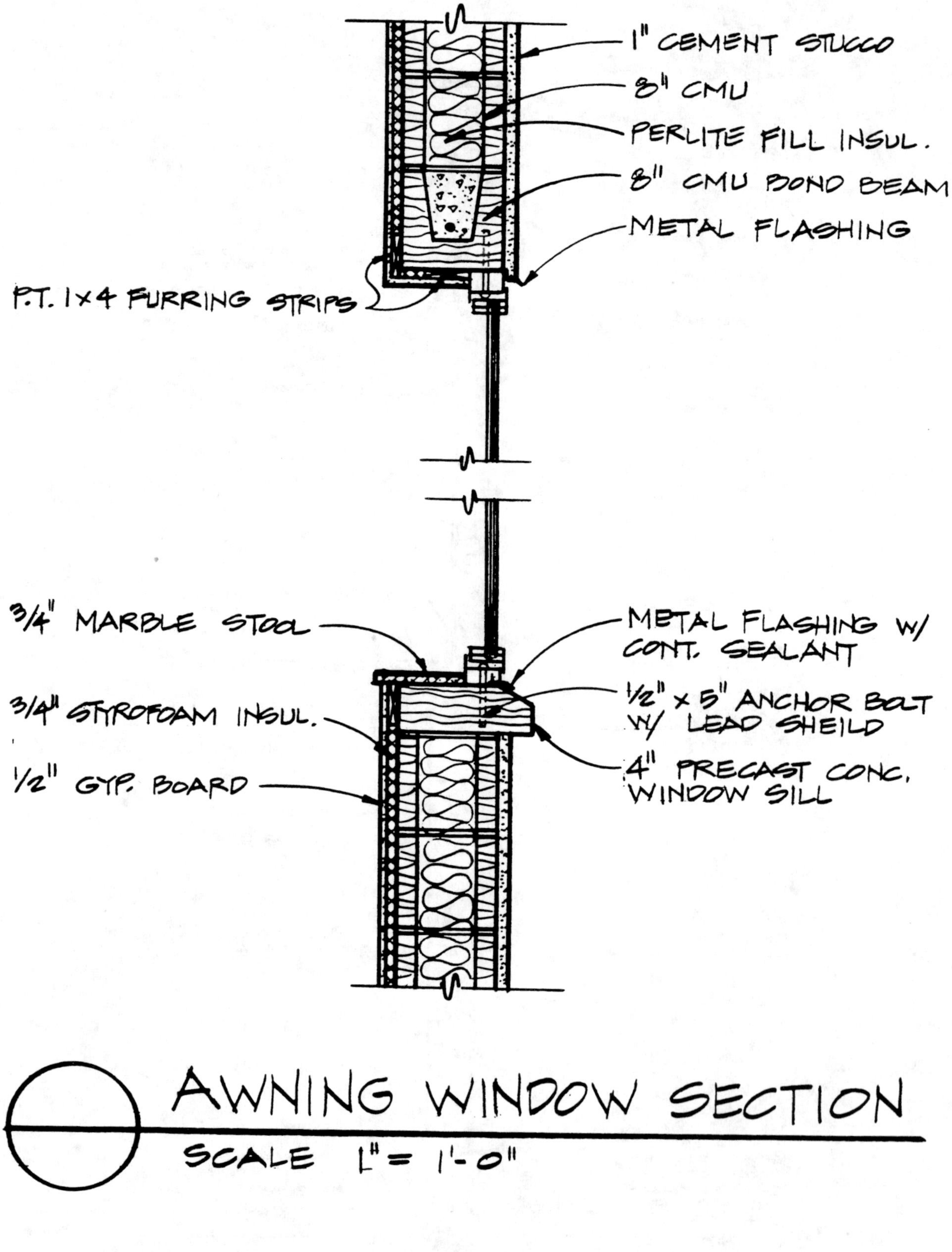

CHAPTER 14, EXERCISE 4

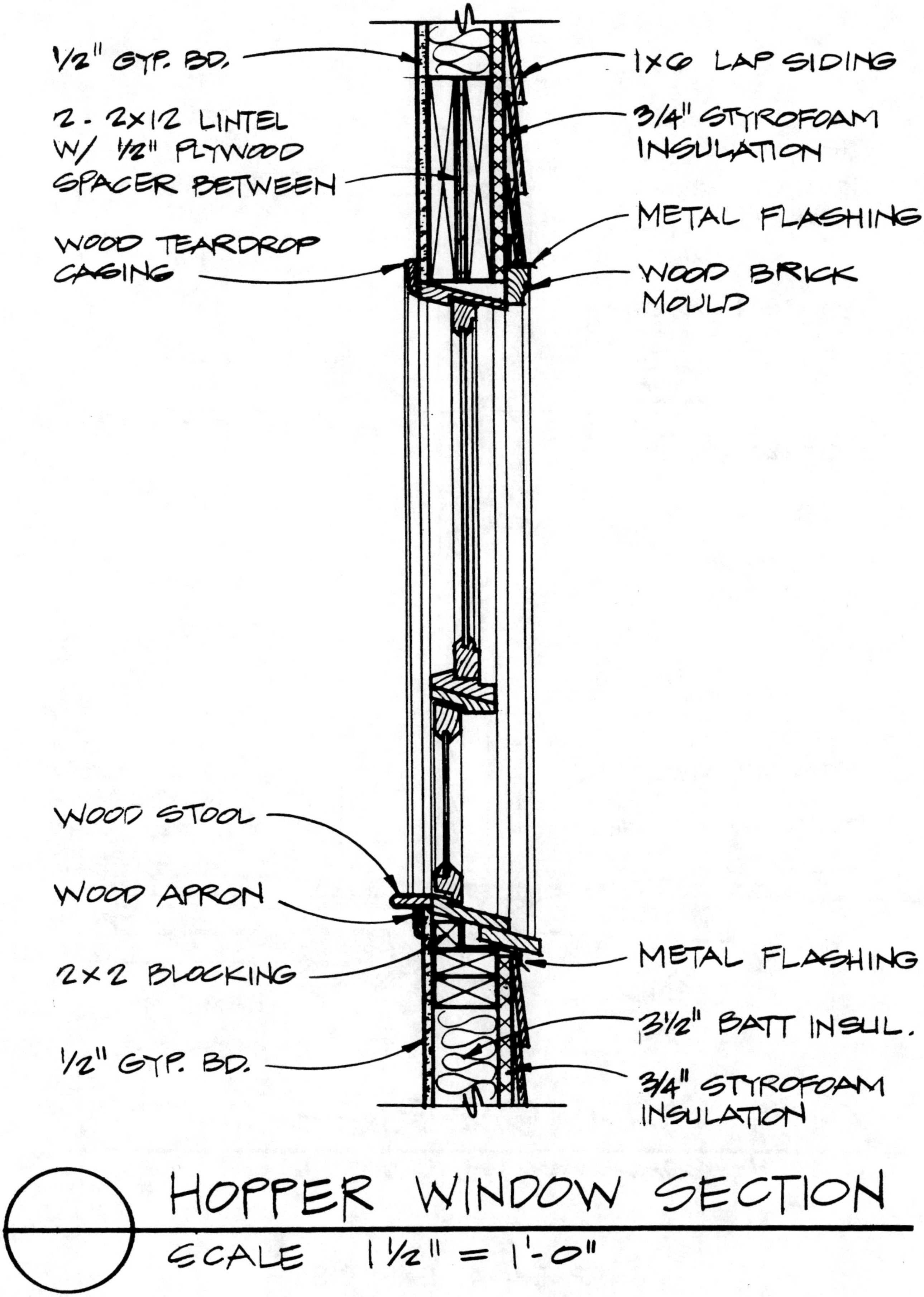

CHAPTER 14, EXERCISE 5

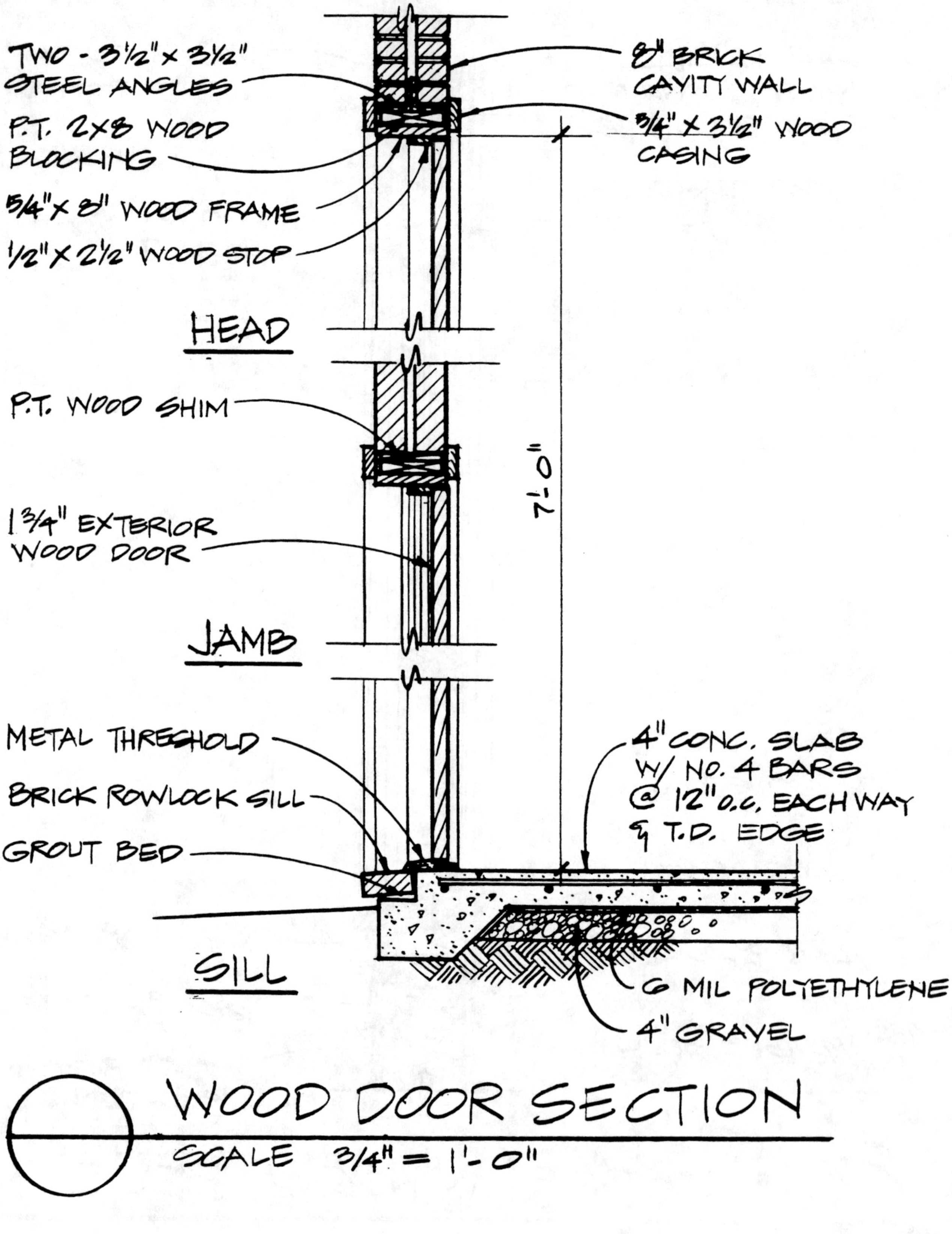

CHAPTER 14, EXERCISE 6

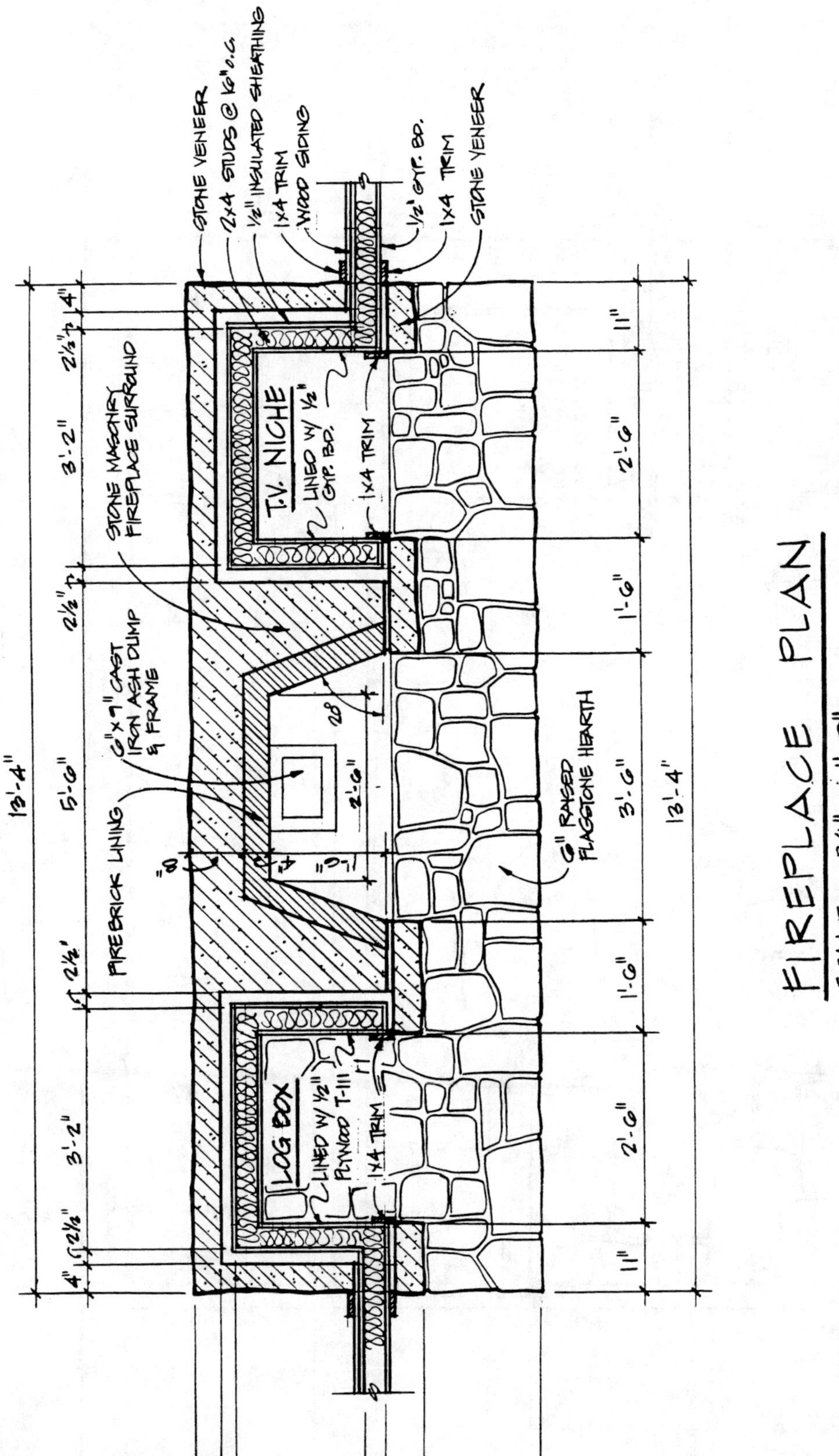

CHAPTER 14, EXERCISE 7

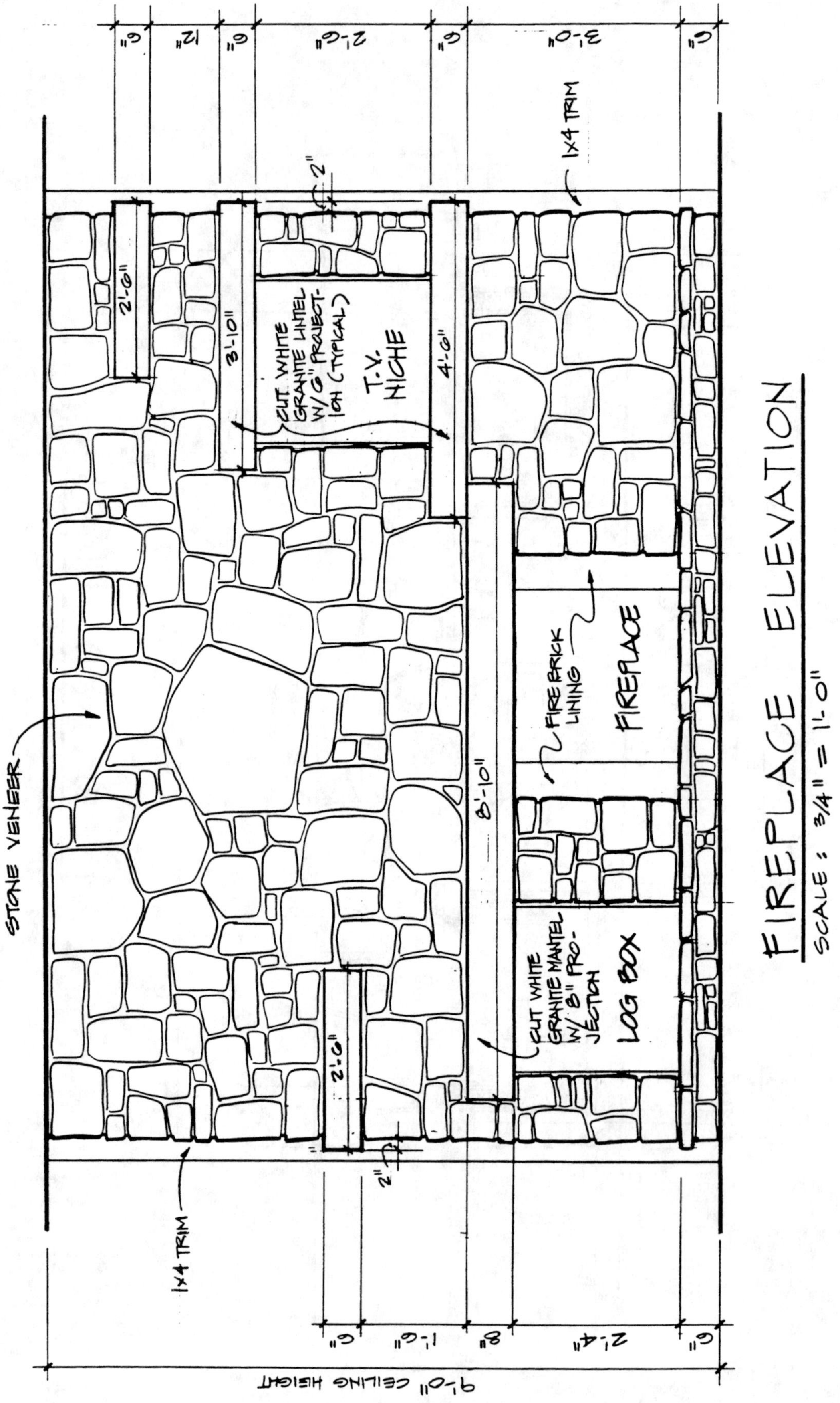

CHAPTER 14, EXERCISE 7

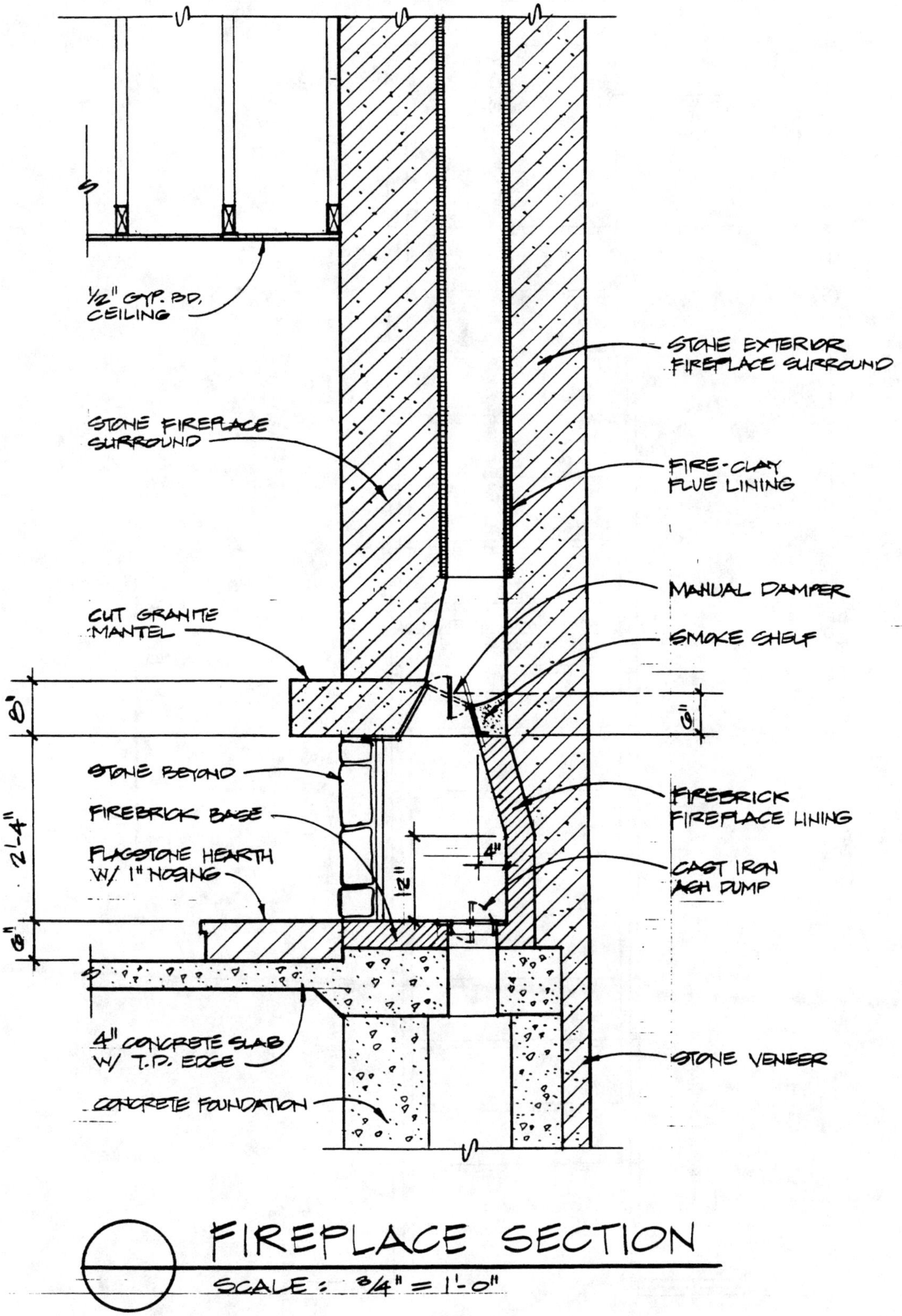

CHAPTER 14, EXERCISE 7

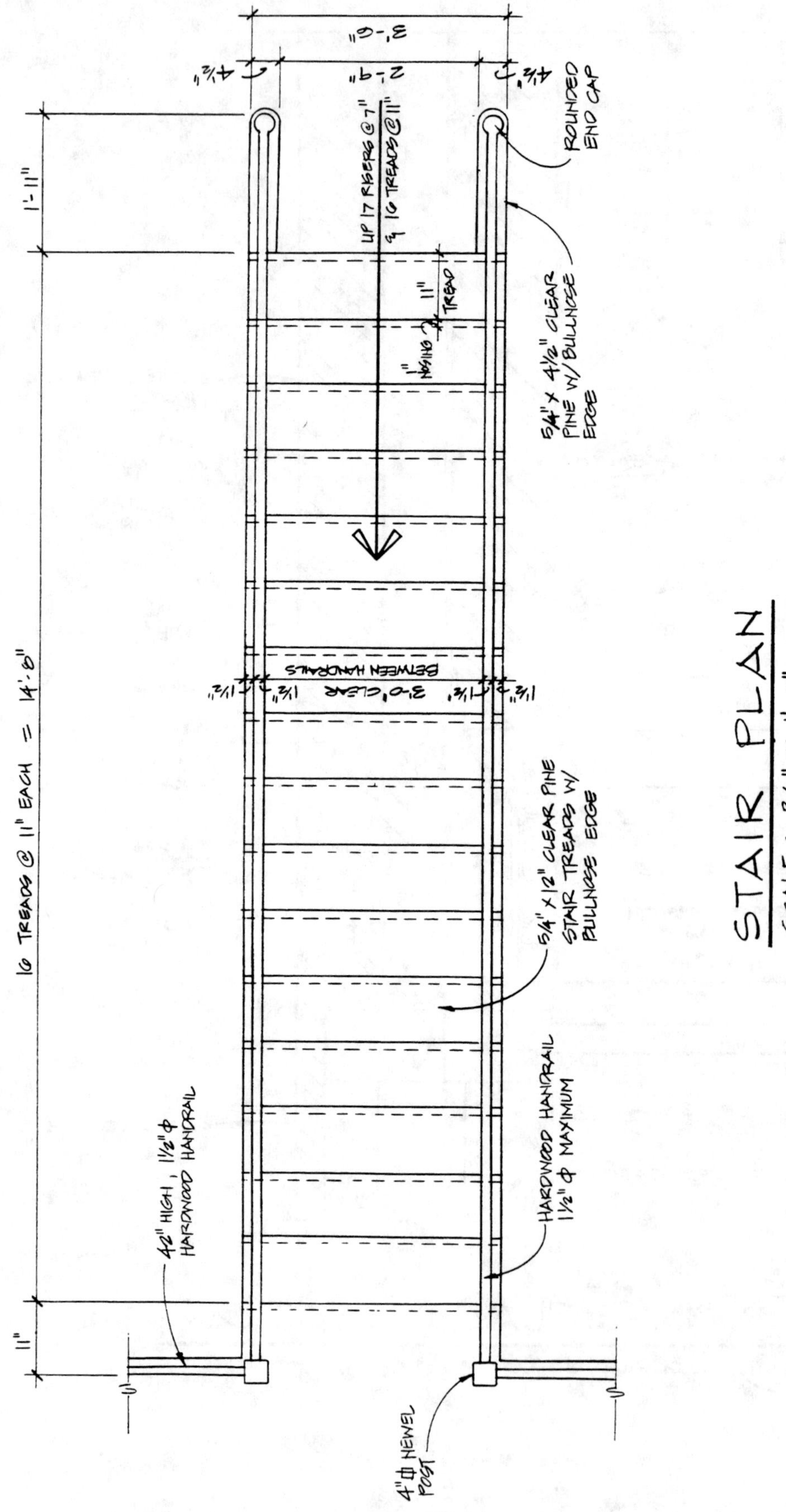

CHAPTER 14, EXERCISE 8

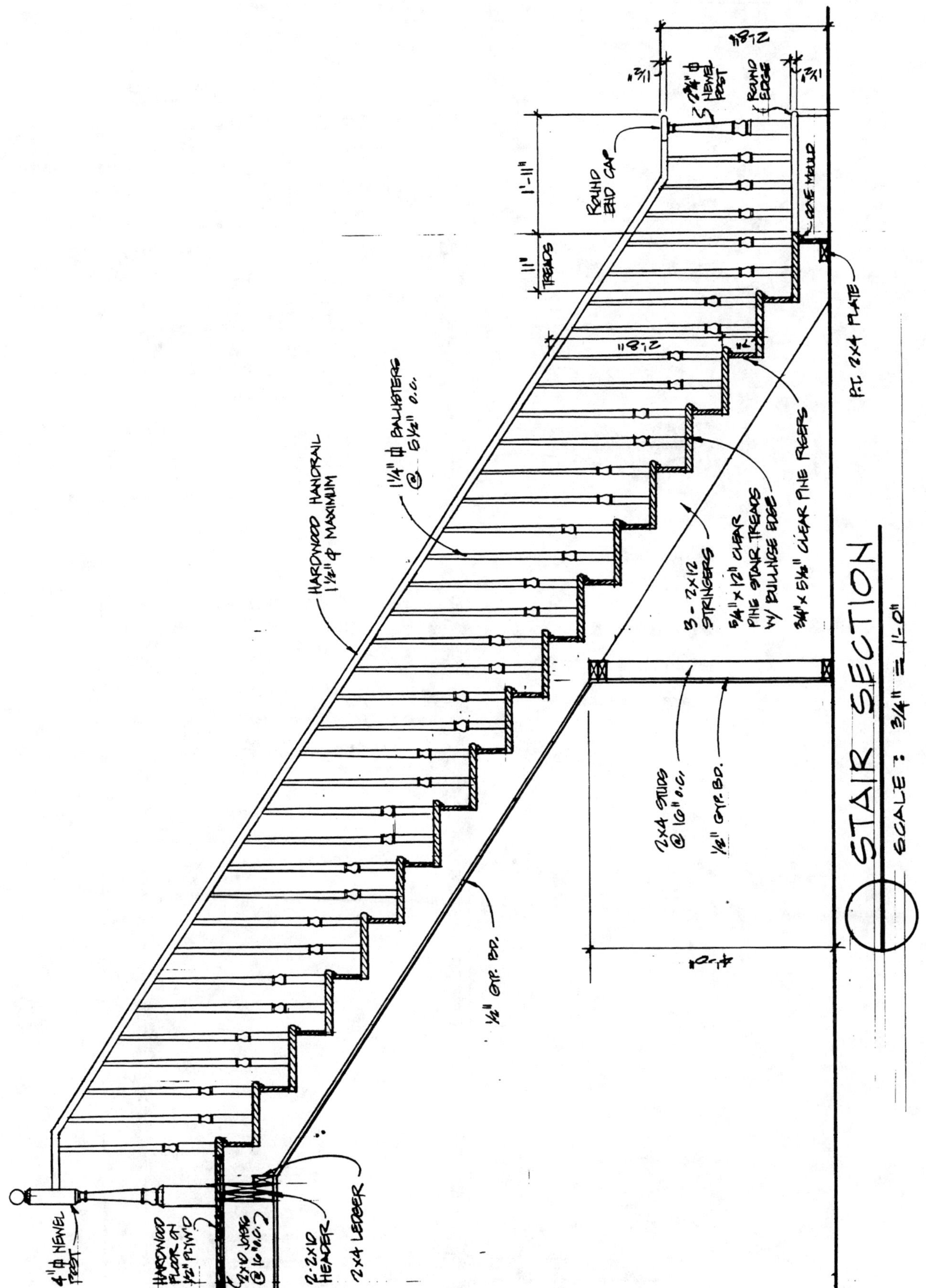

CHAPTER 14, EXERCISE 8

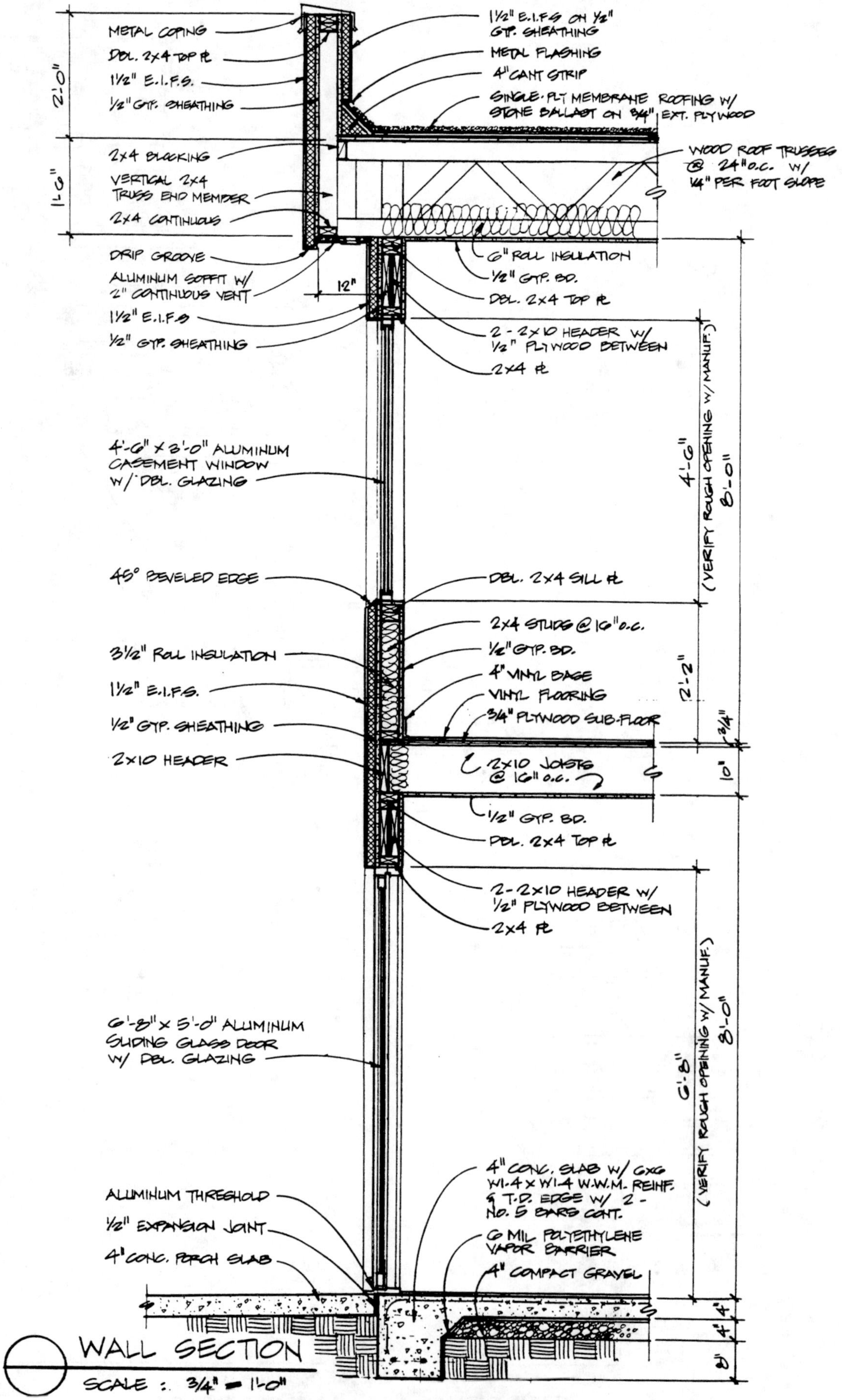

CHAPTER 14, EXERCISE 9

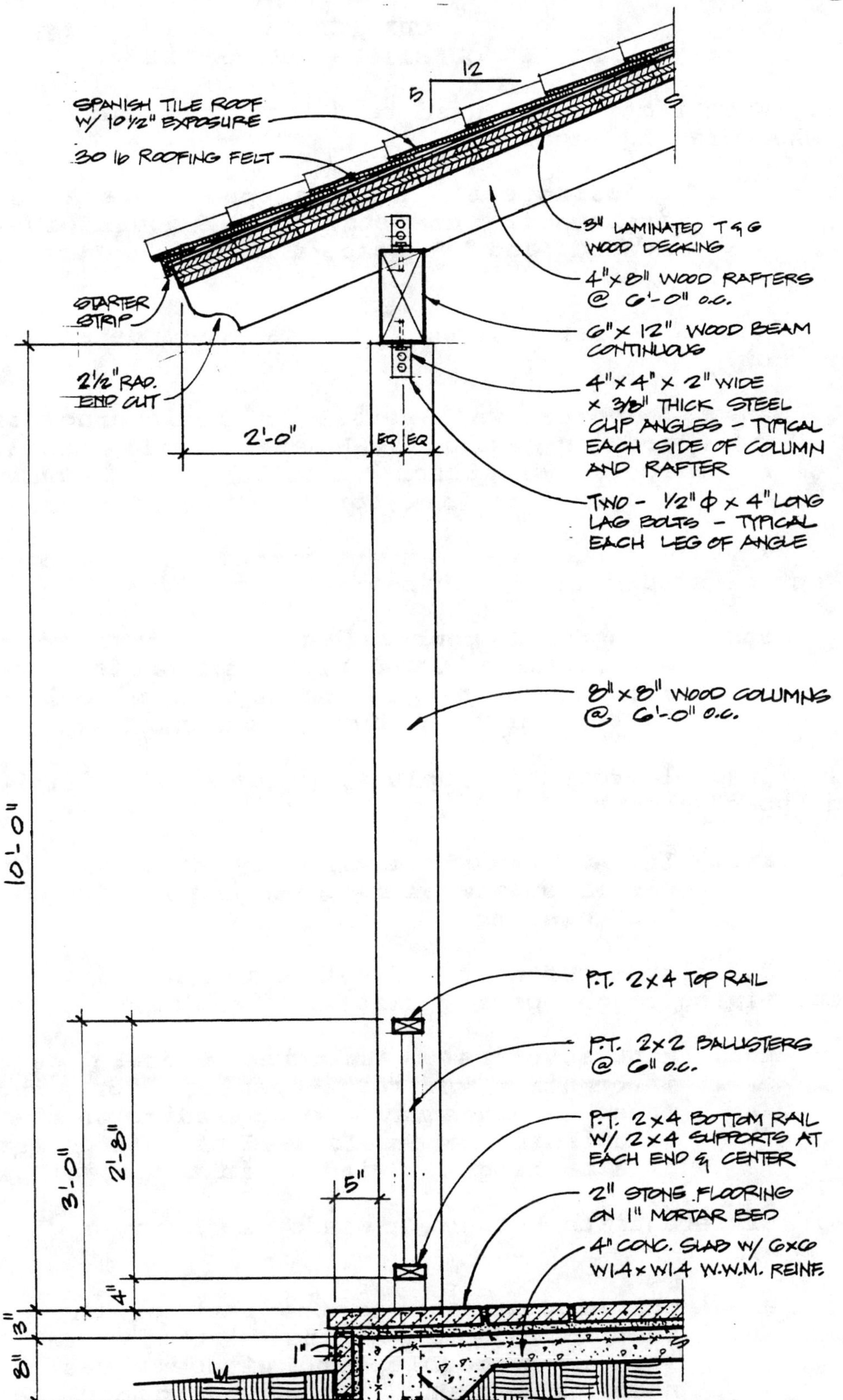

SECTION @ COVERED PATIO

SCALE: 1" = 1'-0"

CHAPTER 14, EXERCISE 10

CHAPTER 14
REVIEW QUESTIONS AND ANSWERS

1. What factors are used to determine the choice of scale when drawing details?

ans. Choosing scale depends upon the size of the members in the detail, the amount of detail needed, and the space available on the layout sheet.

2. What information does a typical wall detail usually show?

ans. A typical wall detail should incorporate the footing detail, sill detail, wall detail, and roof connection detail; all should be properly in line for relative reference.

3. Why are structural members in detail drawings drawn actual size rather than nominal size?

ans. Structural members must be drawn to their actual size in details since the details illustrate the precise way the materials are to be assembled during construction.

4. In gable-roof terminology, what is the difference between "span" and "run"?

ans. In gable-roof terminology the span is the distance between supports and run is one half that distance.

5. Why must manufacturers' catalogues be consulted when determining rough-opening sizes for windows?

ans. Manufacturers' catalogues contain detailed information on rough-openings for windows. These openings may vary depending on the type of building materials used as well as methods of attaching the windows in the openings.

6. Differentiate between a window sash and a window frame.

ans. The window sash is the part of the window that usually moves inside the frame. The sash of a double hung window moves up and down. The sash of a casement window opens to the exterior. The frame is secured in the

rough opening and holds the sash in place. Some window frames have a fixed sash that does not move.

7. Why are door jambs usually the only sections needed when drawing door details?

ans. **Door jambs are usually the only sections needed when detailing a door since the door head detail is in most instances similar to the jamb and does not need to be drawn.**

8. What dimensions are first selected in fireplace design, and what should be the basis for their selection?

ans. **The first dimensions selected in fireplace design are the openings. Openings should not only have correct proportions to insure proper functioning but also have a pleasing proportion in relation to the size of the room. Rectangles appear more desirable than squares.**

9. For a workable fireplace, what should be the proportion of the cross-sectional flue area to the fireplace opening area?

ans. **Fireplaces should have a flue area one-tenth the size of the fireplace opening area. Chimney heights under 14′ may require even larger flue sizes.**

10. What two dimensions are the most critical in satisfactory stair design?

ans. **The most important dimensions in the stairs are the risers and treads.**

11. Describe how an architect's scale can be used to lay out the riser height and tread width of stairs in elevation or section without measuring each riser and tread from floor to floor.

ans. **The best way to lay out stairs on a drawing is with an architect's scale. Establish the floor to floor height and draw floor lines between which the stair is to be drawn. Divide the distance (in inches) between floors by seven to determine the number of risers needed. If 16 risers are required, place the same scale used for the layout with**

0 (zero) on the scale located on the top floor and place 16 on the scale on the lower floor and mark off the risers. If 16 risers are required, the stair will need 15 treads. Measure 11" for the first tread at the top of the stair. Place a scale with the 15th increment on the first floor level directly below the top riser on the second floor. Incline the scale until the 14th increment aligns with the vertical line that you drew to locate the first 11" tread at the top of the stair. Mark off each full number increment on the scale to locate the treads.

12. Write the three formulas for checking riser and tread proportions.

ans. There are three formulas for figuring riser and tread: 2 risers + 1 tread = between 24" and 25" Riser X tread = between 72" and 77" Riser + tread = between 17" and 18"

13. What is the fire door and what do the labels A, B, and C designate?

ans. A fire rated door is a door that will withstand a fire for a designated time before disintegrating. Fire doors have class ratings or labels showing how long they will last during a fire. A 'C' rated door will withstand fire for 45 minutes; and 'B' rated doors will withstand fire for 1 hour and 1 1/2 hours; and an 'A' rated door will withstand fire for 3 hours.

14. What are anchor bolts and where are they used in wood frame construction?

ans. Anchor bolts are steel bolts placed in foundation walls and used to hold sill plates to the foundation.

15. What is used to support brick masonry above a door or window opening?

ans. Steel angles (lintels) are used to support brick over windows and doors.

16. What type of cut is usually placed on a rafter where it rests on a bearing wall?

ans. A bird's-mouth cut is usually placed on a rafter where the rafter rests on a bearing wall.

17. Residential doors are usually 6'-8" high. What is the common height of commercial doors?

ans. The common height for a commercial door is 7'-0".

18. What is the minimum headroom above stairs?

ans. The minimum headroom above stairs is 6'-8" on major stairways and 6'-6" on secondary stairways.

19. Where is a brick rowlock used in window detailing?

ans. A brick rowlock is used as a window sill.

20. What is a clerestory window?

ans. A clerestory window is so named because of its placement above lower roof lines. Clerestory windows admit light and offer privacy because they are placed high on a wall above eye level.

The following page contains an example of the stair calculation procedure which can be copied and handed to students for reference.

THE PURPOSE OF STAIRS IS TO GET THE FEET FROM ONE HORIZONTAL PLANE TO ANOTHER.

1.	DETERMINE FLOOR TO FLOOR HEIGHT.	EXAMPLE: 10'-3"
2.	CONVERT TO INCHES.	10 X 12 + 3 = 123"
3.	DIVIDE BY SEVEN.	123 / 7 = 17 PLUS
4.	USE RESULT AS NUMBER OF RISERS.	17 RISERS
5.	DIVIDE HEIGHT BY NUMBER OF RISERS.	123 / 17 = 7.23"
6.	CHECK RESULT: SHOULD BE 7" TO 7.5".	OK
7.	TRY ONE LESS RISER.	123 / 16 = 7.688" : OK
8.	TRY ONE MORE RISER.	123 / 18 = 6.83" : TOO SHORT
9.	LIST CHOICES.	17 OR 16 RISERS
10.	SUBTRACT ONE FROM THE NUMBER OF RISERS.	17 - 1 = 16
11.	SUBTRACT ONE FOR EACH LANDING.	16 - 0 = 16
12.	USE RESULT AS THE NUMBER OF TREADS.	16 TREADS
13.	SELECT TREAD SIZE - 10 1/2". 10 3/4". 11"	10 1/2"
14.	MULTIPLY TREADS BY SIZE CHOSEN.	16 X 10.5" = 14'- 0"
15.	LAYOUT STAIRS IN SECTION.	SEE BELOW
16.	DRAW HEADROOM REQUIREMENTS.	SEE BELOW

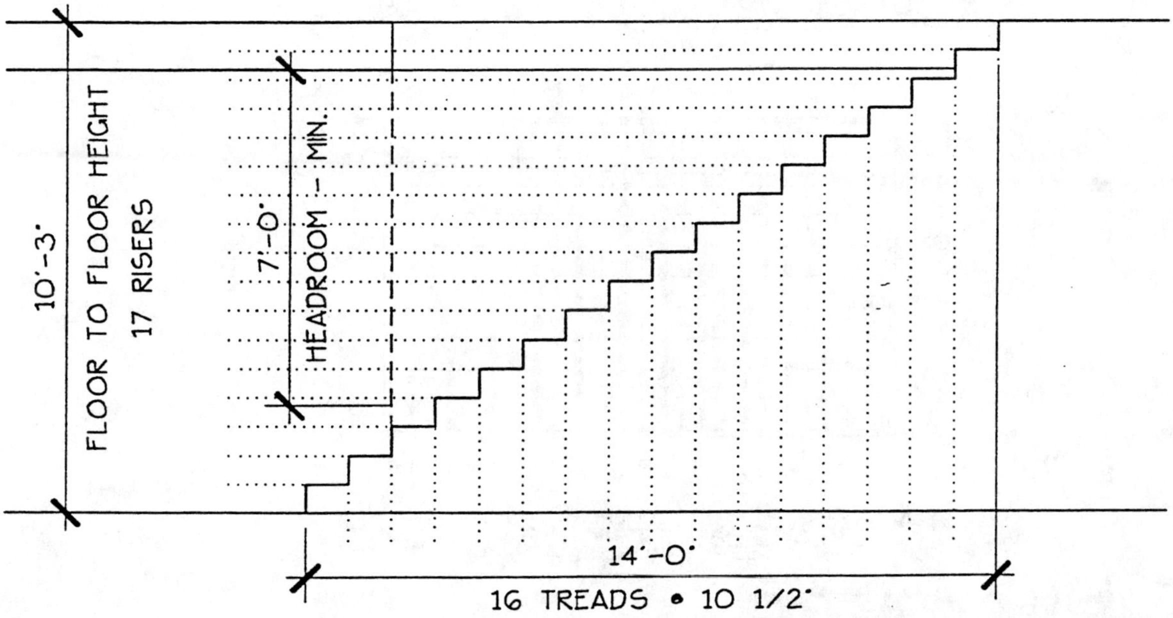

STAIR CALCULATIONS

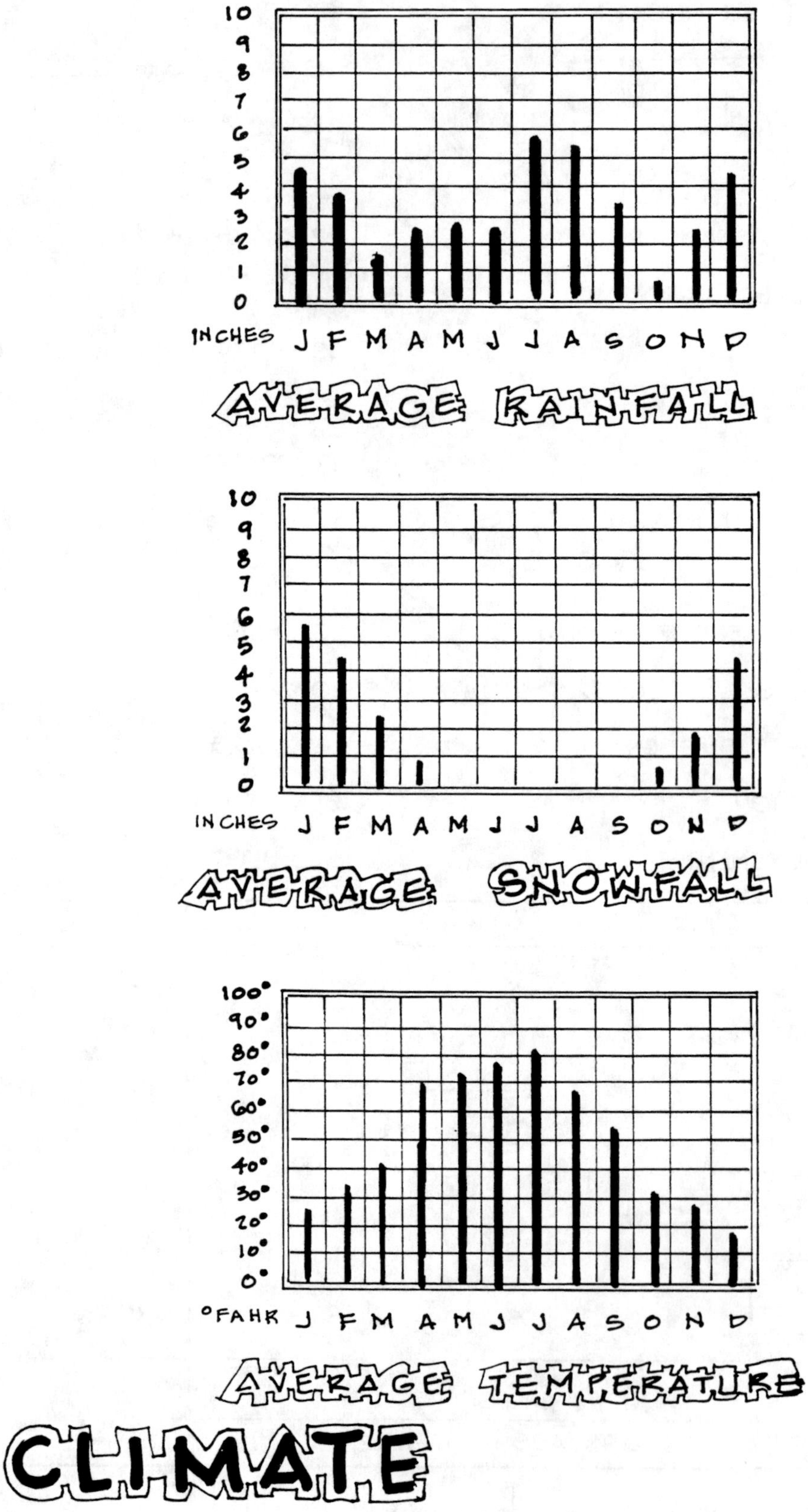

CHAPTER 15, EXERCISE 1, FIG. 15-85

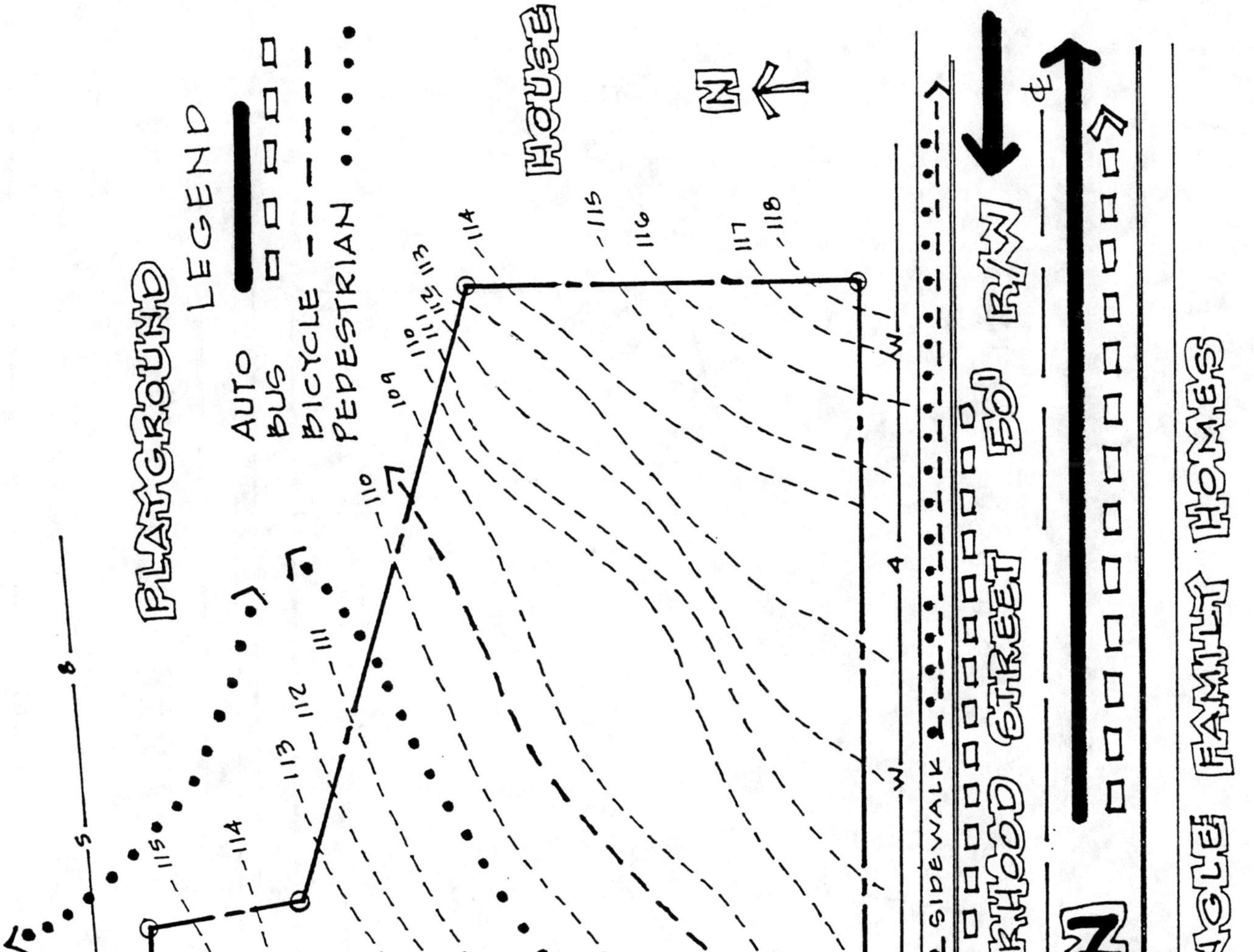

CHAPTER 15, EXERCISE 1, FIG. 15-85

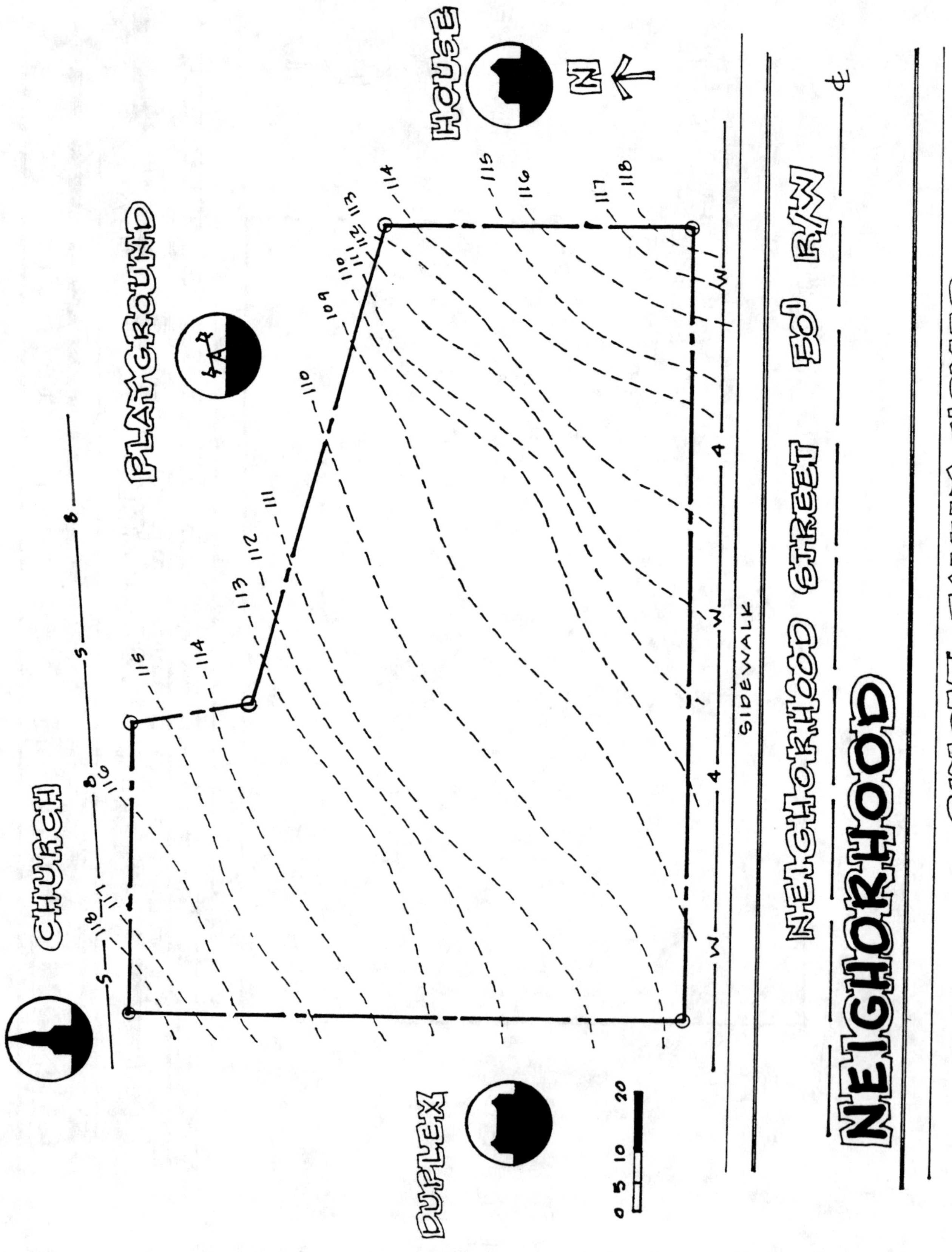

CHAPTER 15, EXERCISE 1, FIG. 15-85

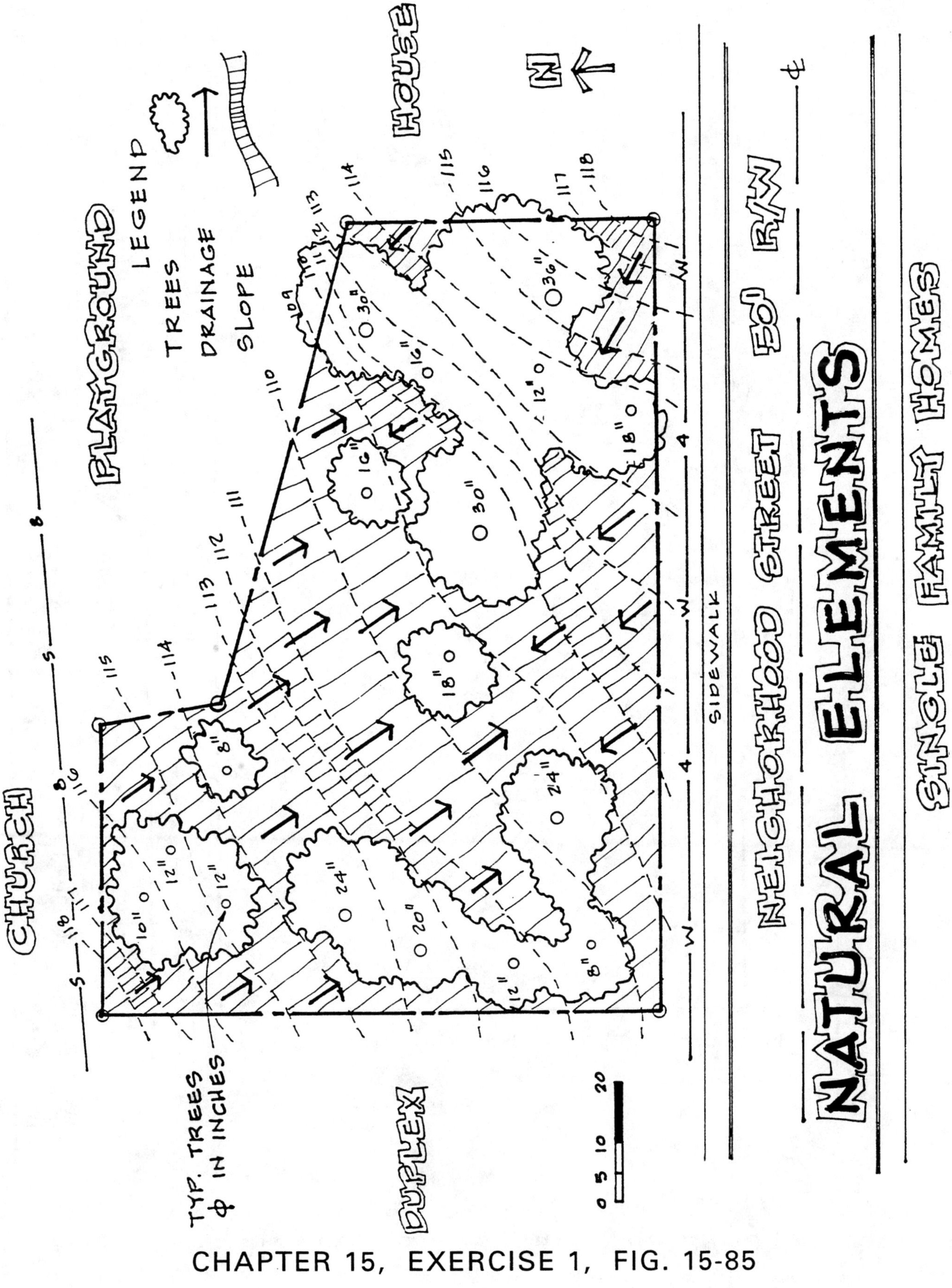

CHAPTER 15, EXERCISE 1, FIG. 15-85

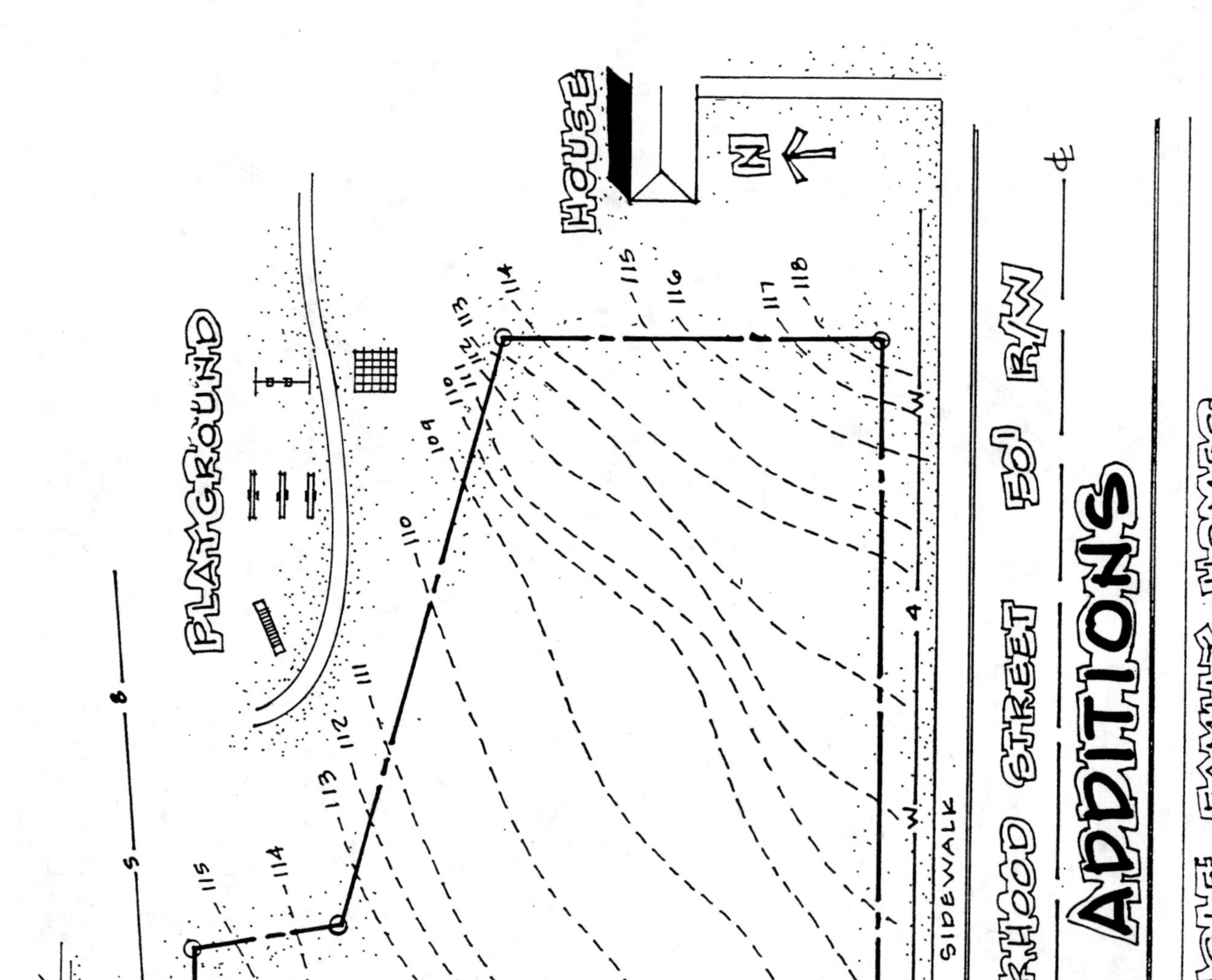

CHAPTER 15, EXERCISE 1, FIG. 15-85

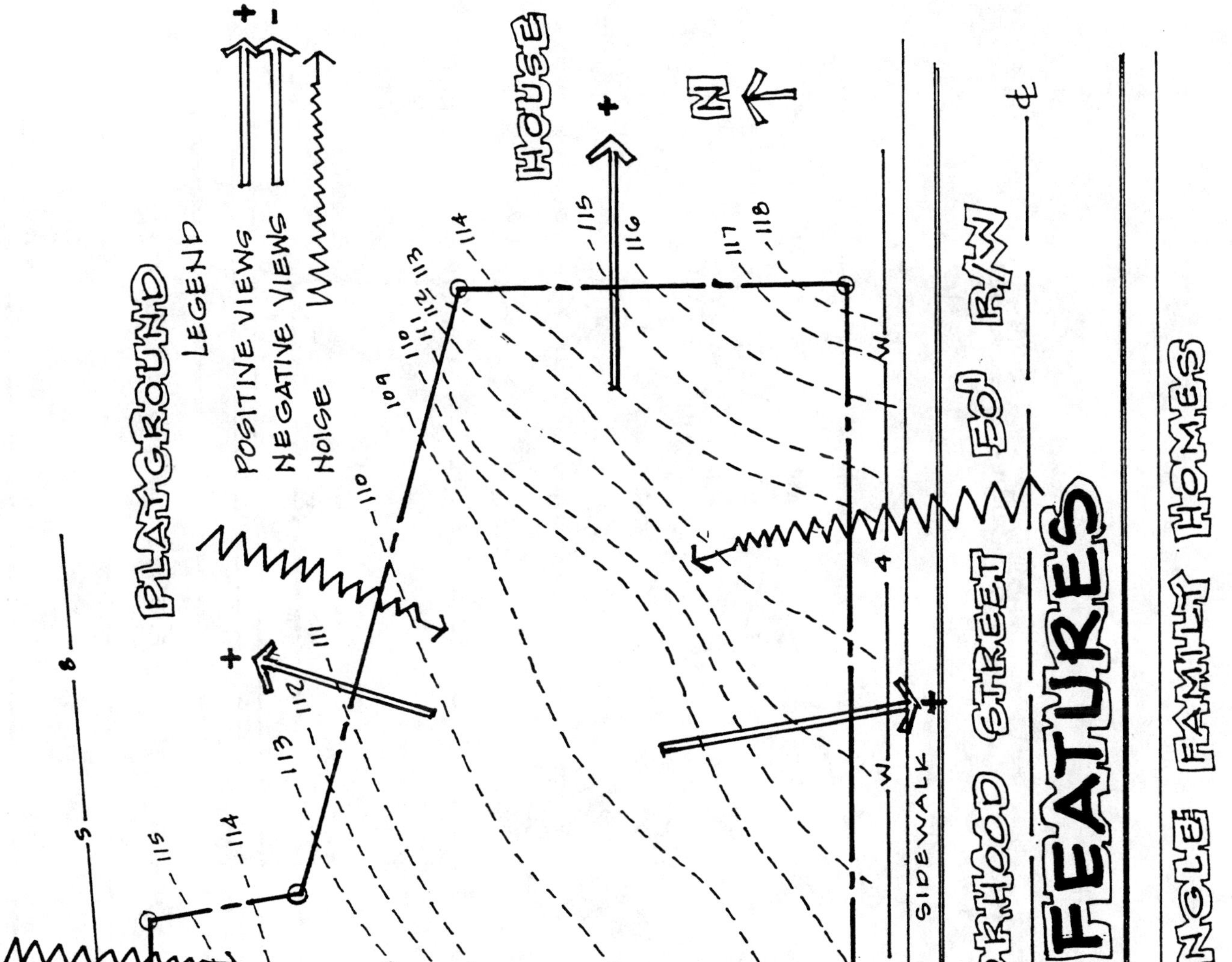

CHAPTER 15, EXERCISE 1, FIG. 15-85

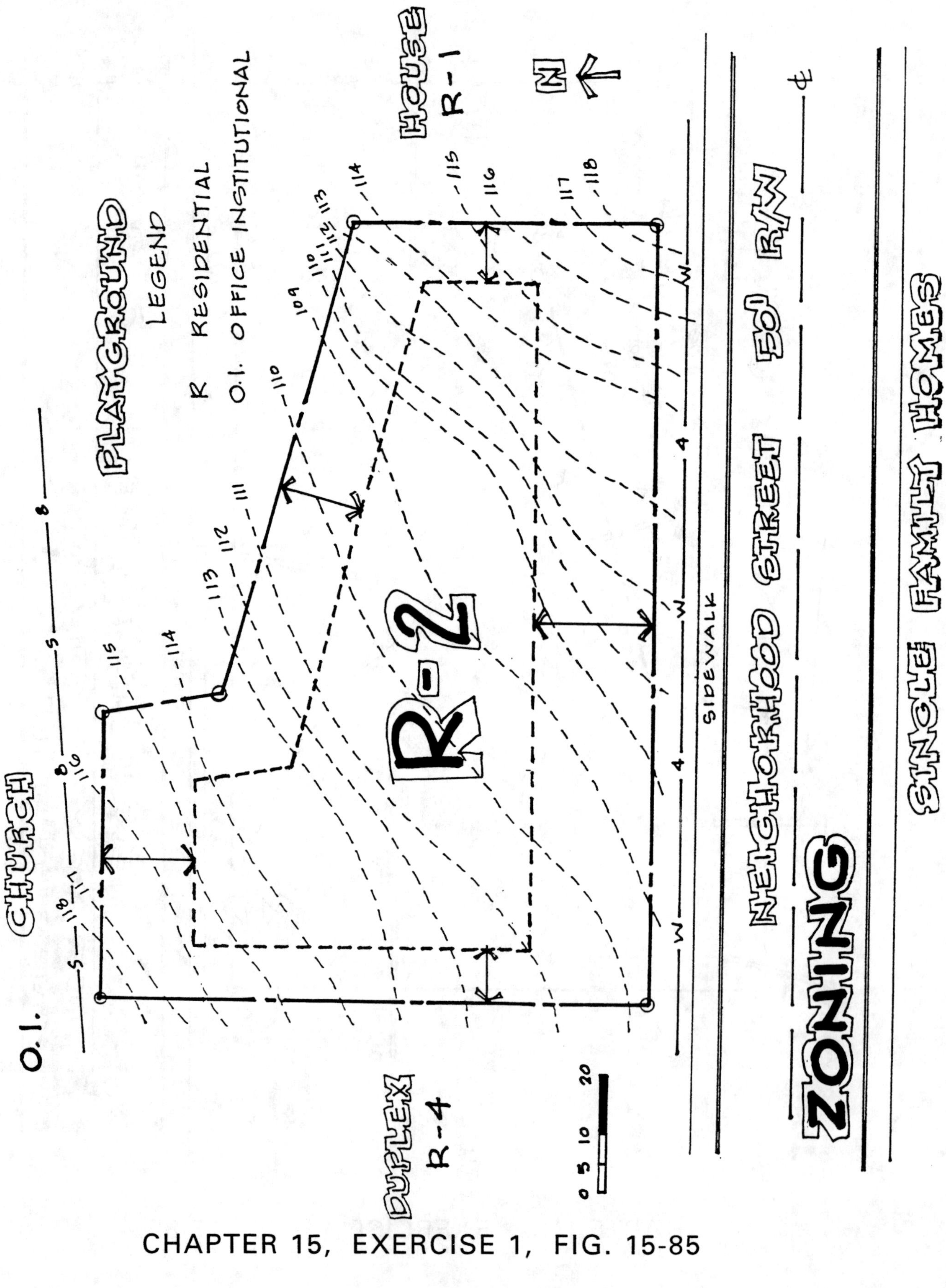

CHAPTER 15, EXERCISE 1, FIG. 15-85

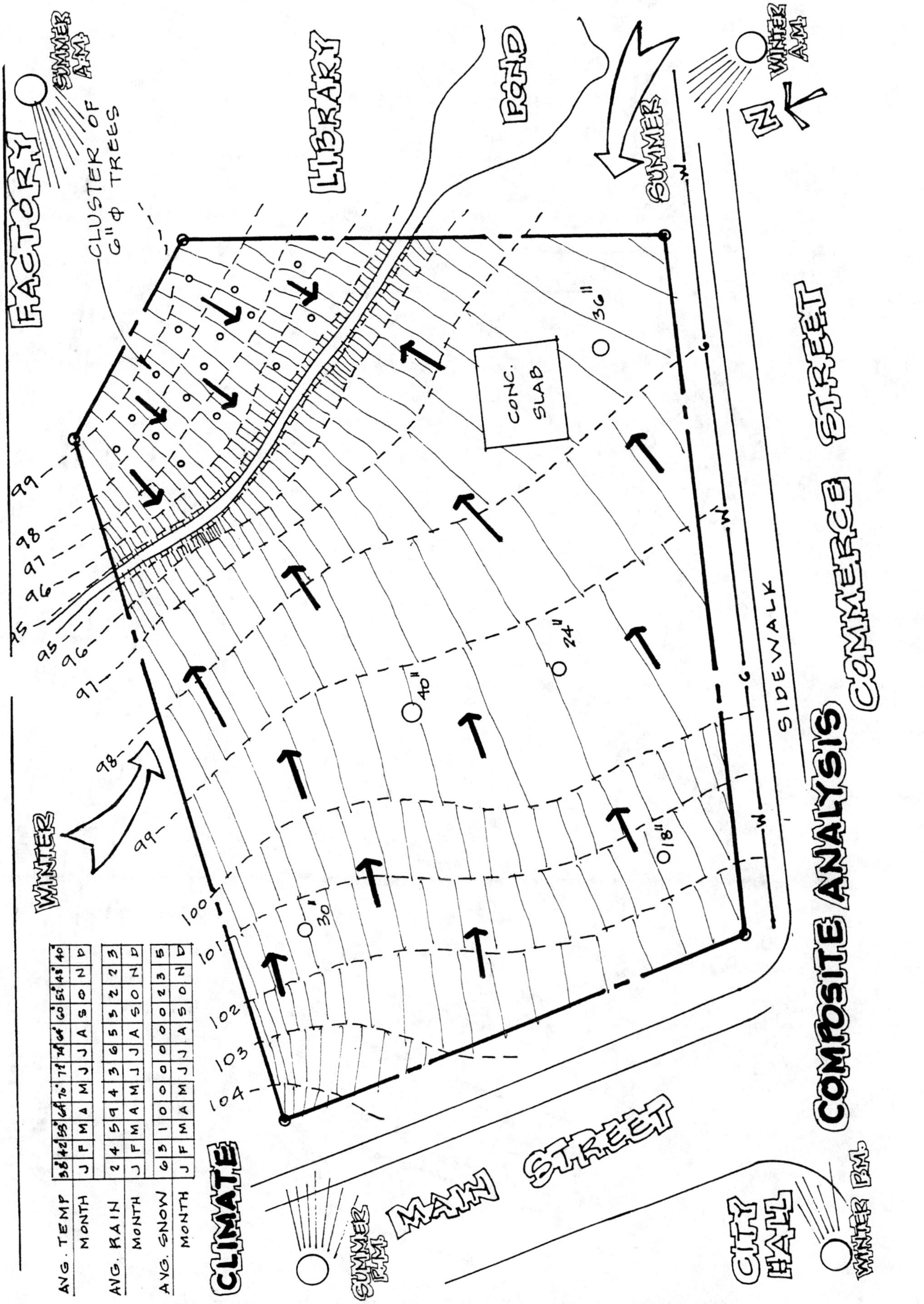

CHAPTER 15, EXERCISE 2, FIG. 15-86

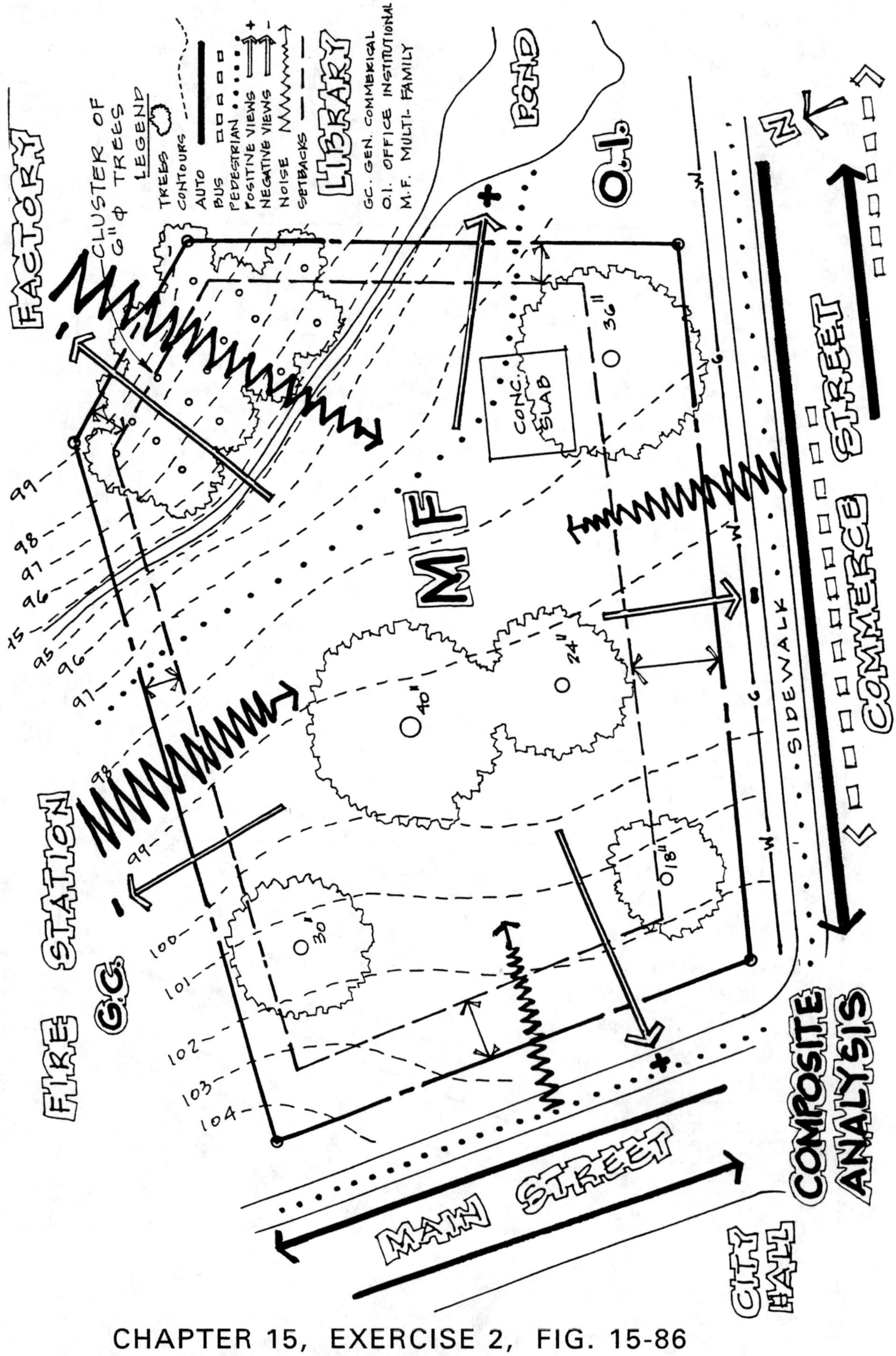

CHAPTER 15, EXERCISE 2, FIG. 15-86

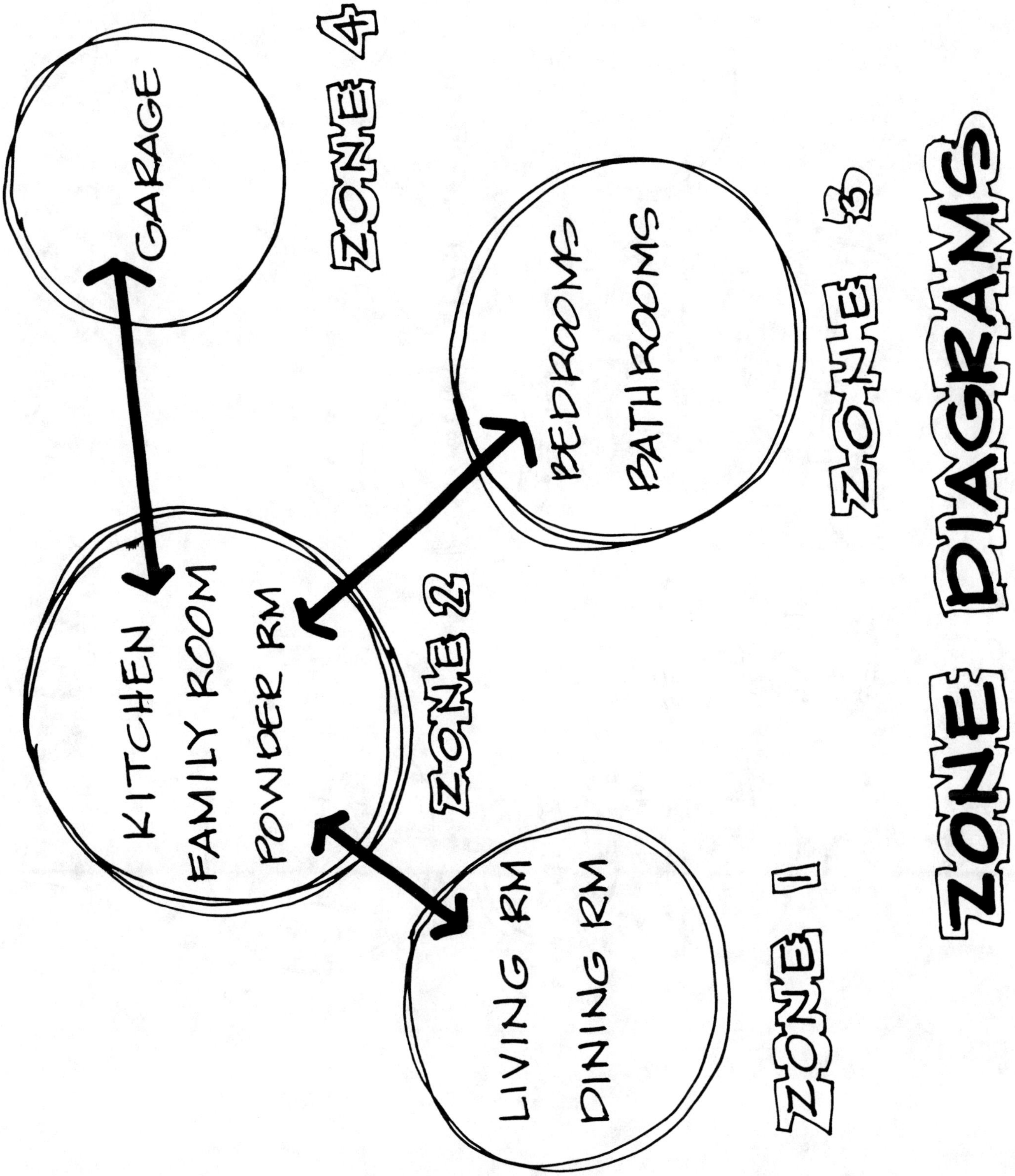

CHAPTER 15, EXERCISE 3

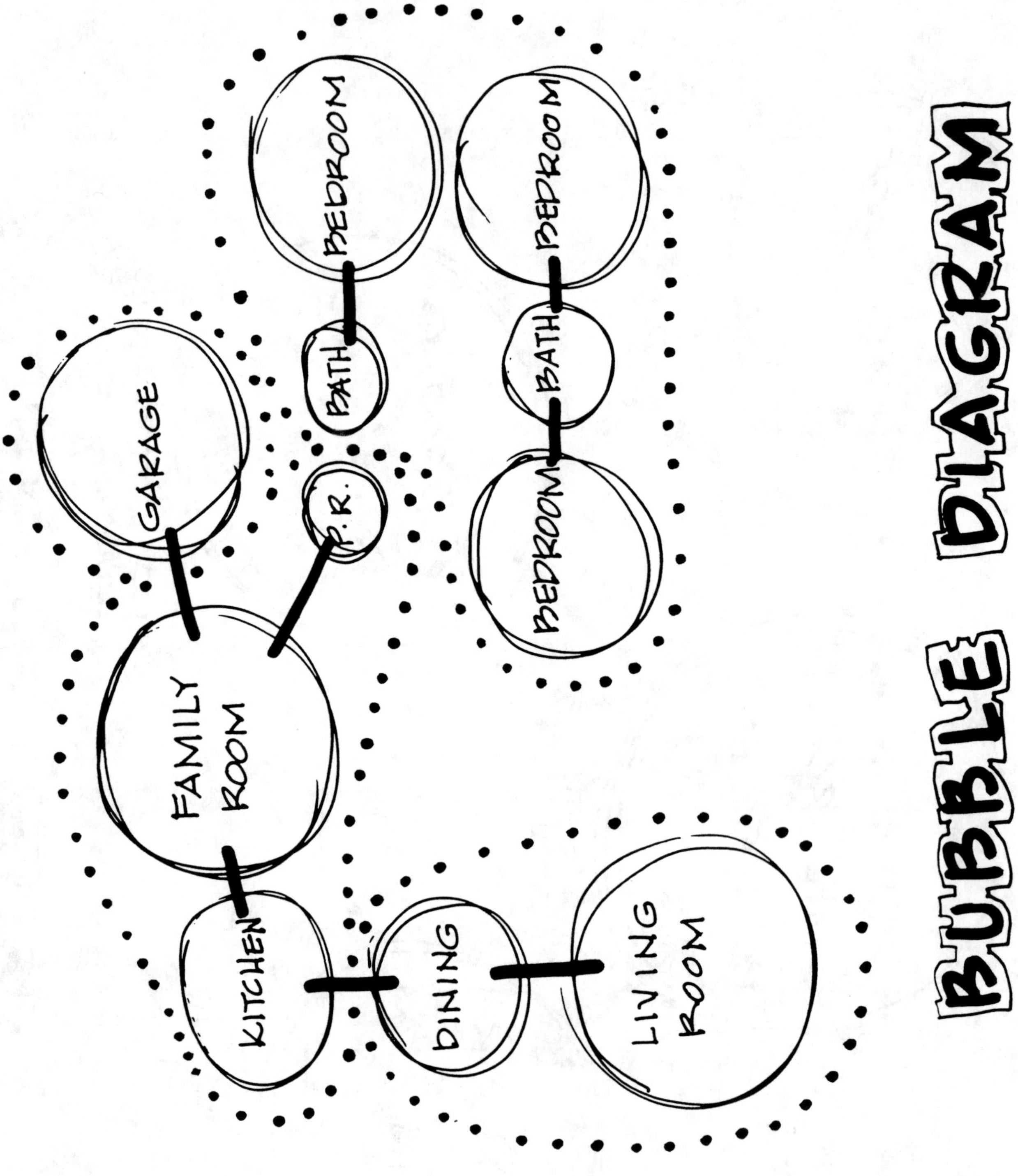

CHAPTER 15, EXERCISE 4

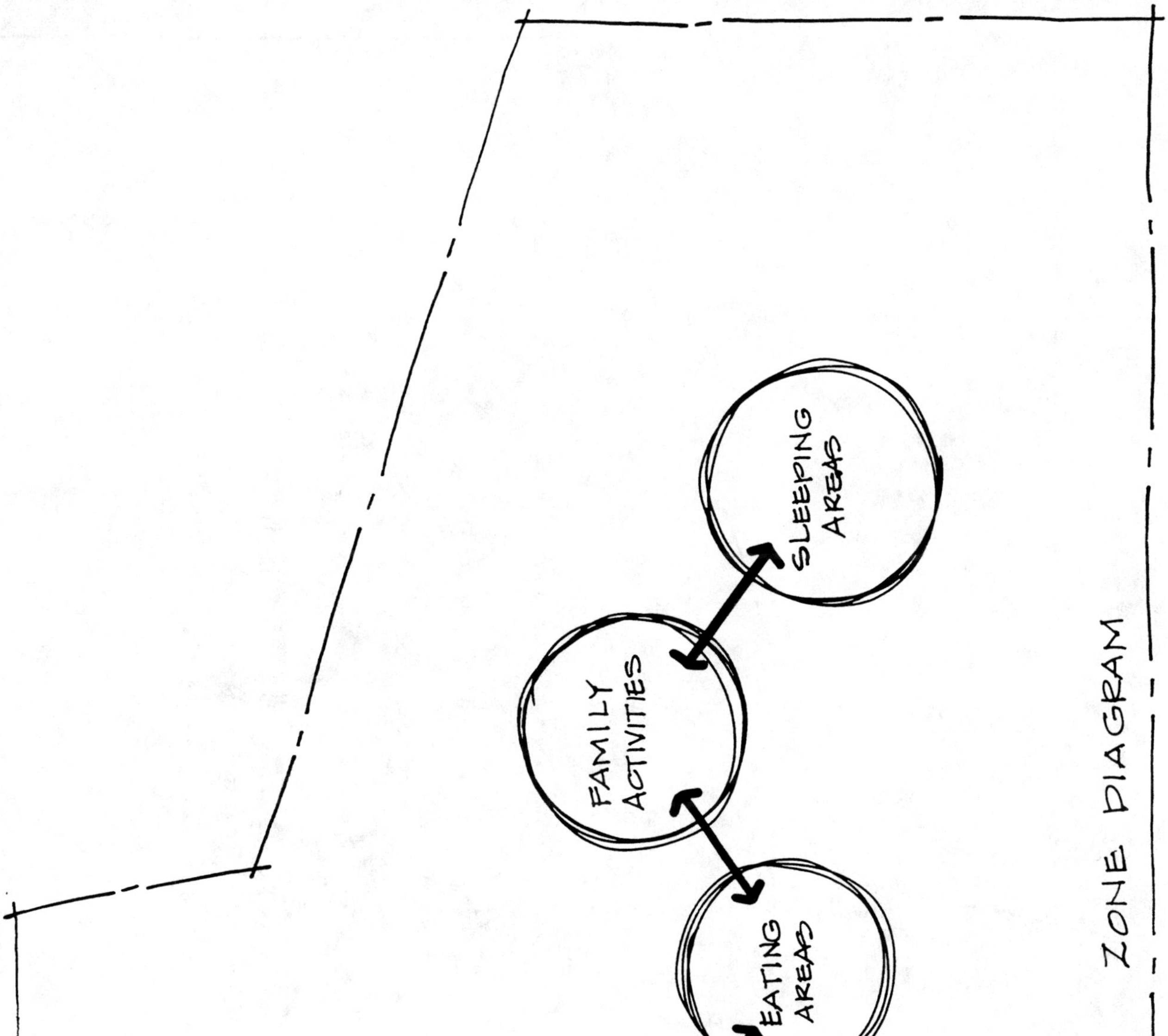

CHAPTER 15, EXERCISE 5

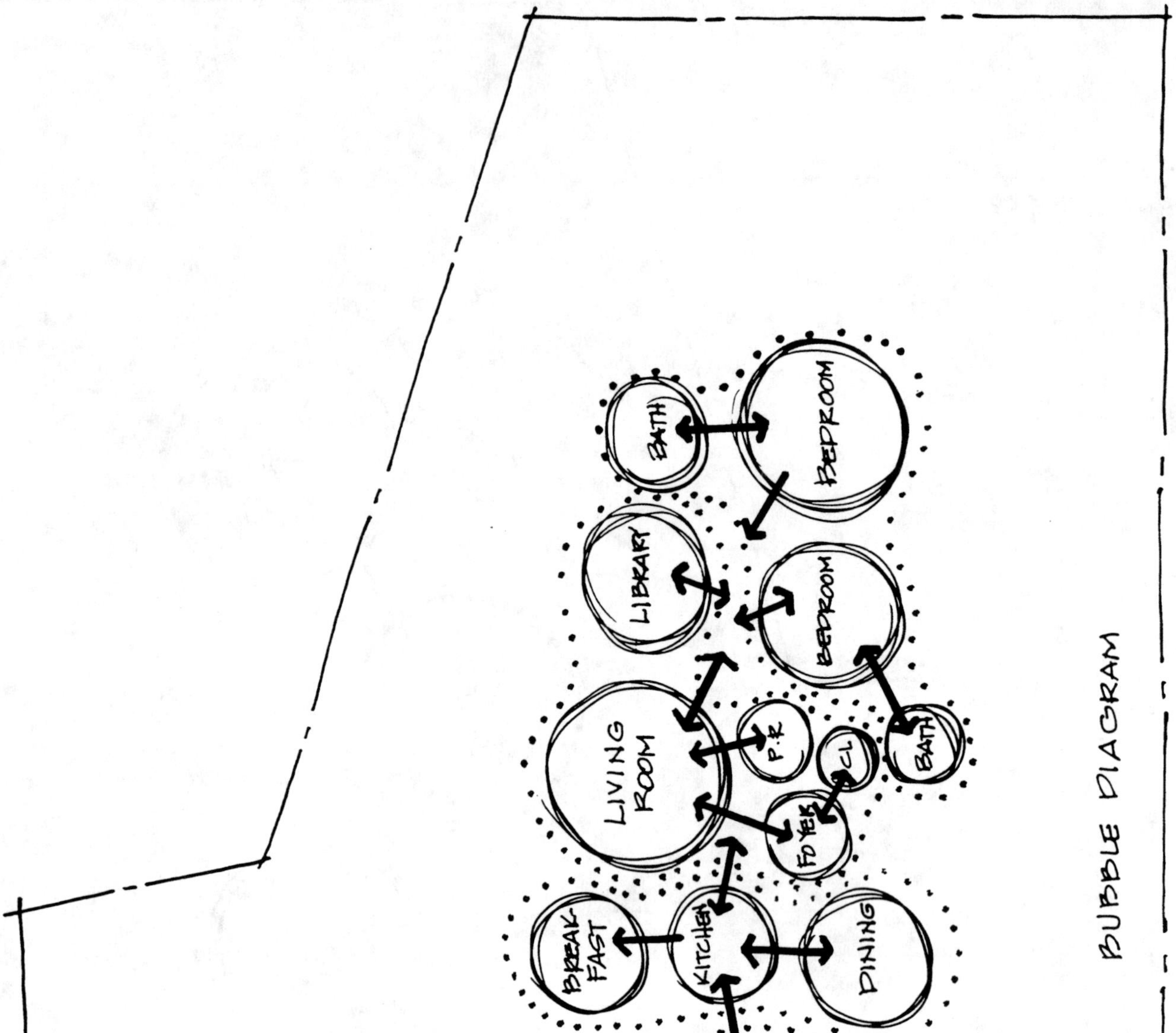

CHAPTER 15, EXERCISE 5

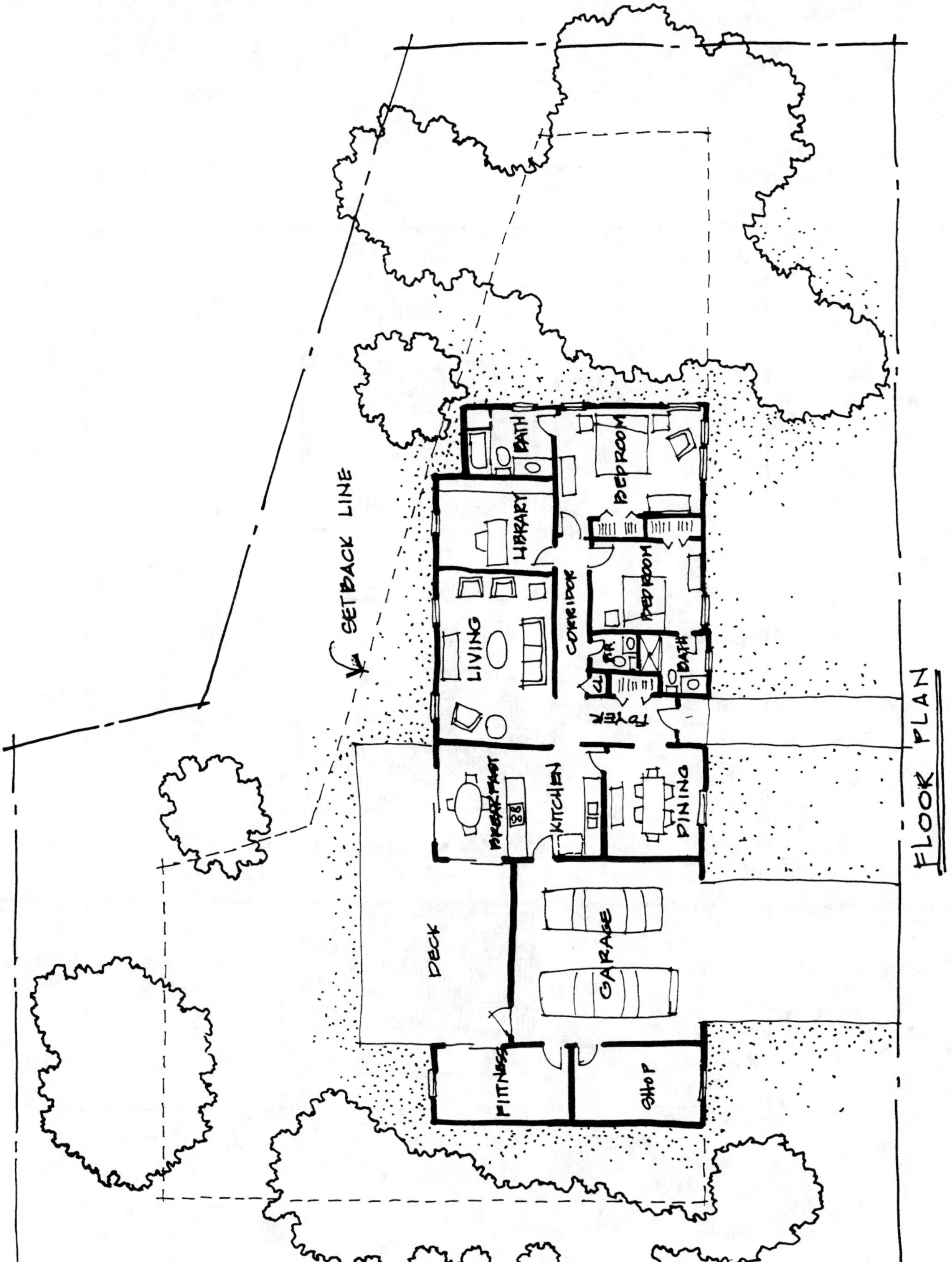

CHAPTER 15, EXERCISE 5

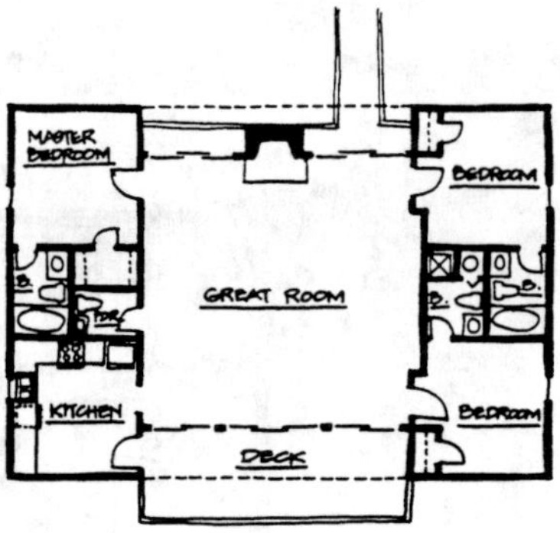

FLOOR PLAN 1,396 SF

REAR ELEVATION

SIDE ELEVATION

CHAPTER 15, EXERCISE 6

CHAPTER 15
REVIEW QUESTIONS AND ANSWERS

1. Why is it important to use a planning checklist?

ans. It is important to use a planning checklist to ensure that no important spaces or details have been overlooked or forgotten. The checklist helps to organize these requirements before planning is started.

2. What is meant by an easement?

ans. Easements are the legal means by which a party other than the owner has been given access or certain rights to the property for various reasons. The rights are irrevocable and must be honored by the owner and future owners.

3. Do contour lines crossing a small stream point upstream or downstream?

ans. Contour lines crossing a small stream point upstream.

4. Why is a southern exposure generally the most satisfactory direction in solar orienting a window wall?

ans. A southern exposure is generally the most satisfactory direction in solar orienting a window wall, because with correctly designed overhangs and sunshades, window walls can restrict the sun in summer and provide warmth and light within the house in the winter.

5. Which part of a home should have the most isolation and quiet?

ans. Bedrooms, libraries and private spaces should have the most isolation and quiet.

6. What geometric shape is the most economical for a basic plan?

ans. The square shape is the most economical for a basic plan because it has the least exterior surface which is the most expensive to construct.

7. Evaluate the traffic flow in your own home from

the standpoint of convenience.

ans. **The front door opens into a foyer which conveniently leads to a living room on the left, a dining room on the right and a hall at the rear. Immediately across the hall is the family room. Rooms accessible from the hall are the kitchen, bedrooms, and bathrooms. The foyer and hall organize the traffic pattern for the home thus preventing cross circulation in all the rooms.**

8. What is the maximum length of a satisfactory kitchen work triangle?

ans. **The maximum length of a satisfactory kitchen work triangle is 20 feet.**

9. Define the word fenestration:

ans. **Fenestration is the placement and sizing of window and door openings.**

10. Why are simple, uncomplicated exteriors usually the most pleasing?

ans. **Simple, uncomplicated exteriors are usually the most pleasing because the designer can create unity, harmony, scale, balance, emphasis, and focal point. Complicated exteriors often have competing elements that de-emphasize important features and over-power the focal point.**

CHAPTER 16
REVIEW QUESTIONS AND ANSWERS

1. What part does the model of a building play in architectural service?

ans. Models are an important part of the architectural service because architects rely on three dimensional models for final evaluation for their designs.

2. What characteristics of an architectural proposal does a model most effectively show?

ans. The model effectively shows aspects of the building such as proportion, relationship of features, appearance of materials, and spatial concepts.

3. Why is balsa wood a favorite material for many model builders?

ans. Balsa wood is a favorite material for many model builders, since it is a soft wood that is easy to score and cut.

4. How are site contours usually represented on architectural models?

ans. Site contours are usually cut from chip board, the thickness of which represents a contour interval such as 1′, 2′, or 5′. Contours on large scale models may be constructed with wire screen and blocking that is covered with papier-maché.

5. Why is the scale so important when selecting model building materials?

ans. It is important to select model-building materials of the proper scale so that the model will appear realistic and be an accurate representation of the building.

6. Why must the model builder use particular care as to the direction in which wood grain is placed on exterior textures?

ans. Care must be used as to the direction in which wood grain is placed on exterior textures since the wood grain has a different

appearance when it is placed vertically versus horizontally.

7. Why is soft pine recommended for structural lumber rather than balsa wood?

ans. **Soft pine is recommended for structural lumber rather than balsa wood because the soft pine has more stability.**

8. What is the disadvantage of using glossy enamels on model surfaces?

ans. **Glossy enamel paints have the disadvantage of being reflective and emphasizing imperfections in materials and craftsmanship.**

9. Name various materials convenient for representing roofing textures.

ans. **The following materials are convenient for representing roof structures: black construction paper represents roofing felt; sand paper represents composition shingles; small wood shingles cut from an actual cedar or redwood shingle represents the wood shakes or shingles.**

10. Why can landscaping problems be more easily solved on a model than on a landscaping plan?

ans. **Landscape problems can be more easily solved on a model than a landscaping plan because the model has three dimensional scale and contours which only appear flat on the landscape plan.**

CHAPTER 17
REVIEW QUESTIONS AND ANSWERS

1. What qualifications are required of a construction specification writer?

> ans. **A specification writer should have experience with construction materials, technical writing, contracts, and working drawings to qualify as a construction specification writer.**

2. Drawings depict the quantity of certain materials. What do specifications depict?

> ans. **Specifications depict the quality of certain building materials.**

3. List five sources for specification reference material.

> ans. **The following is a list of five sources for specification reference material: federal specifications, manufacturers' catalogs, national standards organizations, trade associations, and files of previously written specifications.**

4. Why are construction material manufacturers' associations interested in furnishing materials to specification writers?

> ans. **Construction material manufactures' associations are interested in furnishing information to specification writers because they hope the specifications writer will specify building products that the material manufacturers' association represents.**

5. Who requires a copy of the specifications? How are these copies usually made?

> ans. **The architect, bidders, general contractor, sub-contractors, owner, and lending institutions require copies of specifications. Most copies of specifications are reproduced on high speed copiers.**

6. How is the information in the general conditions related to the other technical sections?

ans. The information in the general conditions applies to the other technical sections?

7. How do dimensions given in the specifications differ from the dimensions required on the working drawings?

ans. Dimensions in specifications usually define the size of an individual unit such as a standard brick 2 1/4" X 3 3/4" x 7 5/8". Dimensions on drawings define the size of the building such as the length, width, and height.

8. Why must requirements in specifications be made fair and just to all parties of the contract?

ans. The contractor and the owner are parties to the contract for construction. Each is to perform strictly in accordance with the provisions of the contract of which the specifications are a part; therefore, the requirements in the specifications should not require either party to do things that are not fair.

9. List the three recommended parts of a typical technical section.

ans. The three recommended parts of a typical technical section are: Part 1-General; Part 2-Products; and Part 3-Execution.

10. What are the major advantages in using the five-digit numbering system in spec writing?

ans. The major advantage of using the five-digit numbering system is that it unifies the 16-division, three-part format. The first two digits identify the division, the remaining three digits represent a sequence of sections. The specifier may create numbers for narrowscope sections using the last three digits.

11. Name several architectural or construction books that follow the five-digit numbering format.

ans. Architectural Graphic Standards and Sweet's Architectural Catalog Files are both organized on the 16-division CSI format.

12. What organization originated the 16-division uniform construction specification system?

ans. The Construction Specification Institute (CSI) originated the 16-division uniform system.

13. Describe the difference between broadscope, mediumscope, and narrowscope?

ans. Broadscope sections cover a series of materials which are closely related such as "acoustical ceilings." Mediumscope sections may address "lay-in acoustical ceilings" consisting of a suspension system and lay-in tiles. A narrowscope section may include "ceiling suspension systems."

14. List and describe the three-part section in specification writing.

ans. The three part section in specification writing consists of Part-1 General, such as shop drawings and delivery process; Part-2 Products, relates to the material; Part-3 Execution, relates to the installation of the materials.

15. What is a master specification?

ans. A master specification is a previously written specification or computerized system which has a bank of specification material stored in memory. The specifier can edit the written or computerized specification and tailor it to the need of a new construction project.

16. Who generally writes specifications in a small architectural firm?

ans. The principle who is the registered architect and owner usually writes specifications for the small firm.

17. What is an allowance and why would it be used?

ans. An allowance is an amount of money or quantity of materials for which the quantity can be determined from the working drawing but a decision as to the actual material to

be used has not been selected. Such as, "500 yards of carpet at $20.00 per yard is the allowance." The owner then later selects a carpet which costs $20.00 per yard.

18. What is an alternate and why would it be used?

    ans. **An alternate is often included in the architect's bidding documents in order to get a price for an alternative system or material from the contractor. An alternate may be "additive" or "deductive" from the contract sum. Such as, "the contractor shall state the amount to be deducted from the base bid, if vinyl wall coverings are deleted and paint is substituted."**

19. What is a proprietary specification?

    ans. **A proprietary specification is a specification which names the manufacturer or products acceptable to the architect.**

20. How do computers aid the specification writer?

    ans. **Computers aid the specification writer in achieving greater speed in specification preparation. Specification data can be taken from a CD ROM disk and reader and stored on a personal computer hard disk. The specifier can generate an entire specification on the computer.**

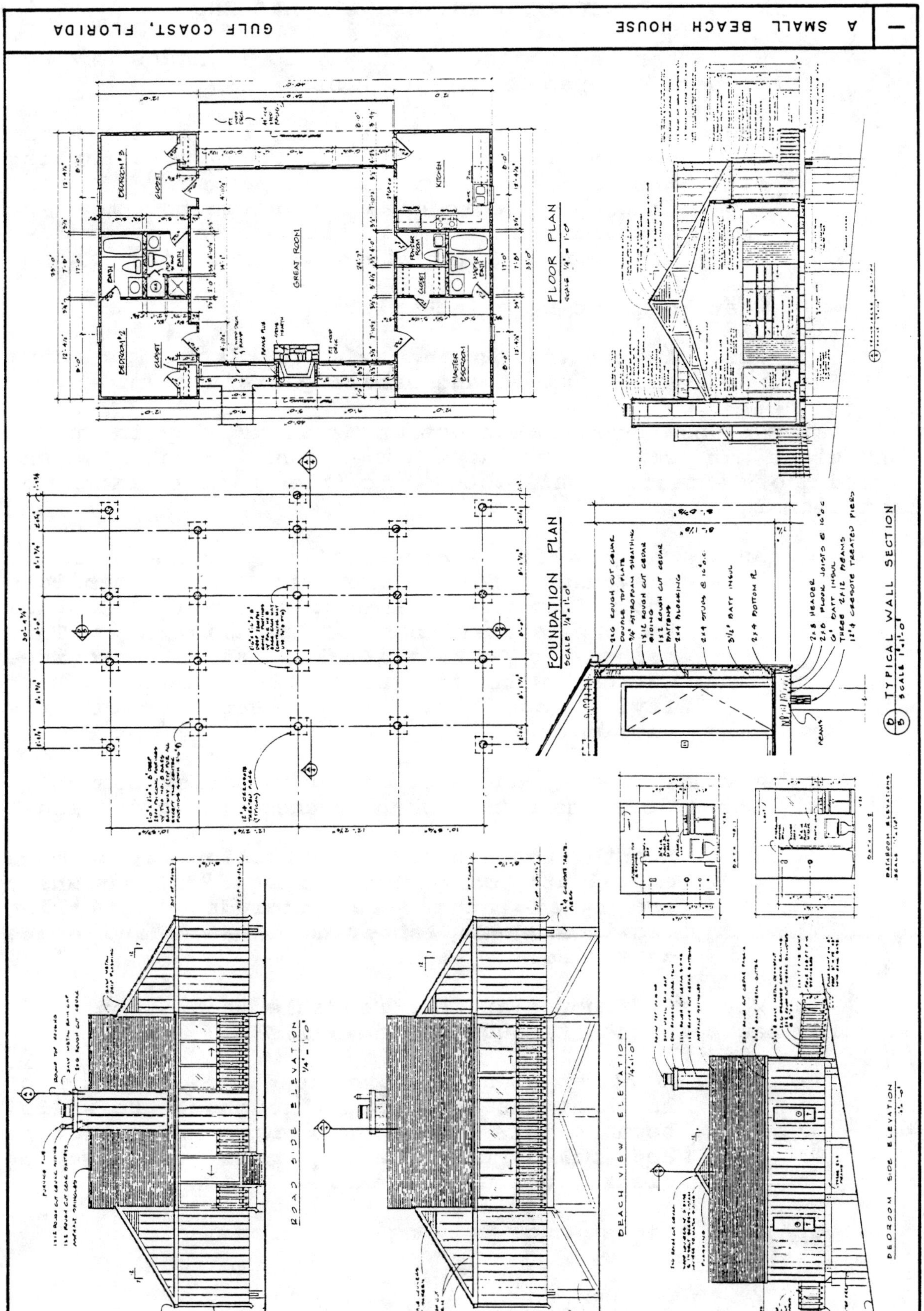

CHAPTER 18, EXERCISE 5

CHAPTER 18
REVIEW QUESTIONS AND ANSWERS

1. When starting a floor plan why is it necessary to begin with general shapes and light lines?

ans. **When starting a floor plan, one begins with general shapes and light lines to establish the overall form of the house. As the drawing progresses, adjustments may be necessary in the location of walls, windows and doors. Light lines may be easily erased.**

2. What is meant by a wet-wall?

ans. **A wet-wall is the wall that contains water supply pipes and sanitary drainage pipes.**

3. On wood frame construction drawings, why is it convenient for workers to have dimensions shown from the outside of exterior wall studs to the center lines of partitions?

ans. **On wood frame construction drawings, it is convenient for workers to have dimensions shown from the outside of exterior wall studs to the centerlines of partitions. This method is conventional, and it provides workers with the necessary dimensions for laying out the sole plates over the subfloors.**

4. Why are lengthy notes about construction commonly put in the specifications rather than on the working drawings?

ans. **Lengthy notes about construction may be more expediently contained in specifications which are typed rather than included in working drawings where lettering is time and space consuming.**

5. Why is a floor plan more readable when symbol hatching has been used throughout the walls?

ans. **A floor plan is more readable when symbol hatching has been used throughout the walls, because this gives the drawing an even tone and makes the drawing more readable by clearly defining rooms.**

6. Does a joist note, giving size, spacing, and

direction and shown on a floor plan, pertain to the framing above or below?

ans. **The joist note giving size, spacing and direction and shown on a floor plan pertains to the framing above.**

7. Why are piers within a crawl space generally masonry? How is this indicated?

ans. **Piers within a crawl space are generally constructed of masonry because they are more durable than medal or wood. They are shown on the foundation plan and hatched with the proper symbol which designates the material required for the construction of the pier.**

8. What does the term unexcavated mean when shown on part of a foundation plan?

ans. **Unexcavated when noted on a foundation plan means the earth is not to be removed.**

9. Of what value is the finish floor line indication on an elevation view?

ans. **The finish floor line indication on an elevation view is of value as an important reference line so that the contractor can locate the floor at the proper position above grade.**

10. What dimensions must necessarily be put on an elevation view?

ans. **Dimensions on elevations need be only those that cannot be shown on details and plans. Dimension the floor and ceiling heights, chimney heights, extended wall heights, window heights, and other features requiring a vertical dimension.**

11. What is the minimum width for a residential driveway for one-way traffic?

ans. **The minimum width for a residential driveway for one-way traffic is 10′-0".**

12. At what scale are bathroom elevations usually drawn?

ans. **Bathroom elevations are usually drawn to the scale of 1/2" = 1'0".**

13. How can columns and load-bearing walls be eliminated from a basement and at the same time maintain the structural integrity of the floor above?

ans. **Columns and load bearing walls can be eliminated from a basement by using floor trusses that can span from exterior wall to exterior wall and maintain the structural integrity of the floor above.**

14. What is the standard height from the floor to the top of doors and windows in residences?

ans. **The standard height from the floor to the top of doors and windows in a residence is 6'-8".**

15. Why is the floor plan developed before the foundation plan in working drawings?

ans. **The floor plan is developed before the foundation plan in working drawings because the foundation plan requires information about the total concept of the structure before it can be drawn.**

16. Place the following drawings in the order they would appear in a set of residential working drawings: exterior elevations, foundation plan, bathroom and kitchen details, site plan, typical wall sections, and floor plan.

ans. **The drawing in a set of residential working drawing would appear in the following order: site plan, foundation plan, floor plan, exterior elevations, typical wall sections, and bathroom and kitchen details.**

17. Why are doors numbered on a working drawing floor plan?

ans. **Doors are numbered on working drawings to cross reference the door to the corresponding number on the door schedule which indicates the type and size of the door.**

18. How are section cuts referenced on floor plans?

ans. **Section cuts are referenced on the floor plan by a cutting plane symbol that is shown by a**

bold line drawn through the point where the section is cut and a circle is attached to the cutting plane line. The circle is divided into halves by a line. A detail number or letter is placed in the upper half of the circle and a page reference number is placed in the lower half of the circle.

19. What working drawing contains the most information about the construction of the residence from the foundation to the roof?

ans. The wall section contains detailed information about the construction of the residence from the foundation to the roof.

20. How far should wood siding be placed above the exterior grade at the perimeter of the building?

ans. Wood siding should be placed 8" above the exterior grade at the perimeter of the building.

The following pages contain suggested guidelines for adding notes and dimensions to construction drawings as well as a handout exercise, along with the solution, which can be used to familiarize the student with calculating dimensions on a construction floor plan. Students should fill in the missing dimensions. This exercise can be used prior to assigning a floor plan design/drafting exercise.

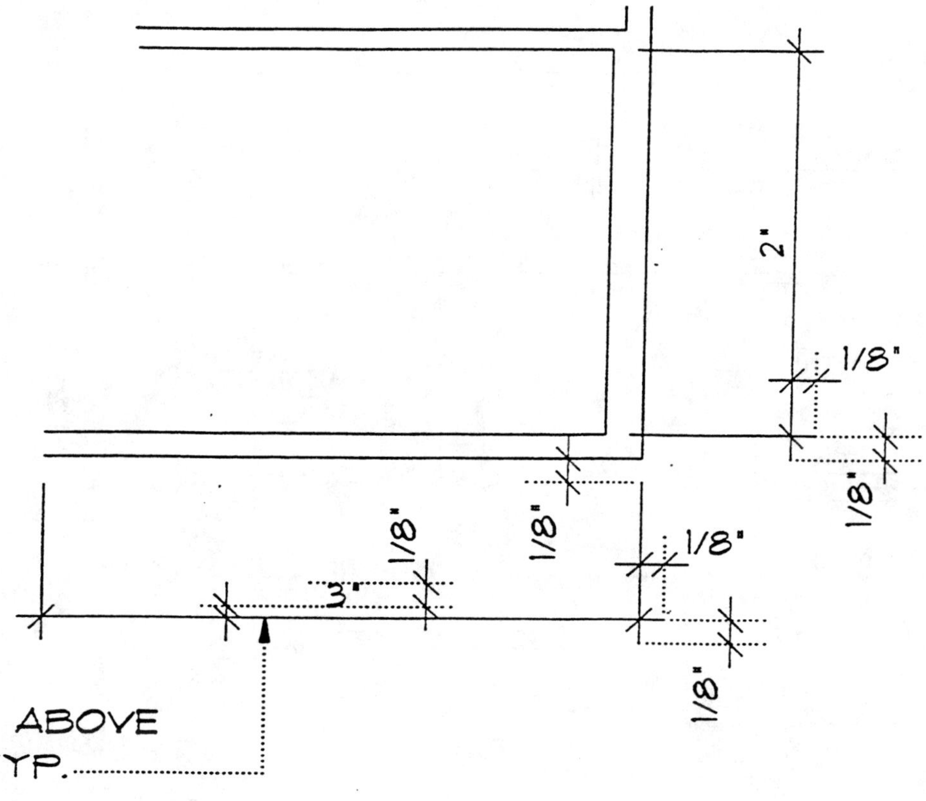

NOTES:
LINE UP
ALWAYS USE GUIDELINES
ALWAYS USE TRIANGLE
TITLES - 1/4"
GENERAL - 1/8"
SPACES BETWEEN LINES
MINIMUM 1/16"

DIMENSIONS:
1/8" HIGH
ALWAYS USE GUIDELINES
ALWAYS USE TRIANGLE
ABOVE LINE
CENTERED
LEFT TO RIGHT
BOTTOM TO TOP

SLASHES:
45 DEGREES WITH TRIANGLE
NO ARROWS

NOTES AND DIMENSIONS ON DRAWINGS

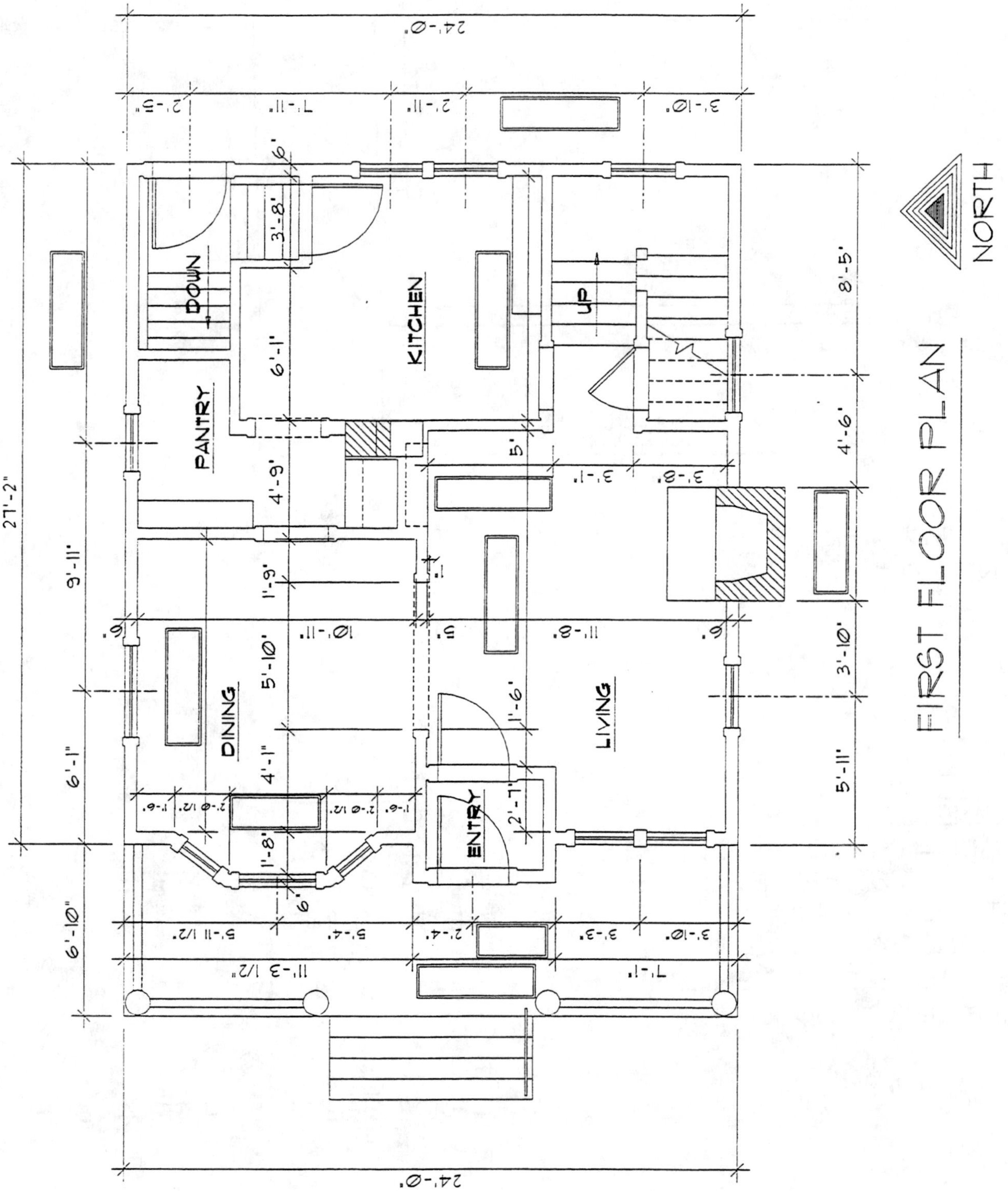
FIRST FLOOR PLAN
NORTH
KITCHEN
PANTRY
DINING
LIVING
ENTRY
UP
DOWN
24'-0"
27'-2"

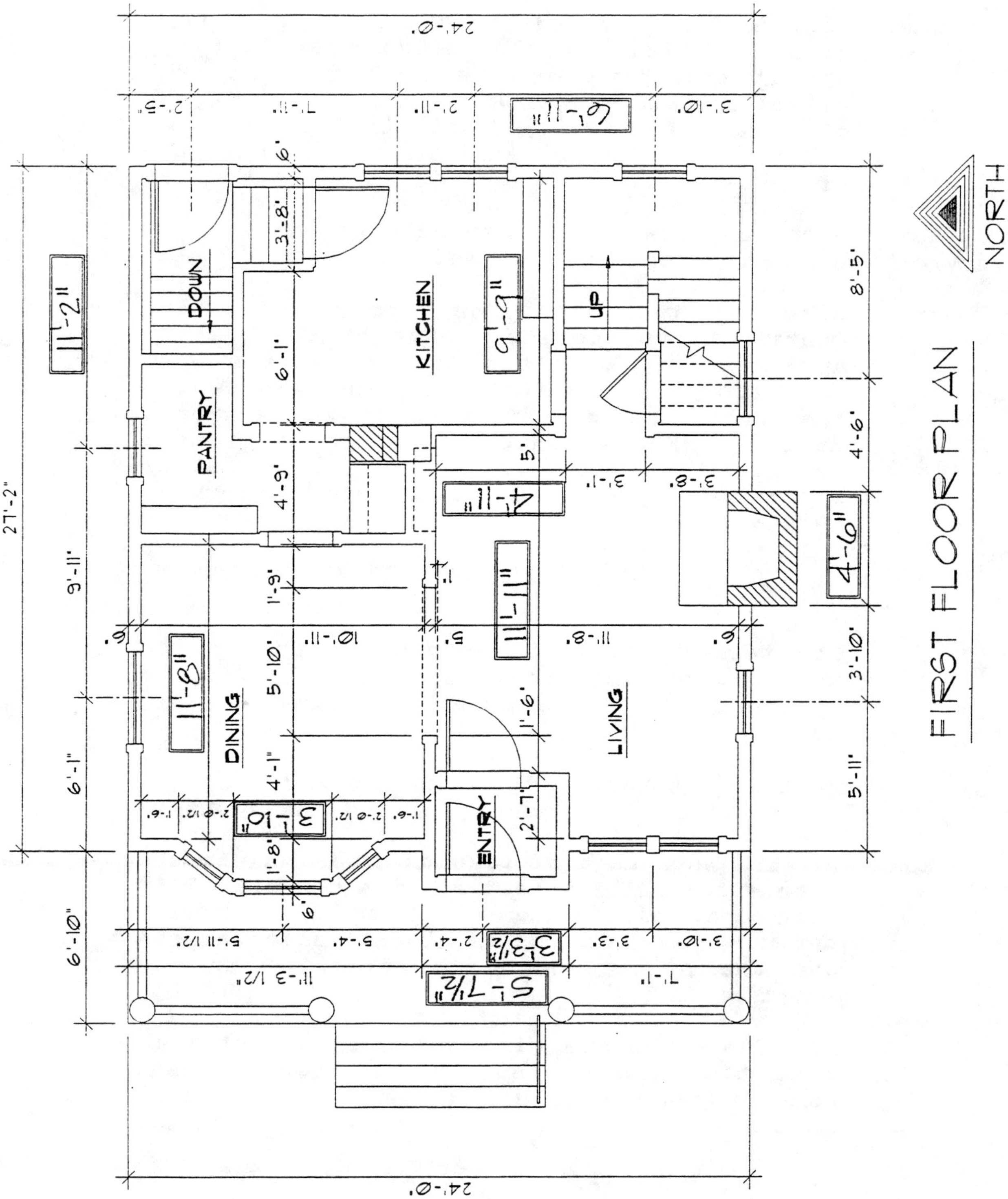
FIRST FLOOR PLAN
NORTH
KITCHEN
PANTRY
DINING
LIVING
ENTRY
DOWN
UP
27'-2"
24'-0"

CHAPTER 19
REVIEW QUESTIONS AND ANSWERS

1. In planning a satisfactory residential heating system, what basic factors must be considered?

ans. **When designing a heating and cooling system several factors should be considered: type, and availability of the fuel to be used, client preferences, local climate, the degree of comfort desired, initial cost of equipment, operating efficiency, and the type of insulation.**

2. How can the architecture contribute to the efficiency of the heating-cooling systems?

ans. **Some of the ways the architecture can contribute to the efficiency of the heating and cooling system are to protect the west wall from solar radiation; place windows on the south side; specify a light colored roof; design the house with a barrier to protect against the winter winds; specify weather stripping, insulated glass, and adequate insulation.**

3. What is meant by "degree of comfort" in reference to heating-cooling systems?

ans. **The term "degree of comfort" refers to the temperature range that is comfortable to the home owner. The temperature range may vary from person to person.**

4. What are the advantages of the forced warm-air heating systems? The hydronic systems? The radiant systems?

ans. **a. The advantage of forced air is mainly the economical initial cost and its compatibility with cool air systems. Heat distribution through out the house is almost instantaneous and the system is not restrictive in its location.**

b. The advantage of the hydronic system is that the same boiler can be used to heat water for domestic use as well as for space heating.

c. The advantage of the radiant system is

even distribution of heat, no noise, and the pipes can be concealed in floors, walls or ceilings.

5. Would a heat-pump system be efficient for heating a home in your locality?

ans. **The most practical adoption of the heat pump for home heating is in regions where the outside temperatures seldom drop below 30°F.**

6. Why are filters placed in the return-duct side of a warm-air heating system?

ans. **The filters are placed on the return duct side of the warm air heating system to keep dust from collecting in the heat exchange unit.**

7. What type of warm-air furnace must be used with heat ducts embedded in a concrete slab-on-ground floor?

ans. **When ducts are put in concrete floors or on the ground floor, a counter-flow system must be used to push the heat down into the ducts.**

8. How is the air that is removed by kitchen and bath exhaust fans usually replaced in a well designed system?

ans. **The air lost from the house because of vent fans in the bathrooms and kitchens is now being replaced with fresh air in return ducts to equalize return air pressures and keep a continual supply of fresh air in the house.**

9. What three controls are necessary in making a warm-air system fully automatic?

ans. **To have a fully automatic warm air heating system one must have the following controls: room thermostat, fan thermostat, and a high limit control switch.**

10. Why has electricity become popular as a home-heating energy source?

ans. **Electricity has become a very popular heating source where electricity is economical; it is clean heat that is very easy to control and distribute.**

11. Why would the 2-pipe hot water system be more satisfactory than the 1-pipe system in home heating?

ans. **The two pipe hot water system would be more desirable because the system produces more even heat throughout the house.**

12. What general type of insulation is the most efficient with radiant heating systems?

ans. **A good type of insulation to use with radiant heating is a reflective insulation.**

13. What two methods of home heating commonly employ baseboard registers?

ans. **The two methods of home heating that commonly employ base board registers are hot water systems and electric strip heat systems.**

14. Which type of heating system is most easily combined with conventional equipment?

ans. **The forced warm air systems are most suitable when combined with a cooling system.**

15. If a room has a calculated heat loss of 3,200 Btu per hr., what wattage resistance wire would be needed to satisfy the heat?

ans. **3,200 Btu ÷ 3.41 Btu per watt = 938.42 watts resistance wiring is needed.**

16. In heat-pump installation, what is the primary source of heat supplied to the rooms?

ans. **Exterior heat is transferred through a heat pump to heat the interior.**

17. What mechanism reverses the cycles from heating to cooling in the heat pump?

ans. **To change a heat pump from heating to cooling you must reverse the refrigeration cycle.**

18. What is the purpose of an outside thermostat?

ans. **The outside thermostat keeps the radiant heating system from getting too far behind.**

19. What are the disadvantages of water chillers in residential cooling?

ans. **The main problem with water chillers for residential use is that their size, complexity and demand for power make them uneconomical.**

20. Are partitions between heated rooms considered when calculating heat losses?

ans. **Partitions between heated rooms are not considered in heat loss calculations; they balance each other out.**

21. Which part of a residential plumbing system operates by gravity? Which part by pressure?

ans. **In residential plumbing the waste system operates by gravity while the fresh water system operates by pressure.**

22. How can initial plumbing costs be reduced when designing a home?

ans. **The best way to lower plumbing costs is to centralize all plumbing in one wall if possible and keep the fixtures as close to each other as possible.**

23. What is the purpose of a soil trap in plumbing fixtures?

ans. **The purpose of a soil trap is to prevent sewer gases from entering a building through the sanitary sewer system.**

24. What size hot-water heater would be sufficient for a family of three, where the home contains automatic laundry equipment?

ans. **The average family needs a 30 gallon hot water tank.**

25. What factors determine the correct size septic tank and the length of the tile drainage lines?

ans. **The size of the septic tank is determined by local codes according to the size of the dwelling and the number of occupants. The length of the tile drainage lines is based on the percolation rate of the soil.**

26. What size electrical service panel should be

selected for a home of 2,000 sq. ft.?

ans. **A 2,000 square foot house would need a 150 ampere service; if the house has electric heating it will need a 200 ampere service.**

27. What is a "feeder" circuit?

ans. **A feeder circuit connects power from the main power panel to sub-panel.**

28. What should be analyzed to determine the location of wall switches?

ans. **When placing wall switches, one factor to be considered would be that switches are generally placed 4′ above the floor in the direction of the flow of traffic so one can turn lights off and on when leaving or entering a room.**

29. What types of switches are needed to operate an outlet from three locations?

ans. **A switch which can operate at three different locations is a low-voltage four way switch.**

30. Why must lighting be considered in the total concept of a home?

ans. **Well lighted interiors are often decidedly more interesting in the evening than during the day light. Artificial lighting must be regarded as an important part of the total design of the building.**

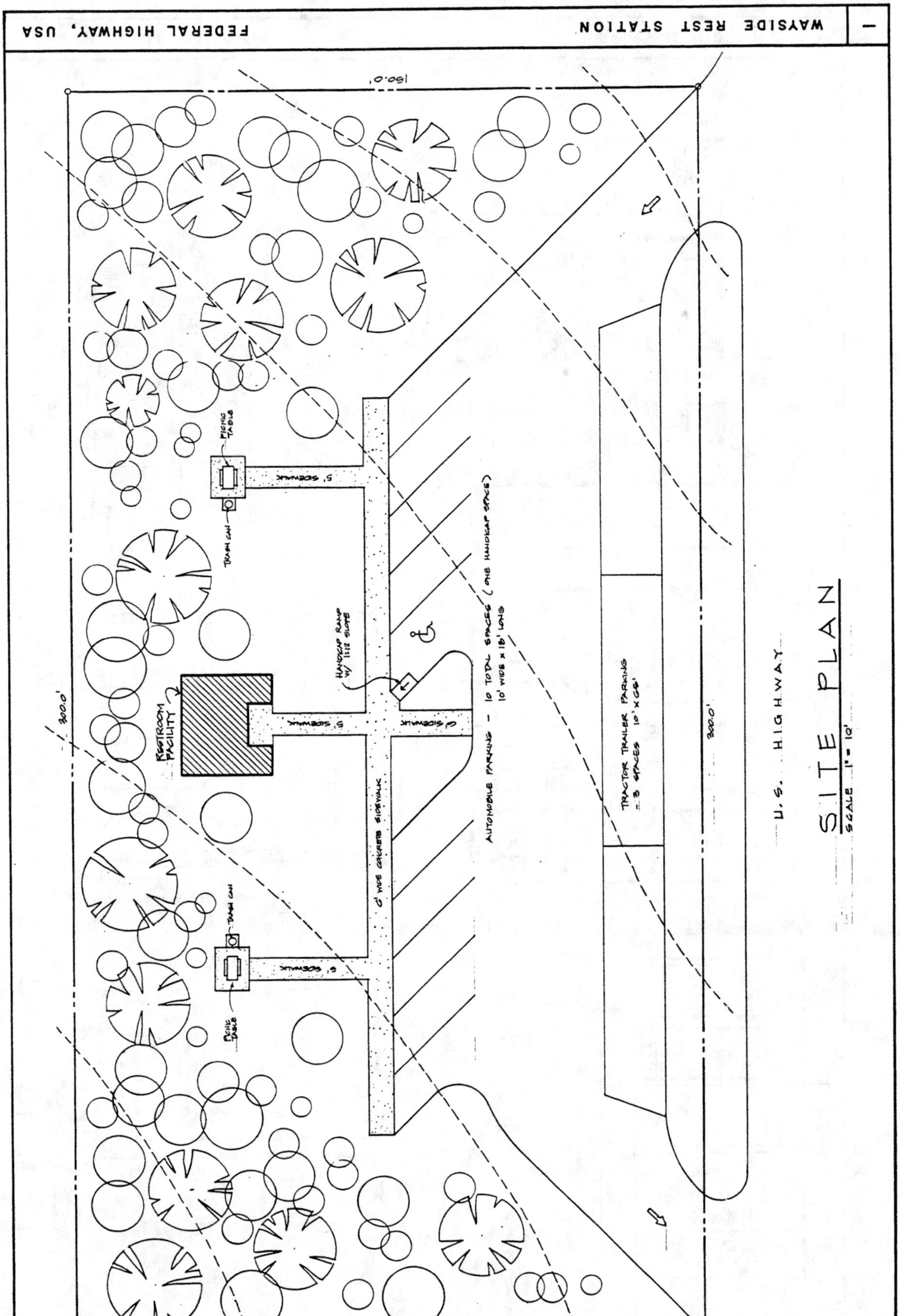

CHAPTER 20, EXERCISE 1

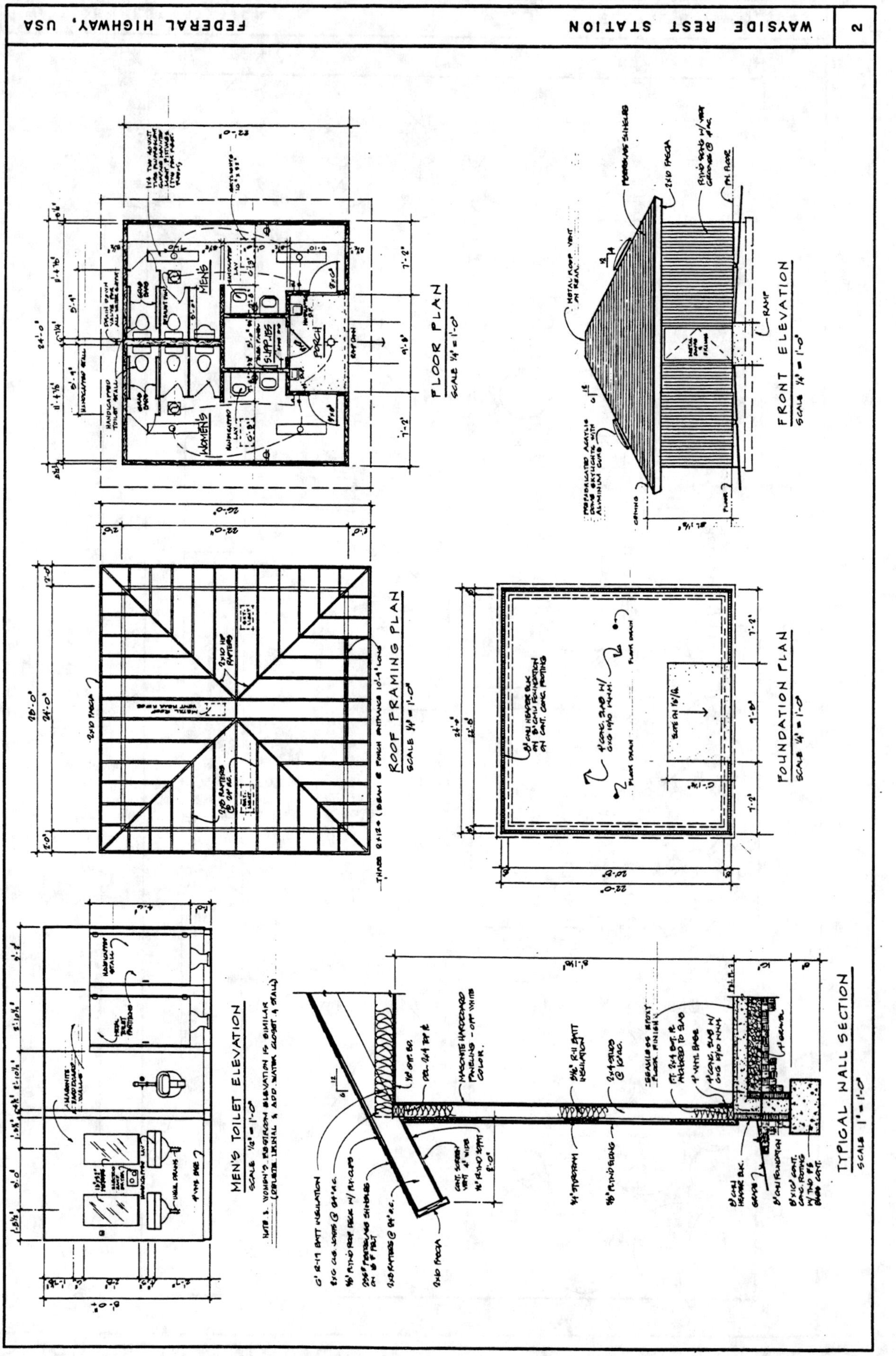

CHAPTER 20, EXERCISE 1

CHAPTER 20
REVIEW QUESTIONS AND ANSWERS

1. Why must codes dealing with public buildings be carefully regulated?

ans. Codes dealing with public buildings must be carefully regulated to protect life, property, and the welfare of occupants.

2. List three general structural systems commonly used in commercial buildings.

ans. Three general structural systems commonly used in commercial buildings are load bearing masonry walls, steel frame structures, and concrete frame structures.

3. Why are reflected ceiling plans commonly drawn for commercial buildings?

ans. Reflected ceiling plans are drawn for most commercial buildings because an extensive amount of lighting and HVAC equipment must be mounted on the ceilings.

4. Why are enclosed vestibules often used in public entrances?

ans. Enclosed vestibules are often used in public entrances to prevent loss of heating and cooling.

5. When laying out plan views of buildings with multiple floor levels, why is it important for the drafter to reserve suitable space for vertical plumbing and mechanical chases?

ans. Plumbing pipe, electrical wire, and HVAC duct work must be run vertically in a multi-story building; therefore it is necessary to plan for these mechanical services.

6. What detail is commonly drawn before starting the plans and elevations?

ans. The wall section detail is commonly drawn before starting the plans and elevations.

7. What factors must be considered in deciding on the

spacing of modular columns in the planning of a commercial building?

ans. **Limitations of the span of the beams framing the floor or roof structure would determine the spacing of modular columns in the planning of a commercial building.**

8. In dimensioning, how are features in detail views made to relate to major features on plan and elevation views?

ans. **There are more dimensions on detailed views than on plan and elevation views. Such dimensions clarify information which cannot be shown on plans and elevations.**

9. Why must masonry coursing sizes be accurately drawn on details?

ans. **It is critical to draw masonry coursing sizes accurately on details so that the construction materials will fit properly.**

10. What types of professional services are usually engaged by architectural firms to complete their sets of working drawings for commercial buildings?

ans. **The professional services of civil, structural, electrical, and mechanical engineers are usually engaged by architectural firms to complete their sets of working drawings for commercial buildings.**